CORPSE TALK

QUEENS & KINGS

AND OTHER ROYAL ROTTERS

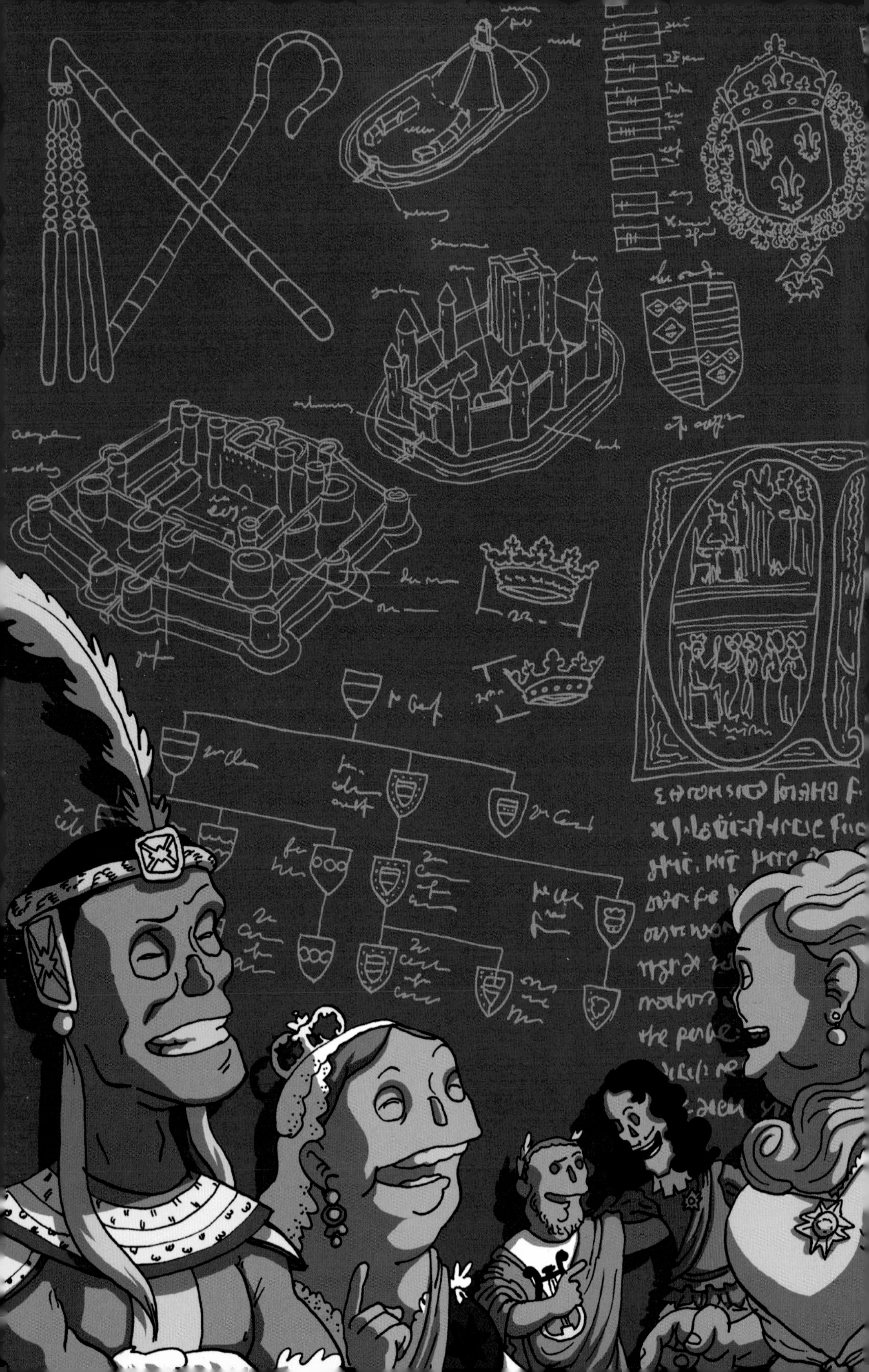

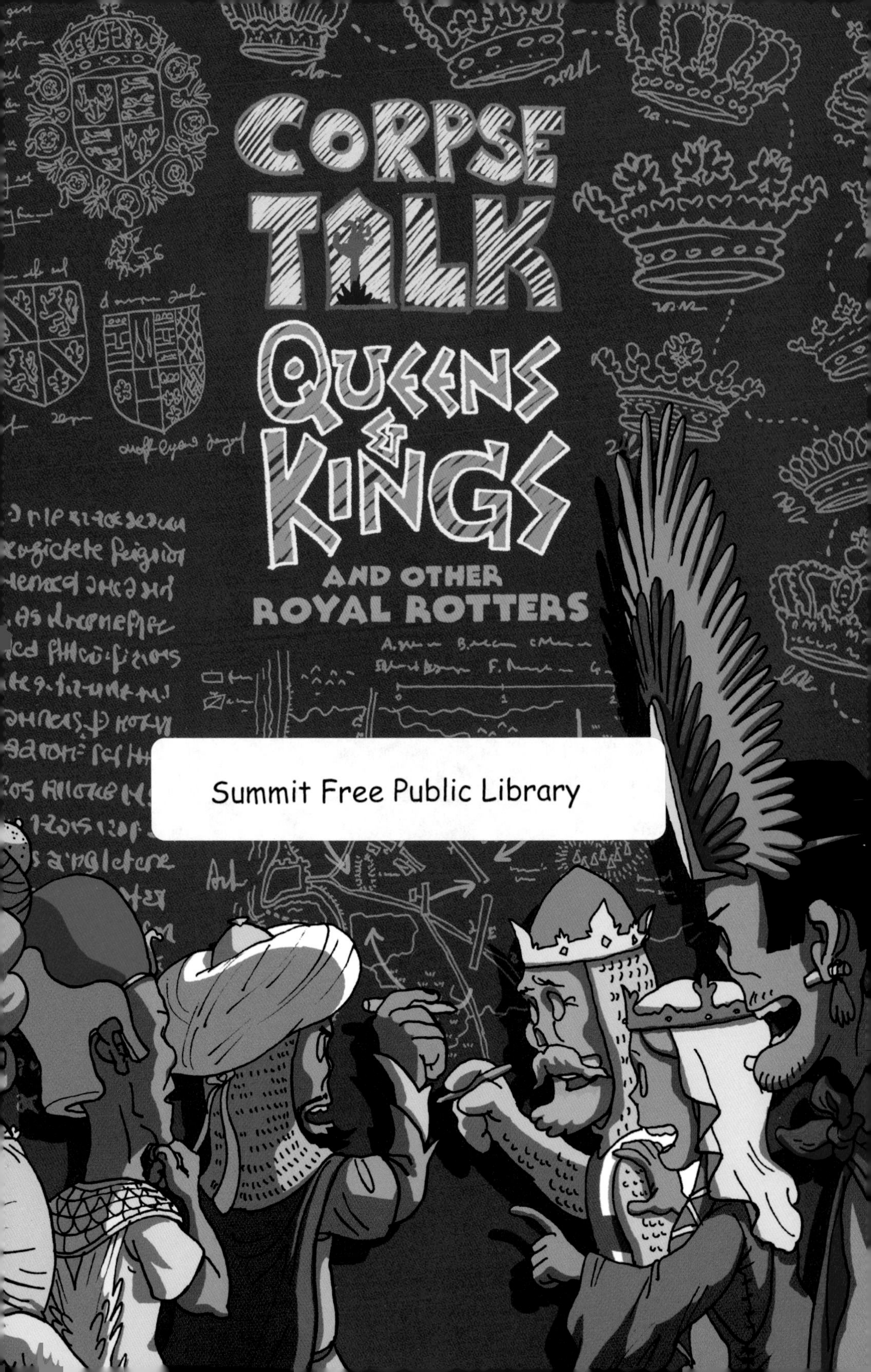
CORPSE TALK
QUEENS & KINGS
AND OTHER ROYAL ROTTERS

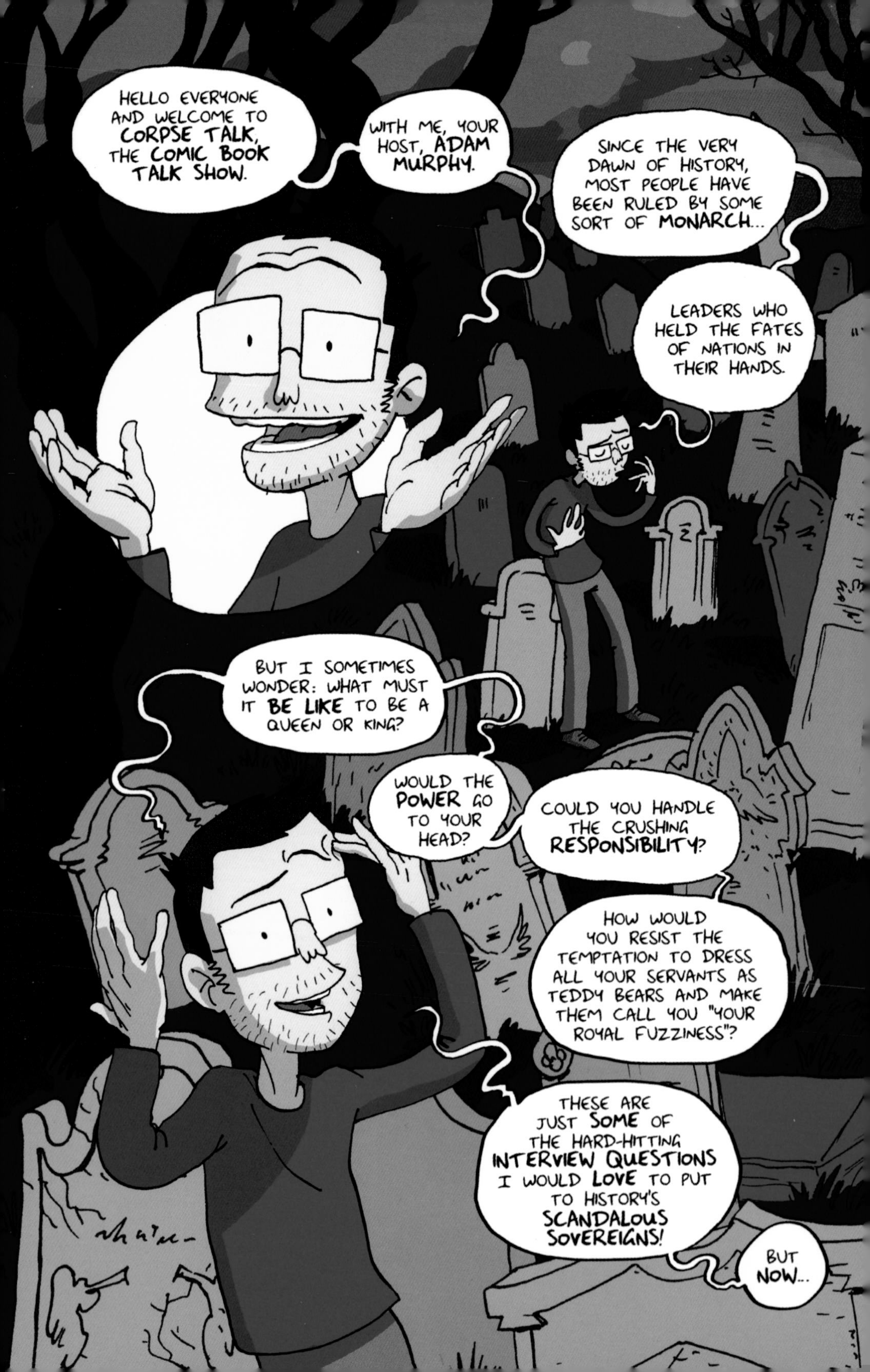
HELLO EVERYONE AND WELCOME TO CORPSE TALK, THE COMIC BOOK TALK SHOW.
WITH ME, YOUR HOST, ADAM MURPHY.
SINCE THE VERY DAWN OF HISTORY, MOST PEOPLE HAVE BEEN RULED BY SOME SORT OF MONARCH...
LEADERS WHO HELD THE FATES OF NATIONS IN THEIR HANDS.
BUT I SOMETIMES WONDER: WHAT MUST IT BE LIKE TO BE A QUEEN OR KING?
WOULD THE POWER GO TO YOUR HEAD?
COULD YOU HANDLE THE CRUSHING RESPONSIBILITY?
HOW WOULD YOU RESIST THE TEMPTATION TO DRESS ALL YOUR SERVANTS AS TEDDY BEARS AND MAKE THEM CALL YOU "YOUR ROYAL FUZZINESS"?
THESE ARE JUST SOME OF THE HARD-HITTING INTERVIEW QUESTIONS I WOULD LOVE TO PUT TO HISTORY'S SCANDALOUS SOVEREIGNS!
BUT NOW...

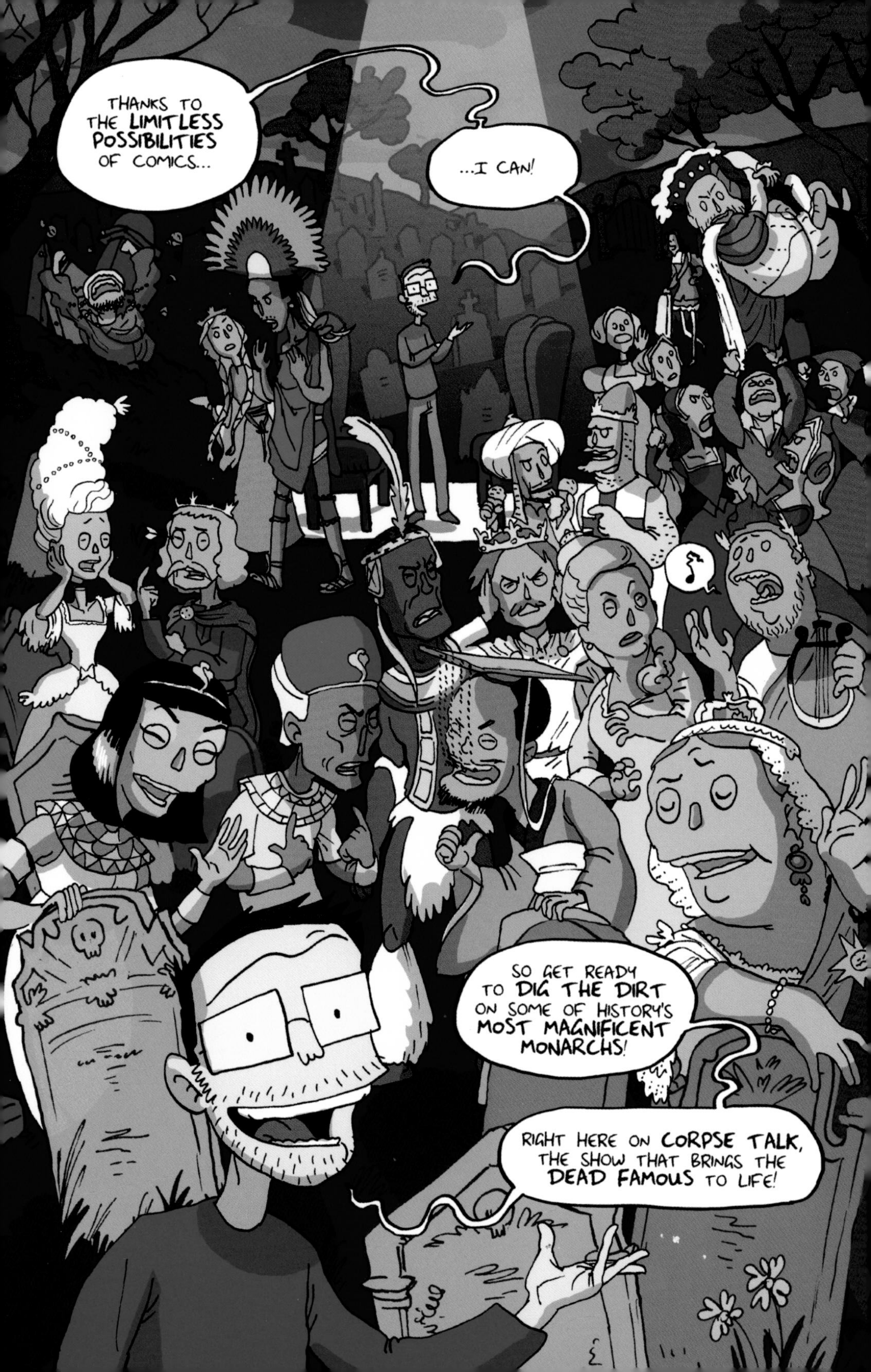
THANKS TO THE LIMITLESS POSSIBILITIES OF COMICS...
...I CAN!
SO GET READY TO DIG THE DIRT ON SOME OF HISTORY'S MOST MAGNIFICENT MONARCHS!
RIGHT HERE ON CORPSE TALK, THE SHOW THAT BRINGS THE DEAD FAMOUS TO LIFE!

CONTENTS

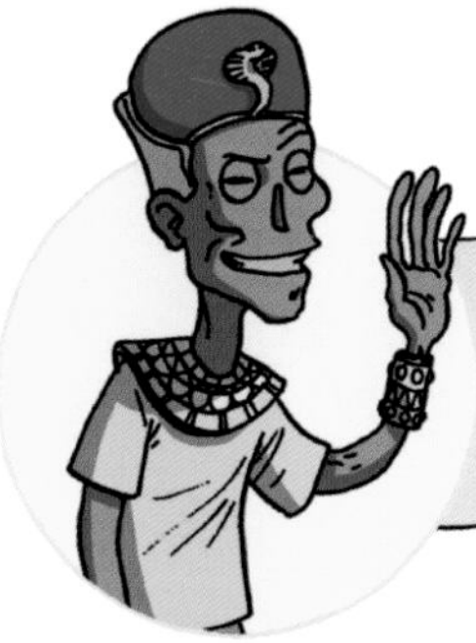

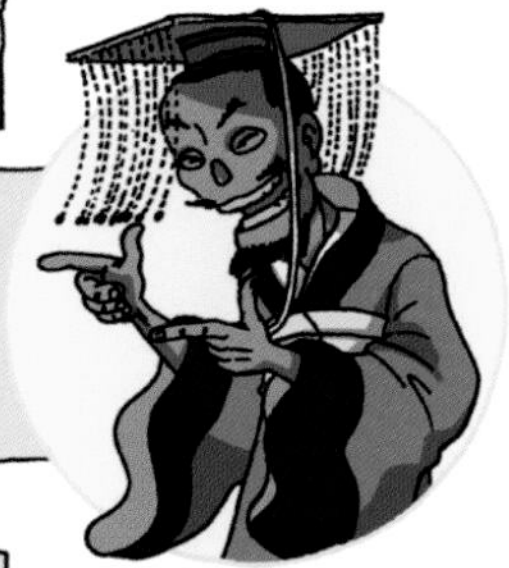

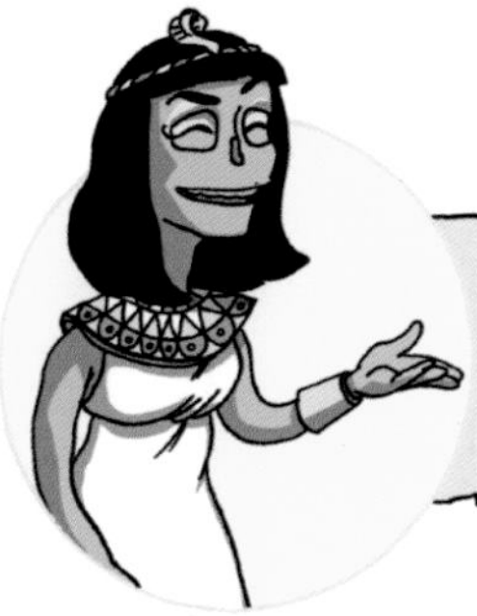

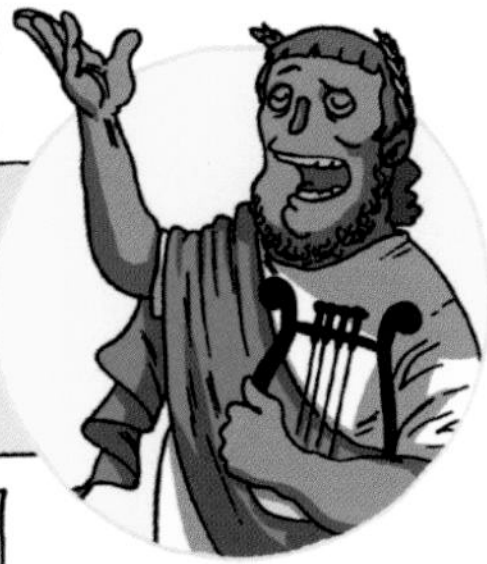

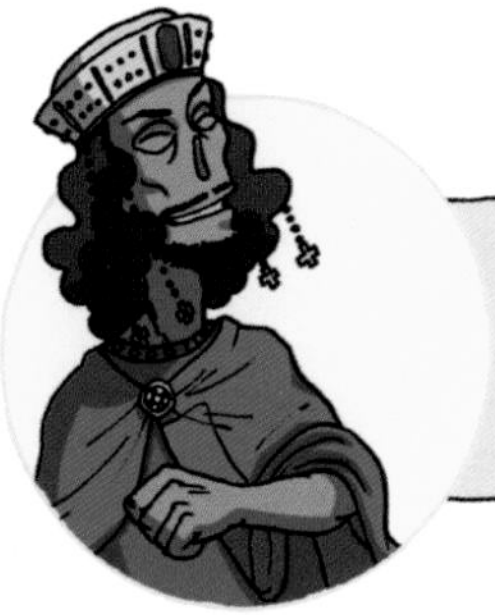

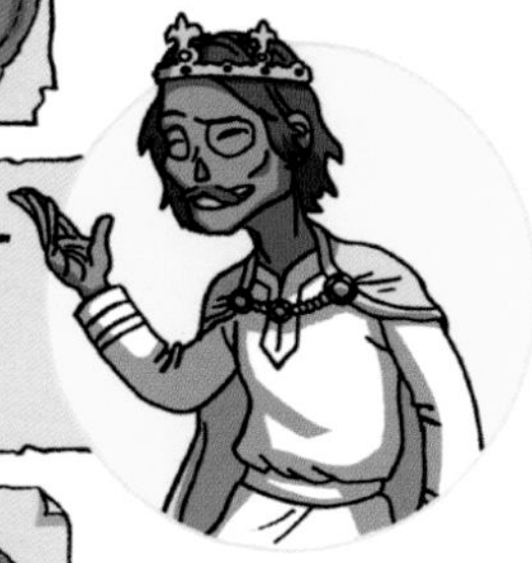

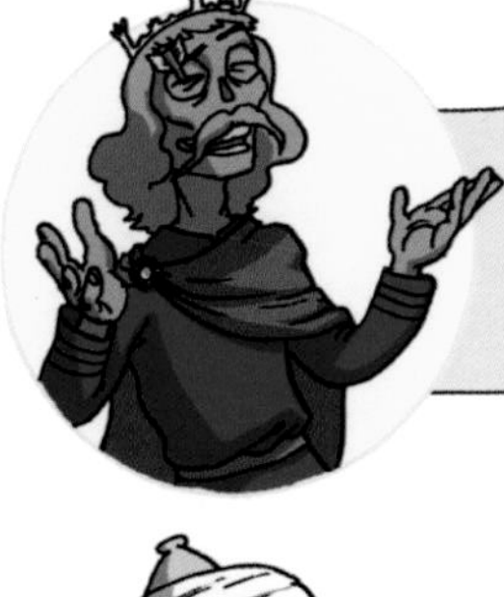

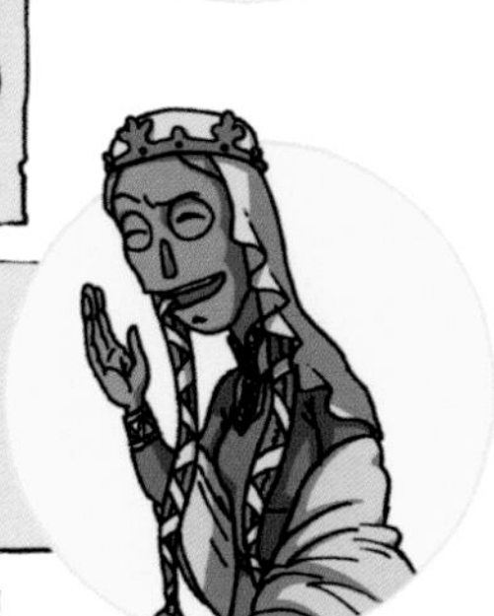

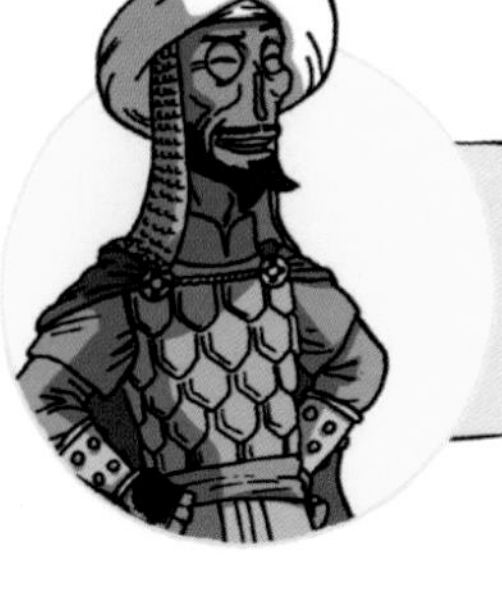

64 RICHARD THE LIONHEART
ENGLISH KING 1157–1199

MOCTEZUMA II
AZTEC EMPEROR 1466–1520 70

76 HENRY VIII
ENGLISH KING 1491–1547

HENRY VIII'S WIVES
ENGLISH QUEENS
1480s–1500s 82

92 CHARLES II
BRITISH KING 1630–1685

MARIE ANTOINETTE
FRENCH QUEEN 1755–1793 100

106 CATHERINE THE GREAT
RUSSIAN EMPRESS 1729–1796

SHAKA ZULU
ZULU KING 1787–1828 112

118 QUEEN VICTORIA
BRITISH QUEEN 1819–1901

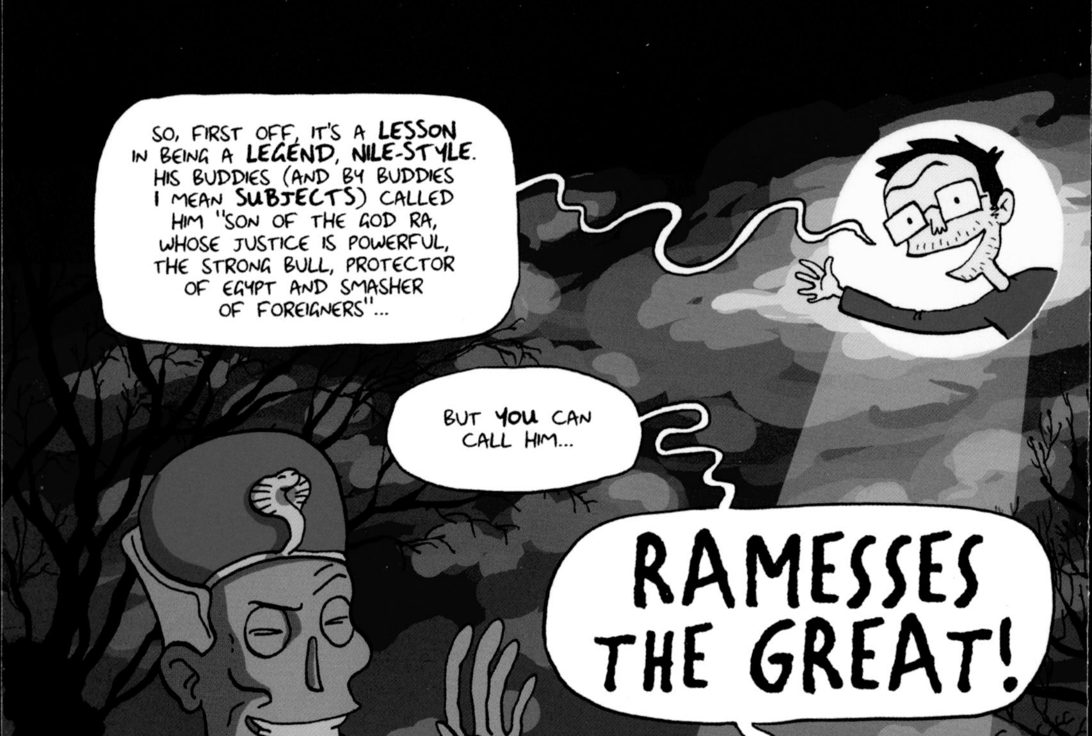
SO, FIRST OFF, IT'S A **LESSON** IN BEING A **LEGEND, NILE-STYLE**. HIS BUDDIES (AND BY BUDDIES I MEAN **SUBJECTS**) CALLED HIM "SON OF THE GOD RA, WHOSE JUSTICE IS POWERFUL, THE STRONG BULL, PROTECTOR OF EGYPT AND SMASHER OF FOREIGNERS"...
BUT **YOU** CAN CALL HIM...
RAMESSES THE GREAT!
RAMESSES II
PHARAOH OF EGYPT
c.1303 BCE–1213 BCE

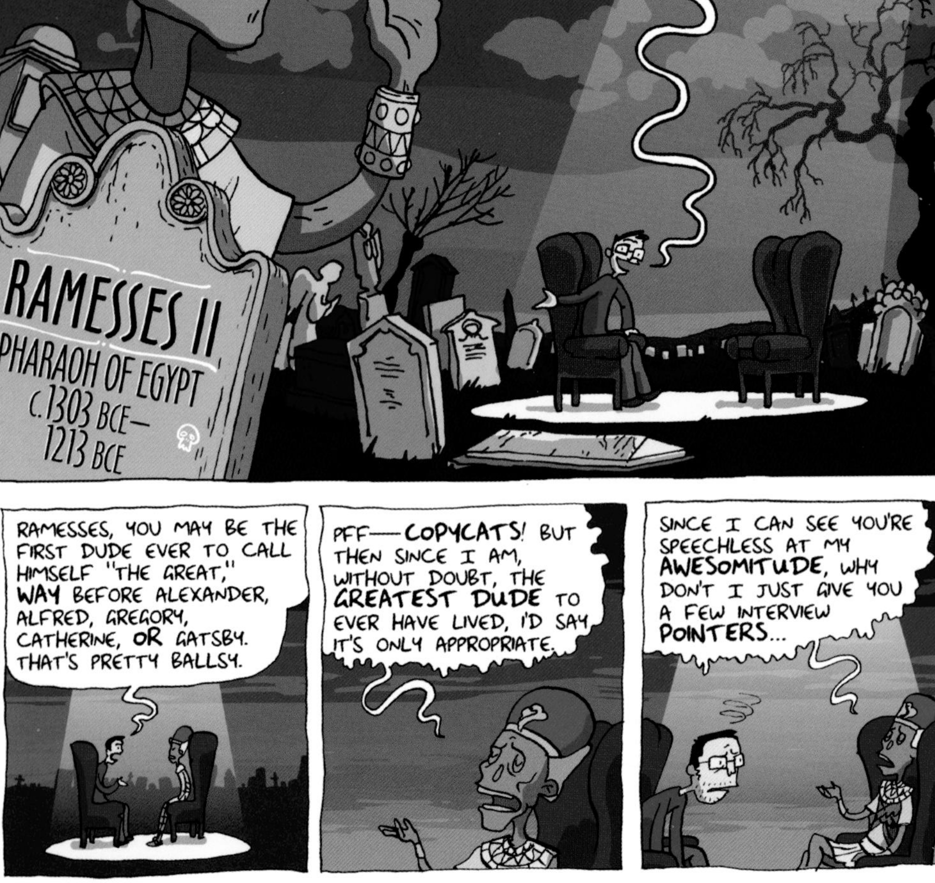
RAMESSES, YOU MAY BE THE FIRST DUDE EVER TO CALL HIMSELF "THE GREAT," **WAY** BEFORE ALEXANDER, ALFRED, GREGORY, CATHERINE, **OR** GATSBY. THAT'S PRETTY BALLSY.
PFF—**COPYCATS**! BUT THEN SINCE I AM, WITHOUT DOUBT, THE **GREATEST DUDE** TO EVER HAVE LIVED, I'D SAY IT'S ONLY APPROPRIATE.
SINCE I CAN SEE YOU'RE SPEECHLESS AT MY **AWESOMITUDE**, WHY DON'T I JUST GIVE YOU A FEW INTERVIEW **POINTERS**...

FOR EXAMPLE, YOU SHOULD CERTAINLY ASK ABOUT MY AMAZING VICTORIES AGAINST EGYPT'S ANCIENT ENEMIES, THE **HITTITES**.

OOH, I **HATE** THOSE GUYS! THOSE HALF-BAKED ANCIENT EMPIRE WANNABES, COMING OVER HERE, STEALING **MY** CITIES...

WELL, THEY SOON FOUND OUT THEY'D MESSED WITH THE **WRONG PHARAOH!**

BOOYAH!

OH YES, YOU TANGLE WITH THE RAM-MAN, YOU GONNA **FEEL THE PAIN!**

BUT THE RAM COULD ALSO SHOW **MERCY**...

DID YOU KNOW I SIGNED THE WORLD'S **VERY FIRST PEACE** TREATY, WITH THOSE SAME HITTITES...

I DIDN'T **HAVE** TO DO THAT... I'M JUST SUCH A NICE GUY.

THEN PERHAPS YOUR READERS WOULD WANT TO HEAR ABOUT MY AWESOME MONUMENTS.

LIKE I BUILT BASICALLY THE BIGGEST STATUE **EVER. OH YEAH!** YOU LIKE THAT?

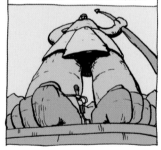

AND WHEN I SAY I BUILT IT, I MEAN THE PEOPLE I ENSLAVED BUILT IT.

HOLD ON, THERE'S MORE. DON'T FORGET TO ASK ABOUT HOW MANY TIMES I WAS MADE **A GOD**.

IT WAS LIKE **20** TIMES OR SOMETHING BECAUSE I LIVED SO LONG, AND JUST KEPT ON DOING SO MUCH AWESOME STUFF.

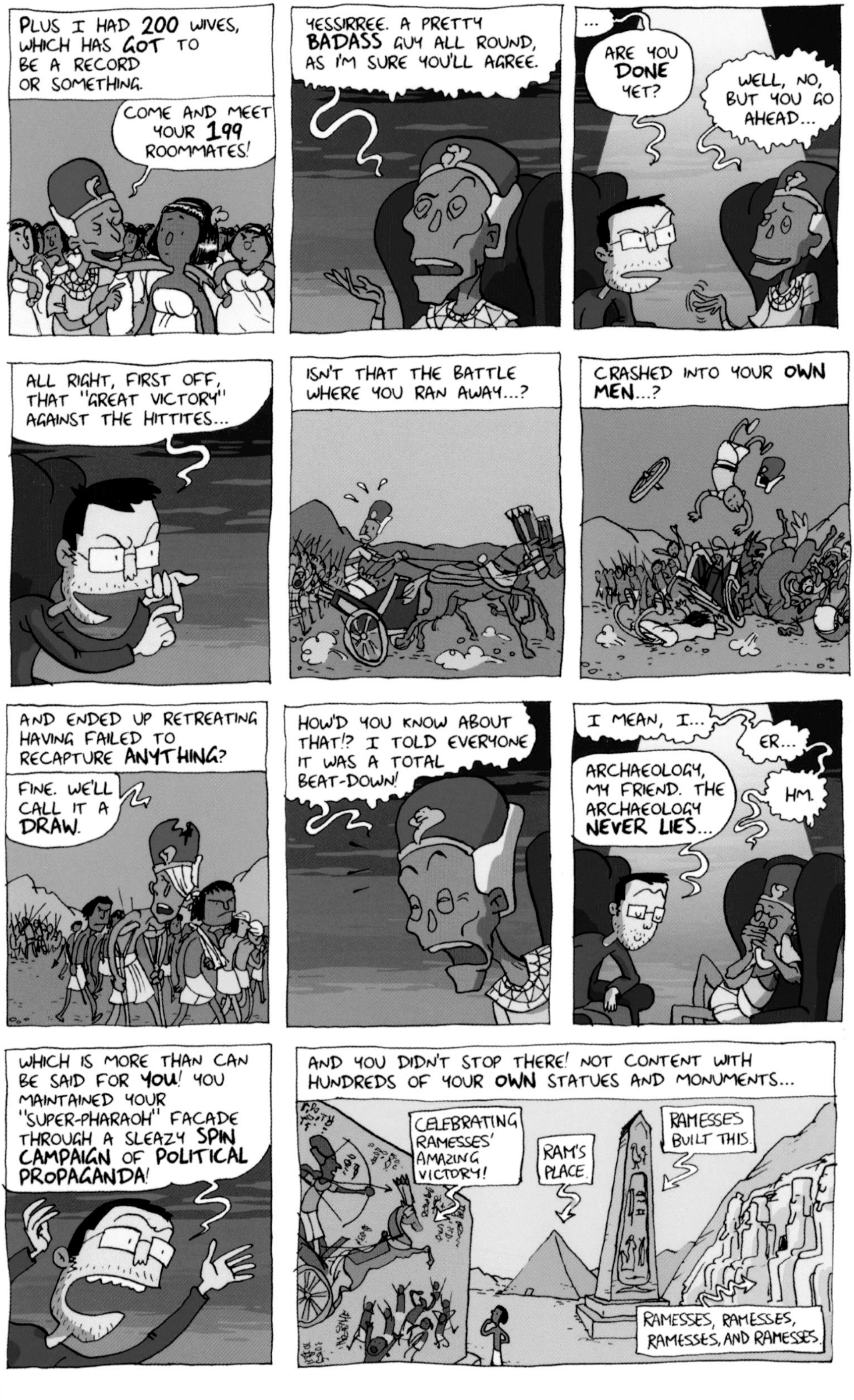
PLUS I HAD 200 WIVES, WHICH HAS GOT TO BE A RECORD OR SOMETHING.
COME AND MEET YOUR 199 ROOMMATES!
YESSIRREE. A PRETTY BADASS GUY ALL ROUND, AS I'M SURE YOU'LL AGREE.
...
ARE YOU DONE YET?
WELL, NO, BUT YOU GO AHEAD...
ALL RIGHT, FIRST OFF, THAT "GREAT VICTORY" AGAINST THE HITTITES...
ISN'T THAT THE BATTLE WHERE YOU RAN AWAY...?
CRASHED INTO YOUR OWN MEN...?
AND ENDED UP RETREATING HAVING FAILED TO RECAPTURE ANYTHING?
FINE. WE'LL CALL IT A DRAW.
HOW'D YOU KNOW ABOUT THAT!? I TOLD EVERYONE IT WAS A TOTAL BEAT-DOWN!
I MEAN, I...
ER...
ARCHAEOLOGY, MY FRIEND. THE ARCHAEOLOGY NEVER LIES...
HM.
WHICH IS MORE THAN CAN BE SAID FOR YOU! YOU MAINTAINED YOUR "SUPER-PHARAOH" FACADE THROUGH A SLEAZY SPIN CAMPAIGN OF POLITICAL PROPAGANDA!
AND YOU DIDN'T STOP THERE! NOT CONTENT WITH HUNDREDS OF YOUR OWN STATUES AND MONUMENTS...
CELEBRATING RAMESSES' AMAZING VICTORY!
RAM'S PLACE.
RAMESSES BUILT THIS.
RAMESSES, RAMESSES, RAMESSES, AND RAMESSES.

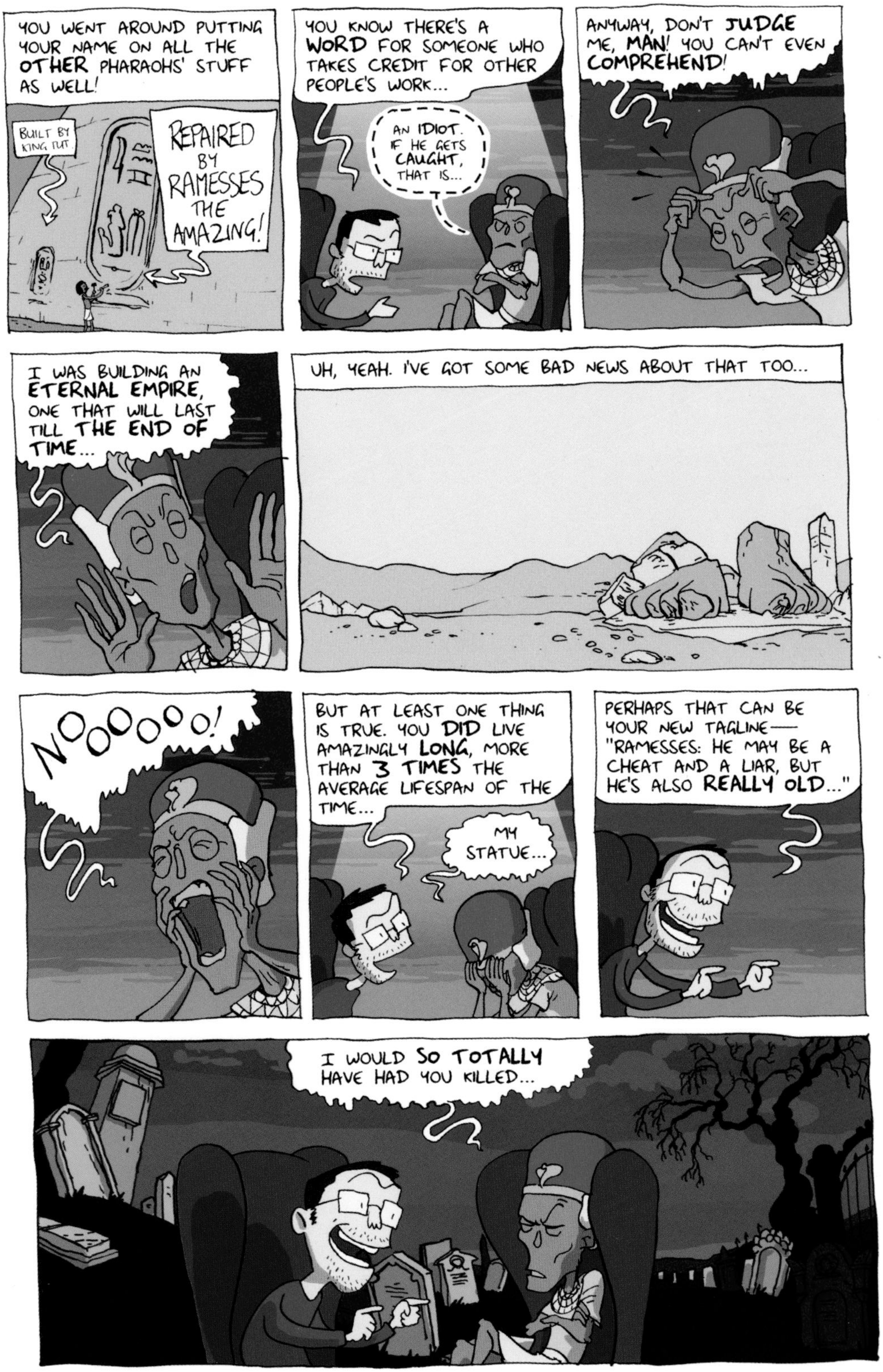
YOU WENT AROUND PUTTING YOUR NAME ON ALL THE OTHER PHARAOHS' STUFF AS WELL!
BUILT BY KING TUT.
REPAIRED BY RAMESSES THE AMAZING!
YOU KNOW THERE'S A WORD FOR SOMEONE WHO TAKES CREDIT FOR OTHER PEOPLE'S WORK...
AN IDIOT. IF HE GETS CAUGHT, THAT IS...
ANYWAY, DON'T JUDGE ME, MAN! YOU CAN'T EVEN COMPREHEND!
I WAS BUILDING AN ETERNAL EMPIRE, ONE THAT WILL LAST TILL THE END OF TIME...
UH, YEAH. I'VE GOT SOME BAD NEWS ABOUT THAT TOO...
NOOOOOO!
BUT AT LEAST ONE THING IS TRUE. YOU DID LIVE AMAZINGLY LONG, MORE THAN 3 TIMES THE AVERAGE LIFESPAN OF THE TIME...
MY STATUE...
PERHAPS THAT CAN BE YOUR NEW TAGLINE— "RAMESSES: HE MAY BE A CHEAT AND A LIAR, BUT HE'S ALSO REALLY OLD..."
I WOULD SO TOTALLY HAVE HAD YOU KILLED...

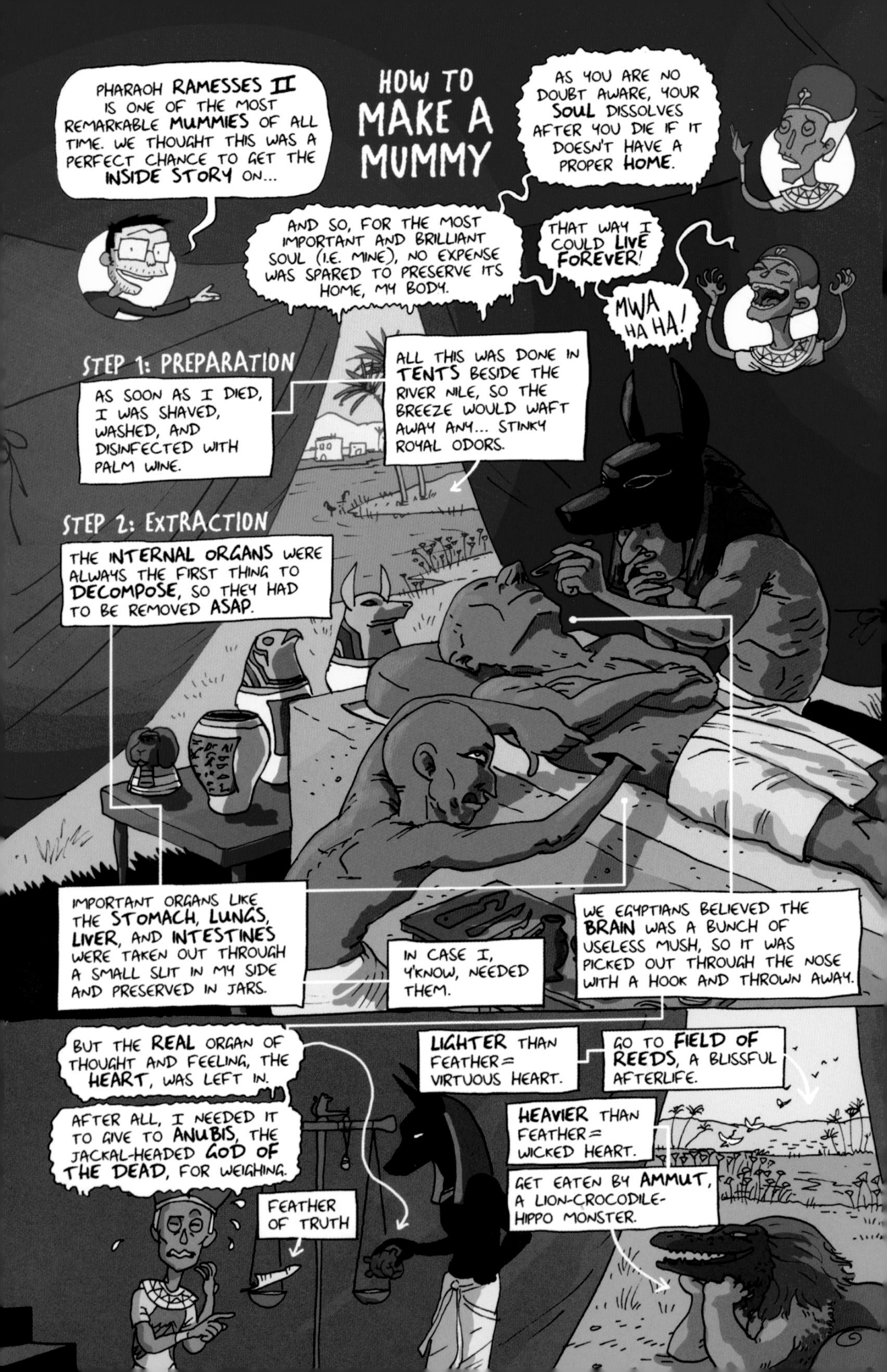

HOW TO MAKE A MUMMY
PHARAOH RAMESSES II IS ONE OF THE MOST REMARKABLE MUMMIES OF ALL TIME. WE THOUGHT THIS WAS A PERFECT CHANCE TO GET THE INSIDE STORY ON...
AS YOU ARE NO DOUBT AWARE, YOUR SOUL DISSOLVES AFTER YOU DIE IF IT DOESN'T HAVE A PROPER HOME.
AND SO, FOR THE MOST IMPORTANT AND BRILLIANT SOUL (I.E. MINE), NO EXPENSE WAS SPARED TO PRESERVE ITS HOME, MY BODY.
THAT WAY I COULD LIVE FOREVER!
MWA HA HA!
STEP 1: PREPARATION
AS SOON AS I DIED, I WAS SHAVED, WASHED, AND DISINFECTED WITH PALM WINE.
ALL THIS WAS DONE IN TENTS BESIDE THE RIVER NILE, SO THE BREEZE WOULD WAFT AWAY ANY... STINKY ROYAL ODORS.
STEP 2: EXTRACTION
THE INTERNAL ORGANS WERE ALWAYS THE FIRST THING TO DECOMPOSE, SO THEY HAD TO BE REMOVED ASAP.
IMPORTANT ORGANS LIKE THE STOMACH, LUNGS, LIVER, AND INTESTINES WERE TAKEN OUT THROUGH A SMALL SLIT IN MY SIDE AND PRESERVED IN JARS.
IN CASE I, Y'KNOW, NEEDED THEM.
WE EGYPTIANS BELIEVED THE BRAIN WAS A BUNCH OF USELESS MUSH, SO IT WAS PICKED OUT THROUGH THE NOSE WITH A HOOK AND THROWN AWAY.
BUT THE REAL ORGAN OF THOUGHT AND FEELING, THE HEART, WAS LEFT IN.
AFTER ALL, I NEEDED IT TO GIVE TO ANUBIS, THE JACKAL-HEADED GOD OF THE DEAD, FOR WEIGHING.
FEATHER OF TRUTH
LIGHTER THAN FEATHER = VIRTUOUS HEART.
GO TO FIELD OF REEDS, A BLISSFUL AFTERLIFE.
HEAVIER THAN FEATHER = WICKED HEART.
GET EATEN BY AMMUT, A LION-CROCODILE-HIPPO MONSTER.

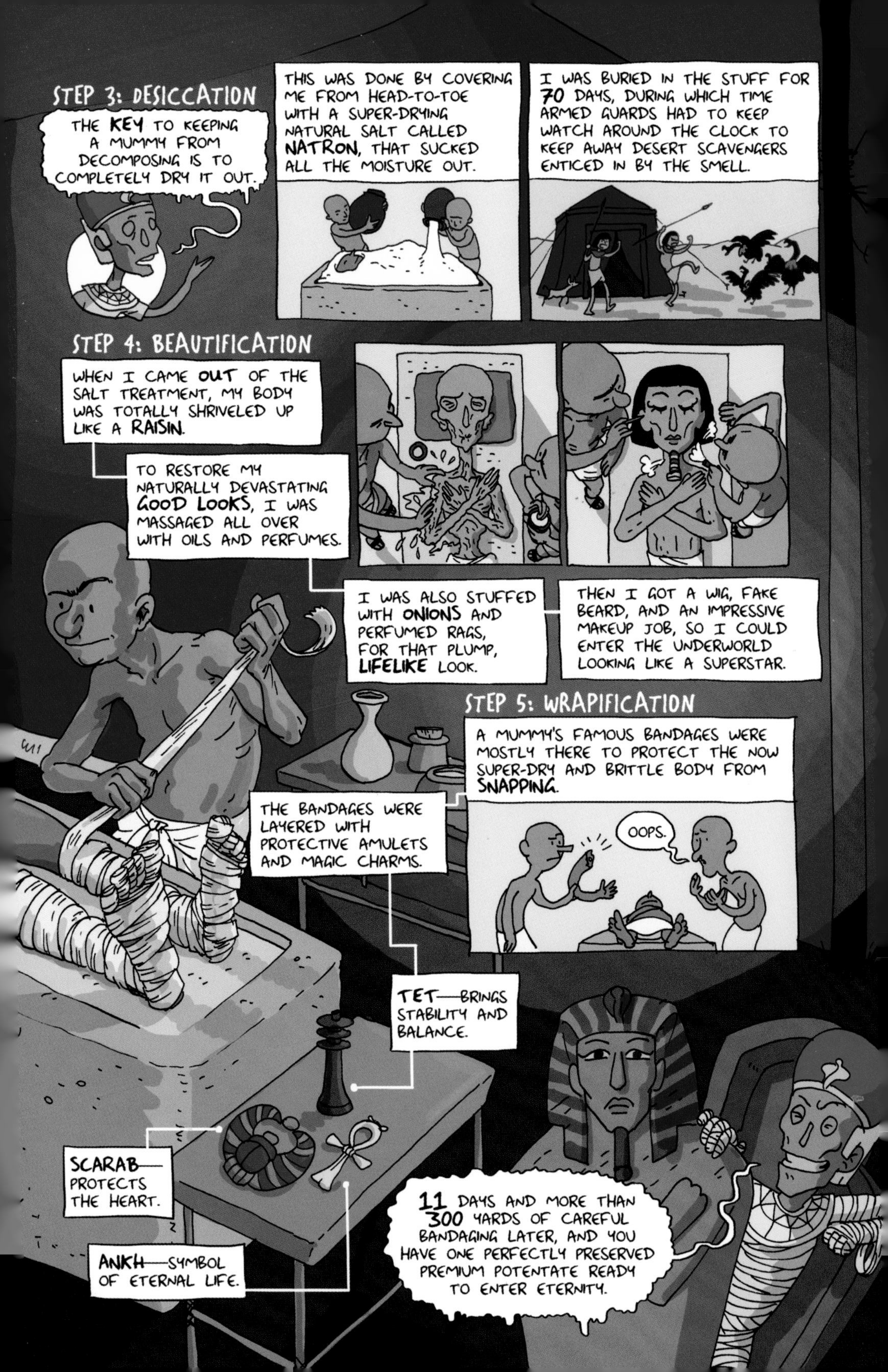
STEP 3: DESICCATION
THE KEY TO KEEPING A MUMMY FROM DECOMPOSING IS TO COMPLETELY DRY IT OUT.
THIS WAS DONE BY COVERING ME FROM HEAD-TO-TOE WITH A SUPER-DRYING NATURAL SALT CALLED NATRON, THAT SUCKED ALL THE MOISTURE OUT.
I WAS BURIED IN THE STUFF FOR 70 DAYS, DURING WHICH TIME ARMED GUARDS HAD TO KEEP WATCH AROUND THE CLOCK TO KEEP AWAY DESERT SCAVENGERS ENTICED IN BY THE SMELL.
STEP 4: BEAUTIFICATION
WHEN I CAME OUT OF THE SALT TREATMENT, MY BODY WAS TOTALLY SHRIVELED UP LIKE A RAISIN.
TO RESTORE MY NATURALLY DEVASTATING GOOD LOOKS, I WAS MASSAGED ALL OVER WITH OILS AND PERFUMES.
I WAS ALSO STUFFED WITH ONIONS AND PERFUMED RAGS, FOR THAT PLUMP, LIFELIKE LOOK.
THEN I GOT A WIG, FAKE BEARD, AND AN IMPRESSIVE MAKEUP JOB, SO I COULD ENTER THE UNDERWORLD LOOKING LIKE A SUPERSTAR.
STEP 5: WRAPIFICATION
A MUMMY'S FAMOUS BANDAGES WERE MOSTLY THERE TO PROTECT THE NOW SUPER-DRY AND BRITTLE BODY FROM SNAPPING.
OOPS.
THE BANDAGES WERE LAYERED WITH PROTECTIVE AMULETS AND MAGIC CHARMS.
TET—BRINGS STABILITY AND BALANCE.
SCARAB—PROTECTS THE HEART.
ANKH—SYMBOL OF ETERNAL LIFE.
11 DAYS AND MORE THAN 300 YARDS OF CAREFUL BANDAGING LATER, AND YOU HAVE ONE PERFECTLY PRESERVED PREMIUM POTENTATE READY TO ENTER ETERNITY.

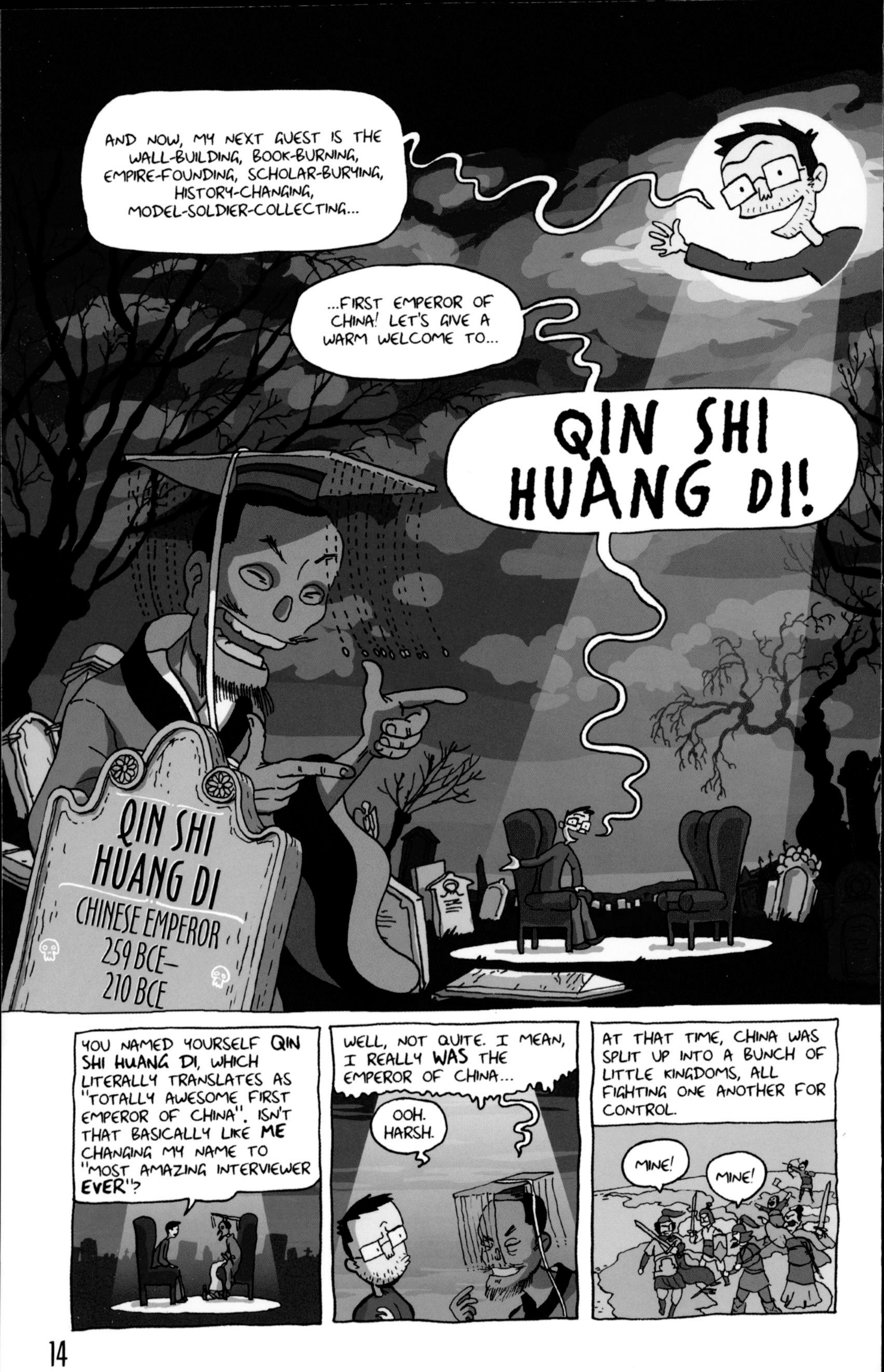
AND NOW, MY NEXT GUEST IS THE WALL-BUILDING, BOOK-BURNING, EMPIRE-FOUNDING, SCHOLAR-BURYING, HISTORY-CHANGING, MODEL-SOLDIER-COLLECTING...
...FIRST EMPEROR OF CHINA! LET'S GIVE A WARM WELCOME TO...
QIN SHI HUANG DI!
QIN SHI HUANG DI
CHINESE EMPEROR
259 BCE–
210 BCE
YOU NAMED YOURSELF QIN SHI HUANG DI, WHICH LITERALLY TRANSLATES AS "TOTALLY AWESOME FIRST EMPEROR OF CHINA". ISN'T THAT BASICALLY LIKE ME CHANGING MY NAME TO "MOST AMAZING INTERVIEWER EVER"?
WELL, NOT QUITE. I MEAN, I REALLY WAS THE EMPEROR OF CHINA...
OOH. HARSH.
AT THAT TIME, CHINA WAS SPLIT UP INTO A BUNCH OF LITTLE KINGDOMS, ALL FIGHTING ONE ANOTHER FOR CONTROL.
MINE!
MINE!

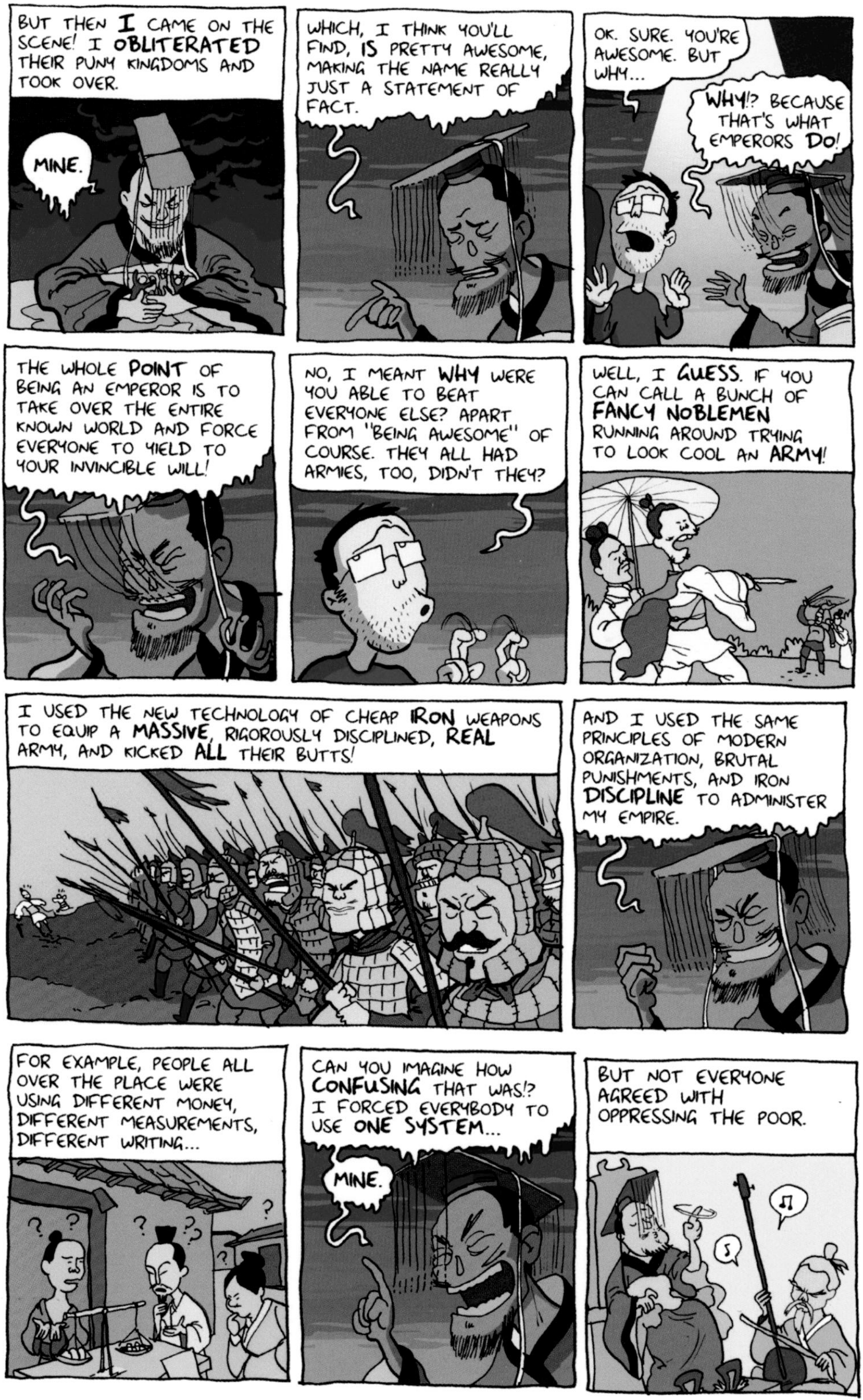
BUT THEN I CAME ON THE SCENE! I OBLITERATED THEIR PUNY KINGDOMS AND TOOK OVER.
MINE.
WHICH, I THINK YOU'LL FIND, IS PRETTY AWESOME, MAKING THE NAME REALLY JUST A STATEMENT OF FACT.
OK. SURE. YOU'RE AWESOME. BUT WHY...
WHY!? BECAUSE THAT'S WHAT EMPERORS DO!
THE WHOLE POINT OF BEING AN EMPEROR IS TO TAKE OVER THE ENTIRE KNOWN WORLD AND FORCE EVERYONE TO YIELD TO YOUR INVINCIBLE WILL!
NO, I MEANT WHY WERE YOU ABLE TO BEAT EVERYONE ELSE? APART FROM "BEING AWESOME" OF COURSE. THEY ALL HAD ARMIES, TOO, DIDN'T THEY?
WELL, I GUESS. IF YOU CAN CALL A BUNCH OF FANCY NOBLEMEN RUNNING AROUND TRYING TO LOOK COOL AN ARMY!
I USED THE NEW TECHNOLOGY OF CHEAP IRON WEAPONS TO EQUIP A MASSIVE, RIGOROUSLY DISCIPLINED, REAL ARMY, AND KICKED ALL THEIR BUTTS!
AND I USED THE SAME PRINCIPLES OF MODERN ORGANIZATION, BRUTAL PUNISHMENTS, AND IRON DISCIPLINE TO ADMINISTER MY EMPIRE.
FOR EXAMPLE, PEOPLE ALL OVER THE PLACE WERE USING DIFFERENT MONEY, DIFFERENT MEASUREMENTS, DIFFERENT WRITING...
CAN YOU IMAGINE HOW CONFUSING THAT WAS!? I FORCED EVERYBODY TO USE ONE SYSTEM...
MINE.
BUT NOT EVERYONE AGREED WITH OPPRESSING THE POOR.

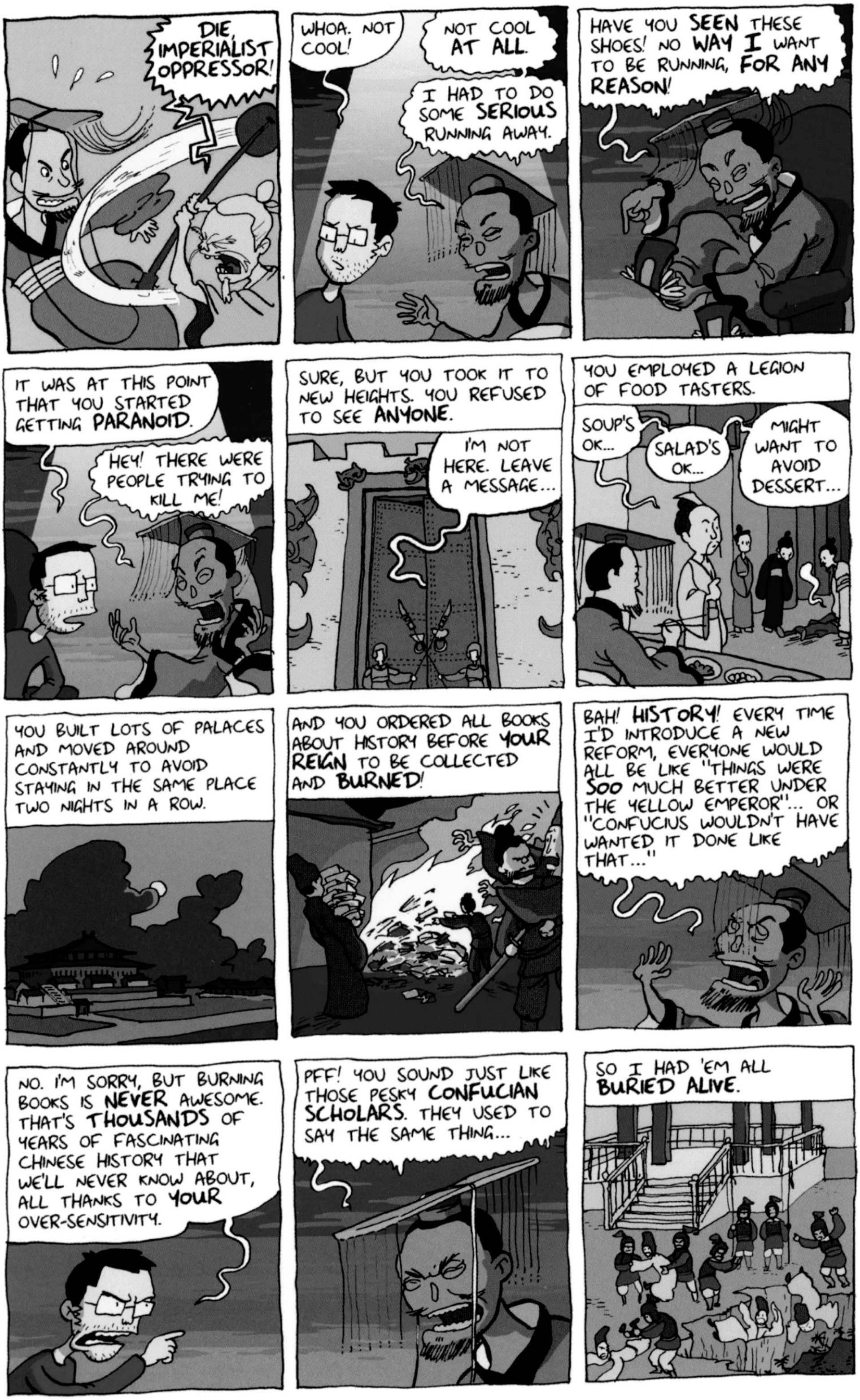
DIE, IMPERIALIST OPPRESSOR!
WHOA. NOT COOL!
NOT COOL AT ALL.
I HAD TO DO SOME SERIOUS RUNNING AWAY.
HAVE YOU SEEN THESE SHOES! NO WAY I WANT TO BE RUNNING, FOR ANY REASON!
IT WAS AT THIS POINT THAT YOU STARTED GETTING PARANOID.
HEY! THERE WERE PEOPLE TRYING TO KILL ME!
SURE, BUT YOU TOOK IT TO NEW HEIGHTS. YOU REFUSED TO SEE ANYONE.
I'M NOT HERE. LEAVE A MESSAGE...
YOU EMPLOYED A LEGION OF FOOD TASTERS.
SOUP'S OK...
SALAD'S OK...
MIGHT WANT TO AVOID DESSERT...
YOU BUILT LOTS OF PALACES AND MOVED AROUND CONSTANTLY TO AVOID STAYING IN THE SAME PLACE TWO NIGHTS IN A ROW.
AND YOU ORDERED ALL BOOKS ABOUT HISTORY BEFORE YOUR REIGN TO BE COLLECTED AND BURNED!
BAH! HISTORY! EVERY TIME I'D INTRODUCE A NEW REFORM, EVERYONE WOULD ALL BE LIKE "THINGS WERE SOO MUCH BETTER UNDER THE YELLOW EMPEROR"... OR "CONFUCIUS WOULDN'T HAVE WANTED IT DONE LIKE THAT..."
NO. I'M SORRY, BUT BURNING BOOKS IS NEVER AWESOME. THAT'S THOUSANDS OF YEARS OF FASCINATING CHINESE HISTORY THAT WE'LL NEVER KNOW ABOUT, ALL THANKS TO YOUR OVER-SENSITIVITY.
PFF! YOU SOUND JUST LIKE THOSE PESKY CONFUCIAN SCHOLARS. THEY USED TO SAY THE SAME THING...
SO I HAD 'EM ALL BURIED ALIVE.

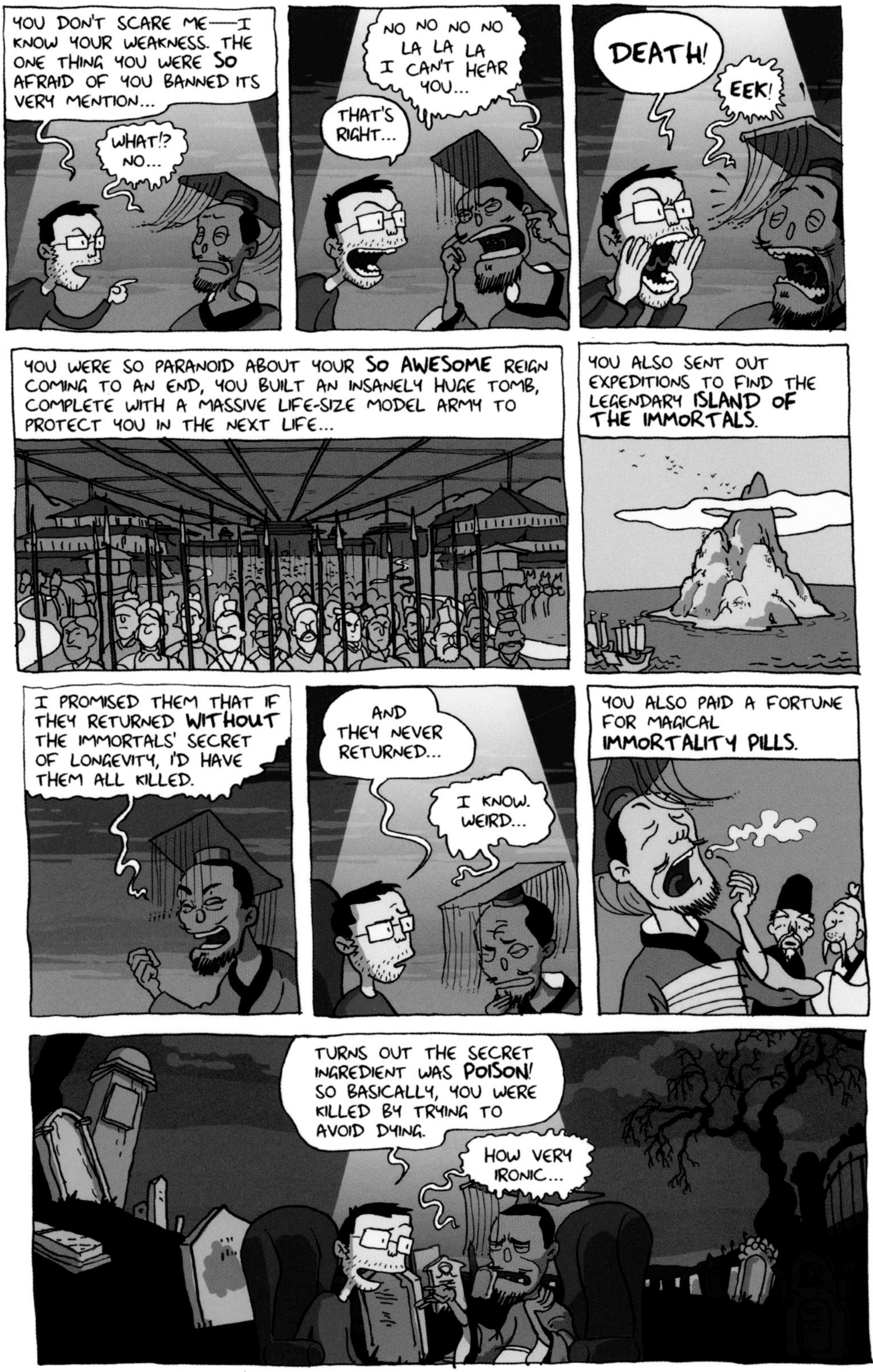
YOU DON'T SCARE ME—I KNOW YOUR WEAKNESS. THE ONE THING YOU WERE SO AFRAID OF YOU BANNED ITS VERY MENTION...
WHAT!? NO...
NO NO NO NO LA LA LA I CAN'T HEAR YOU...
THAT'S RIGHT...
DEATH!
EEK!
YOU WERE SO PARANOID ABOUT YOUR SO AWESOME REIGN COMING TO AN END, YOU BUILT AN INSANELY HUGE TOMB, COMPLETE WITH A MASSIVE LIFE-SIZE MODEL ARMY TO PROTECT YOU IN THE NEXT LIFE...
YOU ALSO SENT OUT EXPEDITIONS TO FIND THE LEGENDARY ISLAND OF THE IMMORTALS.
I PROMISED THEM THAT IF THEY RETURNED WITHOUT THE IMMORTALS' SECRET OF LONGEVITY, I'D HAVE THEM ALL KILLED.
AND THEY NEVER RETURNED...
I KNOW. WEIRD...
YOU ALSO PAID A FORTUNE FOR MAGICAL IMMORTALITY PILLS.
TURNS OUT THE SECRET INGREDIENT WAS POISON! SO BASICALLY, YOU WERE KILLED BY TRYING TO AVOID DYING.
HOW VERY IRONIC...

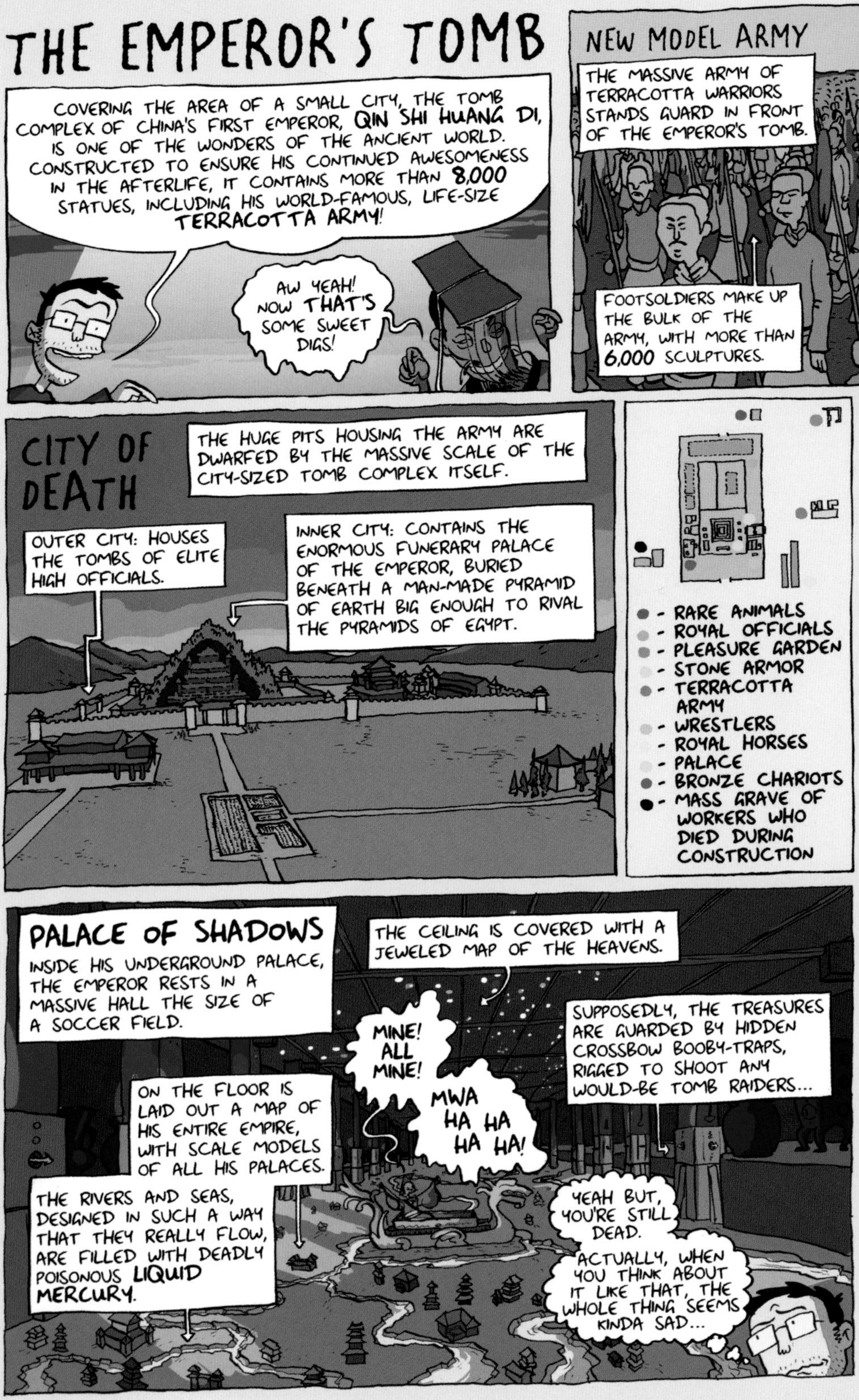
THE EMPEROR'S TOMB
COVERING THE AREA OF A SMALL CITY, THE TOMB COMPLEX OF CHINA'S FIRST EMPEROR, QIN SHI HUANG DI, IS ONE OF THE WONDERS OF THE ANCIENT WORLD. CONSTRUCTED TO ENSURE HIS CONTINUED AWESOMENESS IN THE AFTERLIFE, IT CONTAINS MORE THAN 8,000 STATUES, INCLUDING HIS WORLD-FAMOUS, LIFE-SIZE TERRACOTTA ARMY!
AW YEAH! NOW THAT'S SOME SWEET DIGS!
NEW MODEL ARMY
THE MASSIVE ARMY OF TERRACOTTA WARRIORS STANDS GUARD IN FRONT OF THE EMPEROR'S TOMB.
FOOTSOLDIERS MAKE UP THE BULK OF THE ARMY, WITH MORE THAN 6,000 SCULPTURES.
CITY OF DEATH
THE HUGE PITS HOUSING THE ARMY ARE DWARFED BY THE MASSIVE SCALE OF THE CITY-SIZED TOMB COMPLEX ITSELF.
OUTER CITY: HOUSES THE TOMBS OF ELITE HIGH OFFICIALS.
INNER CITY: CONTAINS THE ENORMOUS FUNERARY PALACE OF THE EMPEROR, BURIED BENEATH A MAN-MADE PYRAMID OF EARTH BIG ENOUGH TO RIVAL THE PYRAMIDS OF EGYPT.
- RARE ANIMALS
- ROYAL OFFICIALS
- PLEASURE GARDEN
- STONE ARMOR
- TERRACOTTA ARMY
- WRESTLERS
- ROYAL HORSES
- PALACE
- BRONZE CHARIOTS
- MASS GRAVE OF WORKERS WHO DIED DURING CONSTRUCTION
PALACE OF SHADOWS
INSIDE HIS UNDERGROUND PALACE, THE EMPEROR RESTS IN A MASSIVE HALL THE SIZE OF A SOCCER FIELD.
THE CEILING IS COVERED WITH A JEWELED MAP OF THE HEAVENS.
MINE! ALL MINE!
MWA HA HA HA HA!
SUPPOSEDLY, THE TREASURES ARE GUARDED BY HIDDEN CROSSBOW BOOBY-TRAPS, RIGGED TO SHOOT ANY WOULD-BE TOMB RAIDERS...
ON THE FLOOR IS LAID OUT A MAP OF HIS ENTIRE EMPIRE, WITH SCALE MODELS OF ALL HIS PALACES.
THE RIVERS AND SEAS, DESIGNED IN SUCH A WAY THAT THEY REALLY FLOW, ARE FILLED WITH DEADLY POISONOUS LIQUID MERCURY.
YEAH BUT, YOU'RE STILL DEAD.
ACTUALLY, WHEN YOU THINK ABOUT IT LIKE THAT, THE WHOLE THING SEEMS KINDA SAD...

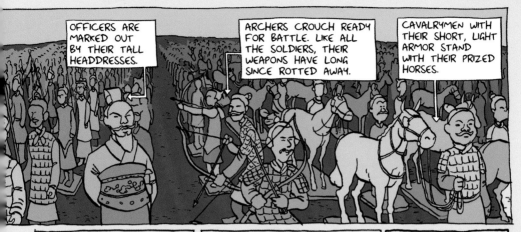

OFFICERS ARE MARKED OUT BY THEIR TALL HEADDRESSES.

ARCHERS CROUCH READY FOR BATTLE. LIKE ALL THE SOLDIERS, THEIR WEAPONS HAVE LONG SINCE ROTTED AWAY.

CAVALRYMEN WITH THEIR SHORT, LIGHT ARMOR STAND WITH THEIR PRIZED HORSES.

NOW FADED, THE WARRIORS WERE ORIGINALLY PAINTED IN BRIGHT COLORS!

EACH STATUE WAS MODELED ON ONE OF THE EMPEROR'S REAL-LIFE ELITE SOLDIERS.

EVEN THE HAIRSTYLES!

BURIED TREASURES

IN ADDITION TO THE TERRACOTTA WARRIORS, ARCHAEOLOGISTS HAVE RECENTLY DISCOVERED ALL SORTS OF OTHER FANTASTIC TREASURES IN THE PALACE COMPLEX.

BURIED ALIVE

THE EMPEROR WAS **SO AFRAID** OF THE BUILDERS REVEALING THE SECRETS OF THE TOMB'S DEFENSES THAT, WHILE THEY WERE PUTTING ON THE LAST FINISHING TOUCHES, THEY WERE ALL SHUT UP INSIDE!

SLAM!

LIKE A **MASSIVE** SUIT OF **STONE ARMOR**. TOO HEAVY TO WEAR, IT IS THOUGHT TO BE DESIGNED TO PROTECT THE EMPEROR FROM UNDERWORLD SPIRITS.

HE HAD A **PLEASURE GARDEN** FILLED WITH LIFELIKE STATUES OF HIS FAVORITE MUSICIANS AND EXOTIC BIRDS.

RECENTLY UNEARTHED: A TEAM OF **BRONZE WRESTLERS**. LIKE HAVING WWE IN YOUR LIVING ROOM!

LUCKY FIND

THE TERRACOTTA WARRIORS, AND THE ENTIRE TOMB COMPLEX, WERE DISCOVERED BY **ACCIDENT** BY THREE FARMERS, WHILE THEY WERE DIGGING A WELL...

BEHIND THE TOMB IS A SET OF **BRONZE CHARIOTS**, COMPLETE WITH HORSES AND DRIVERS, READY FOR A SIGHTSEEING TRIP AROUND THE KINGDOM.

YEAH! VROOM VROOM! LET'S GO!

THE EMPEROR'S **CENTRAL PALACE MOUND** IS YET TO BE OPENED. NO ONE KNOWS FOR SURE WHAT AMAZING STUFF IT HOLDS.

EXCEPT MEEE!

AND I'M NOT TELLING!

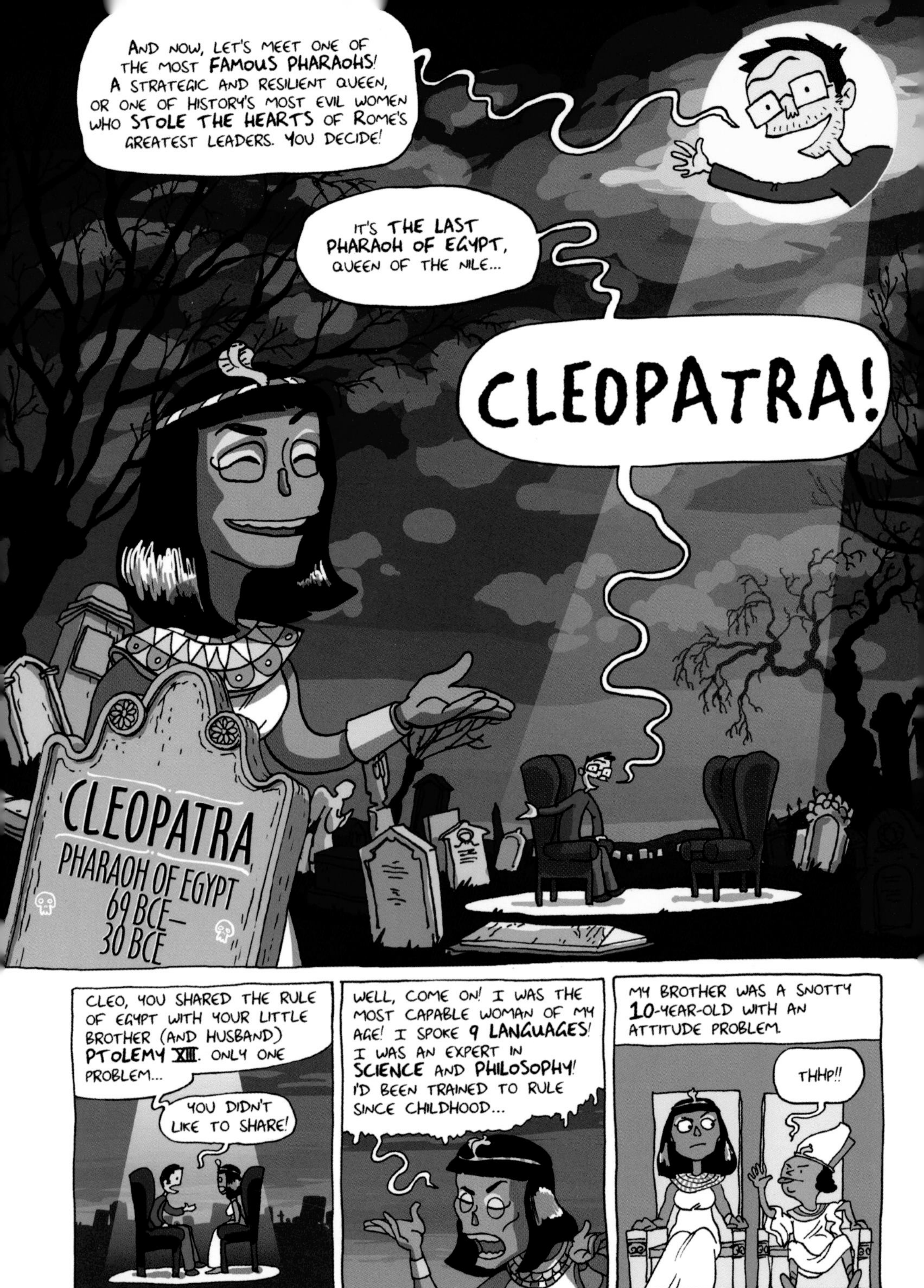
AND NOW, LET'S MEET ONE OF THE MOST FAMOUS PHARAOHS! A STRATEGIC AND RESILIENT QUEEN, OR ONE OF HISTORY'S MOST EVIL WOMEN WHO STOLE THE HEARTS OF ROME'S GREATEST LEADERS. YOU DECIDE!
IT'S THE LAST PHARAOH OF EGYPT, QUEEN OF THE NILE...
CLEOPATRA!
CLEOPATRA
PHARAOH OF EGYPT
69 BCE–
30 BCE
CLEO, YOU SHARED THE RULE OF EGYPT WITH YOUR LITTLE BROTHER (AND HUSBAND) PTOLEMY XIII. ONLY ONE PROBLEM...
YOU DIDN'T LIKE TO SHARE!
WELL, COME ON! I WAS THE MOST CAPABLE WOMAN OF MY AGE! I SPOKE 9 LANGUAGES! I WAS AN EXPERT IN SCIENCE AND PHILOSOPHY! I'D BEEN TRAINED TO RULE SINCE CHILDHOOD...
MY BROTHER WAS A SNOTTY 10-YEAR-OLD WITH AN ATTITUDE PROBLEM.
THHP!!

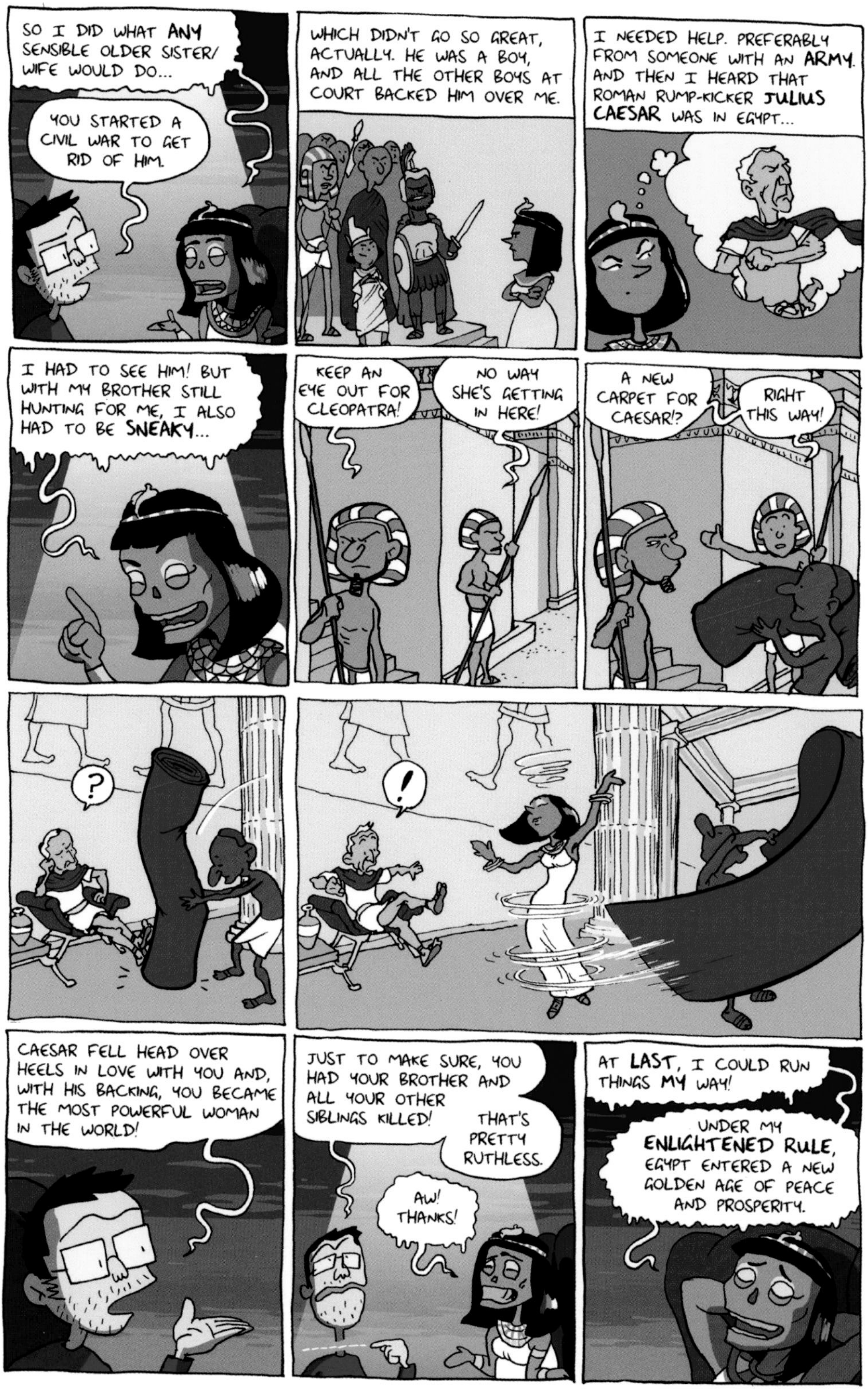

SO I DID WHAT ANY SENSIBLE OLDER SISTER/WIFE WOULD DO...
YOU STARTED A CIVIL WAR TO GET RID OF HIM.
WHICH DIDN'T GO SO GREAT, ACTUALLY. HE WAS A BOY, AND ALL THE OTHER BOYS AT COURT BACKED HIM OVER ME.
I NEEDED HELP. PREFERABLY FROM SOMEONE WITH AN ARMY. AND THEN I HEARD THAT ROMAN RUMP-KICKER JULIUS CAESAR WAS IN EGYPT...
I HAD TO SEE HIM! BUT WITH MY BROTHER STILL HUNTING FOR ME, I ALSO HAD TO BE SNEAKY...
KEEP AN EYE OUT FOR CLEOPATRA!
NO WAY SHE'S GETTING IN HERE!
A NEW CARPET FOR CAESAR!?
RIGHT THIS WAY!
?
!
CAESAR FELL HEAD OVER HEELS IN LOVE WITH YOU AND, WITH HIS BACKING, YOU BECAME THE MOST POWERFUL WOMAN IN THE WORLD!
JUST TO MAKE SURE, YOU HAD YOUR BROTHER AND ALL YOUR OTHER SIBLINGS KILLED!
THAT'S PRETTY RUTHLESS.
AW! THANKS!
AT LAST, I COULD RUN THINGS MY WAY!
UNDER MY ENLIGHTENED RULE, EGYPT ENTERED A NEW GOLDEN AGE OF PEACE AND PROSPERITY.

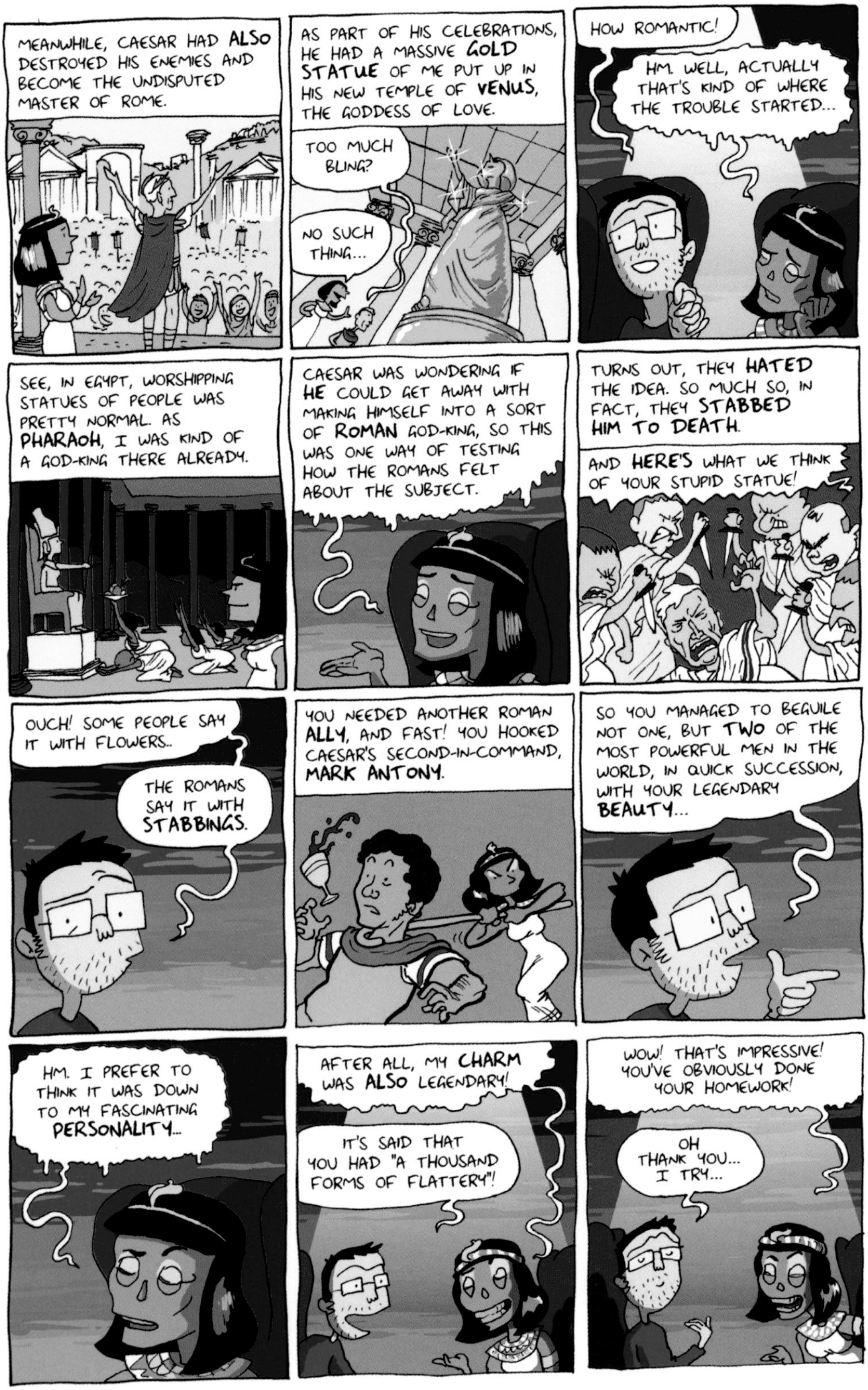
MEANWHILE, CAESAR HAD ALSO DESTROYED HIS ENEMIES AND BECOME THE UNDISPUTED MASTER OF ROME.
AS PART OF HIS CELEBRATIONS, HE HAD A MASSIVE GOLD STATUE OF ME PUT UP IN HIS NEW TEMPLE OF VENUS, THE GODDESS OF LOVE.
TOO MUCH BLING?
NO SUCH THING...
HOW ROMANTIC!
HM. WELL, ACTUALLY THAT'S KIND OF WHERE THE TROUBLE STARTED...
SEE, IN EGYPT, WORSHIPPING STATUES OF PEOPLE WAS PRETTY NORMAL. AS PHARAOH, I WAS KIND OF A GOD-KING THERE ALREADY.
CAESAR WAS WONDERING IF HE COULD GET AWAY WITH MAKING HIMSELF INTO A SORT OF ROMAN GOD-KING, SO THIS WAS ONE WAY OF TESTING HOW THE ROMANS FELT ABOUT THE SUBJECT.
TURNS OUT, THEY HATED THE IDEA. SO MUCH SO, IN FACT, THEY STABBED HIM TO DEATH.
AND HERE'S WHAT WE THINK OF YOUR STUPID STATUE!
OUCH! SOME PEOPLE SAY IT WITH FLOWERS..
THE ROMANS SAY IT WITH STABBINGS.
YOU NEEDED ANOTHER ROMAN ALLY, AND FAST! YOU HOOKED CAESAR'S SECOND-IN-COMMAND, MARK ANTONY.
SO YOU MANAGED TO BEGUILE NOT ONE, BUT TWO OF THE MOST POWERFUL MEN IN THE WORLD, IN QUICK SUCCESSION, WITH YOUR LEGENDARY BEAUTY...
HM. I PREFER TO THINK IT WAS DOWN TO MY FASCINATING PERSONALITY...
AFTER ALL, MY CHARM WAS ALSO LEGENDARY!
IT'S SAID THAT YOU HAD "A THOUSAND FORMS OF FLATTERY"!
WOW! THAT'S IMPRESSIVE! YOU'VE OBVIOUSLY DONE YOUR HOMEWORK!
OH THANK YOU... I TRY...

PLUS, I WAS STINKIN' RICH!

ANTONY ONCE BET ME I COULDN'T SPEND A MILLION DOLLARS ON ONE MEAL...

OH YEAH?

CHALLENGE ACCEPTED!

ENORMOUS PEARL

VINEGAR

PLOP!

PEARLS **DISSOLVE** IN VINEGAR...

DOOK
DOOK
DOOK

CLAP CLAP

ROME DECLARED WAR ON YOU, CLAIMING THAT YOUR LIFE OF LUXURY HAD MADE ANTONY DISTRACTED, AND THAT YOU WANTED TO TAKE OVER THEIR EMPIRE.

BUT I DID!

WELL, ANTONY'S SOLDIERS CERTAINLY BELIEVED IT. THEY **DESERTED** HIM EN MASSE AND JOINED HIS ENEMY'S ARMY.

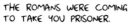

GUYS!

COME BACK!

GUYS!

SO LONG...

SOFTY!

DESERTED AND DEFEATED, HE FELL ON HIS SWORD. EXCEPT HE MESSED THAT UP, TOO...

THIS... DOESN'T SEEM TO HAVE WORKED. COULD SOMEONE HELP ME OUT HERE...?

THE ROMANS WERE COMING TO TAKE YOU PRISONER.

BUT I WOULDN'T GIVE THEM THE SATISFACTION!

I ENDED MY LIFE WITH A POISONOUS ASP!

G-ASP!

OH PLEASE TELL ME YOU DID NOT JUST SAY THAT...

BARGING IN

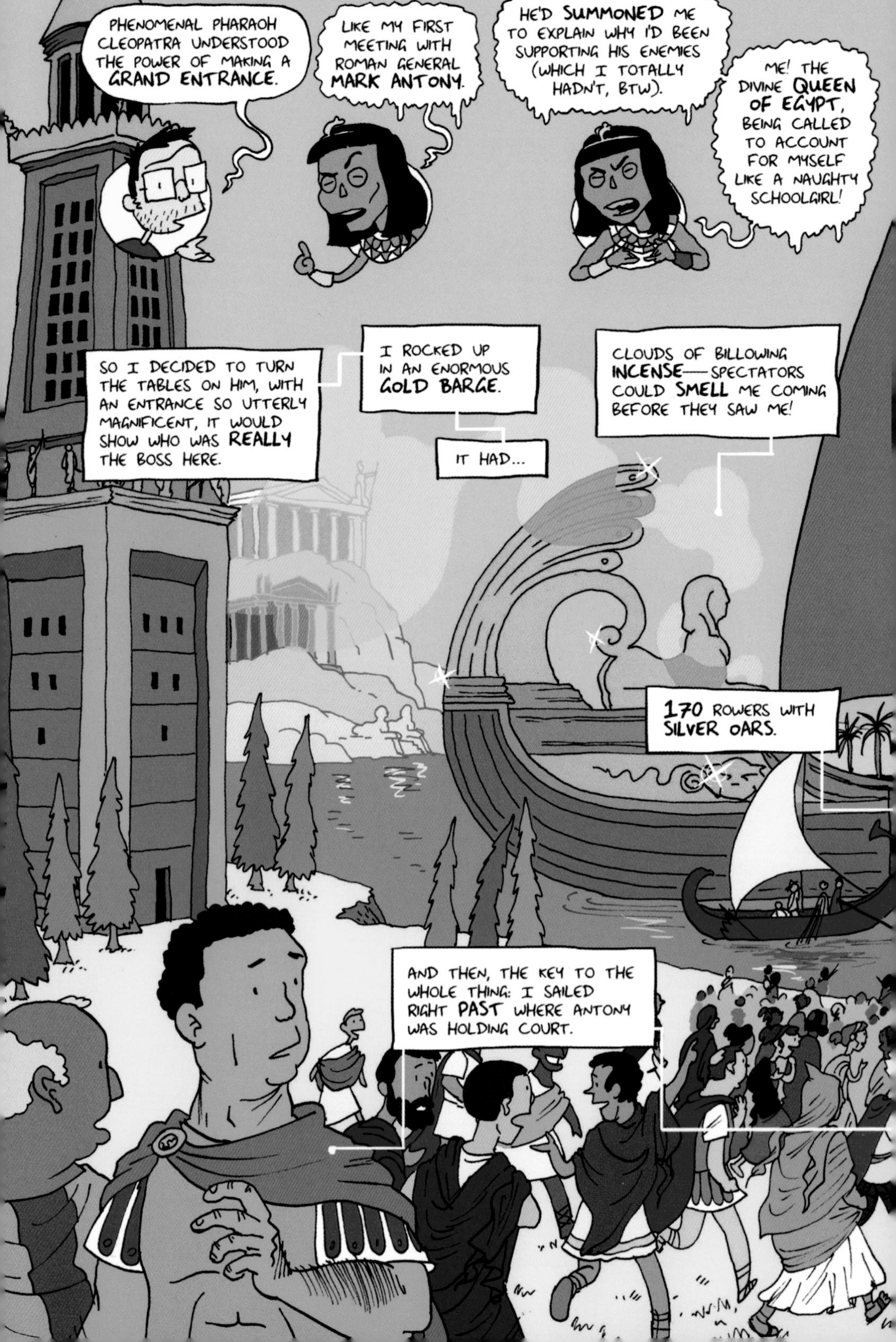
PHENOMENAL PHARAOH CLEOPATRA UNDERSTOOD THE POWER OF MAKING A GRAND ENTRANCE.
LIKE MY FIRST MEETING WITH ROMAN GENERAL MARK ANTONY.
HE'D SUMMONED ME TO EXPLAIN WHY I'D BEEN SUPPORTING HIS ENEMIES (WHICH I TOTALLY HADN'T, BTW).
ME! THE DIVINE QUEEN OF EGYPT, BEING CALLED TO ACCOUNT FOR MYSELF LIKE A NAUGHTY SCHOOLGIRL!
SO I DECIDED TO TURN THE TABLES ON HIM, WITH AN ENTRANCE SO UTTERLY MAGNIFICENT, IT WOULD SHOW WHO WAS REALLY THE BOSS HERE.
I ROCKED UP IN AN ENORMOUS GOLD BARGE.
IT HAD...
CLOUDS OF BILLOWING INCENSE—SPECTATORS COULD SMELL ME COMING BEFORE THEY SAW ME!
170 ROWERS WITH SILVER OARS.
AND THEN, THE KEY TO THE WHOLE THING: I SAILED RIGHT PAST WHERE ANTONY WAS HOLDING COURT.

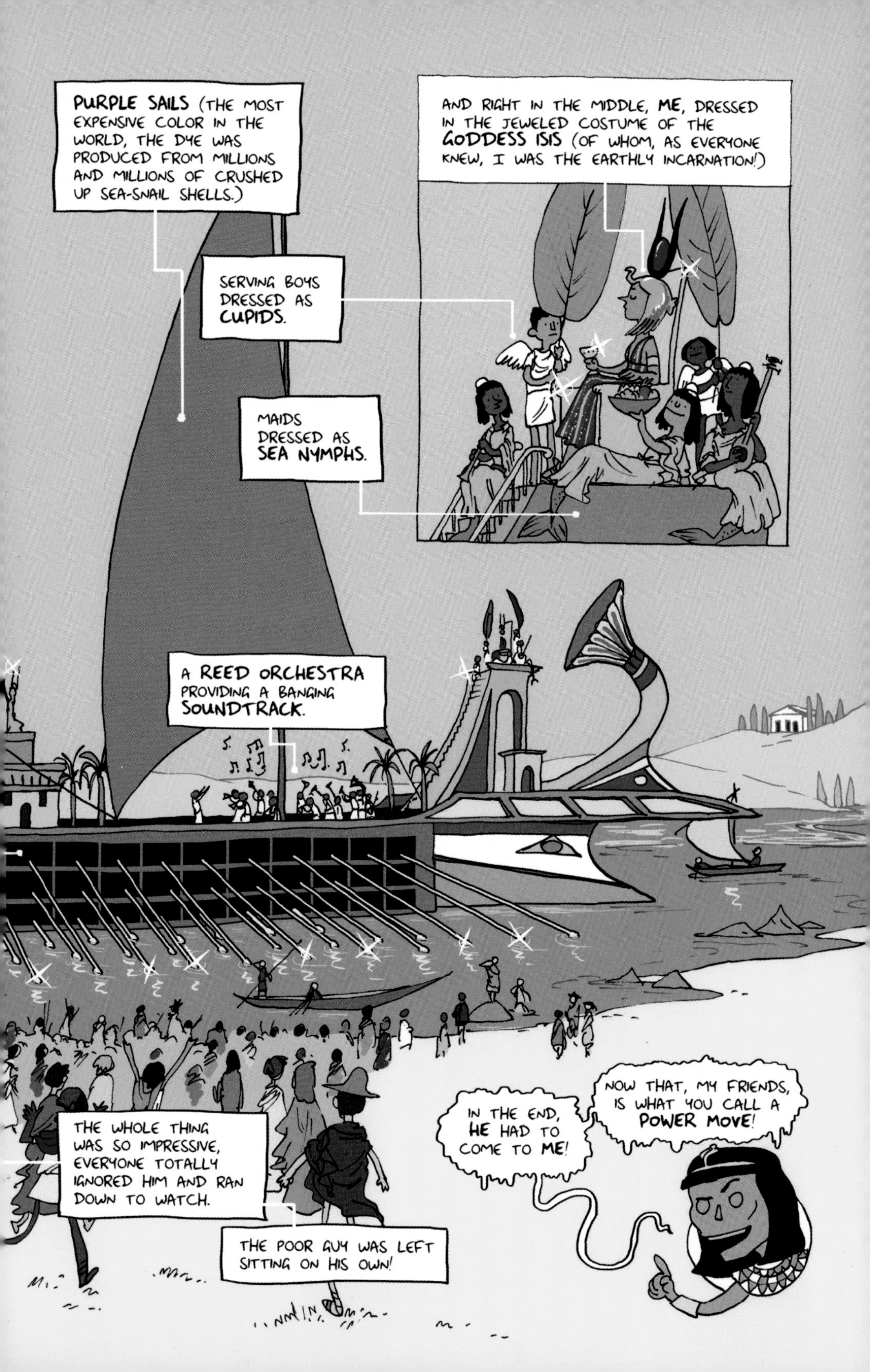
PURPLE SAILS (THE MOST EXPENSIVE COLOR IN THE WORLD, THE DYE WAS PRODUCED FROM MILLIONS AND MILLIONS OF CRUSHED UP SEA-SNAIL SHELLS.)
AND RIGHT IN THE MIDDLE, ME, DRESSED IN THE JEWELED COSTUME OF THE GODDESS ISIS (OF WHOM, AS EVERYONE KNEW, I WAS THE EARTHLY INCARNATION!)
SERVING BOYS DRESSED AS CUPIDS.
MAIDS DRESSED AS SEA NYMPHS.
A REED ORCHESTRA PROVIDING A BANGING SOUNDTRACK.
THE WHOLE THING WAS SO IMPRESSIVE, EVERYONE TOTALLY IGNORED HIM AND RAN DOWN TO WATCH.
THE POOR GUY WAS LEFT SITTING ON HIS OWN!
IN THE END, HE HAD TO COME TO ME!
NOW THAT, MY FRIENDS, IS WHAT YOU CALL A POWER MOVE!

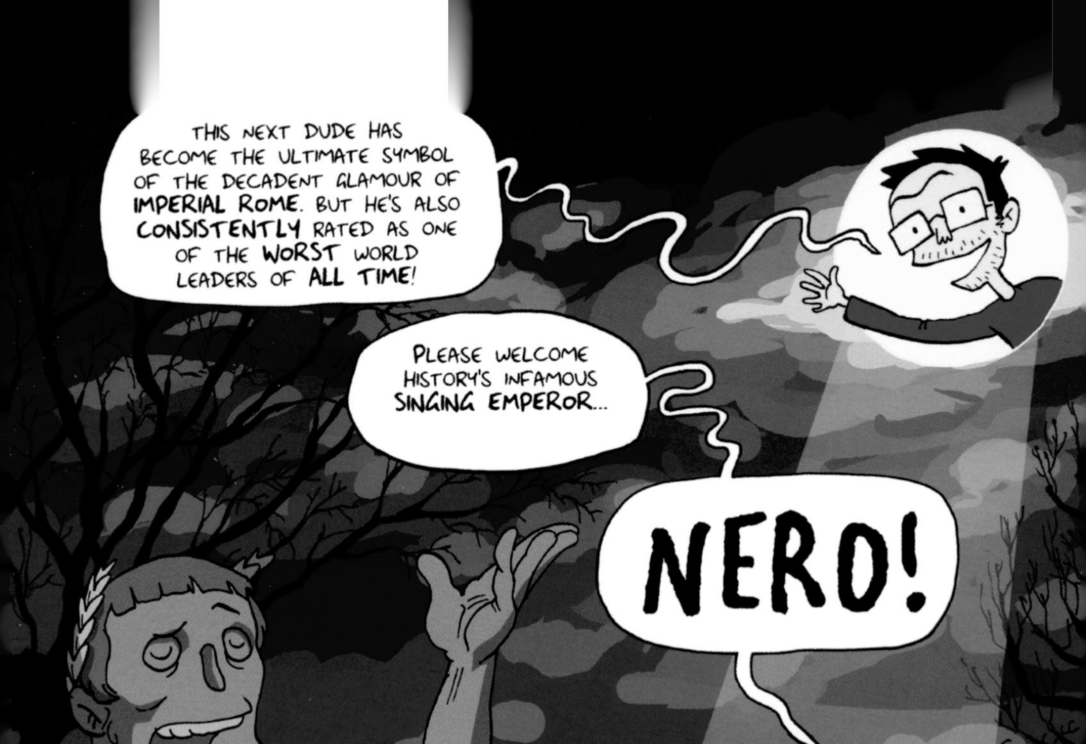
THIS NEXT DUDE HAS BECOME THE ULTIMATE SYMBOL OF THE DECADENT GLAMOUR OF IMPERIAL ROME. BUT HE'S ALSO CONSISTENTLY RATED AS ONE OF THE WORST WORLD LEADERS OF ALL TIME!
PLEASE WELCOME HISTORY'S INFAMOUS SINGING EMPEROR...
NERO!
NERO
ROMAN EMPEROR
37–68

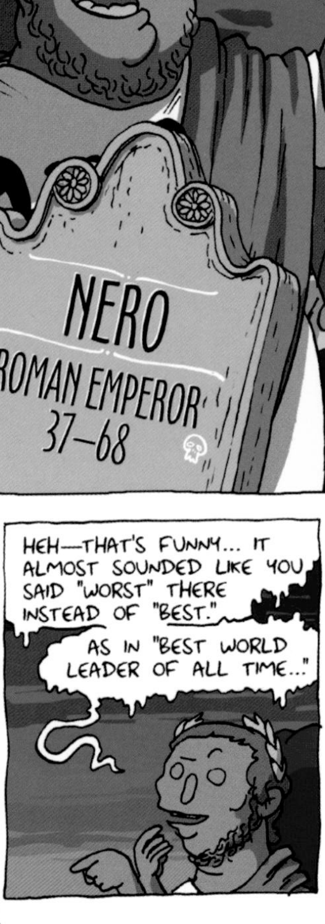
HEH—THAT'S FUNNY... IT ALMOST SOUNDED LIKE YOU SAID "WORST" THERE INSTEAD OF "BEST."
AS IN "BEST WORLD LEADER OF ALL TIME..."

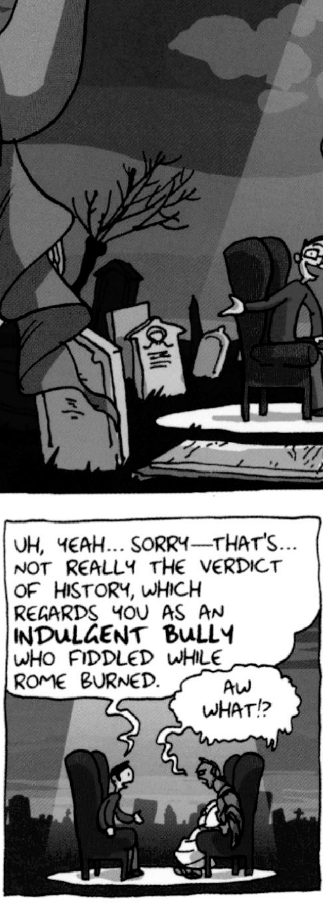
UH, YEAH... SORRY—THAT'S... NOT REALLY THE VERDICT OF HISTORY, WHICH REGARDS YOU AS AN INDULGENT BULLY WHO FIDDLED WHILE ROME BURNED.
AW WHAT!?

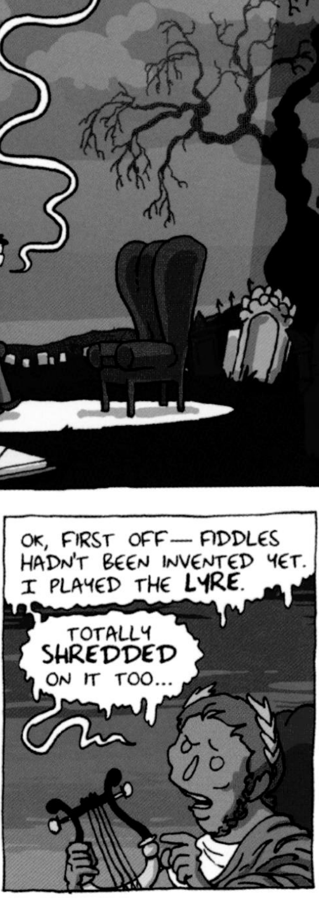
OK, FIRST OFF— FIDDLES HADN'T BEEN INVENTED YET. I PLAYED THE LYRE.
TOTALLY SHREDDED ON IT TOO...

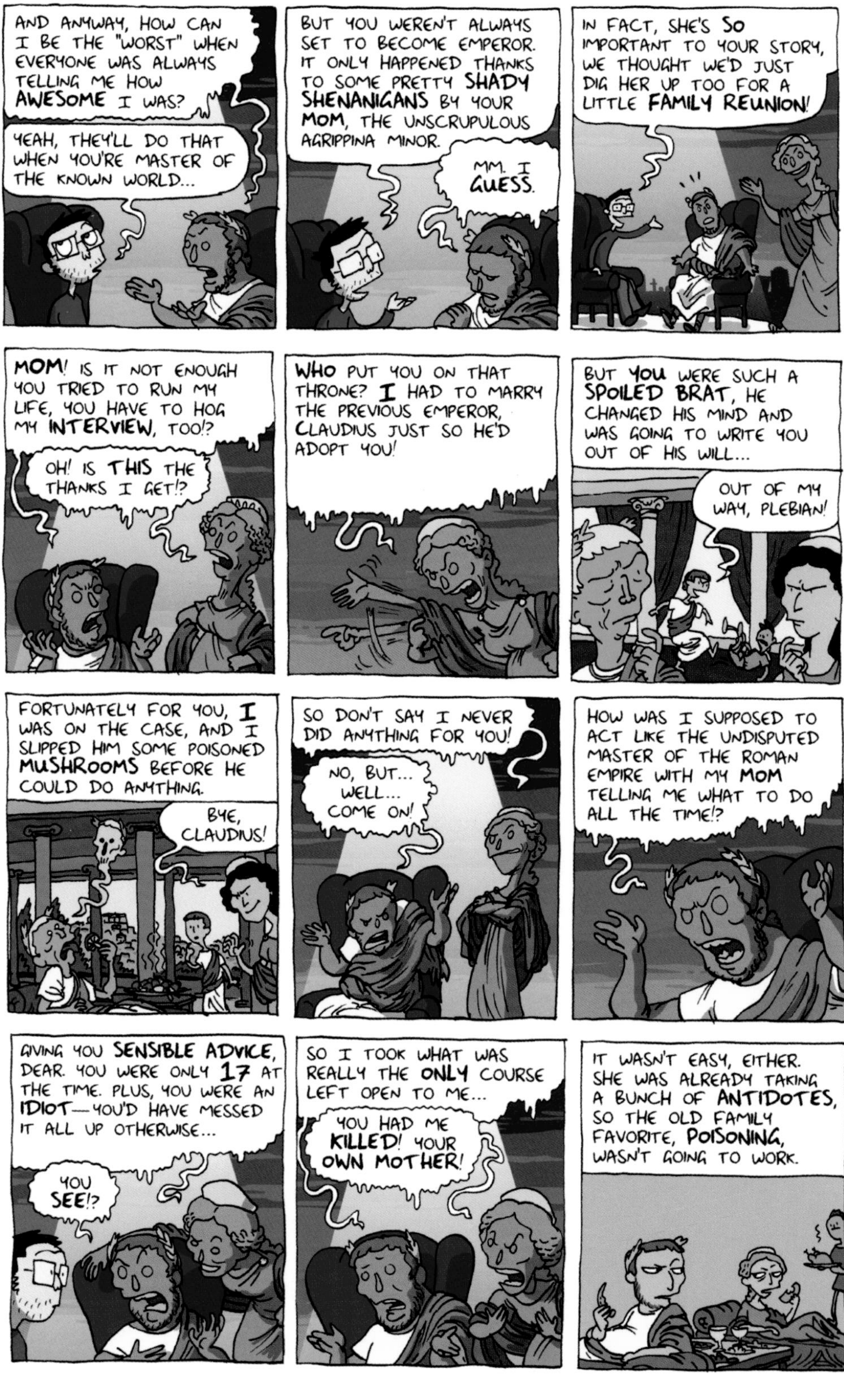
AND ANYWAY, HOW CAN I BE THE "WORST" WHEN EVERYONE WAS ALWAYS TELLING ME HOW AWESOME I WAS?
YEAH, THEY'LL DO THAT WHEN YOU'RE MASTER OF THE KNOWN WORLD...
BUT YOU WEREN'T ALWAYS SET TO BECOME EMPEROR. IT ONLY HAPPENED THANKS TO SOME PRETTY SHADY SHENANIGANS BY YOUR MOM, THE UNSCRUPULOUS AGRIPPINA MINOR.
MM. I GUESS.
IN FACT, SHE'S SO IMPORTANT TO YOUR STORY, WE THOUGHT WE'D JUST DIG HER UP TOO FOR A LITTLE FAMILY REUNION!
MOM! IS IT NOT ENOUGH YOU TRIED TO RUN MY LIFE, YOU HAVE TO HOG MY INTERVIEW, TOO!?
OH! IS THIS THE THANKS I GET!?
WHO PUT YOU ON THAT THRONE? I HAD TO MARRY THE PREVIOUS EMPEROR, CLAUDIUS JUST SO HE'D ADOPT YOU!
BUT YOU WERE SUCH A SPOILED BRAT, HE CHANGED HIS MIND AND WAS GOING TO WRITE YOU OUT OF HIS WILL...
OUT OF MY WAY, PLEBIAN!
FORTUNATELY FOR YOU, I WAS ON THE CASE, AND I SLIPPED HIM SOME POISONED MUSHROOMS BEFORE HE COULD DO ANYTHING.
BYE, CLAUDIUS!
SO DON'T SAY I NEVER DID ANYTHING FOR YOU!
NO, BUT... WELL... COME ON!
HOW WAS I SUPPOSED TO ACT LIKE THE UNDISPUTED MASTER OF THE ROMAN EMPIRE WITH MY MOM TELLING ME WHAT TO DO ALL THE TIME!?
GIVING YOU SENSIBLE ADVICE, DEAR. YOU WERE ONLY 17 AT THE TIME. PLUS, YOU WERE AN IDIOT—YOU'D HAVE MESSED IT ALL UP OTHERWISE...
YOU SEE!?
SO I TOOK WHAT WAS REALLY THE ONLY COURSE LEFT OPEN TO ME...
YOU HAD ME KILLED! YOUR OWN MOTHER!
IT WASN'T EASY, EITHER. SHE WAS ALREADY TAKING A BUNCH OF ANTIDOTES, SO THE OLD FAMILY FAVORITE, POISONING, WASN'T GOING TO WORK.

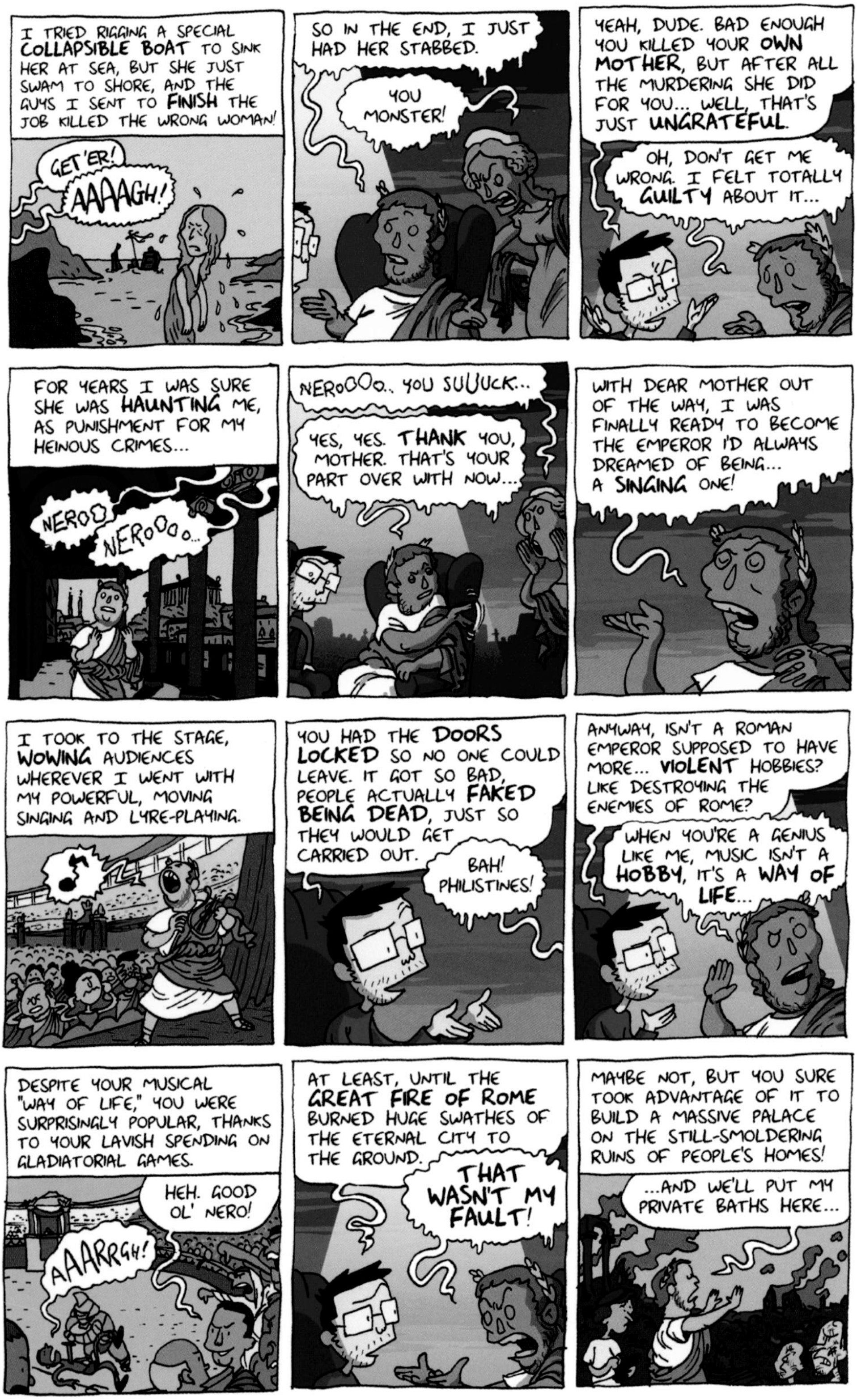
I TRIED RIGGING A SPECIAL COLLAPSIBLE BOAT TO SINK HER AT SEA, BUT SHE JUST SWAM TO SHORE, AND THE GUYS I SENT TO FINISH THE JOB KILLED THE WRONG WOMAN!
GET 'ER!
AAAAGH!
SO IN THE END, I JUST HAD HER STABBED.
YOU MONSTER!
YEAH, DUDE. BAD ENOUGH YOU KILLED YOUR OWN MOTHER, BUT AFTER ALL THE MURDERING SHE DID FOR YOU... WELL, THAT'S JUST UNGRATEFUL.
OH, DON'T GET ME WRONG. I FELT TOTALLY GUILTY ABOUT IT...
FOR YEARS I WAS SURE SHE WAS HAUNTING ME, AS PUNISHMENT FOR MY HEINOUS CRIMES...
NEROO
NEROooo...
NEROOOo.. YOU SUUUCK...
YES, YES. THANK YOU, MOTHER. THAT'S YOUR PART OVER WITH NOW...
WITH DEAR MOTHER OUT OF THE WAY, I WAS FINALLY READY TO BECOME THE EMPEROR I'D ALWAYS DREAMED OF BEING... A SINGING ONE!
I TOOK TO THE STAGE, WOWING AUDIENCES WHEREVER I WENT WITH MY POWERFUL, MOVING SINGING AND LYRE-PLAYING.
YOU HAD THE DOORS LOCKED SO NO ONE COULD LEAVE. IT GOT SO BAD, PEOPLE ACTUALLY FAKED BEING DEAD, JUST SO THEY WOULD GET CARRIED OUT.
BAH! PHILISTINES!
ANYWAY, ISN'T A ROMAN EMPEROR SUPPOSED TO HAVE MORE... VIOLENT HOBBIES? LIKE DESTROYING THE ENEMIES OF ROME?
WHEN YOU'RE A GENIUS LIKE ME, MUSIC ISN'T A HOBBY, IT'S A WAY OF LIFE...
DESPITE YOUR MUSICAL "WAY OF LIFE," YOU WERE SURPRISINGLY POPULAR, THANKS TO YOUR LAVISH SPENDING ON GLADIATORIAL GAMES.
HEH. GOOD OL' NERO!
AAARRGH!
AT LEAST, UNTIL THE GREAT FIRE OF ROME BURNED HUGE SWATHES OF THE ETERNAL CITY TO THE GROUND.
THAT WASN'T MY FAULT!
MAYBE NOT, BUT YOU SURE TOOK ADVANTAGE OF IT TO BUILD A MASSIVE PALACE ON THE STILL-SMOLDERING RUINS OF PEOPLE'S HOMES!
...AND WE'LL PUT MY PRIVATE BATHS HERE...

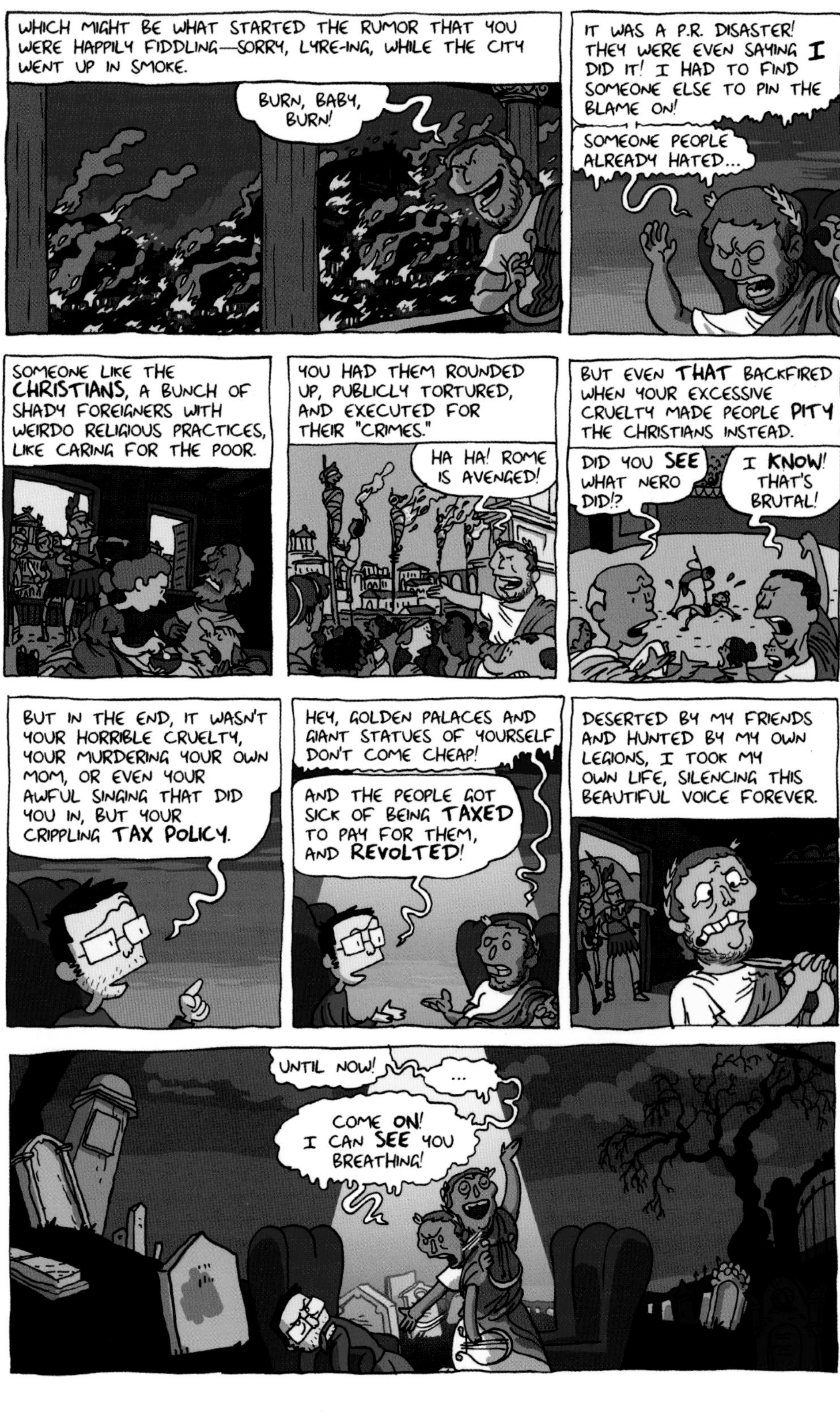
WHICH MIGHT BE WHAT STARTED THE RUMOR THAT YOU WERE HAPPILY FIDDLING—SORRY, LYRE-ING, WHILE THE CITY WENT UP IN SMOKE.
BURN, BABY, BURN!
IT WAS A P.R. DISASTER! THEY WERE EVEN SAYING **I** DID IT! I HAD TO FIND SOMEONE ELSE TO PIN THE BLAME ON!
SOMEONE PEOPLE ALREADY HATED...
SOMEONE LIKE THE **CHRISTIANS**, A BUNCH OF SHADY FOREIGNERS WITH WEIRDO RELIGIOUS PRACTICES, LIKE CARING FOR THE POOR.
YOU HAD THEM ROUNDED UP, PUBLICLY TORTURED, AND EXECUTED FOR THEIR "CRIMES."
HA HA! ROME IS AVENGED!
BUT EVEN **THAT** BACKFIRED WHEN YOUR EXCESSIVE CRUELTY MADE PEOPLE **PITY** THE CHRISTIANS INSTEAD.
DID YOU **SEE** WHAT NERO DID!?
I **KNOW**! THAT'S BRUTAL!
BUT IN THE END, IT WASN'T YOUR HORRIBLE CRUELTY, YOUR MURDERING YOUR OWN MOM, OR EVEN YOUR AWFUL SINGING THAT DID YOU IN, BUT YOUR CRIPPLING **TAX POLICY**.
HEY, GOLDEN PALACES AND GIANT STATUES OF YOURSELF DON'T COME CHEAP!
AND THE PEOPLE GOT SICK OF BEING **TAXED** TO PAY FOR THEM, AND **REVOLTED**!
DESERTED BY MY FRIENDS AND HUNTED BY MY OWN LEGIONS, I TOOK MY OWN LIFE, SILENCING THIS BEAUTIFUL VOICE FOREVER.
UNTIL NOW!
...
COME **ON**! I CAN **SEE** YOU BREATHING!

CAFÉ NERO

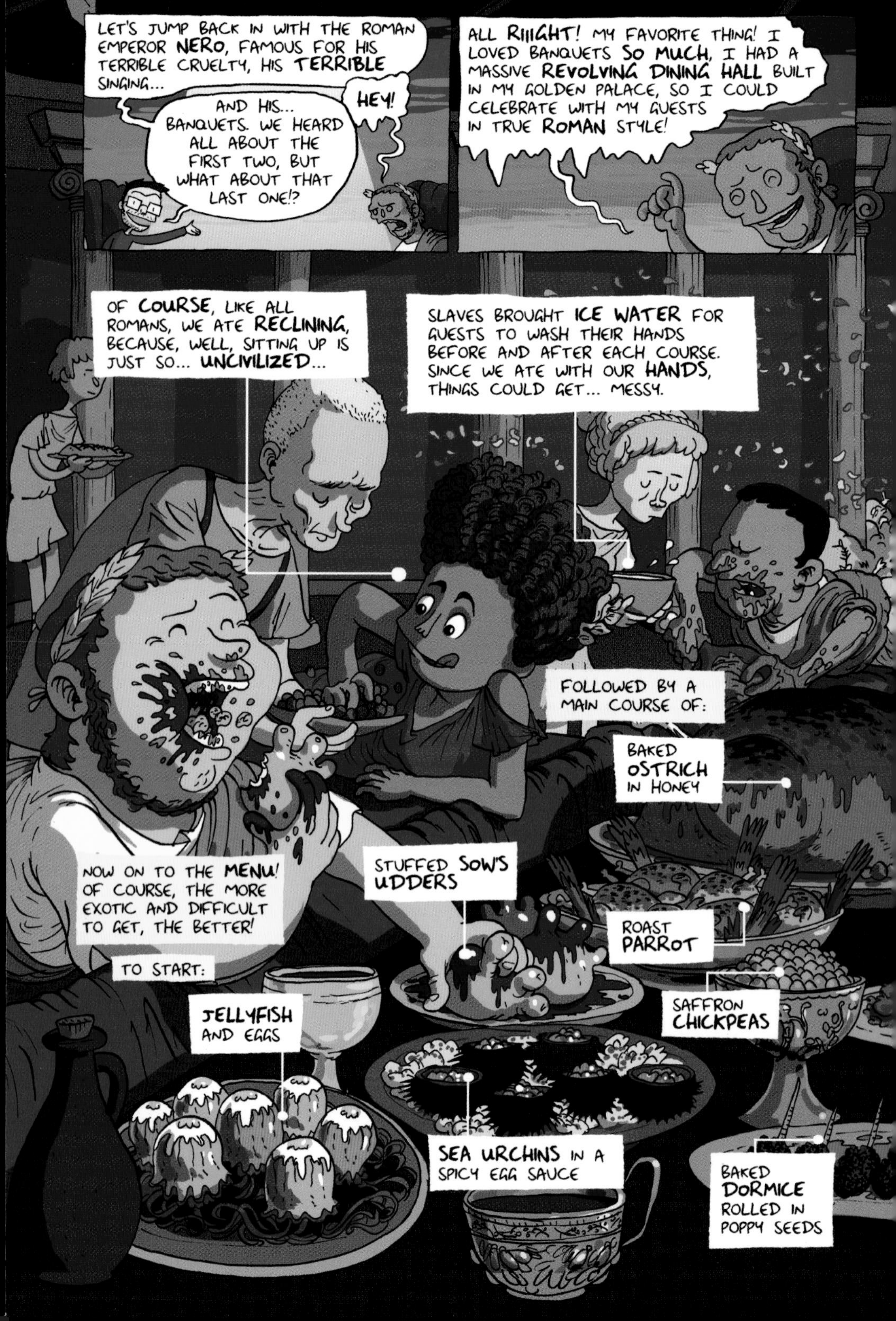
LET'S JUMP BACK IN WITH THE ROMAN EMPEROR NERO, FAMOUS FOR HIS TERRIBLE CRUELTY, HIS TERRIBLE SINGING...
HEY!
AND HIS... BANQUETS. WE HEARD ALL ABOUT THE FIRST TWO, BUT WHAT ABOUT THAT LAST ONE!?
ALL RIIIGHT! MY FAVORITE THING! I LOVED BANQUETS SO MUCH, I HAD A MASSIVE REVOLVING DINING HALL BUILT IN MY GOLDEN PALACE, SO I COULD CELEBRATE WITH MY GUESTS IN TRUE ROMAN STYLE!
OF COURSE, LIKE ALL ROMANS, WE ATE RECLINING, BECAUSE, WELL, SITTING UP IS JUST SO... UNCIVILIZED...
SLAVES BROUGHT ICE WATER FOR GUESTS TO WASH THEIR HANDS BEFORE AND AFTER EACH COURSE. SINCE WE ATE WITH OUR HANDS, THINGS COULD GET... MESSY.
NOW ON TO THE MENU! OF COURSE, THE MORE EXOTIC AND DIFFICULT TO GET, THE BETTER!
TO START:
JELLYFISH AND EGGS
SEA URCHINS IN A SPICY EGG SAUCE
STUFFED SOW'S UDDERS
FOLLOWED BY A MAIN COURSE OF:
BAKED OSTRICH IN HONEY
ROAST PARROT
SAFFRON CHICKPEAS
BAKED DORMICE ROLLED IN POPPY SEEDS

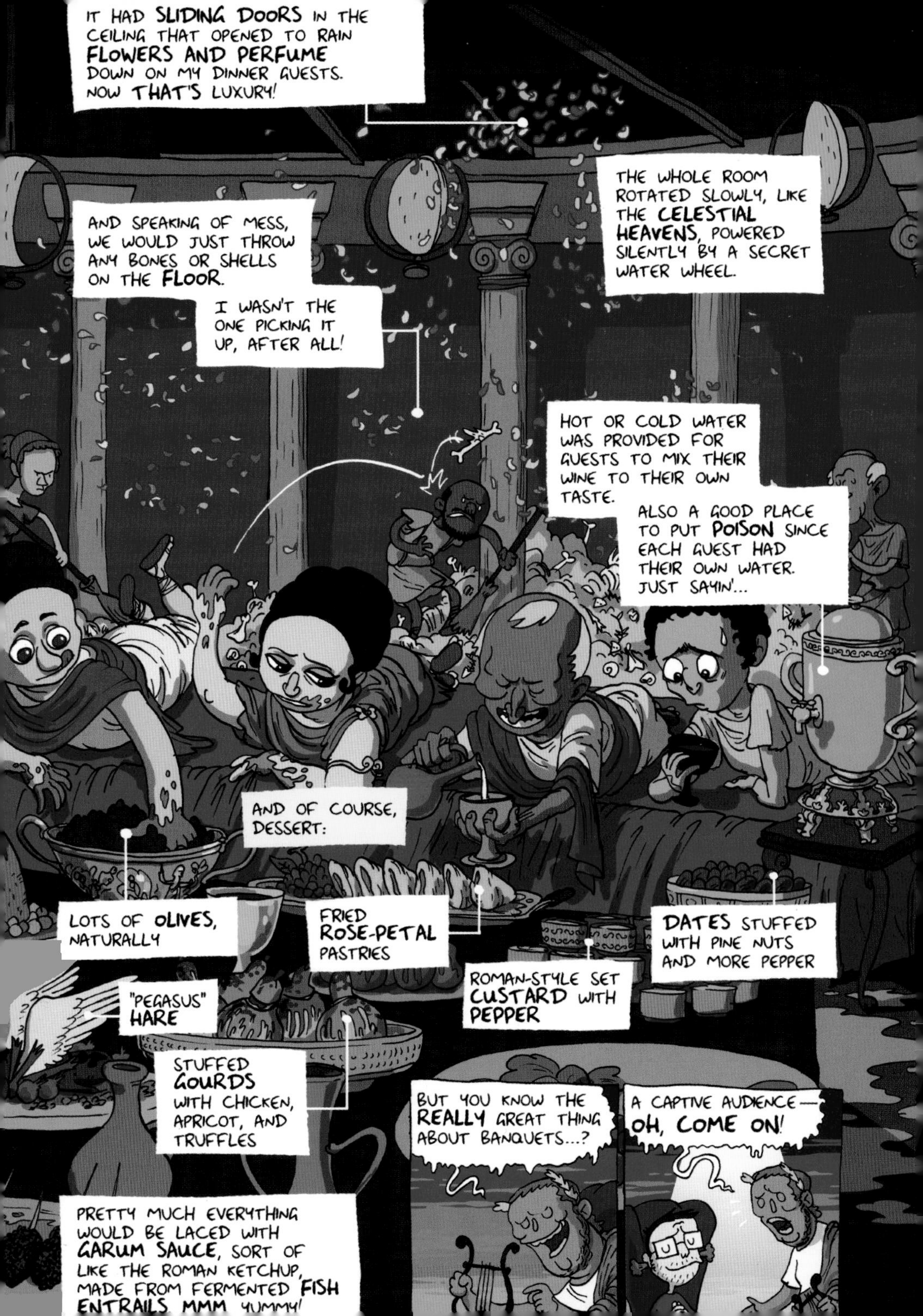
IT HAD SLIDING DOORS IN THE CEILING THAT OPENED TO RAIN FLOWERS AND PERFUME DOWN ON MY DINNER GUESTS. NOW THAT'S LUXURY!
THE WHOLE ROOM ROTATED SLOWLY, LIKE THE CELESTIAL HEAVENS, POWERED SILENTLY BY A SECRET WATER WHEEL.
AND SPEAKING OF MESS, WE WOULD JUST THROW ANY BONES OR SHELLS ON THE FLOOR.
I WASN'T THE ONE PICKING IT UP, AFTER ALL!
HOT OR COLD WATER WAS PROVIDED FOR GUESTS TO MIX THEIR WINE TO THEIR OWN TASTE.
ALSO A GOOD PLACE TO PUT POISON SINCE EACH GUEST HAD THEIR OWN WATER. JUST SAYIN'...
AND OF COURSE, DESSERT:
LOTS OF OLIVES, NATURALLY
FRIED ROSE-PETAL PASTRIES
DATES STUFFED WITH PINE NUTS AND MORE PEPPER
ROMAN-STYLE SET CUSTARD WITH PEPPER
"PEGASUS" HARE
STUFFED GOURDS WITH CHICKEN, APRICOT, AND TRUFFLES
PRETTY MUCH EVERYTHING WOULD BE LACED WITH GARUM SAUCE, SORT OF LIKE THE ROMAN KETCHUP, MADE FROM FERMENTED FISH ENTRAILS. MMM YUMMY!
BUT YOU KNOW THE REALLY GREAT THING ABOUT BANQUETS...?
A CAPTIVE AUDIENCE— OH, COME ON!

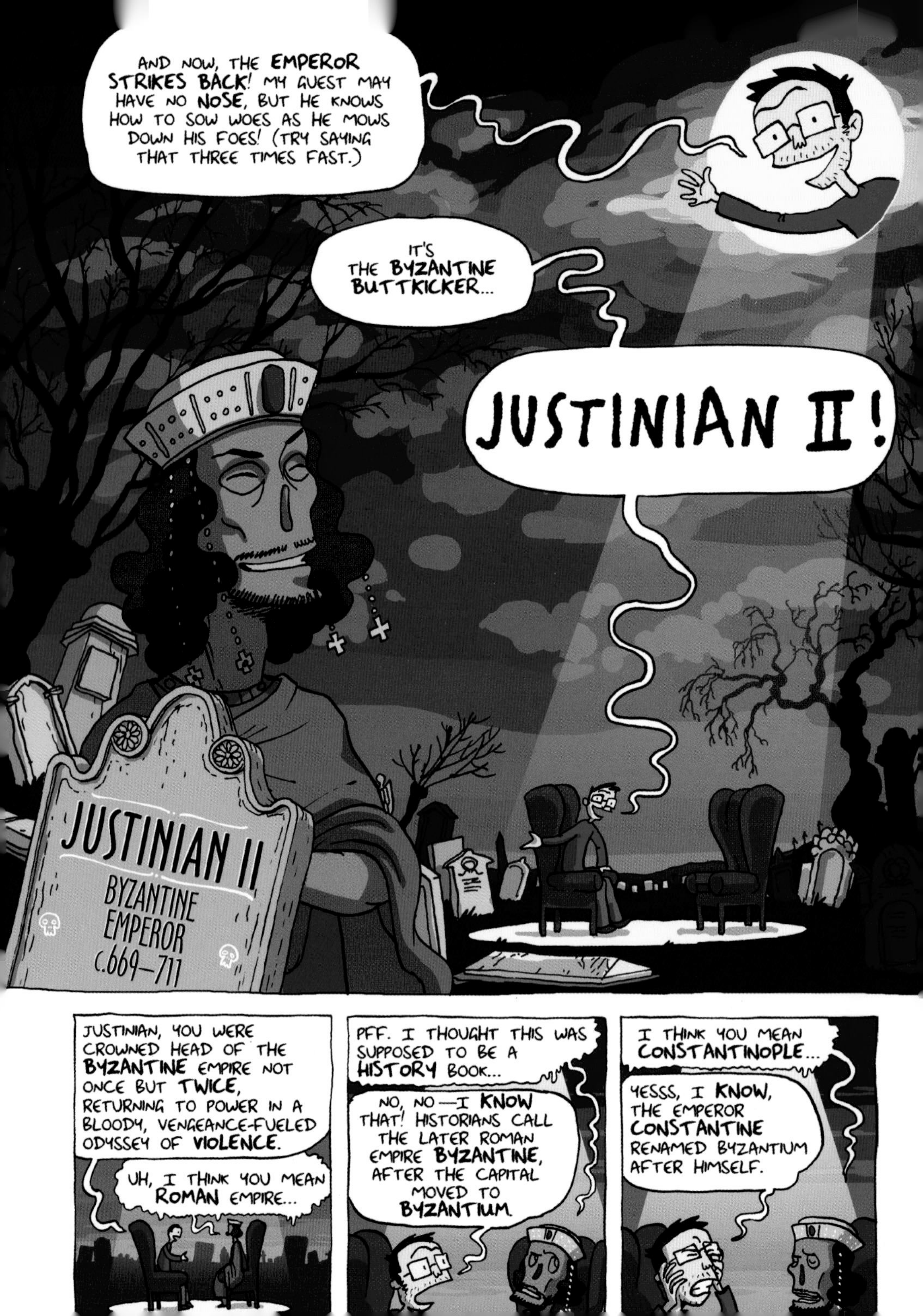
AND NOW, THE EMPEROR STRIKES BACK! MY GUEST MAY HAVE NO NOSE, BUT HE KNOWS HOW TO SOW WOES AS HE MOWS DOWN HIS FOES! (TRY SAYING THAT THREE TIMES FAST.)
IT'S THE BYZANTINE BUTTKICKER...
JUSTINIAN II!
JUSTINIAN II
BYZANTINE EMPEROR
c.669–711
JUSTINIAN, YOU WERE CROWNED HEAD OF THE BYZANTINE EMPIRE NOT ONCE BUT TWICE, RETURNING TO POWER IN A BLOODY, VENGEANCE-FUELED ODYSSEY OF VIOLENCE.
UH, I THINK YOU MEAN ROMAN EMPIRE...
PFF. I THOUGHT THIS WAS SUPPOSED TO BE A HISTORY BOOK...
NO, NO—I KNOW THAT! HISTORIANS CALL THE LATER ROMAN EMPIRE BYZANTINE, AFTER THE CAPITAL MOVED TO BYZANTIUM.
I THINK YOU MEAN CONSTANTINOPLE...
YESSS, I KNOW, THE EMPEROR CONSTANTINE RENAMED BYZANTIUM AFTER HIMSELF.

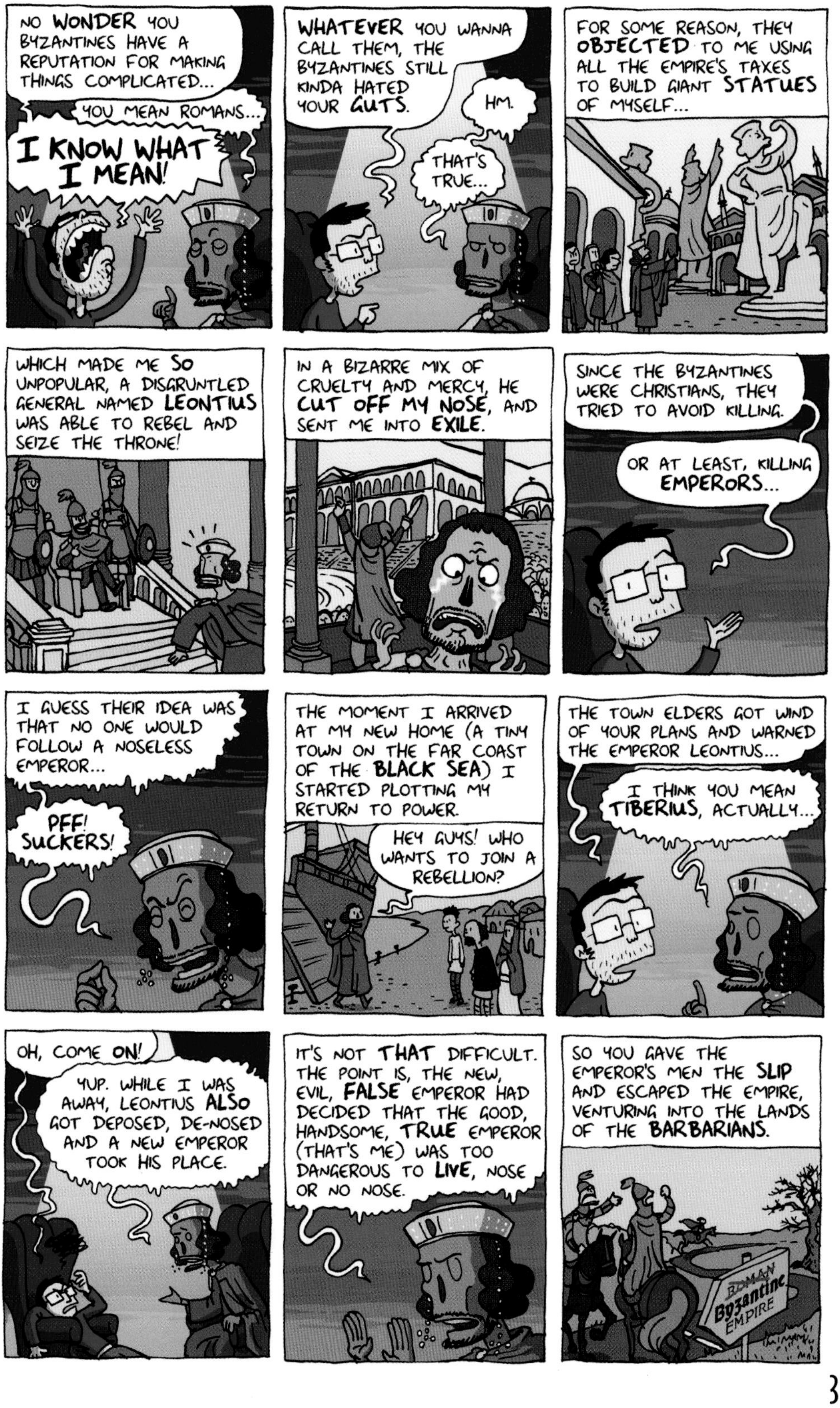
NO WONDER YOU BYZANTINES HAVE A REPUTATION FOR MAKING THINGS COMPLICATED...
YOU MEAN ROMANS...
I KNOW WHAT I MEAN!
WHATEVER YOU WANNA CALL THEM, THE BYZANTINES STILL KINDA HATED YOUR GUTS.
HM.
THAT'S TRUE...
FOR SOME REASON, THEY OBJECTED TO ME USING ALL THE EMPIRE'S TAXES TO BUILD GIANT STATUES OF MYSELF...
WHICH MADE ME SO UNPOPULAR, A DISGRUNTLED GENERAL NAMED LEONTIUS WAS ABLE TO REBEL AND SEIZE THE THRONE!
IN A BIZARRE MIX OF CRUELTY AND MERCY, HE CUT OFF MY NOSE, AND SENT ME INTO EXILE.
SINCE THE BYZANTINES WERE CHRISTIANS, THEY TRIED TO AVOID KILLING.
OR AT LEAST, KILLING EMPERORS...
I GUESS THEIR IDEA WAS THAT NO ONE WOULD FOLLOW A NOSELESS EMPEROR...
PFF! SUCKERS!
THE MOMENT I ARRIVED AT MY NEW HOME (A TINY TOWN ON THE FAR COAST OF THE BLACK SEA) I STARTED PLOTTING MY RETURN TO POWER.
HEY GUYS! WHO WANTS TO JOIN A REBELLION?
THE TOWN ELDERS GOT WIND OF YOUR PLANS AND WARNED THE EMPEROR LEONTIUS...
I THINK YOU MEAN TIBERIUS, ACTUALLY...
OH, COME ON!
YUP. WHILE I WAS AWAY, LEONTIUS ALSO GOT DEPOSED, DE-NOSED AND A NEW EMPEROR TOOK HIS PLACE.
IT'S NOT THAT DIFFICULT. THE POINT IS, THE NEW, EVIL, FALSE EMPEROR HAD DECIDED THAT THE GOOD, HANDSOME, TRUE EMPEROR (THAT'S ME) WAS TOO DANGEROUS TO LIVE, NOSE OR NO NOSE.
SO YOU GAVE THE EMPEROR'S MEN THE SLIP AND ESCAPED THE EMPIRE, VENTURING INTO THE LANDS OF THE BARBARIANS.
~~ROMAN~~
Byzantine EMPIRE

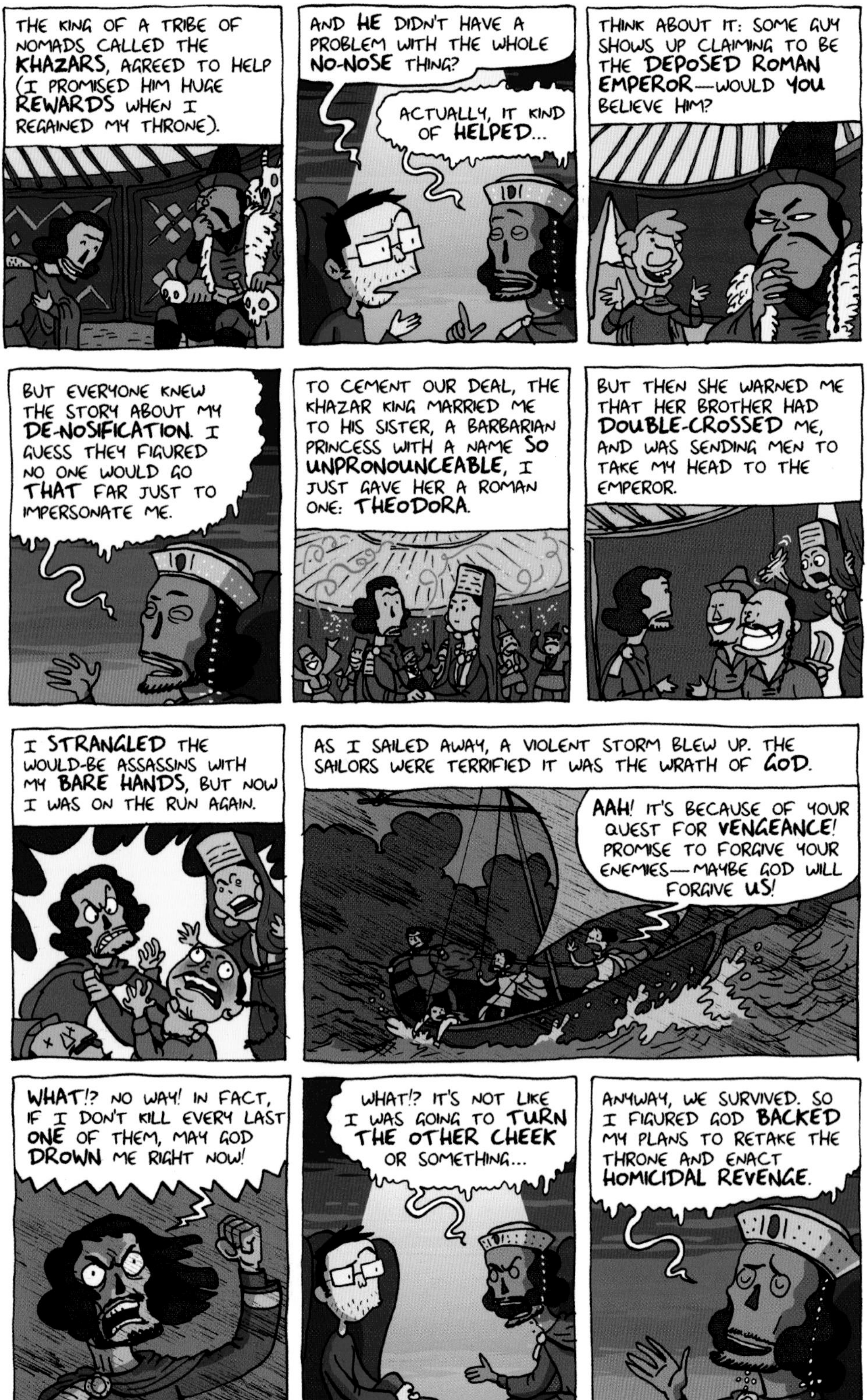
THE KING OF A TRIBE OF NOMADS CALLED THE KHAZARS, AGREED TO HELP (I PROMISED HIM HUGE REWARDS WHEN I REGAINED MY THRONE).
AND HE DIDN'T HAVE A PROBLEM WITH THE WHOLE NO-NOSE THING?
ACTUALLY, IT KIND OF HELPED...
THINK ABOUT IT: SOME GUY SHOWS UP CLAIMING TO BE THE DEPOSED ROMAN EMPEROR—WOULD YOU BELIEVE HIM?
BUT EVERYONE KNEW THE STORY ABOUT MY DE-NOSIFICATION. I GUESS THEY FIGURED NO ONE WOULD GO THAT FAR JUST TO IMPERSONATE ME.
TO CEMENT OUR DEAL, THE KHAZAR KING MARRIED ME TO HIS SISTER, A BARBARIAN PRINCESS WITH A NAME SO UNPRONOUNCEABLE, I JUST GAVE HER A ROMAN ONE: THEODORA.
BUT THEN SHE WARNED ME THAT HER BROTHER HAD DOUBLE-CROSSED ME, AND WAS SENDING MEN TO TAKE MY HEAD TO THE EMPEROR.
I STRANGLED THE WOULD-BE ASSASSINS WITH MY BARE HANDS, BUT NOW I WAS ON THE RUN AGAIN.
AS I SAILED AWAY, A VIOLENT STORM BLEW UP. THE SAILORS WERE TERRIFIED IT WAS THE WRATH OF GOD.
AAH! IT'S BECAUSE OF YOUR QUEST FOR VENGEANCE! PROMISE TO FORGIVE YOUR ENEMIES—MAYBE GOD WILL FORGIVE US!
WHAT!? NO WAY! IN FACT, IF I DON'T KILL EVERY LAST ONE OF THEM, MAY GOD DROWN ME RIGHT NOW!
WHAT!? IT'S NOT LIKE I WAS GOING TO TURN THE OTHER CHEEK OR SOMETHING...
ANYWAY, WE SURVIVED. SO I FIGURED GOD BACKED MY PLANS TO RETAKE THE THRONE AND ENACT HOMICIDAL REVENGE.

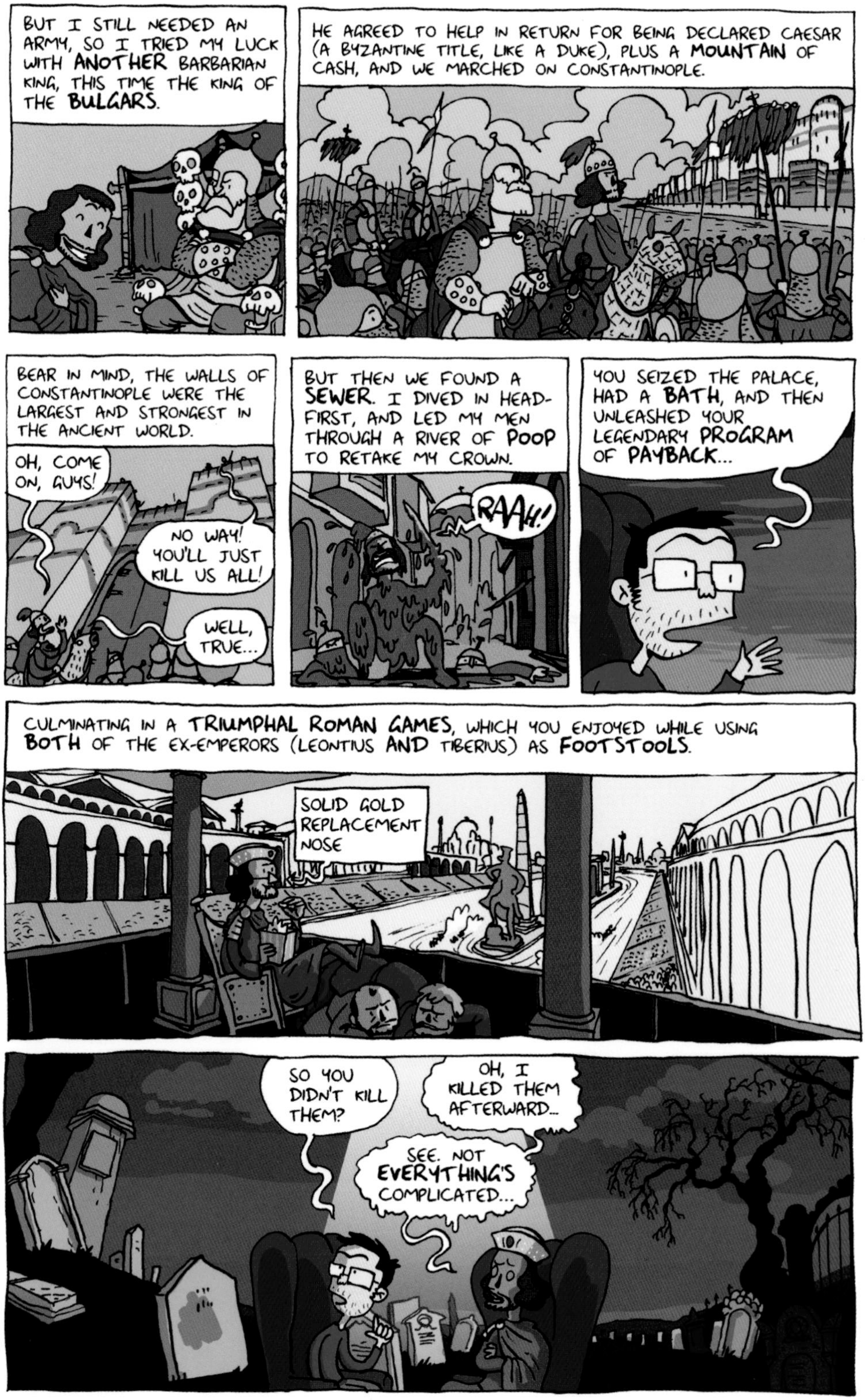
BUT I STILL NEEDED AN ARMY, SO I TRIED MY LUCK WITH ANOTHER BARBARIAN KING, THIS TIME THE KING OF THE BULGARS.
HE AGREED TO HELP IN RETURN FOR BEING DECLARED CAESAR (A BYZANTINE TITLE, LIKE A DUKE), PLUS A MOUNTAIN OF CASH, AND WE MARCHED ON CONSTANTINOPLE.
BEAR IN MIND, THE WALLS OF CONSTANTINOPLE WERE THE LARGEST AND STRONGEST IN THE ANCIENT WORLD.
OH, COME ON, GUYS!
NO WAY! YOU'LL JUST KILL US ALL!
WELL, TRUE...
BUT THEN WE FOUND A SEWER. I DIVED IN HEAD-FIRST, AND LED MY MEN THROUGH A RIVER OF POOP TO RETAKE MY CROWN.
RAAH!
YOU SEIZED THE PALACE, HAD A BATH, AND THEN UNLEASHED YOUR LEGENDARY PROGRAM OF PAYBACK...
CULMINATING IN A TRIUMPHAL ROMAN GAMES, WHICH YOU ENJOYED WHILE USING BOTH OF THE EX-EMPERORS (LEONTIUS AND TIBERIUS) AS FOOTSTOOLS.
SOLID GOLD REPLACEMENT NOSE
SO YOU DIDN'T KILL THEM?
OH, I KILLED THEM AFTERWARD...
SEE. NOT EVERYTHING'S COMPLICATED...

THE WALLED CITY

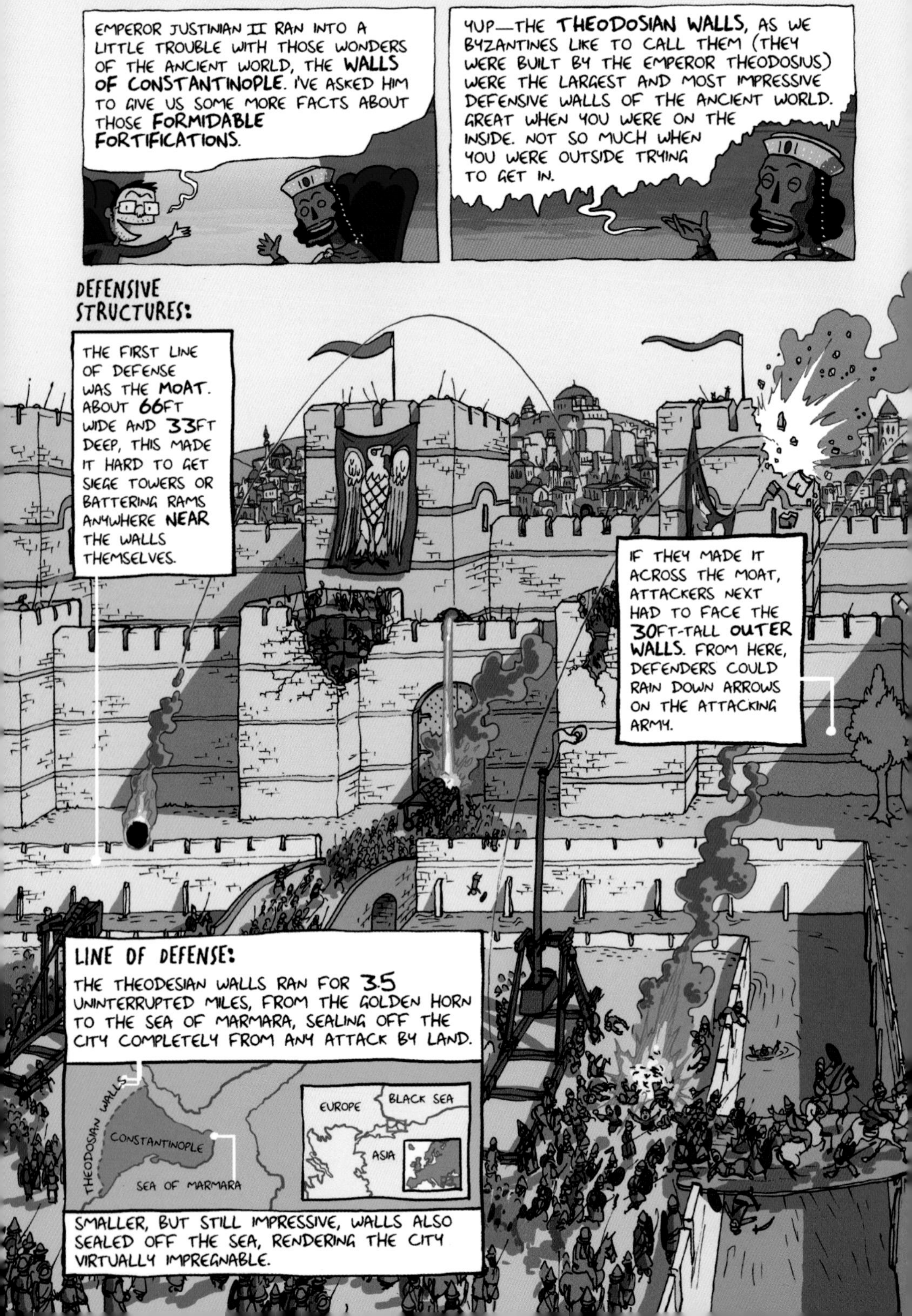
EMPEROR JUSTINIAN II RAN INTO A LITTLE TROUBLE WITH THOSE WONDERS OF THE ANCIENT WORLD, THE **WALLS OF CONSTANTINOPLE**. I'VE ASKED HIM TO GIVE US SOME MORE FACTS ABOUT THOSE **FORMIDABLE FORTIFICATIONS**.
YUP—THE **THEODOSIAN WALLS**, AS WE BYZANTINES LIKE TO CALL THEM (THEY WERE BUILT BY THE EMPEROR THEODOSIUS) WERE THE LARGEST AND MOST IMPRESSIVE DEFENSIVE WALLS OF THE ANCIENT WORLD. GREAT WHEN YOU WERE ON THE INSIDE. NOT SO MUCH WHEN YOU WERE OUTSIDE TRYING TO GET IN.
DEFENSIVE STRUCTURES:
THE FIRST LINE OF DEFENSE WAS THE **MOAT**. ABOUT **66**FT WIDE AND **33**FT DEEP, THIS MADE IT HARD TO GET SIEGE TOWERS OR BATTERING RAMS ANYWHERE **NEAR** THE WALLS THEMSELVES.
IF THEY MADE IT ACROSS THE MOAT, ATTACKERS NEXT HAD TO FACE THE **30**FT-TALL **OUTER WALLS**. FROM HERE, DEFENDERS COULD RAIN DOWN ARROWS ON THE ATTACKING ARMY.
LINE OF DEFENSE:
THE THEODESIAN WALLS RAN FOR **3.5** UNINTERRUPTED MILES, FROM THE GOLDEN HORN TO THE SEA OF MARMARA, SEALING OFF THE CITY COMPLETELY FROM ANY ATTACK BY LAND.
THEODOSIAN WALLS
CONSTANTINOPLE
SEA OF MARMARA
EUROPE
BLACK SEA
ASIA
SMALLER, BUT STILL IMPRESSIVE, WALLS ALSO SEALED OFF THE SEA, RENDERING THE CITY VIRTUALLY IMPREGNABLE.

FOILED BY THE WALL

IT WASN'T JUST ME! THESE ARE JUST SOME OF THE YOUNG HOPEFULS WHO WERE...

ATTILA THE HUN: TOOK ONE LOOK AT THE WALLS, AND DECIDED TO ATTACK ROME INSTEAD.

THE AVARS: BEATEN SO BADLY, THEY BELIEVED *GOD* WAS ON THE BYZANTINE SIDE.

THE ARABS: CONQUERED MOST OF BYZANTINE TERRITORY, BUT WERE UNABLE TO CAPTURE THE CITY.

THE CRUSADERS: MANAGED TO SACK THE CITY, BUT ONLY BY GOING OVER THE LOWER, WEAKER SEAWALLS.

THE BYZANTINES: TRIED SEVERAL TIMES TO GET THE CITY BACK FROM THE CRUSADERS, BUT COULDN'T BREAK THROUGH THEIR *OWN* WALLS! THEY SUCCEEDED BY WAITING UNTIL THE CRUSADERS LEFT!

NEVERMIND...

BAH!

POOP!

THAT'S NOT CHEATING!

I DON'T **BELIEVE** THIS!

ANYONE WHO SOMEHOW SCALED THE FORMIDABLE OUTER WALL WOULD FIND THEMSELVES TRAPPED AND SURROUNDED IN THE **PERIBOLOS**, THE 50-FT-WIDE ENCLOSED WALKWAY BETWEEN THE WALLS.

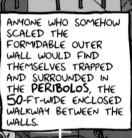

AND IF THEY SOMEHOW CLEARED THE PERIBOLOS, ATTACKERS WERE NOW FACED WITH THE MOST MASSIVE DEFENSIVE STRUCTURE OF THE ANCIENT WORLD, THE **INNER WALLS. 16**FT THICK AND **39**FT HIGH, STUDDED WITH **96** MASSIVE TOWERS, THE WALLS WERE LARGE ENOUGH FOR DEFENDERS TO MOUNT CATAPULTS AND EVEN CANNON, TO RAIN TERROR ON THE ARMY OUTSIDE.

THE WALL FALLS:

CONSTANTINOPLE'S AMAZING WALLS FINALLY FELL TO THE MASSIVE CANNONS OF THE TURKISH SULTAN **MEHMED II** IN **1453**, MARKING THE END OF ALMOST **1,500** YEARS OF THE ROMAN EMPIRE.

HEH HEH...

JUST WAIT...

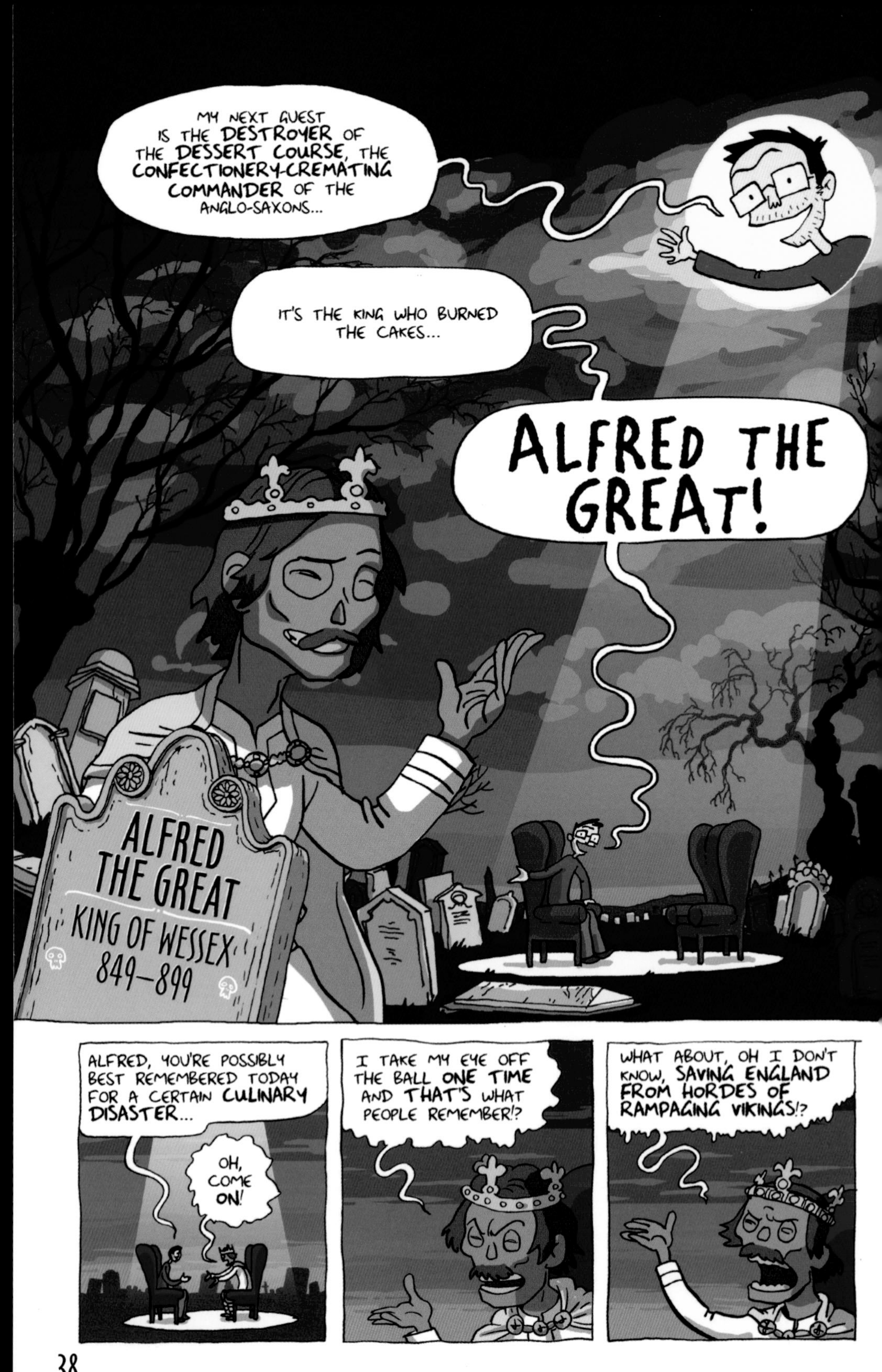
MY NEXT GUEST IS THE DESTROYER OF THE DESSERT COURSE, THE CONFECTIONERY-CREMATING COMMANDER OF THE ANGLO-SAXONS...
IT'S THE KING WHO BURNED THE CAKES...
ALFRED THE GREAT!
ALFRED THE GREAT
KING OF WESSEX
849–899
ALFRED, YOU'RE POSSIBLY BEST REMEMBERED TODAY FOR A CERTAIN CULINARY DISASTER...
OH, COME ON!
I TAKE MY EYE OFF THE BALL ONE TIME AND THAT'S WHAT PEOPLE REMEMBER!?
WHAT ABOUT, OH I DON'T KNOW, SAVING ENGLAND FROM HORDES OF RAMPAGING VIKINGS!?

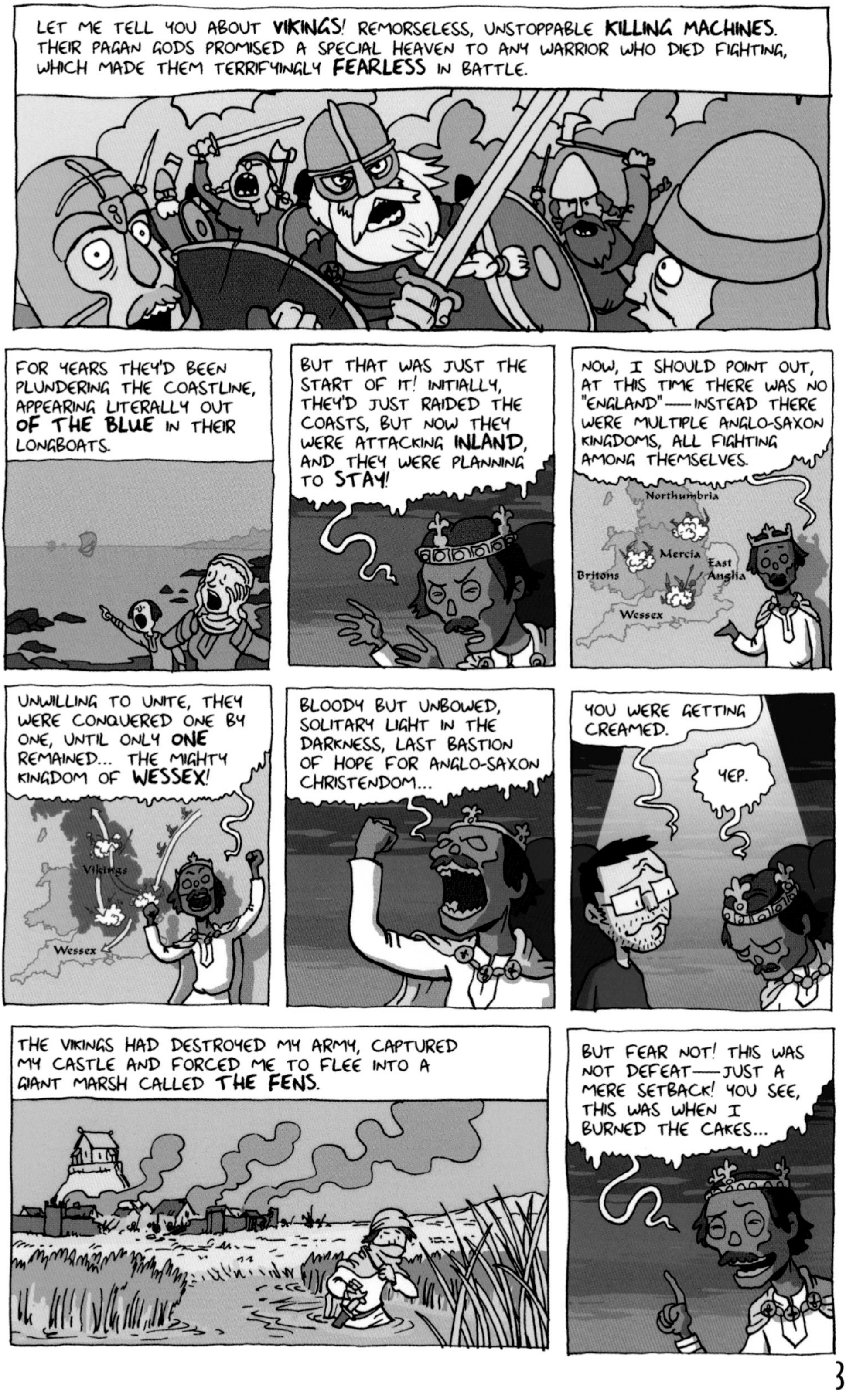

LET ME TELL YOU ABOUT **VIKINGS**! REMORSELESS, UNSTOPPABLE **KILLING MACHINES**. THEIR PAGAN GODS PROMISED A SPECIAL HEAVEN TO ANY WARRIOR WHO DIED FIGHTING, WHICH MADE THEM TERRIFYINGLY **FEARLESS** IN BATTLE.
FOR YEARS THEY'D BEEN PLUNDERING THE COASTLINE, APPEARING LITERALLY OUT **OF THE BLUE** IN THEIR LONGBOATS.
BUT THAT WAS JUST THE START OF IT! INITIALLY, THEY'D JUST RAIDED THE COASTS, BUT NOW THEY WERE ATTACKING **INLAND**, AND THEY WERE PLANNING TO **STAY**!
NOW, I SHOULD POINT OUT, AT THIS TIME THERE WAS NO "ENGLAND"——INSTEAD THERE WERE MULTIPLE ANGLO-SAXON KINGDOMS, ALL FIGHTING AMONG THEMSELVES.
Northumbria
Mercia
East Anglia
Britons
Wessex
UNWILLING TO UNITE, THEY WERE CONQUERED ONE BY ONE, UNTIL ONLY **ONE** REMAINED... THE MIGHTY KINGDOM OF **WESSEX**!
Vikings
Wessex
BLOODY BUT UNBOWED, SOLITARY LIGHT IN THE DARKNESS, LAST BASTION OF HOPE FOR ANGLO-SAXON CHRISTENDOM...
YOU WERE GETTING CREAMED.
YEP.
THE VIKINGS HAD DESTROYED MY ARMY, CAPTURED MY CASTLE AND FORCED ME TO FLEE INTO A GIANT MARSH CALLED **THE FENS**.
BUT FEAR NOT! THIS WAS NOT DEFEAT——JUST A MERE SETBACK! YOU SEE, THIS WAS WHEN I BURNED THE CAKES...

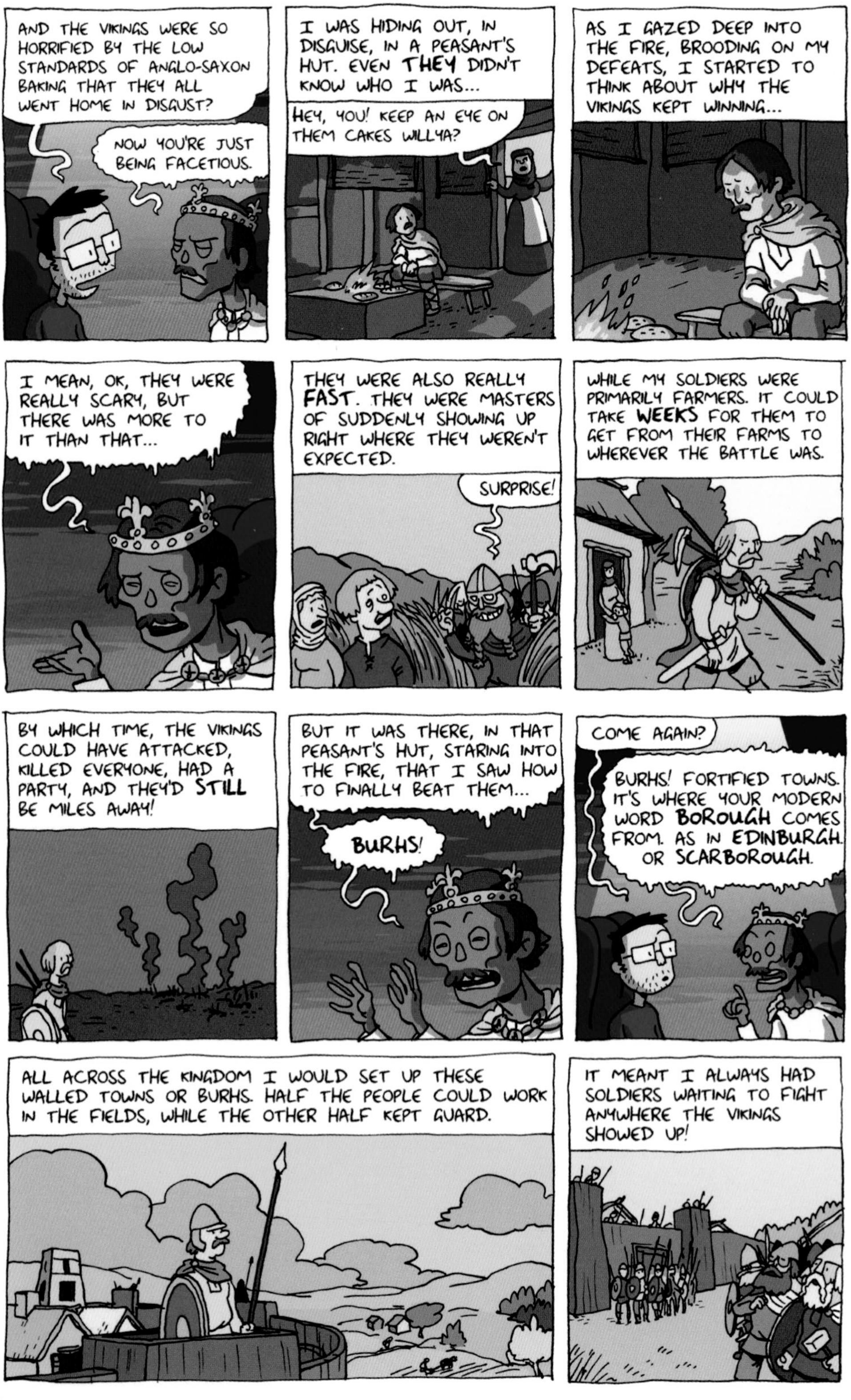
AND THE VIKINGS WERE SO HORRIFIED BY THE LOW STANDARDS OF ANGLO-SAXON BAKING THAT THEY ALL WENT HOME IN DISGUST?
NOW YOU'RE JUST BEING FACETIOUS.
I WAS HIDING OUT, IN DISGUISE, IN A PEASANT'S HUT. EVEN THEY DIDN'T KNOW WHO I WAS...
HEY, YOU! KEEP AN EYE ON THEM CAKES WILLYA?
AS I GAZED DEEP INTO THE FIRE, BROODING ON MY DEFEATS, I STARTED TO THINK ABOUT WHY THE VIKINGS KEPT WINNING...
I MEAN, OK, THEY WERE REALLY SCARY, BUT THERE WAS MORE TO IT THAN THAT...
THEY WERE ALSO REALLY FAST. THEY WERE MASTERS OF SUDDENLY SHOWING UP RIGHT WHERE THEY WEREN'T EXPECTED.
SURPRISE!
WHILE MY SOLDIERS WERE PRIMARILY FARMERS. IT COULD TAKE WEEKS FOR THEM TO GET FROM THEIR FARMS TO WHEREVER THE BATTLE WAS.
BY WHICH TIME, THE VIKINGS COULD HAVE ATTACKED, KILLED EVERYONE, HAD A PARTY, AND THEY'D STILL BE MILES AWAY!
BUT IT WAS THERE, IN THAT PEASANT'S HUT, STARING INTO THE FIRE, THAT I SAW HOW TO FINALLY BEAT THEM...
BURHS!
COME AGAIN?
BURHS! FORTIFIED TOWNS. IT'S WHERE YOUR MODERN WORD BOROUGH COMES FROM. AS IN EDINBURGH OR SCARBOROUGH.
ALL ACROSS THE KINGDOM I WOULD SET UP THESE WALLED TOWNS OR BURHS. HALF THE PEOPLE COULD WORK IN THE FIELDS, WHILE THE OTHER HALF KEPT GUARD.
IT MEANT I ALWAYS HAD SOLDIERS WAITING TO FIGHT ANYWHERE THE VIKINGS SHOWED UP!

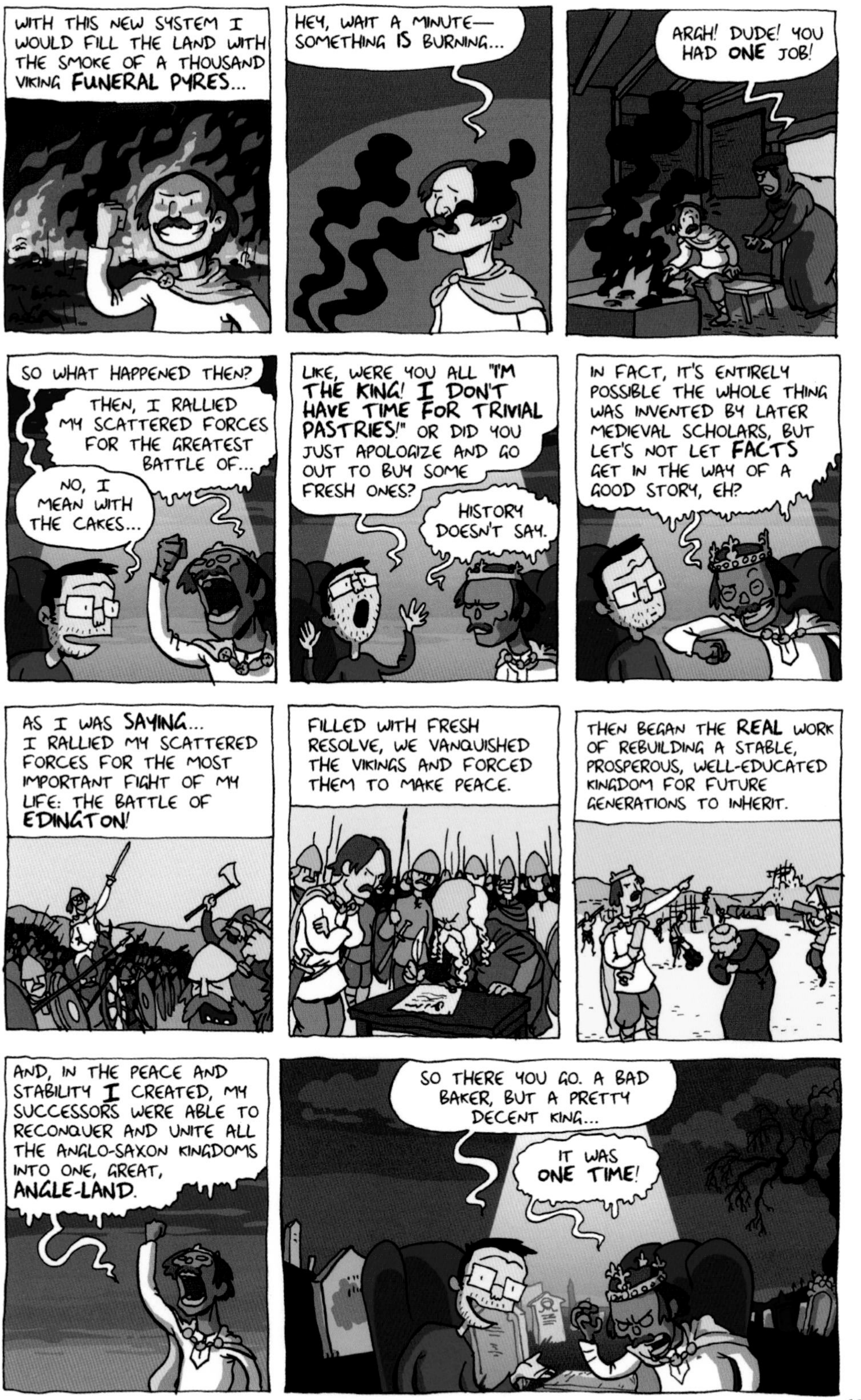
WITH THIS NEW SYSTEM I WOULD FILL THE LAND WITH THE SMOKE OF A THOUSAND VIKING FUNERAL PYRES...
HEY, WAIT A MINUTE— SOMETHING IS BURNING...
ARGH! DUDE! YOU HAD ONE JOB!
SO WHAT HAPPENED THEN?
THEN, I RALLIED MY SCATTERED FORCES FOR THE GREATEST BATTLE OF...
NO, I MEAN WITH THE CAKES...
LIKE, WERE YOU ALL "I'M THE KING! I DON'T HAVE TIME FOR TRIVIAL PASTRIES!" OR DID YOU JUST APOLOGIZE AND GO OUT TO BUY SOME FRESH ONES?
HISTORY DOESN'T SAY.
IN FACT, IT'S ENTIRELY POSSIBLE THE WHOLE THING WAS INVENTED BY LATER MEDIEVAL SCHOLARS, BUT LET'S NOT LET FACTS GET IN THE WAY OF A GOOD STORY, EH?
AS I WAS SAYING... I RALLIED MY SCATTERED FORCES FOR THE MOST IMPORTANT FIGHT OF MY LIFE: THE BATTLE OF EDINGTON!
FILLED WITH FRESH RESOLVE, WE VANQUISHED THE VIKINGS AND FORCED THEM TO MAKE PEACE.
THEN BEGAN THE REAL WORK OF REBUILDING A STABLE, PROSPEROUS, WELL-EDUCATED KINGDOM FOR FUTURE GENERATIONS TO INHERIT.
AND, IN THE PEACE AND STABILITY I CREATED, MY SUCCESSORS WERE ABLE TO RECONQUER AND UNITE ALL THE ANGLO-SAXON KINGDOMS INTO ONE, GREAT, ANGLE-LAND.
SO THERE YOU GO. A BAD BAKER, BUT A PRETTY DECENT KING...
IT WAS ONE TIME!

THE DARK ISLAND

KING ALFRED THE GREAT IS BACK TO SHED LIGHT ON DARK AGES BRITAIN!

ACTUALLY, I PREFER THE TERM EARLY MIDDLE AGES. "DARK AGES" MAKES IT SOUND SO GLOOMY.

EUROPE WAS A COMPLEX NETWORK OF DIFFERENT PEOPLES, ALL WITH THEIR OWN UNIQUE HISTORIES, LANGUAGES, AND CULTURES; ALL STRUGGLING FOR SUPREMACY AND SURVIVAL.

Britons

THIS WAS THE ROMANS' NAME FOR THE NATIVE PEOPLE. THEY SPOKE THE CELTIC LANGUAGE THAT SPREAD THROUGHOUT EUROPE AT THE START OF THE IRON AGE.

THEY WERE ORIGINALLY PAGANS, WHOSE PRIESTS (DRUIDS) CONDUCTED HUMAN SACRIFICES!

THE BRITONS MOSTLY CONVERTED TO CHRISTIANITY DURING THE ROMAN OCCUPATION.

Vikings

Picts

Irish

Britons

Angles

Irish

Vikings

Britons

Angles

Vikings

Angles

Saxons

Jutes

Irish and Picts

THESE GROUPS OF BRITONS WERE NEVER CONQUERED BY THE ROMANS, AND SO KEPT THEIR OWN RULERS AND THEIR OWN CULTURE.

Romano-Britons

THESE WERE BRITONS WHO EVENTUALLY BECAME PROUD ROMAN CITIZENS, SPEAKING LATIN AND ENJOYING THE PEACE AND SECURITY OF THE ROMAN EMPIRE.

BUT WHEN THE ROMAN ARMY LEFT, THE ROMANO-BRITONS HAD GOTTEN SO USED TO ROMAN PROTECTION, THEY COULDN'T REALLY DEFEND THEM-SELVES ANY MORE...

SO THEY HIRED A BUNCH OF TOUGH BARBARIANS FROM GERMANY CALLED SAXONS TO PROTECT THEM FROM IRISH AND PICTISH RAIDERS. SMART MOVE, RIGHT?

WHAT COULD POSSIBLY GO WRONG!?

Anglo-Saxons

GERMANIC-SPEAKING TRIBES FROM THE **ANGELN** PENINSULA (DENMARK) AND **SAXONY** (NORTH GERMANY), THESE PEOPLE WERE THEMSELVES BEING PUSHED OUT BY EVEN **TOUGHER** TRIBES FROM THE **E**AST!

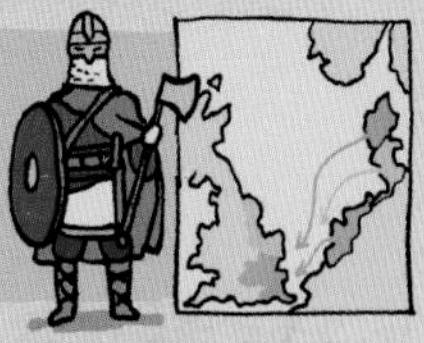

BROUGHT IN TO HELP **DEFEND** THE NATIVE BRITONS, THE **SAXONS** LIKED IT SO MUCH, THEY STAYED. (AND ENSLAVED THE BRITONS!)

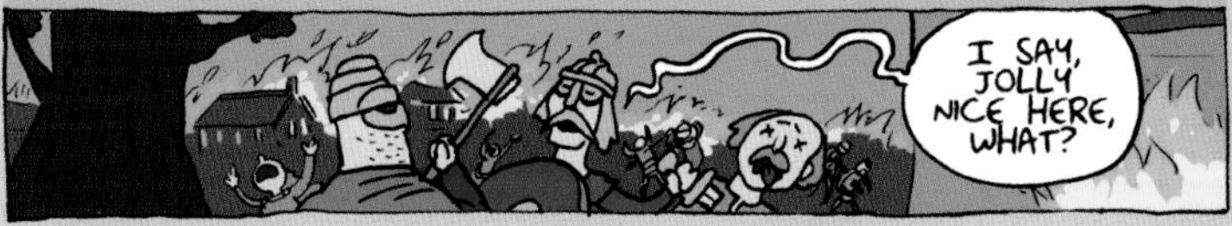
I SAY, JOLLY NICE HERE, WHAT?

TRIBES LIKE THE **ANGLES** AND **JUTES** STARTED INVADING, TOO. EVENTUALLY, THEY ALL MERGED INTO THE **ANGLO-SAXONS**.

THE ANGLO-SAXON INVADERS COULDN'T READ. THE ONLY PEOPLE WHO COULD WERE MONKS, WHO KEPT KNOWLEDGE ALIVE IN REMOTE IRISH MONASTERIES.

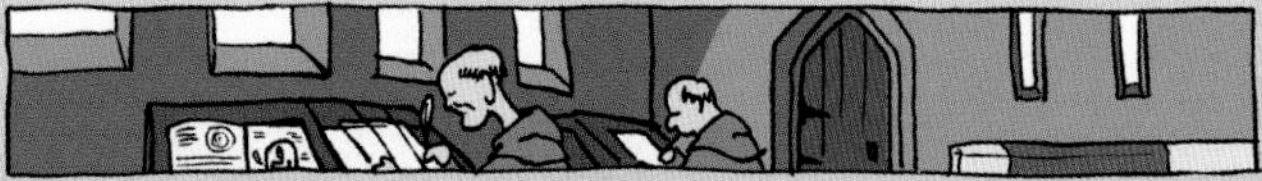

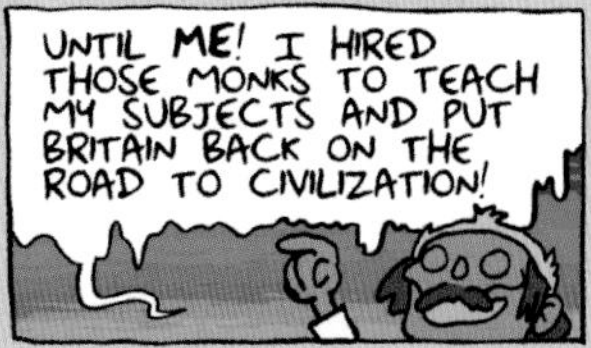
UNTIL **ME**! I HIRED THOSE MONKS TO TEACH MY SUBJECTS AND PUT BRITAIN BACK ON THE ROAD TO CIVILIZATION!

ORIGINALLY PAGANS, THE ANGLO-SAXONS CONVERTED TO CHRISTIANITY, TOO. IRONICALLY, THEY BECAME LIKE THEIR BRITON FOREBEARS: VULNERABLE TO **INVASION**, THIS TIME BY...

Vikings

RAIDING PARTIES FROM NORWAY AND DENMARK BEGAN BY ATTACKING MONASTERIES AND COASTAL TOWNS, AND SOON CONCLUDED BRITAIN WAS READY FOR A TAKEOVER!

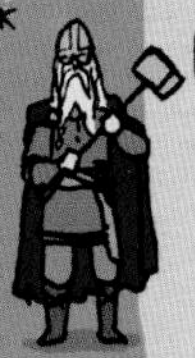

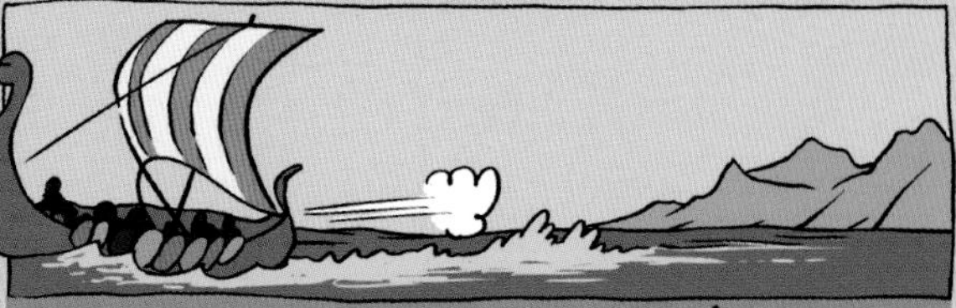

THE BEST SHIP OF THE AGE, THE **VIKING LONGBOAT**, ALLOWED THEM TO STRIKE ANYWHERE ALONG THE COAST WITHOUT WARNING!

VIKINGS TRAVELED AS FAR AS RUSSIA AND THE MIDDLE EAST. THEY EVEN MADE IT AS FAR AS **CANADA**!

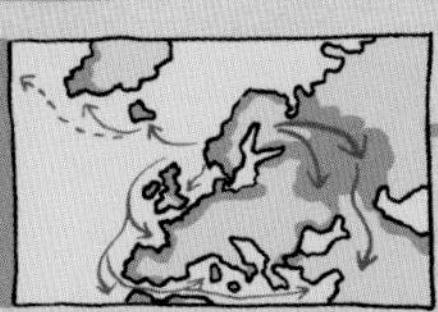

DESPITE AN UNCIVILIZED REPUTATION, THE VIKINGS WERE COMPARATIVELY HYGIENIC, BATHING ONCE A WEEK AND COMBING AND BRAIDING THEIR HAIR DAILY.

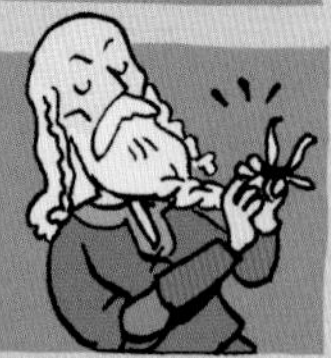

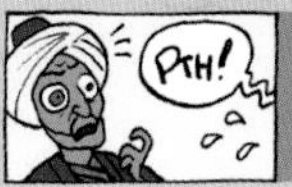
PTH!

NOTE: "COMPARATIVELY HYGIENIC"—ISLAMIC OBSERVERS WERE **TOTALLY** GROSSED OUT BY THEIR HABIT OF **SPITTING** IN THEIR FACE-WASHING WATER BEFORE **PASSING IT TO SOMEONE ELSE**!

ROMANS LEAVE **400** CE, IRISH AND ANGLO-SAXONS INVADE: ~**450** CE.

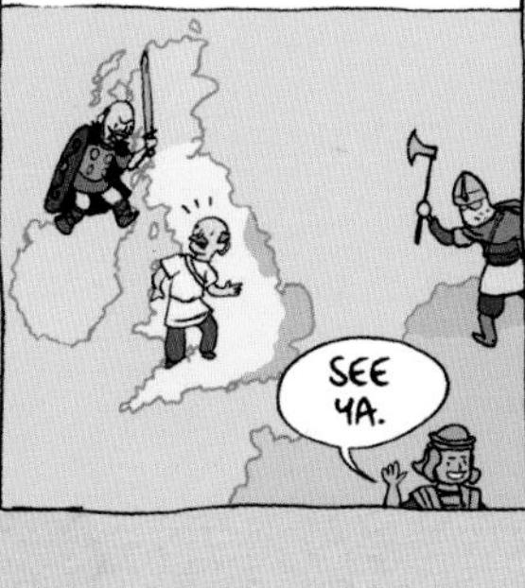
SEE YA.

ANGLO-SAXONS EXPAND, BRITONS RETREAT: ~**450-800** CE.

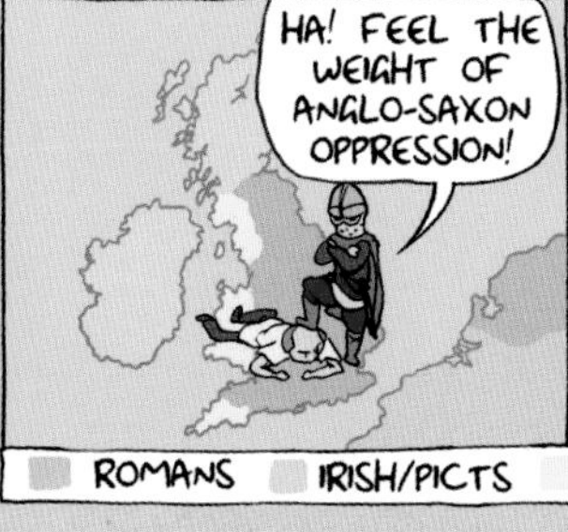
HA! FEEL THE WEIGHT OF ANGLO-SAXON OPPRESSION!

VIKINGS CONQUER LARGE AREAS BEFORE MAKING PEACE WITH ALFRED IN **898** CE.

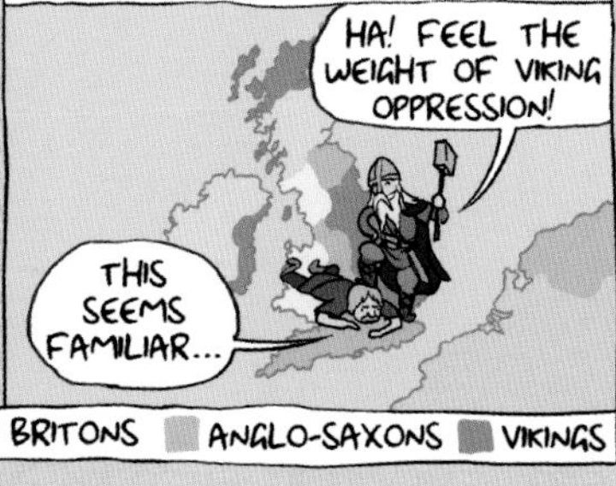
HA! FEEL THE WEIGHT OF VIKING OPPRESSION!
THIS SEEMS FAMILIAR...

ROMANS | IRISH/PICTS | BRITONS | ANGLO-SAXONS | VIKINGS

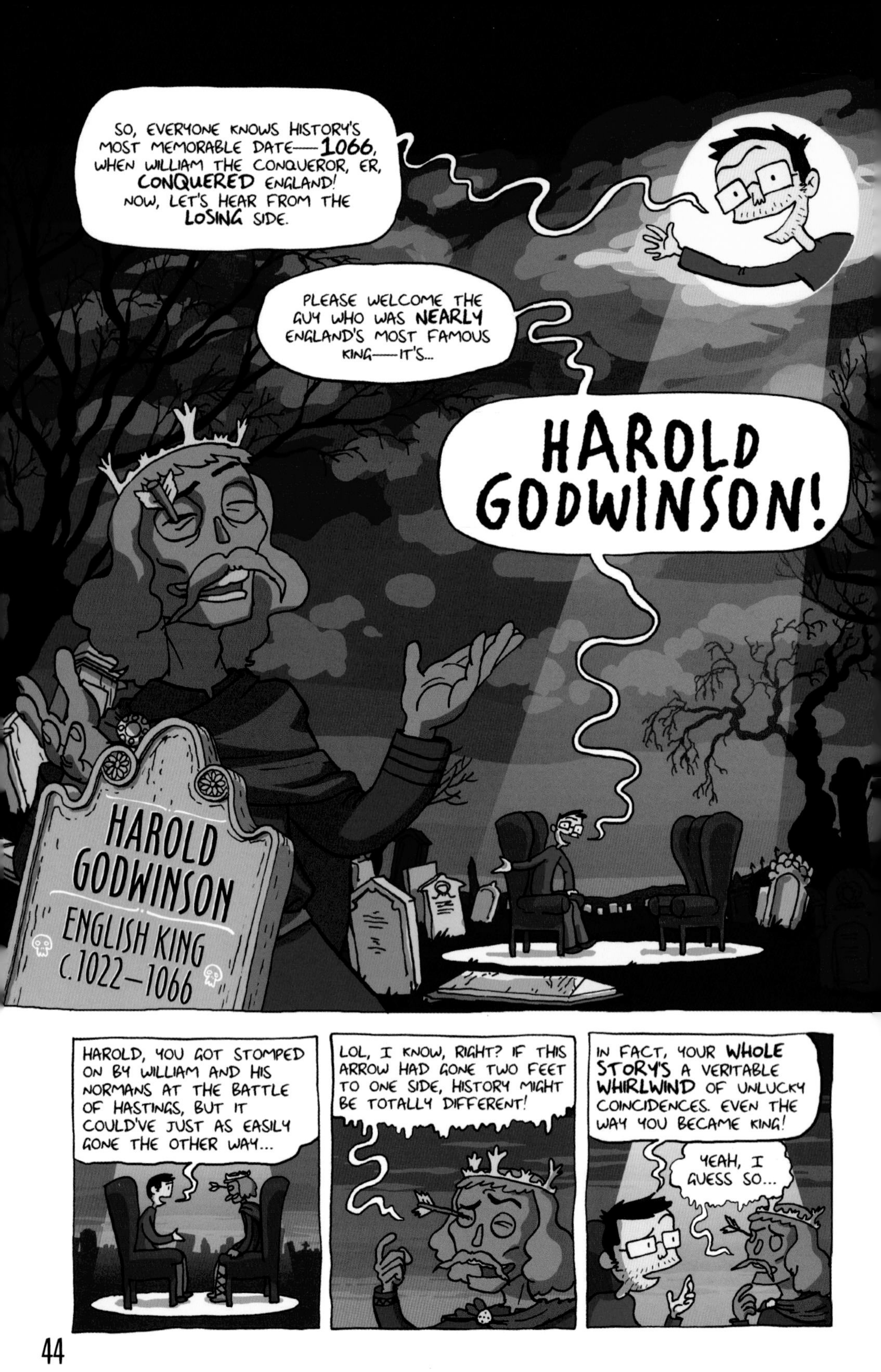
SO, EVERYONE KNOWS HISTORY'S MOST MEMORABLE DATE—1066, WHEN WILLIAM THE CONQUEROR, ER, CONQUERED ENGLAND! NOW, LET'S HEAR FROM THE LOSING SIDE.
PLEASE WELCOME THE GUY WHO WAS NEARLY ENGLAND'S MOST FAMOUS KING—IT'S...
HAROLD GODWINSON!
HAROLD GODWINSON
ENGLISH KING
c.1022–1066
HAROLD, YOU GOT STOMPED ON BY WILLIAM AND HIS NORMANS AT THE BATTLE OF HASTINGS, BUT IT COULD'VE JUST AS EASILY GONE THE OTHER WAY...
LOL, I KNOW, RIGHT? IF THIS ARROW HAD GONE TWO FEET TO ONE SIDE, HISTORY MIGHT BE TOTALLY DIFFERENT!
IN FACT, YOUR WHOLE STORY'S A VERITABLE WHIRLWIND OF UNLUCKY COINCIDENCES. EVEN THE WAY YOU BECAME KING!
YEAH, I GUESS SO...

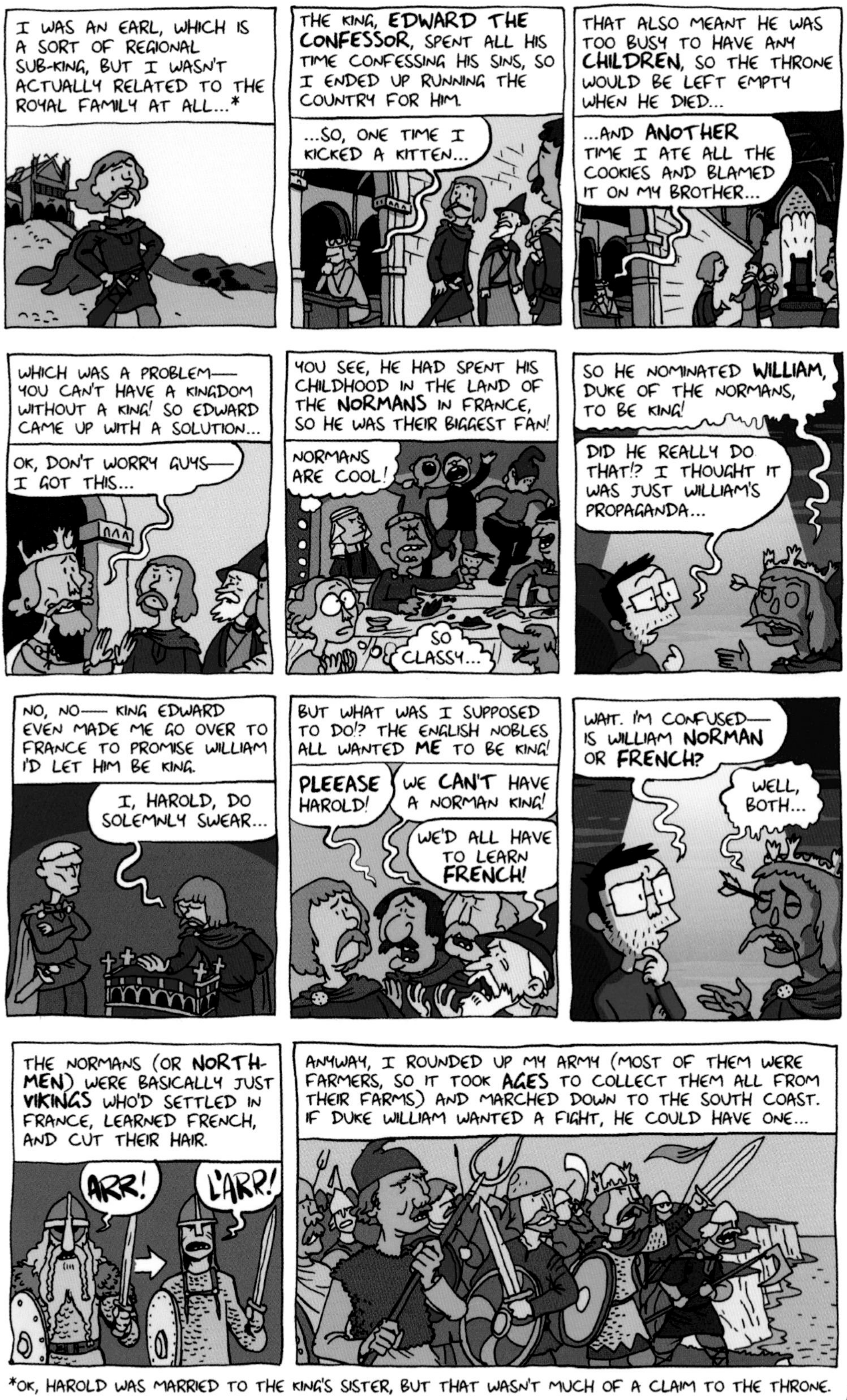
I WAS AN EARL, WHICH IS A SORT OF REGIONAL SUB-KING, BUT I WASN'T ACTUALLY RELATED TO THE ROYAL FAMILY AT ALL...*
THE KING, EDWARD THE CONFESSOR, SPENT ALL HIS TIME CONFESSING HIS SINS, SO I ENDED UP RUNNING THE COUNTRY FOR HIM.
...SO, ONE TIME I KICKED A KITTEN...
THAT ALSO MEANT HE WAS TOO BUSY TO HAVE ANY CHILDREN, SO THE THRONE WOULD BE LEFT EMPTY WHEN HE DIED...
...AND ANOTHER TIME I ATE ALL THE COOKIES AND BLAMED IT ON MY BROTHER...
WHICH WAS A PROBLEM— YOU CAN'T HAVE A KINGDOM WITHOUT A KING! SO EDWARD CAME UP WITH A SOLUTION...
OK, DON'T WORRY GUYS— I GOT THIS...
YOU SEE, HE HAD SPENT HIS CHILDHOOD IN THE LAND OF THE NORMANS IN FRANCE, SO HE WAS THEIR BIGGEST FAN!
NORMANS ARE COOL!
SO CLASSY...
SO HE NOMINATED WILLIAM, DUKE OF THE NORMANS, TO BE KING!
DID HE REALLY DO THAT!? I THOUGHT IT WAS JUST WILLIAM'S PROPAGANDA...
NO, NO— KING EDWARD EVEN MADE ME GO OVER TO FRANCE TO PROMISE WILLIAM I'D LET HIM BE KING.
I, HAROLD, DO SOLEMNLY SWEAR...
BUT WHAT WAS I SUPPOSED TO DO!? THE ENGLISH NOBLES ALL WANTED ME TO BE KING!
PLEEASE HAROLD!
WE CAN'T HAVE A NORMAN KING!
WE'D ALL HAVE TO LEARN FRENCH!
WAIT. I'M CONFUSED— IS WILLIAM NORMAN OR FRENCH?
WELL, BOTH...
THE NORMANS (OR NORTH-MEN) WERE BASICALLY JUST VIKINGS WHO'D SETTLED IN FRANCE, LEARNED FRENCH, AND CUT THEIR HAIR.
ARR!
L'ARR!
ANYWAY, I ROUNDED UP MY ARMY (MOST OF THEM WERE FARMERS, SO IT TOOK AGES TO COLLECT THEM ALL FROM THEIR FARMS) AND MARCHED DOWN TO THE SOUTH COAST. IF DUKE WILLIAM WANTED A FIGHT, HE COULD HAVE ONE...

*OK, HAROLD WAS MARRIED TO THE KING'S SISTER, BUT THAT WASN'T MUCH OF A CLAIM TO THE THRONE.

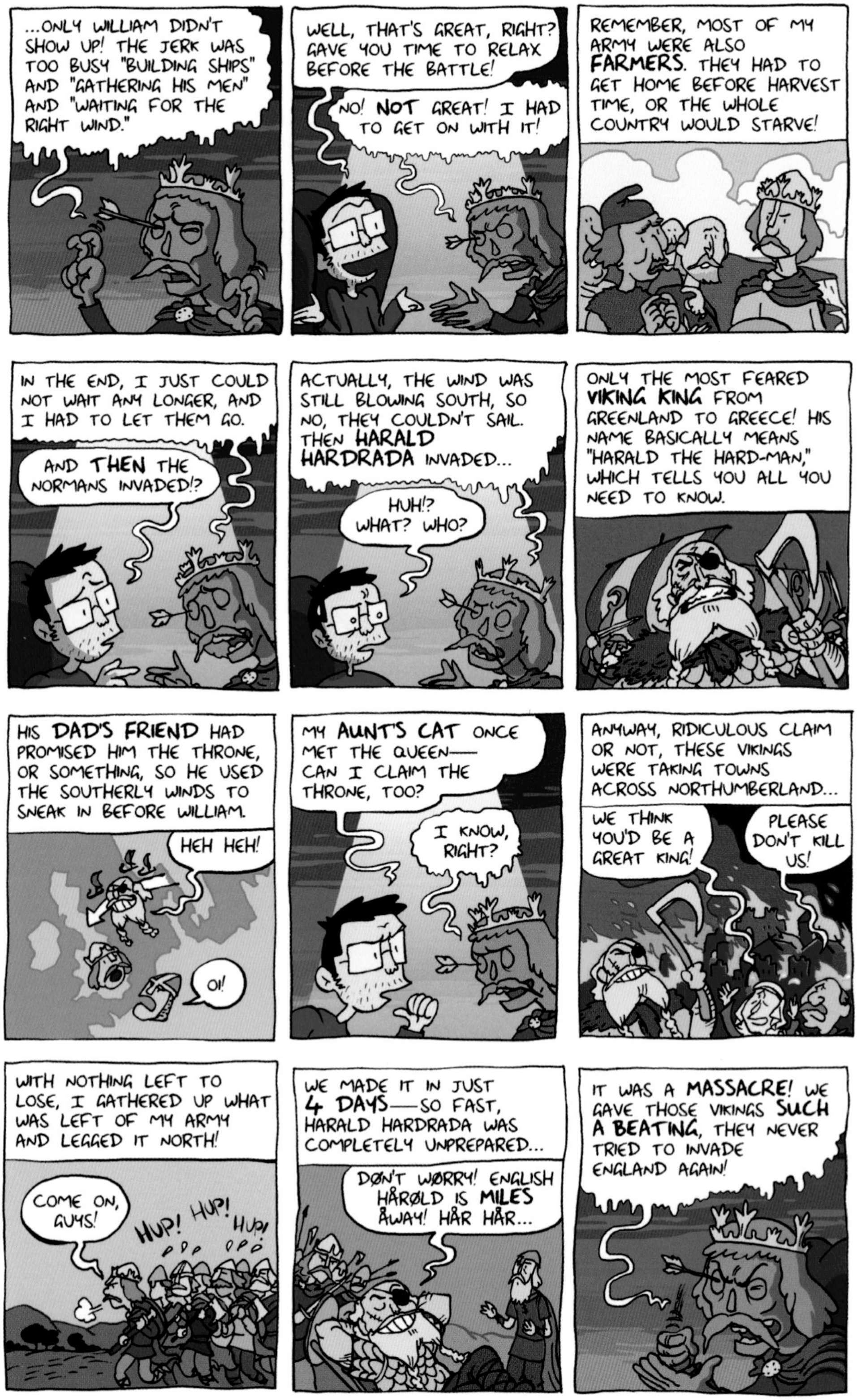
...ONLY WILLIAM DIDN'T SHOW UP! THE JERK WAS TOO BUSY "BUILDING SHIPS" AND "GATHERING HIS MEN" AND "WAITING FOR THE RIGHT WIND."
WELL, THAT'S GREAT, RIGHT? GAVE YOU TIME TO RELAX BEFORE THE BATTLE!
NO! NOT GREAT! I HAD TO GET ON WITH IT!
REMEMBER, MOST OF MY ARMY WERE ALSO FARMERS. THEY HAD TO GET HOME BEFORE HARVEST TIME, OR THE WHOLE COUNTRY WOULD STARVE!
IN THE END, I JUST COULD NOT WAIT ANY LONGER, AND I HAD TO LET THEM GO.
AND THEN THE NORMANS INVADED!?
ACTUALLY, THE WIND WAS STILL BLOWING SOUTH, SO NO, THEY COULDN'T SAIL. THEN HARALD HARDRADA INVADED...
HUH!? WHAT? WHO?
ONLY THE MOST FEARED VIKING KING FROM GREENLAND TO GREECE! HIS NAME BASICALLY MEANS "HARALD THE HARD-MAN," WHICH TELLS YOU ALL YOU NEED TO KNOW.
HIS DAD'S FRIEND HAD PROMISED HIM THE THRONE, OR SOMETHING, SO HE USED THE SOUTHERLY WINDS TO SNEAK IN BEFORE WILLIAM.
HEH HEH!
OI!
MY AUNT'S CAT ONCE MET THE QUEEN— CAN I CLAIM THE THRONE, TOO?
I KNOW, RIGHT?
ANYWAY, RIDICULOUS CLAIM OR NOT, THESE VIKINGS WERE TAKING TOWNS ACROSS NORTHUMBERLAND...
WE THINK YOU'D BE A GREAT KING!
PLEASE DON'T KILL US!
WITH NOTHING LEFT TO LOSE, I GATHERED UP WHAT WAS LEFT OF MY ARMY AND LEGGED IT NORTH!
COME ON, GUYS!
HUP! HUP! HUP!
WE MADE IT IN JUST 4 DAYS—SO FAST, HARALD HARDRADA WAS COMPLETELY UNPREPARED...
DØN'T WØRRY! ENGLISH HÅRØLD IS MILES ÅWAY! HÅR HÅR...
IT WAS A MASSACRE! WE GAVE THOSE VIKINGS SUCH A BEATING, THEY NEVER TRIED TO INVADE ENGLAND AGAIN!

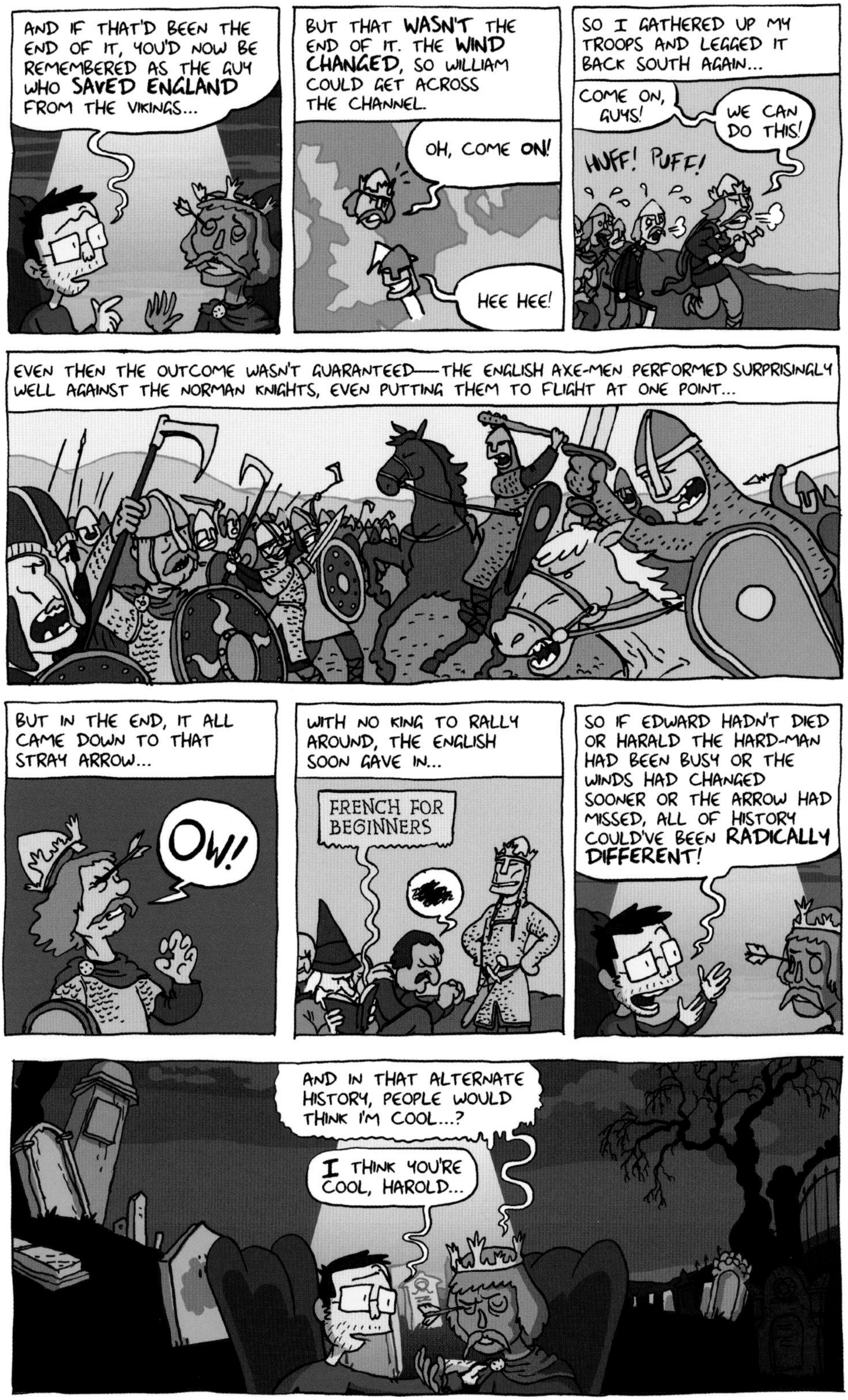
AND IF THAT'D BEEN THE END OF IT, YOU'D NOW BE REMEMBERED AS THE GUY WHO SAVED ENGLAND FROM THE VIKINGS...
BUT THAT WASN'T THE END OF IT. THE WIND CHANGED, SO WILLIAM COULD GET ACROSS THE CHANNEL.
OH, COME ON!
HEE HEE!
SO I GATHERED UP MY TROOPS AND LEGGED IT BACK SOUTH AGAIN...
COME ON, GUYS!
WE CAN DO THIS!
HUFF! PUFF!
EVEN THEN THE OUTCOME WASN'T GUARANTEED—THE ENGLISH AXE-MEN PERFORMED SURPRISINGLY WELL AGAINST THE NORMAN KNIGHTS, EVEN PUTTING THEM TO FLIGHT AT ONE POINT...
BUT IN THE END, IT ALL CAME DOWN TO THAT STRAY ARROW...
OW!
WITH NO KING TO RALLY AROUND, THE ENGLISH SOON GAVE IN...
FRENCH FOR BEGINNERS
SO IF EDWARD HADN'T DIED OR HARALD THE HARD-MAN HAD BEEN BUSY OR THE WINDS HAD CHANGED SOONER OR THE ARROW HAD MISSED, ALL OF HISTORY COULD'VE BEEN RADICALLY DIFFERENT!
AND IN THAT ALTERNATE HISTORY, PEOPLE WOULD THINK I'M COOL...?
I THINK YOU'RE COOL, HAROLD...

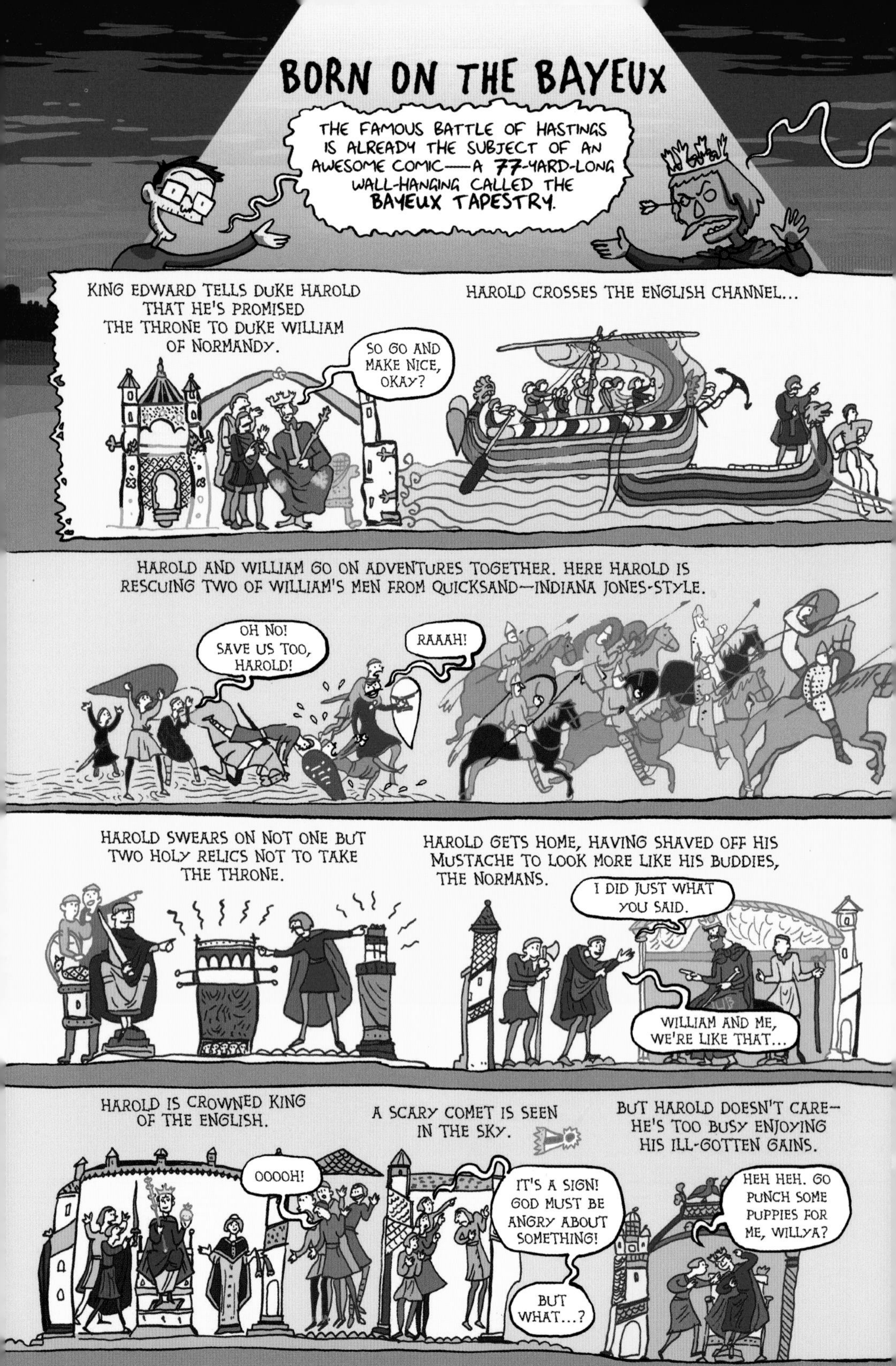
BORN ON THE BAYEUX
THE FAMOUS BATTLE OF HASTINGS IS ALREADY THE SUBJECT OF AN AWESOME COMIC—A 77-YARD-LONG WALL-HANGING CALLED THE BAYEUX TAPESTRY.
KING EDWARD TELLS DUKE HAROLD THAT HE'S PROMISED THE THRONE TO DUKE WILLIAM OF NORMANDY.
SO GO AND MAKE NICE, OKAY?
HAROLD CROSSES THE ENGLISH CHANNEL...
HAROLD AND WILLIAM GO ON ADVENTURES TOGETHER. HERE HAROLD IS RESCUING TWO OF WILLIAM'S MEN FROM QUICKSAND—INDIANA JONES-STYLE.
OH NO! SAVE US TOO, HAROLD!
RAAAH!
HAROLD SWEARS ON NOT ONE BUT TWO HOLY RELICS NOT TO TAKE THE THRONE.
HAROLD GETS HOME, HAVING SHAVED OFF HIS MUSTACHE TO LOOK MORE LIKE HIS BUDDIES, THE NORMANS.
I DID JUST WHAT YOU SAID.
WILLIAM AND ME, WE'RE LIKE THAT...
HAROLD IS CROWNED KING OF THE ENGLISH.
A SCARY COMET IS SEEN IN THE SKY.
OOOOH!
IT'S A SIGN! GOD MUST BE ANGRY ABOUT SOMETHING!
BUT WHAT...?
BUT HAROLD DOESN'T CARE—HE'S TOO BUSY ENJOYING HIS ILL-GOTTEN GAINS.
HEH HEH. GO PUNCH SOME PUPPIES FOR ME, WILLYA?

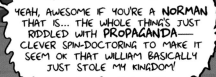

YEAH, AWESOME IF YOU'RE A **NORMAN** THAT IS... THE WHOLE THING'S JUST RIDDLED WITH **PROPAGANDA**—CLEVER SPIN-DOCTORING TO MAKE IT SEEM OK THAT WILLIAM BASICALLY JUST STOLE MY KINGDOM!

SEE IF YOU CAN SPOT ALL THE PLACES WHERE IT MAKES ME LOOK LIKE A **LIAR**...

OK, MAYBE I DID TELL A FEW FIBS NOW AND THEN——THAT'S NOT THE POINT.

TWO WRONGS DON'T MAKE A RIGHT.

...AND IMMEDIATELY GETS CAPTURED.

WHOAH—HOLD ON!

HAROLD IS TAKEN TO WILLIAM'S COURT.

NO, SERIOUSLY! I'M LIKE YOUR BIGGEST FAN!

ASK ANYONE!

IT'S TRUE.

WON'T SHUT UP ABOUT IT...

HERE A PRIEST IS TOUCHING SOME WOMAN IN THE FACE—NO ONE'S REALLY SURE WHY.

UGH! GET OFF!

THEY BEAT UP A GUY CALLED CONAN—NOT THE BARBARIAN, BUT ONE OF WILLIAM'S ENEMIES.

AHH! I'M OUTTA HERE!

CONAN ESCAPING OUT THE BACK OF HIS CASTLE.

IN SHORT—THEY ARE BESTIES FOR LIFE.

I LOVE YOU, MAN...

KING EDWARD PROMPTLY DIES.

THE ENGLISH LORDS ASK HAROLD TO BE KING.

OH, GO ON THEN.

MEANWHILE, WILLIAM HEARS THE NEWS.

I TREAT HIM LIKE A BROTHER, AND THIS IS HOW HE REPAYS ME!?

VERILY, IT IS ON!

HE HAS A BUNCH OF GUYS CHOP DOWN SOME TREES...

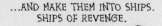
...AND MAKE THEM INTO SHIPS.
SHIPS OF REVENGE.

AND THE FIRST THING THEY DO IS STEAL
SOME POOR PEASANTS' COWS.

LET IT GO, DAD. IT'S JUST A COW...

THEY HAVE A HUGE BARBEUE. THEY
CAN'T GO FIGHTING INJUSTICE ON
AN EMPTY STOMACH...

WILLIAM GIVES A ROUSING SPEECH.

OK, BOYS.

LET'S KICK THEIR BUTTS.

THE NORMANS BEGIN THEIR CAVALRY CHARGE.

THEY SMASH UP AGAINST THE ENGLISH SHIELD-WALL.

HORSES ARE DYING LEFT AND RIGHT.

THE ENGLISH ARE ON TOP OF A HILL, AND FOR
A WHILE IT LOOKS LIKE THEY MIGHT WIN...

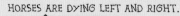

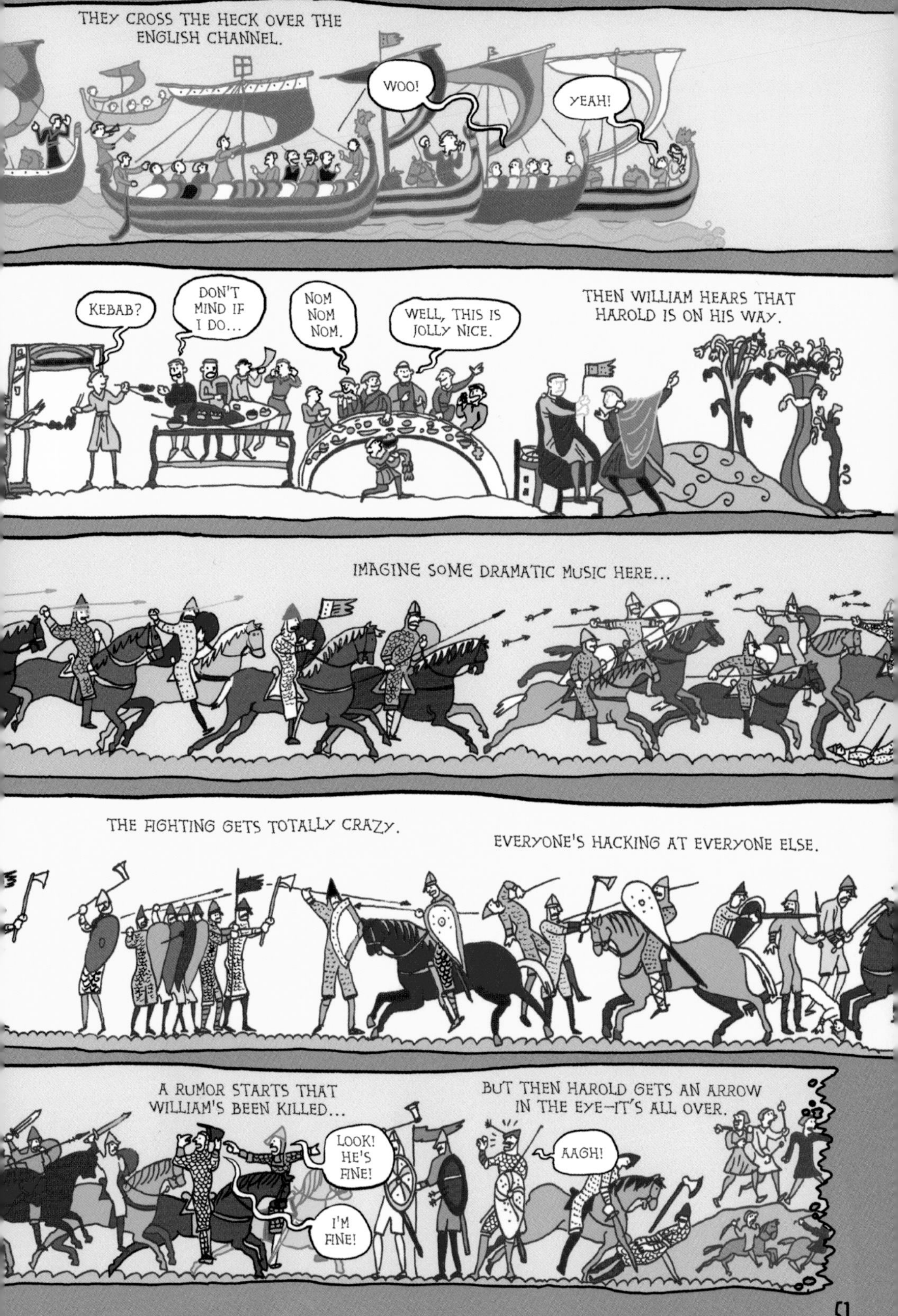
THEY CROSS THE HECK OVER THE ENGLISH CHANNEL.
WOO!
YEAH!
KEBAB?
DON'T MIND IF I DO...
NOM NOM NOM.
WELL, THIS IS JOLLY NICE.
THEN WILLIAM HEARS THAT HAROLD IS ON HIS WAY.
IMAGINE SOME DRAMATIC MUSIC HERE...
THE FIGHTING GETS TOTALLY CRAZY.
EVERYONE'S HACKING AT EVERYONE ELSE.
A RUMOR STARTS THAT WILLIAM'S BEEN KILLED...
LOOK! HE'S FINE!
I'M FINE!
BUT THEN HAROLD GETS AN ARROW IN THE EYE—IT'S ALL OVER.
AAGH!

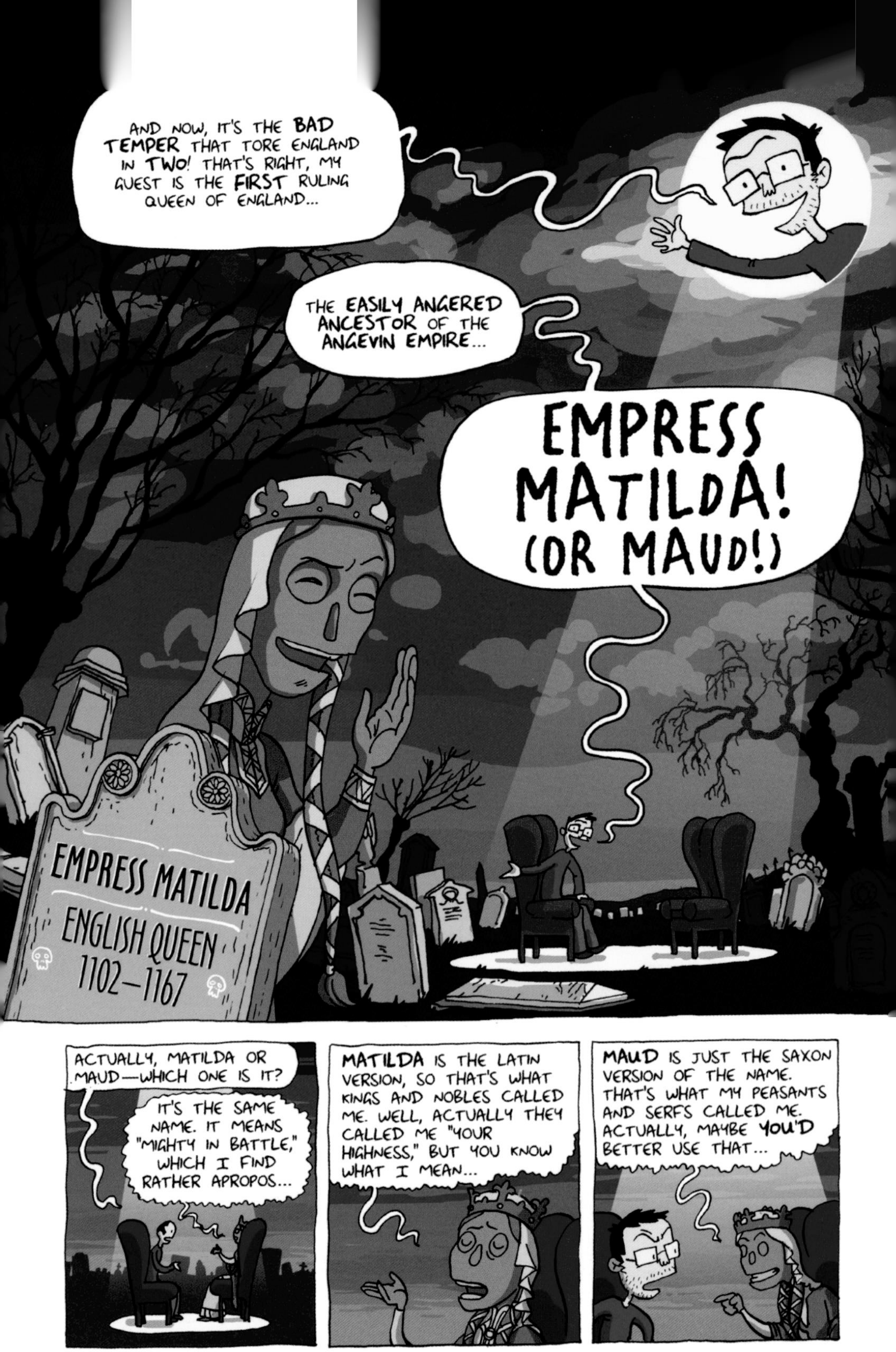

AND NOW, IT'S THE BAD TEMPER THAT TORE ENGLAND IN TWO! THAT'S RIGHT, MY GUEST IS THE FIRST RULING QUEEN OF ENGLAND...
THE EASILY ANGERED ANCESTOR OF THE ANGEVIN EMPIRE...
EMPRESS MATILDA! (OR MAUD!)
EMPRESS MATILDA
ENGLISH QUEEN
1102–1167
ACTUALLY, MATILDA OR MAUD—WHICH ONE IS IT?
IT'S THE SAME NAME. IT MEANS "MIGHTY IN BATTLE," WHICH I FIND RATHER APROPOS...
MATILDA IS THE LATIN VERSION, SO THAT'S WHAT KINGS AND NOBLES CALLED ME. WELL, ACTUALLY THEY CALLED ME "YOUR HIGHNESS," BUT YOU KNOW WHAT I MEAN...
MAUD IS JUST THE SAXON VERSION OF THE NAME. THAT'S WHAT MY PEASANTS AND SERFS CALLED ME. ACTUALLY, MAYBE YOU'D BETTER USE THAT...

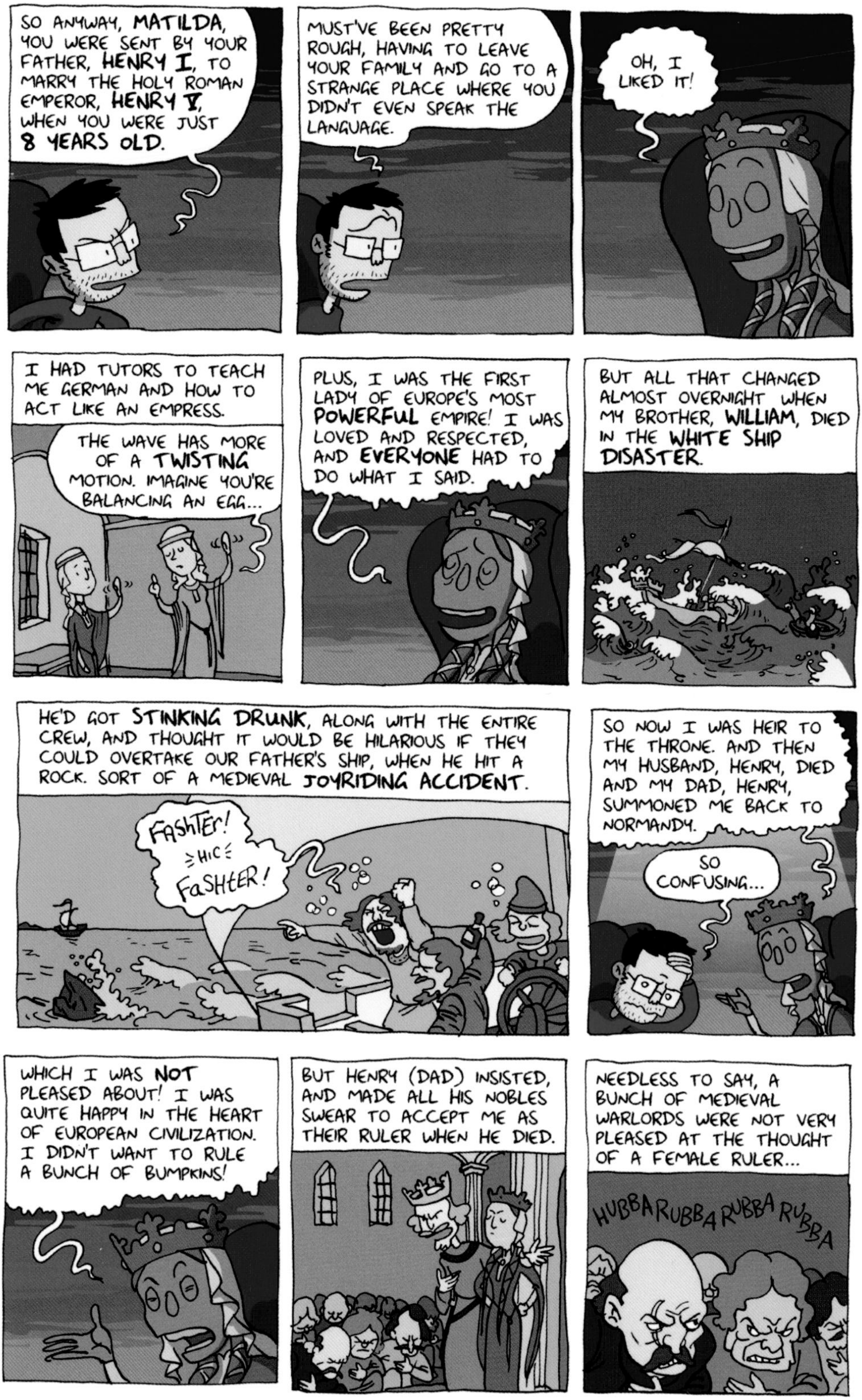

SO ANYWAY, MATILDA, YOU WERE SENT BY YOUR FATHER, HENRY I, TO MARRY THE HOLY ROMAN EMPEROR, HENRY V, WHEN YOU WERE JUST 8 YEARS OLD.
MUST'VE BEEN PRETTY ROUGH, HAVING TO LEAVE YOUR FAMILY AND GO TO A STRANGE PLACE WHERE YOU DIDN'T EVEN SPEAK THE LANGUAGE.
OH, I LIKED IT!
I HAD TUTORS TO TEACH ME GERMAN AND HOW TO ACT LIKE AN EMPRESS.
THE WAVE HAS MORE OF A TWISTING MOTION. IMAGINE YOU'RE BALANCING AN EGG...
PLUS, I WAS THE FIRST LADY OF EUROPE'S MOST POWERFUL EMPIRE! I WAS LOVED AND RESPECTED, AND EVERYONE HAD TO DO WHAT I SAID.
BUT ALL THAT CHANGED ALMOST OVERNIGHT WHEN MY BROTHER, WILLIAM, DIED IN THE WHITE SHIP DISASTER.
HE'D GOT STINKING DRUNK, ALONG WITH THE ENTIRE CREW, AND THOUGHT IT WOULD BE HILARIOUS IF THEY COULD OVERTAKE OUR FATHER'S SHIP, WHEN HE HIT A ROCK. SORT OF A MEDIEVAL JOYRIDING ACCIDENT.
FASHTER! HIC FASHTER!
SO NOW I WAS HEIR TO THE THRONE. AND THEN MY HUSBAND, HENRY, DIED AND MY DAD, HENRY, SUMMONED ME BACK TO NORMANDY.
SO CONFUSING...
WHICH I WAS NOT PLEASED ABOUT! I WAS QUITE HAPPY IN THE HEART OF EUROPEAN CIVILIZATION. I DIDN'T WANT TO RULE A BUNCH OF BUMPKINS!
BUT HENRY (DAD) INSISTED, AND MADE ALL HIS NOBLES SWEAR TO ACCEPT ME AS THEIR RULER WHEN HE DIED.
NEEDLESS TO SAY, A BUNCH OF MEDIEVAL WARLORDS WERE NOT VERY PLEASED AT THE THOUGHT OF A FEMALE RULER...
HUBBA RUBBA RUBBA RUBBA

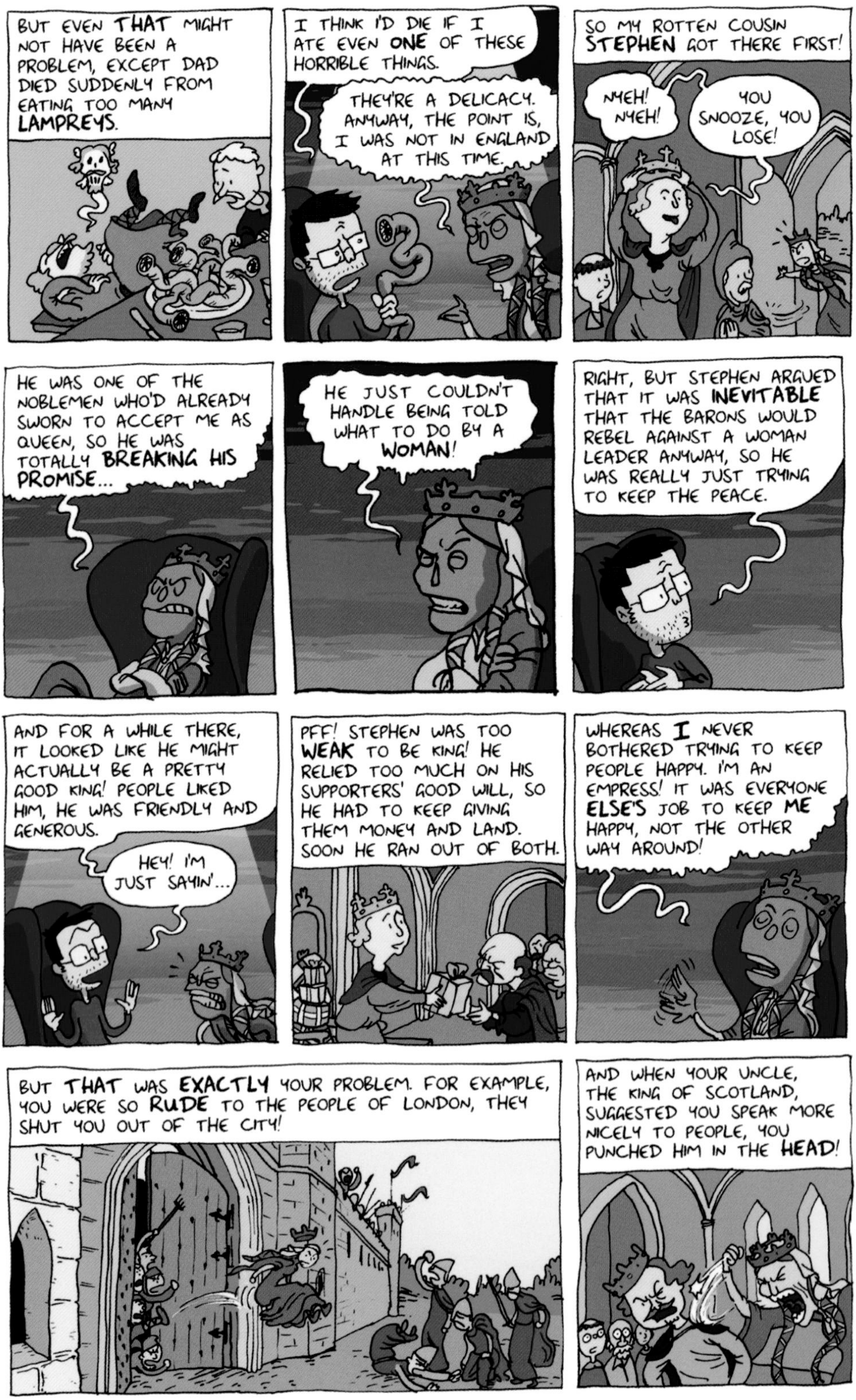
BUT EVEN THAT MIGHT NOT HAVE BEEN A PROBLEM, EXCEPT DAD DIED SUDDENLY FROM EATING TOO MANY LAMPREYS.
I THINK I'D DIE IF I ATE EVEN ONE OF THESE HORRIBLE THINGS.
THEY'RE A DELICACY. ANYWAY, THE POINT IS, I WAS NOT IN ENGLAND AT THIS TIME.
SO MY ROTTEN COUSIN STEPHEN GOT THERE FIRST!
NYEH! NYEH!
YOU SNOOZE, YOU LOSE!
HE WAS ONE OF THE NOBLEMEN WHO'D ALREADY SWORN TO ACCEPT ME AS QUEEN, SO HE WAS TOTALLY BREAKING HIS PROMISE...
HE JUST COULDN'T HANDLE BEING TOLD WHAT TO DO BY A WOMAN!
RIGHT, BUT STEPHEN ARGUED THAT IT WAS INEVITABLE THAT THE BARONS WOULD REBEL AGAINST A WOMAN LEADER ANYWAY, SO HE WAS REALLY JUST TRYING TO KEEP THE PEACE.
AND FOR A WHILE THERE, IT LOOKED LIKE HE MIGHT ACTUALLY BE A PRETTY GOOD KING! PEOPLE LIKED HIM, HE WAS FRIENDLY AND GENEROUS.
HEY! I'M JUST SAYIN'...
PFF! STEPHEN WAS TOO WEAK TO BE KING! HE RELIED TOO MUCH ON HIS SUPPORTERS' GOOD WILL, SO HE HAD TO KEEP GIVING THEM MONEY AND LAND. SOON HE RAN OUT OF BOTH.
WHEREAS I NEVER BOTHERED TRYING TO KEEP PEOPLE HAPPY. I'M AN EMPRESS! IT WAS EVERYONE ELSE'S JOB TO KEEP ME HAPPY, NOT THE OTHER WAY AROUND!
BUT THAT WAS EXACTLY YOUR PROBLEM. FOR EXAMPLE, YOU WERE SO RUDE TO THE PEOPLE OF LONDON, THEY SHUT YOU OUT OF THE CITY!
AND WHEN YOUR UNCLE, THE KING OF SCOTLAND, SUGGESTED YOU SPEAK MORE NICELY TO PEOPLE, YOU PUNCHED HIM IN THE HEAD!

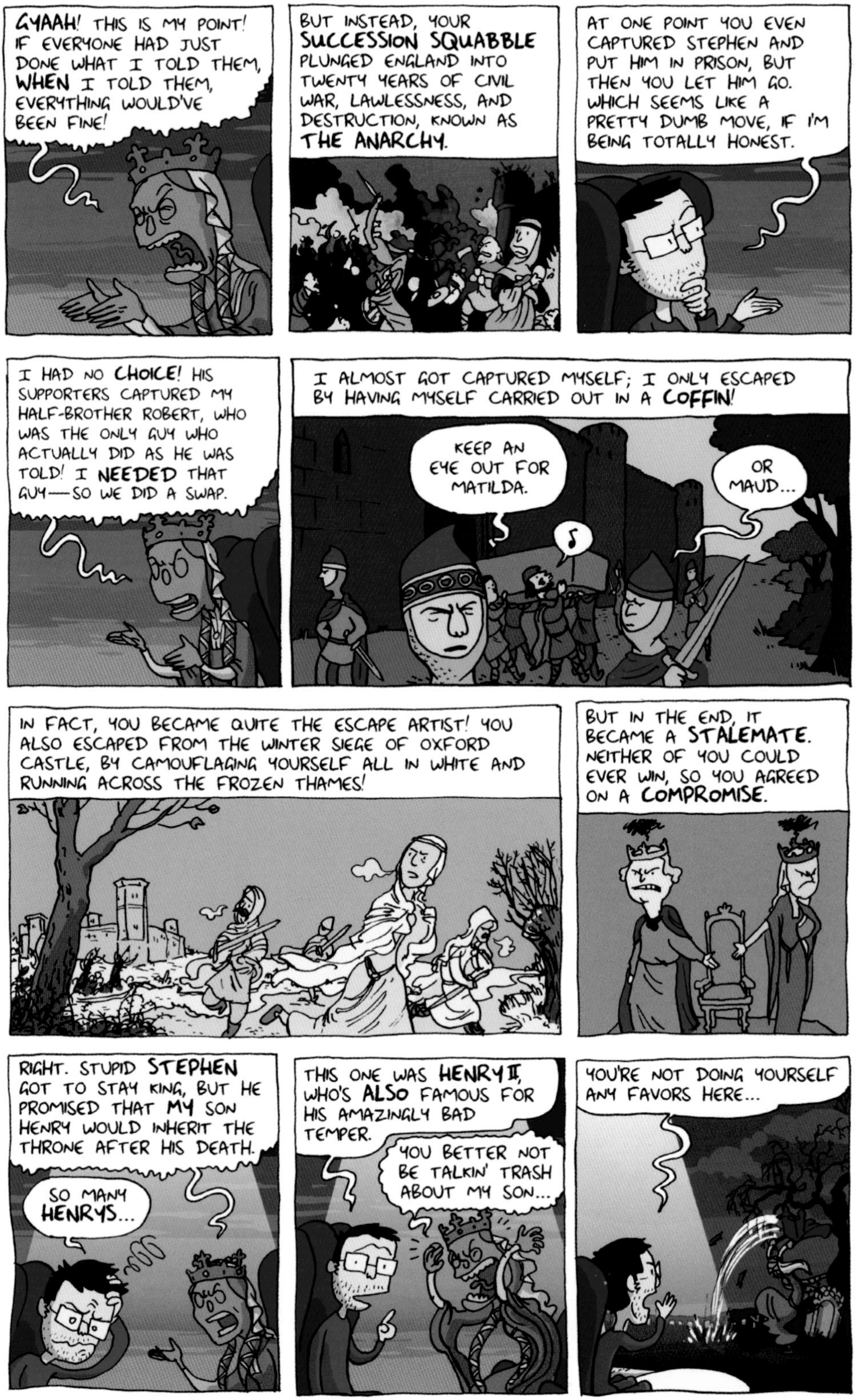
GYAAH! THIS IS MY POINT! IF EVERYONE HAD JUST DONE WHAT I TOLD THEM, WHEN I TOLD THEM, EVERYTHING WOULD'VE BEEN FINE!
BUT INSTEAD, YOUR SUCCESSION SQUABBLE PLUNGED ENGLAND INTO TWENTY YEARS OF CIVIL WAR, LAWLESSNESS, AND DESTRUCTION, KNOWN AS THE ANARCHY.
AT ONE POINT YOU EVEN CAPTURED STEPHEN AND PUT HIM IN PRISON, BUT THEN YOU LET HIM GO. WHICH SEEMS LIKE A PRETTY DUMB MOVE, IF I'M BEING TOTALLY HONEST.
I HAD NO CHOICE! HIS SUPPORTERS CAPTURED MY HALF-BROTHER ROBERT, WHO WAS THE ONLY GUY WHO ACTUALLY DID AS HE WAS TOLD! I NEEDED THAT GUY—SO WE DID A SWAP.
I ALMOST GOT CAPTURED MYSELF; I ONLY ESCAPED BY HAVING MYSELF CARRIED OUT IN A COFFIN!
KEEP AN EYE OUT FOR MATILDA.
OR MAUD...
IN FACT, YOU BECAME QUITE THE ESCAPE ARTIST! YOU ALSO ESCAPED FROM THE WINTER SIEGE OF OXFORD CASTLE, BY CAMOUFLAGING YOURSELF ALL IN WHITE AND RUNNING ACROSS THE FROZEN THAMES!
BUT IN THE END, IT BECAME A STALEMATE. NEITHER OF YOU COULD EVER WIN, SO YOU AGREED ON A COMPROMISE.
RIGHT. STUPID STEPHEN GOT TO STAY KING, BUT HE PROMISED THAT MY SON HENRY WOULD INHERIT THE THRONE AFTER HIS DEATH.
SO MANY HENRYS...
THIS ONE WAS HENRY II, WHO'S ALSO FAMOUS FOR HIS AMAZINGLY BAD TEMPER.
YOU BETTER NOT BE TALKIN' TRASH ABOUT MY SON...
YOU'RE NOT DOING YOURSELF ANY FAVORS HERE...

THE OLD BAILEY

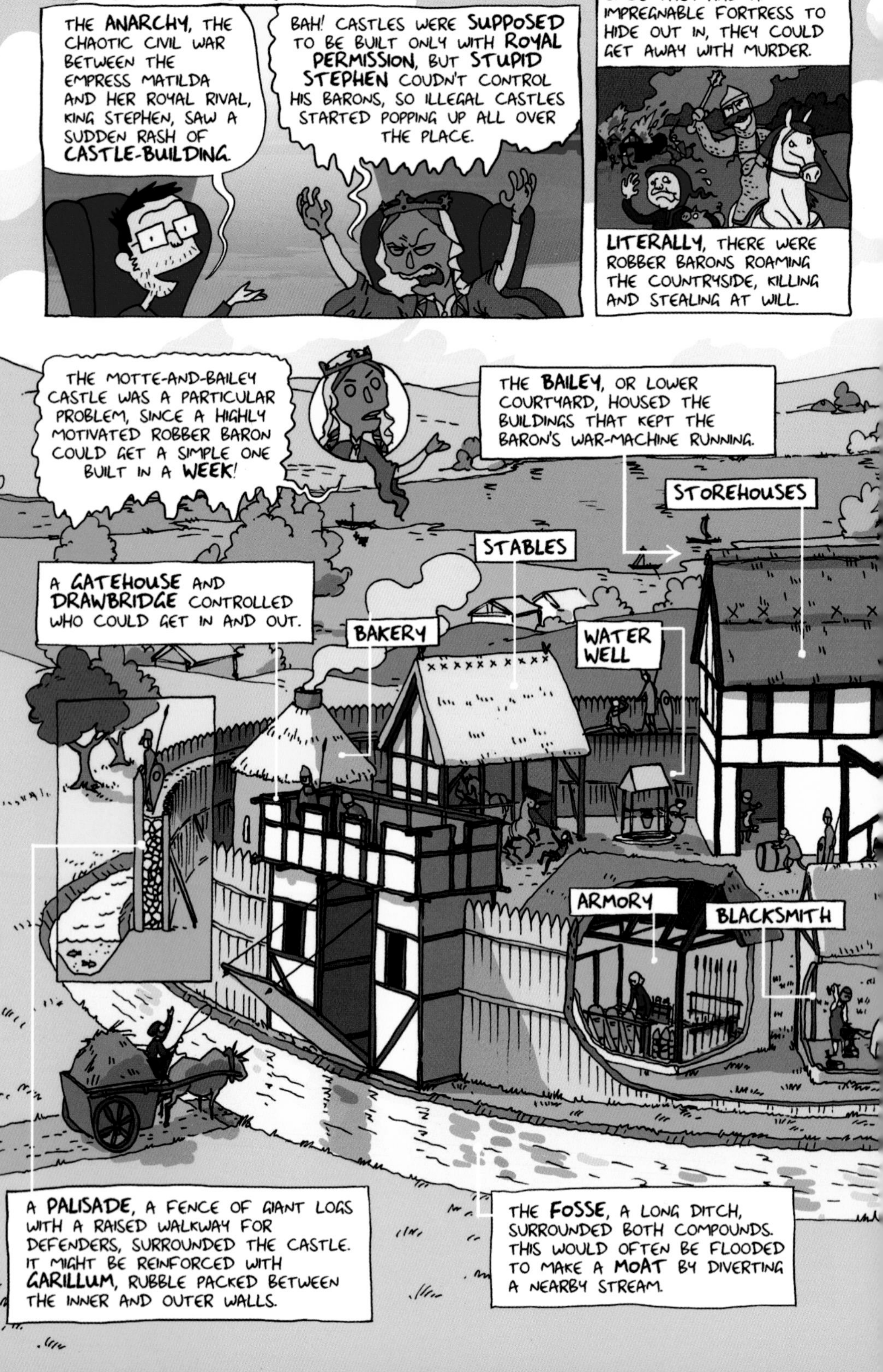
THE ANARCHY, THE CHAOTIC CIVIL WAR BETWEEN THE EMPRESS MATILDA AND HER ROYAL RIVAL, KING STEPHEN, SAW A SUDDEN RASH OF CASTLE-BUILDING.
BAH! CASTLES WERE SUPPOSED TO BE BUILT ONLY WITH ROYAL PERMISSION, BUT STUPID STEPHEN COUDN'T CONTROL HIS BARONS, SO ILLEGAL CASTLES STARTED POPPING UP ALL OVER THE PLACE.
ONCE THEY HAD AN IMPREGNABLE FORTRESS TO HIDE OUT IN, THEY COULD GET AWAY WITH MURDER.
LITERALLY, THERE WERE ROBBER BARONS ROAMING THE COUNTRYSIDE, KILLING AND STEALING AT WILL.
THE MOTTE-AND-BAILEY CASTLE WAS A PARTICULAR PROBLEM, SINCE A HIGHLY MOTIVATED ROBBER BARON COULD GET A SIMPLE ONE BUILT IN A WEEK!
THE BAILEY, OR LOWER COURTYARD, HOUSED THE BUILDINGS THAT KEPT THE BARON'S WAR-MACHINE RUNNING.
STOREHOUSES
STABLES
A GATEHOUSE AND DRAWBRIDGE CONTROLLED WHO COULD GET IN AND OUT.
BAKERY
WATER WELL
ARMORY
BLACKSMITH
A PALISADE, A FENCE OF GIANT LOGS WITH A RAISED WALKWAY FOR DEFENDERS, SURROUNDED THE CASTLE. IT MIGHT BE REINFORCED WITH GARILLUM, RUBBLE PACKED BETWEEN THE INNER AND OUTER WALLS.
THE FOSSE, A LONG DITCH, SURROUNDED BOTH COMPOUNDS. THIS WOULD OFTEN BE FLOODED TO MAKE A MOAT BY DIVERTING A NEARBY STREAM.

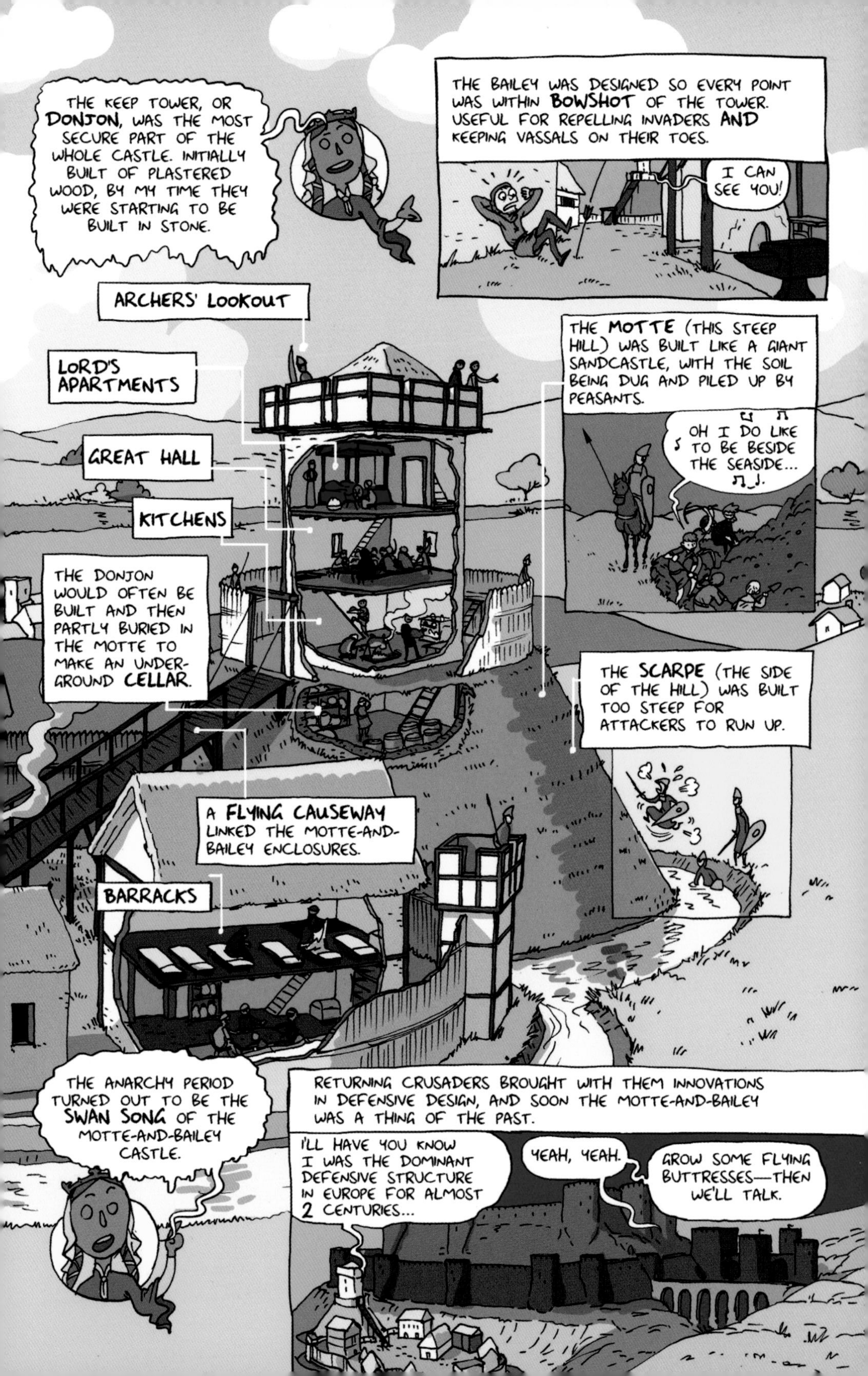
THE KEEP TOWER, OR DONJON, WAS THE MOST SECURE PART OF THE WHOLE CASTLE. INITIALLY BUILT OF PLASTERED WOOD, BY MY TIME THEY WERE STARTING TO BE BUILT IN STONE.
THE BAILEY WAS DESIGNED SO EVERY POINT WAS WITHIN BOWSHOT OF THE TOWER. USEFUL FOR REPELLING INVADERS AND KEEPING VASSALS ON THEIR TOES.
I CAN SEE YOU!
ARCHERS' LOOKOUT
LORD'S APARTMENTS
GREAT HALL
KITCHENS
THE DONJON WOULD OFTEN BE BUILT AND THEN PARTLY BURIED IN THE MOTTE TO MAKE AN UNDERGROUND CELLAR.
THE MOTTE (THIS STEEP HILL) WAS BUILT LIKE A GIANT SANDCASTLE, WITH THE SOIL BEING DUG AND PILED UP BY PEASANTS.
OH I DO LIKE TO BE BESIDE THE SEASIDE...
THE SCARPE (THE SIDE OF THE HILL) WAS BUILT TOO STEEP FOR ATTACKERS TO RUN UP.
A FLYING CAUSEWAY LINKED THE MOTTE-AND-BAILEY ENCLOSURES.
BARRACKS
THE ANARCHY PERIOD TURNED OUT TO BE THE SWAN SONG OF THE MOTTE-AND-BAILEY CASTLE.
RETURNING CRUSADERS BROUGHT WITH THEM INNOVATIONS IN DEFENSIVE DESIGN, AND SOON THE MOTTE-AND-BAILEY WAS A THING OF THE PAST.
I'LL HAVE YOU KNOW I WAS THE DOMINANT DEFENSIVE STRUCTURE IN EUROPE FOR ALMOST 2 CENTURIES...
YEAH, YEAH.
GROW SOME FLYING BUTTRESSES—THEN WE'LL TALK.

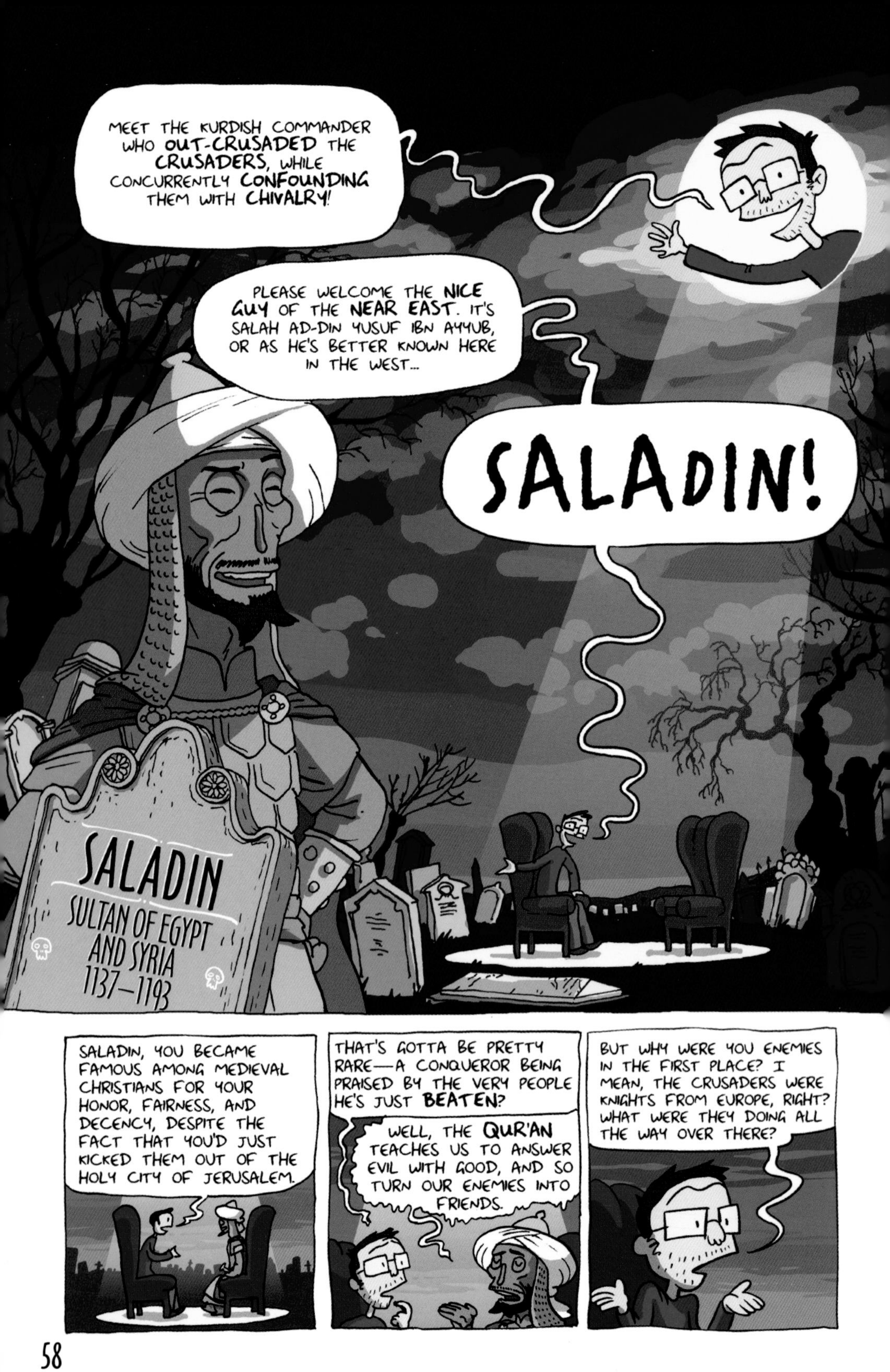
MEET THE KURDISH COMMANDER WHO OUT-CRUSADED THE CRUSADERS, WHILE CONCURRENTLY CONFOUNDING THEM WITH CHIVALRY!
PLEASE WELCOME THE NICE GUY OF THE NEAR EAST. IT'S SALAH AD-DIN YUSUF IBN AYYUB, OR AS HE'S BETTER KNOWN HERE IN THE WEST...
SALADIN!
SALADIN
SULTAN OF EGYPT AND SYRIA
1137–1193
SALADIN, YOU BECAME FAMOUS AMONG MEDIEVAL CHRISTIANS FOR YOUR HONOR, FAIRNESS, AND DECENCY, DESPITE THE FACT THAT YOU'D JUST KICKED THEM OUT OF THE HOLY CITY OF JERUSALEM.
THAT'S GOTTA BE PRETTY RARE—A CONQUEROR BEING PRAISED BY THE VERY PEOPLE HE'S JUST BEATEN?
WELL, THE QUR'AN TEACHES US TO ANSWER EVIL WITH GOOD, AND SO TURN OUR ENEMIES INTO FRIENDS.
BUT WHY WERE YOU ENEMIES IN THE FIRST PLACE? I MEAN, THE CRUSADERS WERE KNIGHTS FROM EUROPE, RIGHT? WHAT WERE THEY DOING ALL THE WAY OVER THERE?

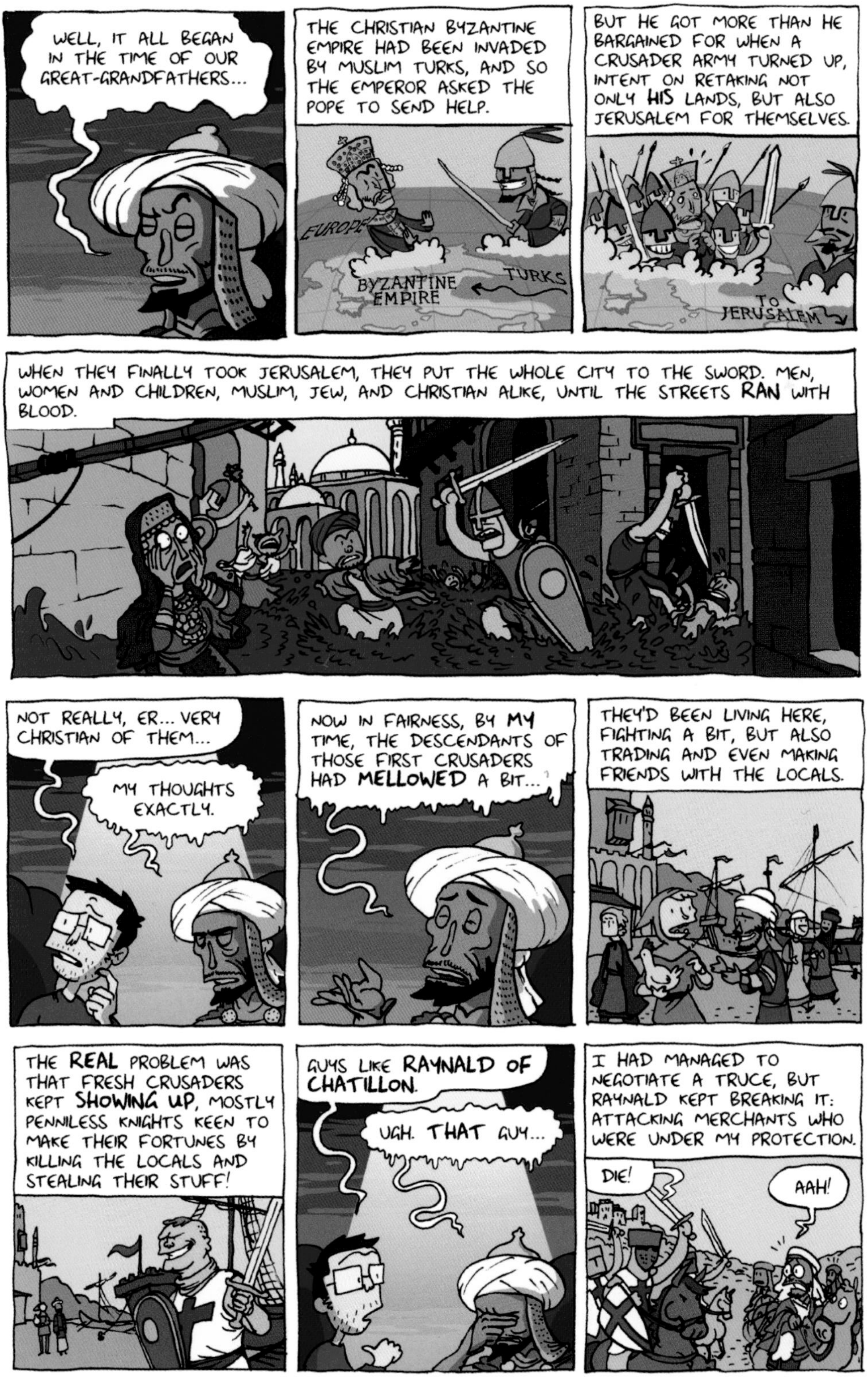
WELL, IT ALL BEGAN IN THE TIME OF OUR GREAT-GRANDFATHERS...
THE CHRISTIAN BYZANTINE EMPIRE HAD BEEN INVADED BY MUSLIM TURKS, AND SO THE EMPEROR ASKED THE POPE TO SEND HELP.
EUROPE
BYZANTINE EMPIRE
TURKS
BUT HE GOT MORE THAN HE BARGAINED FOR WHEN A CRUSADER ARMY TURNED UP, INTENT ON RETAKING NOT ONLY HIS LANDS, BUT ALSO JERUSALEM FOR THEMSELVES.
TO JERUSALEM
WHEN THEY FINALLY TOOK JERUSALEM, THEY PUT THE WHOLE CITY TO THE SWORD. MEN, WOMEN AND CHILDREN, MUSLIM, JEW, AND CHRISTIAN ALIKE, UNTIL THE STREETS RAN WITH BLOOD.
NOT REALLY, ER... VERY CHRISTIAN OF THEM...
MY THOUGHTS EXACTLY.
NOW IN FAIRNESS, BY MY TIME, THE DESCENDANTS OF THOSE FIRST CRUSADERS HAD MELLOWED A BIT...
THEY'D BEEN LIVING HERE, FIGHTING A BIT, BUT ALSO TRADING AND EVEN MAKING FRIENDS WITH THE LOCALS.
THE REAL PROBLEM WAS THAT FRESH CRUSADERS KEPT SHOWING UP, MOSTLY PENNILESS KNIGHTS KEEN TO MAKE THEIR FORTUNES BY KILLING THE LOCALS AND STEALING THEIR STUFF!
GUYS LIKE RAYNALD OF CHATILLON.
UGH. THAT GUY...
I HAD MANAGED TO NEGOTIATE A TRUCE, BUT RAYNALD KEPT BREAKING IT: ATTACKING MERCHANTS WHO WERE UNDER MY PROTECTION.
DIE!
AAH!

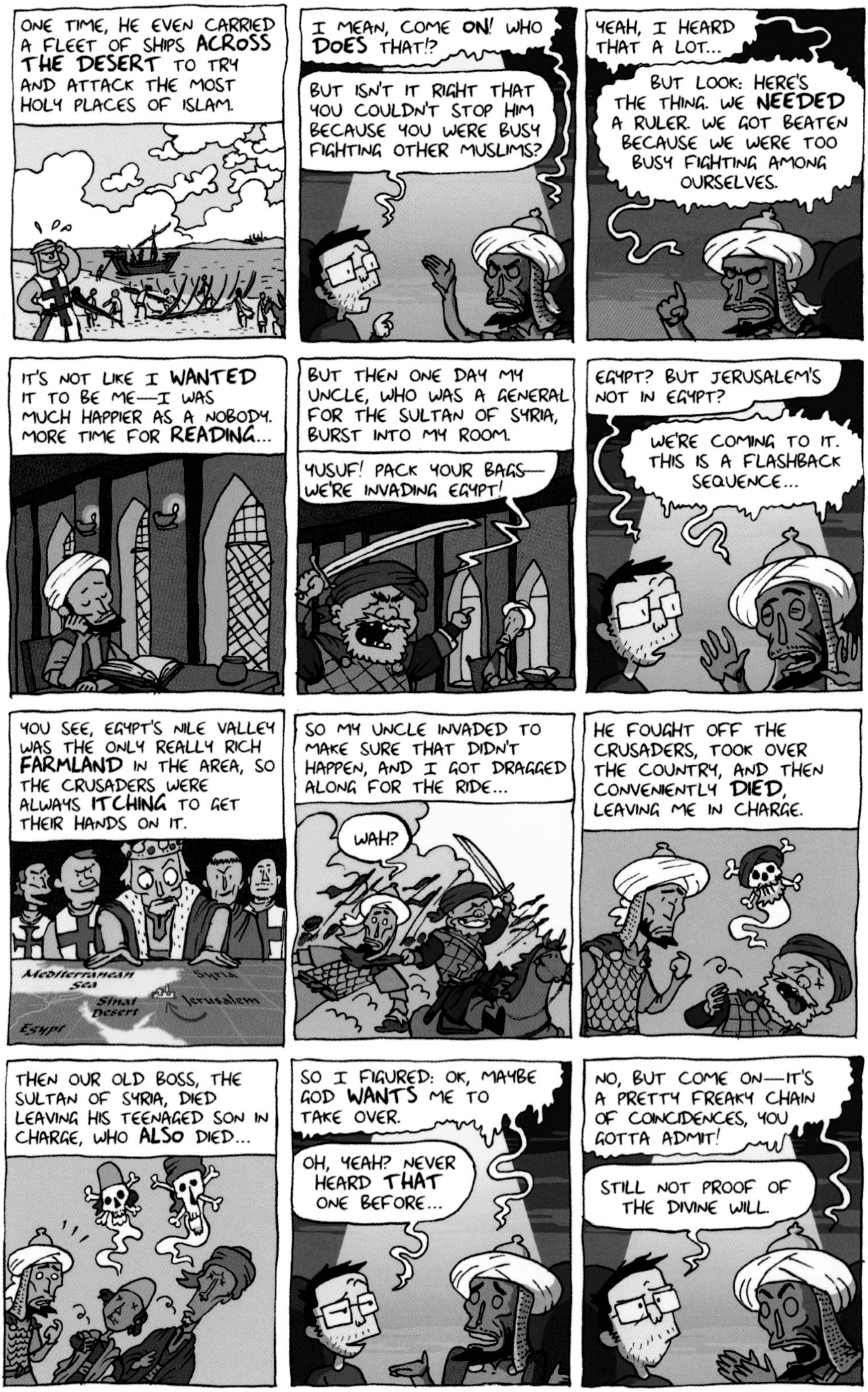
ONE TIME, HE EVEN CARRIED A FLEET OF SHIPS ACROSS THE DESERT TO TRY AND ATTACK THE MOST HOLY PLACES OF ISLAM.
I MEAN, COME ON! WHO DOES THAT!?
BUT ISN'T IT RIGHT THAT YOU COULDN'T STOP HIM BECAUSE YOU WERE BUSY FIGHTING OTHER MUSLIMS?
YEAH, I HEARD THAT A LOT...
BUT LOOK: HERE'S THE THING. WE NEEDED A RULER. WE GOT BEATEN BECAUSE WE WERE TOO BUSY FIGHTING AMONG OURSELVES.
IT'S NOT LIKE I WANTED IT TO BE ME—I WAS MUCH HAPPIER AS A NOBODY. MORE TIME FOR READING...
BUT THEN ONE DAY MY UNCLE, WHO WAS A GENERAL FOR THE SULTAN OF SYRIA, BURST INTO MY ROOM.
YUSUF! PACK YOUR BAGS— WE'RE INVADING EGYPT!
EGYPT? BUT JERUSALEM'S NOT IN EGYPT?
WE'RE COMING TO IT. THIS IS A FLASHBACK SEQUENCE...
YOU SEE, EGYPT'S NILE VALLEY WAS THE ONLY REALLY RICH FARMLAND IN THE AREA, SO THE CRUSADERS WERE ALWAYS ITCHING TO GET THEIR HANDS ON IT.
Mediterranean Sea
Syria
Sinai Desert
Jerusalem
Egypt
SO MY UNCLE INVADED TO MAKE SURE THAT DIDN'T HAPPEN, AND I GOT DRAGGED ALONG FOR THE RIDE...
WAH?
HE FOUGHT OFF THE CRUSADERS, TOOK OVER THE COUNTRY, AND THEN CONVENIENTLY DIED, LEAVING ME IN CHARGE.
THEN OUR OLD BOSS, THE SULTAN OF SYRIA, DIED LEAVING HIS TEENAGED SON IN CHARGE, WHO ALSO DIED...
SO I FIGURED: OK, MAYBE GOD WANTS ME TO TAKE OVER.
OH, YEAH? NEVER HEARD THAT ONE BEFORE...
NO, BUT COME ON—IT'S A PRETTY FREAKY CHAIN OF COINCIDENCES, YOU GOTTA ADMIT!
STILL NOT PROOF OF THE DIVINE WILL.

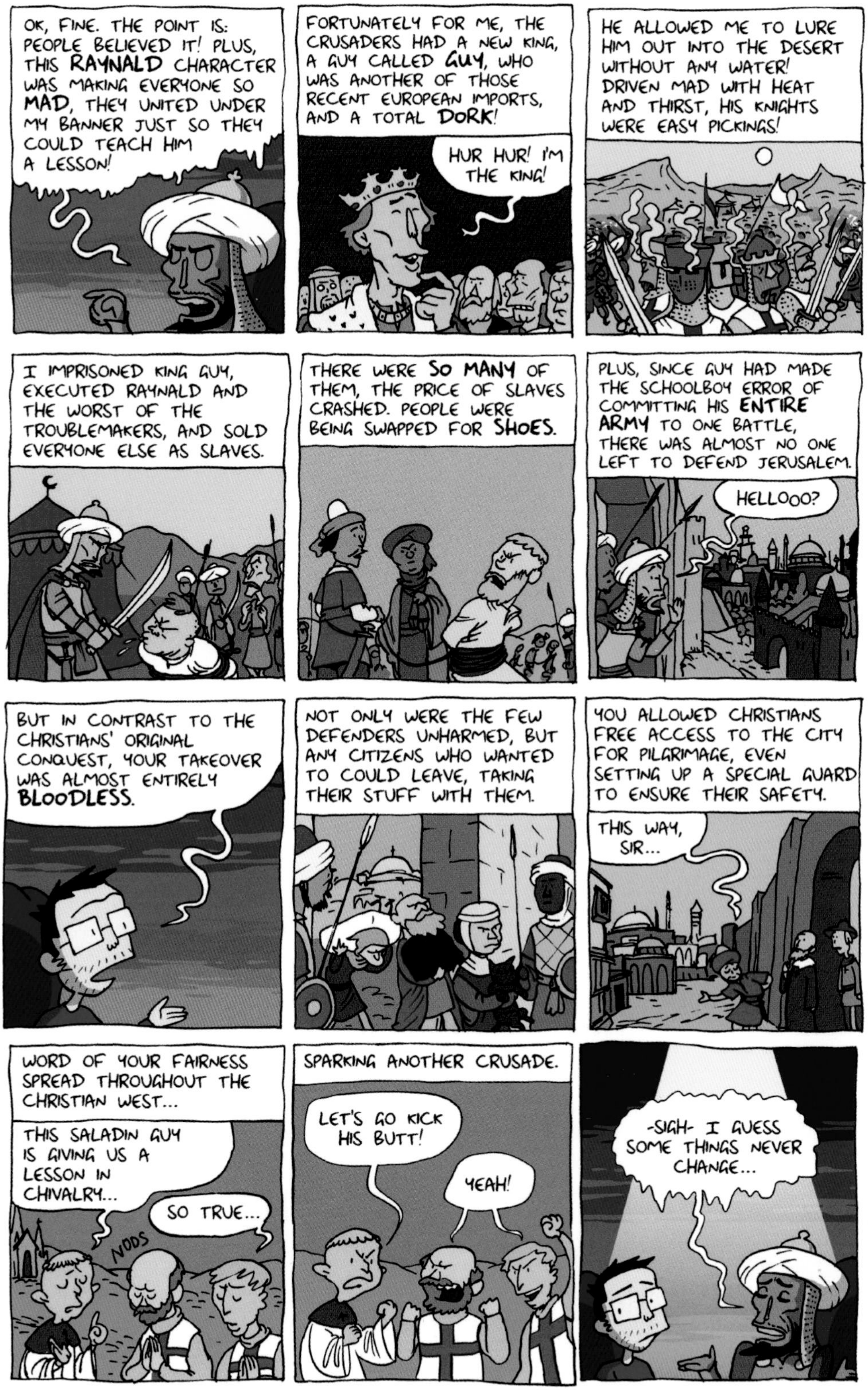
OK, FINE. THE POINT IS: PEOPLE BELIEVED IT! PLUS, THIS RAYNALD CHARACTER WAS MAKING EVERYONE SO MAD, THEY UNITED UNDER MY BANNER JUST SO THEY COULD TEACH HIM A LESSON!
FORTUNATELY FOR ME, THE CRUSADERS HAD A NEW KING, A GUY CALLED GUY, WHO WAS ANOTHER OF THOSE RECENT EUROPEAN IMPORTS, AND A TOTAL DORK!
HUR HUR! I'M THE KING!
HE ALLOWED ME TO LURE HIM OUT INTO THE DESERT WITHOUT ANY WATER! DRIVEN MAD WITH HEAT AND THIRST, HIS KNIGHTS WERE EASY PICKINGS!
I IMPRISONED KING GUY, EXECUTED RAYNALD AND THE WORST OF THE TROUBLEMAKERS, AND SOLD EVERYONE ELSE AS SLAVES.
THERE WERE SO MANY OF THEM, THE PRICE OF SLAVES CRASHED. PEOPLE WERE BEING SWAPPED FOR SHOES.
PLUS, SINCE GUY HAD MADE THE SCHOOLBOY ERROR OF COMMITTING HIS ENTIRE ARMY TO ONE BATTLE, THERE WAS ALMOST NO ONE LEFT TO DEFEND JERUSALEM.
HELLOOO?
BUT IN CONTRAST TO THE CHRISTIANS' ORIGINAL CONQUEST, YOUR TAKEOVER WAS ALMOST ENTIRELY BLOODLESS.
NOT ONLY WERE THE FEW DEFENDERS UNHARMED, BUT ANY CITIZENS WHO WANTED TO COULD LEAVE, TAKING THEIR STUFF WITH THEM.
YOU ALLOWED CHRISTIANS FREE ACCESS TO THE CITY FOR PILGRIMAGE, EVEN SETTING UP A SPECIAL GUARD TO ENSURE THEIR SAFETY.
THIS WAY, SIR...
WORD OF YOUR FAIRNESS SPREAD THROUGHOUT THE CHRISTIAN WEST...
THIS SALADIN GUY IS GIVING US A LESSON IN CHIVALRY...
SO TRUE...
NODS
SPARKING ANOTHER CRUSADE.
LET'S GO KICK HIS BUTT!
YEAH!
-SIGH- I GUESS SOME THINGS NEVER CHANGE...

GIFTS OF GENIUS

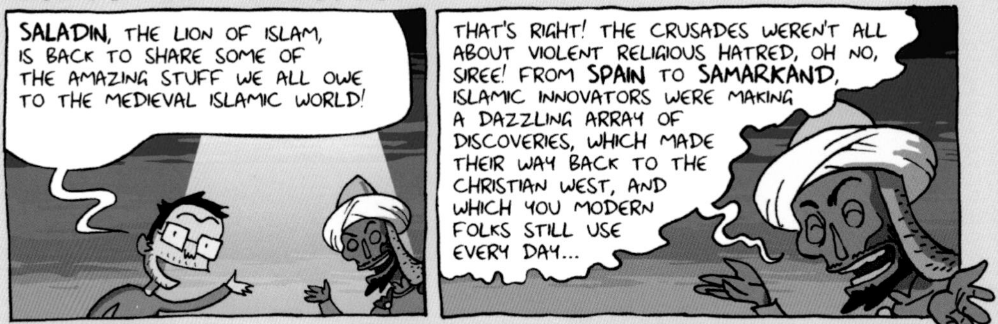
SALADIN, THE LION OF ISLAM, IS BACK TO SHARE SOME OF THE AMAZING STUFF WE ALL OWE TO THE MEDIEVAL ISLAMIC WORLD!
THAT'S RIGHT! THE CRUSADES WEREN'T ALL ABOUT VIOLENT RELIGIOUS HATRED, OH NO, SIREE! FROM SPAIN TO SAMARKAND, ISLAMIC INNOVATORS WERE MAKING A DAZZLING ARRAY OF DISCOVERIES, WHICH MADE THEIR WAY BACK TO THE CHRISTIAN WEST, AND WHICH YOU MODERN FOLKS STILL USE EVERY DAY...

MEDICINE

MUSLIM, CHRISTIAN, AND JEWISH DOCTORS WORKING IN THE EAST WERE FAR MORE ADVANCED THAN THEIR WESTERN COUNTERPARTS. THEY HAD AN ADVANCED UNDERSTANDING OF THINGS LIKE BLOOD CIRCULATION THAT WOULDN'T BE MATCHED IN THE WEST FOR CENTURIES.

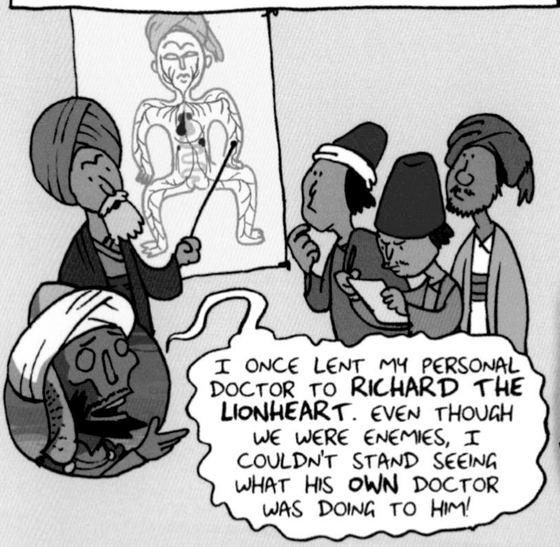
I ONCE LENT MY PERSONAL DOCTOR TO RICHARD THE LIONHEART. EVEN THOUGH WE WERE ENEMIES, I COULDN'T STAND SEEING WHAT HIS OWN DOCTOR WAS DOING TO HIM!

NUMBERS

THE DECIMAL SYSTEM OF NUMBERS FROM 0 TO 9 WAS INVENTED IN INDIA, AND QUICKLY SPREAD THROUGHOUT THE ISLAMIC WORLD.

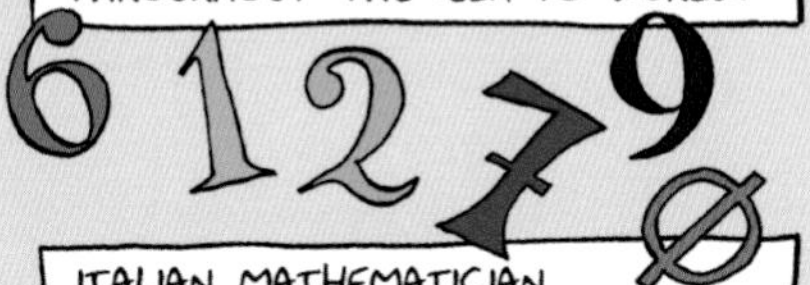
6 1 2 7 9 0

ITALIAN MATHEMATICIAN **LEONARDO FIBONACCI** LEARNED ABOUT THEM WHILE STUDYING IN MUSLIM NORTH AFRICA, AND REALIZED WHAT AN IMPROVEMENT THEY'D BE ON THE OLD ROMAN **IXVC**-TYPE NUMERALS.

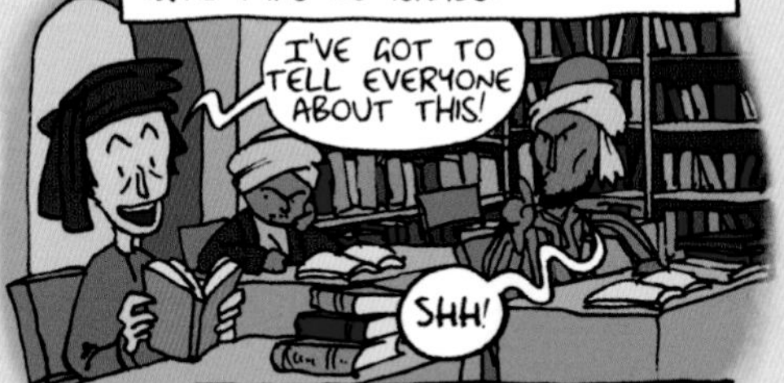
I'VE GOT TO TELL EVERYONE ABOUT THIS!
SHH!

FOODS

JUST SOME OF THE FRUITS AND VEGETABLES THE MUSLIM WORLD INTRODUCED TO EUROPE, WITH THEIR ORIGINAL ARABIC NAMES:

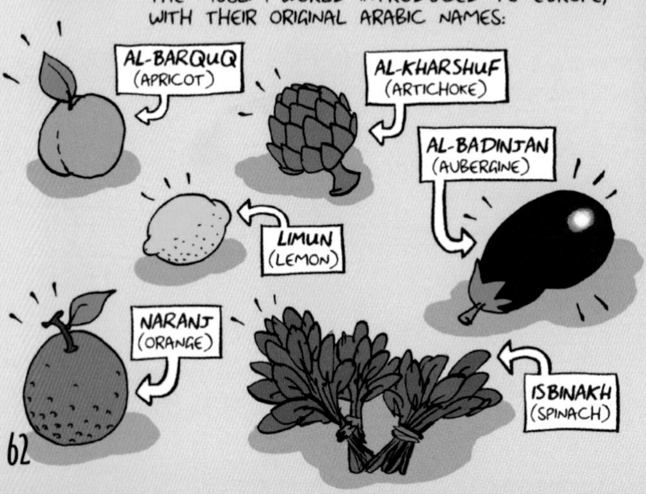
AL-BARQUQ (APRICOT)
AL-KHARSHUF (ARTICHOKE)
AL-BADINJAN (AUBERGINE)
LIMUN (LEMON)
NARANJ (ORANGE)
ISBINAKH (SPINACH)

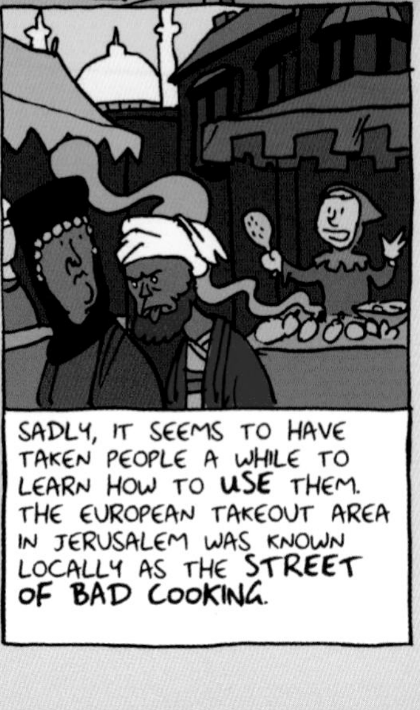
SADLY, IT SEEMS TO HAVE TAKEN PEOPLE A WHILE TO LEARN HOW TO USE THEM. THE EUROPEAN TAKEOUT AREA IN JERUSALEM WAS KNOWN LOCALLY AS THE STREET OF BAD COOKING.

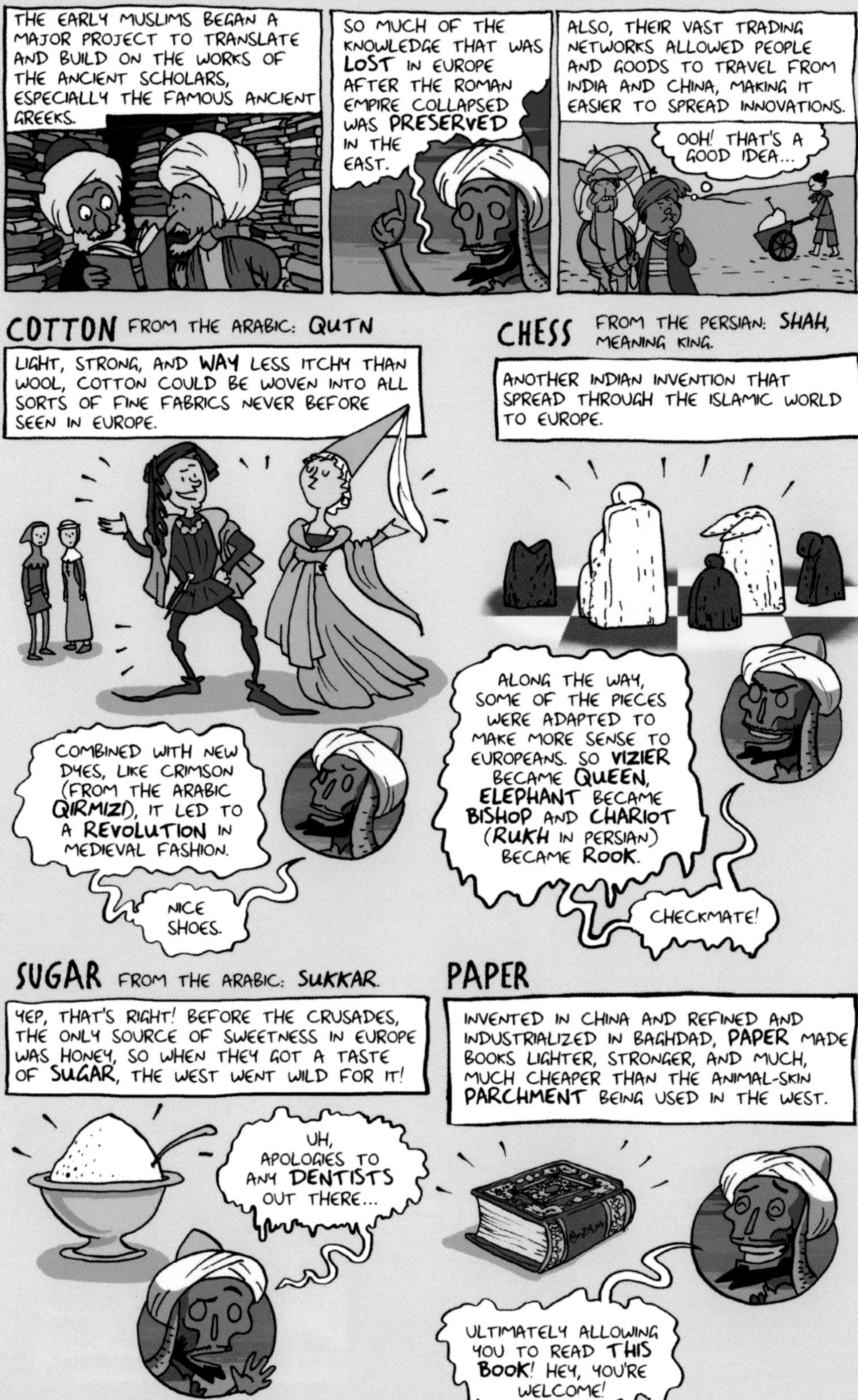
THE EARLY MUSLIMS BEGAN A MAJOR PROJECT TO TRANSLATE AND BUILD ON THE WORKS OF THE ANCIENT SCHOLARS, ESPECIALLY THE FAMOUS ANCIENT GREEKS.
SO MUCH OF THE KNOWLEDGE THAT WAS LOST IN EUROPE AFTER THE ROMAN EMPIRE COLLAPSED WAS PRESERVED IN THE EAST.
ALSO, THEIR VAST TRADING NETWORKS ALLOWED PEOPLE AND GOODS TO TRAVEL FROM INDIA AND CHINA, MAKING IT EASIER TO SPREAD INNOVATIONS.
OOH! THAT'S A GOOD IDEA...
COTTON FROM THE ARABIC: QUTN
LIGHT, STRONG, AND WAY LESS ITCHY THAN WOOL, COTTON COULD BE WOVEN INTO ALL SORTS OF FINE FABRICS NEVER BEFORE SEEN IN EUROPE.
COMBINED WITH NEW DYES, LIKE CRIMSON (FROM THE ARABIC QIRMIZI), IT LED TO A REVOLUTION IN MEDIEVAL FASHION.
NICE SHOES.
CHESS FROM THE PERSIAN: SHAH, MEANING KING.
ANOTHER INDIAN INVENTION THAT SPREAD THROUGH THE ISLAMIC WORLD TO EUROPE.
ALONG THE WAY, SOME OF THE PIECES WERE ADAPTED TO MAKE MORE SENSE TO EUROPEANS. SO VIZIER BECAME QUEEN, ELEPHANT BECAME BISHOP AND CHARIOT (RUKH IN PERSIAN) BECAME ROOK.
CHECKMATE!
SUGAR FROM THE ARABIC: SUKKAR.
YEP, THAT'S RIGHT! BEFORE THE CRUSADES, THE ONLY SOURCE OF SWEETNESS IN EUROPE WAS HONEY, SO WHEN THEY GOT A TASTE OF SUGAR, THE WEST WENT WILD FOR IT!
UH, APOLOGIES TO ANY DENTISTS OUT THERE...
PAPER
INVENTED IN CHINA AND REFINED AND INDUSTRIALIZED IN BAGHDAD, PAPER MADE BOOKS LIGHTER, STRONGER, AND MUCH, MUCH CHEAPER THAN THE ANIMAL-SKIN PARCHMENT BEING USED IN THE WEST.
ULTIMATELY ALLOWING YOU TO READ THIS BOOK! HEY, YOU'RE WELCOME!

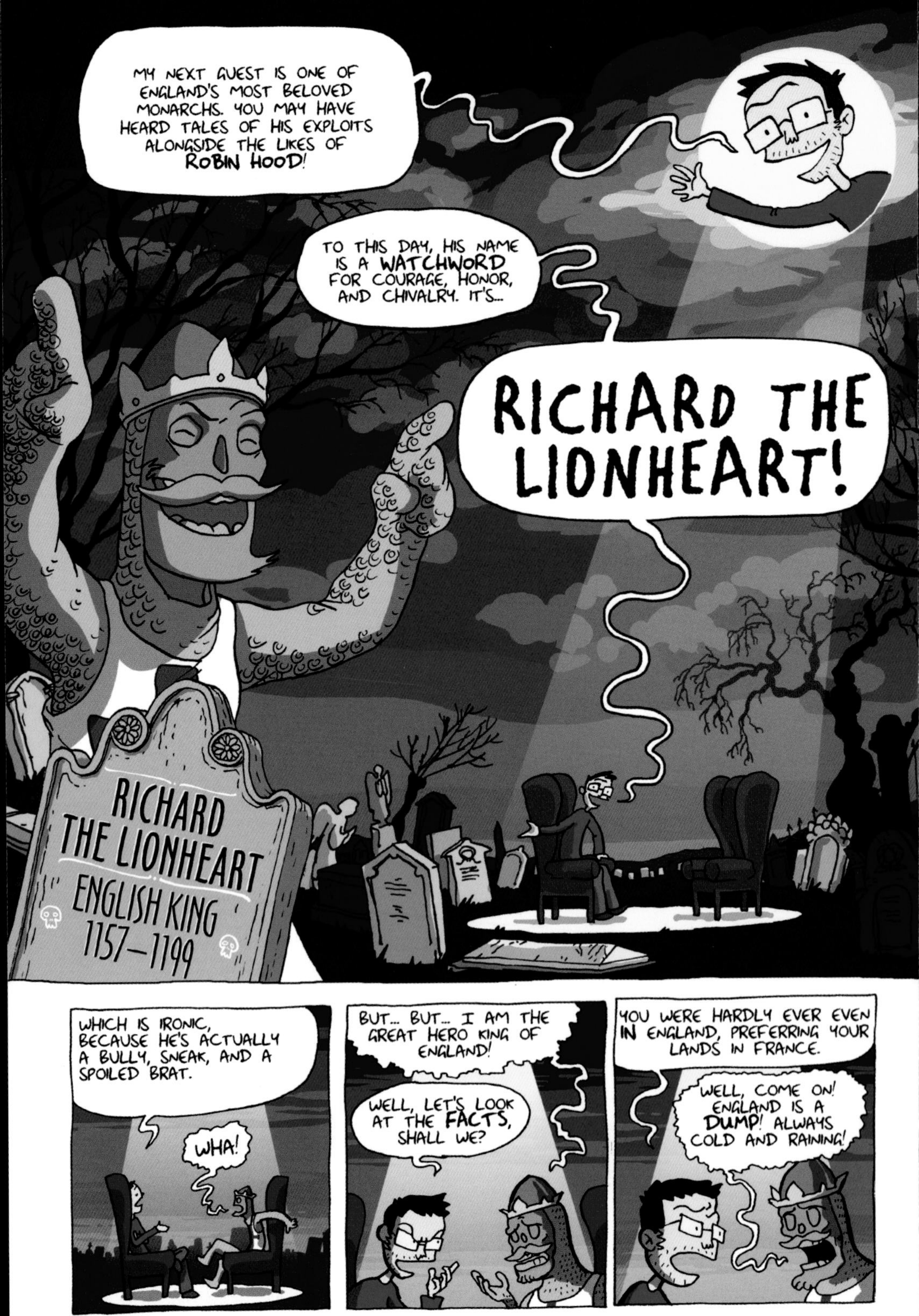
MY NEXT GUEST IS ONE OF ENGLAND'S MOST BELOVED MONARCHS. YOU MAY HAVE HEARD TALES OF HIS EXPLOITS ALONGSIDE THE LIKES OF ROBIN HOOD!
TO THIS DAY, HIS NAME IS A WATCHWORD FOR COURAGE, HONOR, AND CHIVALRY. IT'S...
RICHARD THE LIONHEART!
RICHARD THE LIONHEART
ENGLISH KING 1157–1199
WHICH IS IRONIC, BECAUSE HE'S ACTUALLY A BULLY, SNEAK, AND A SPOILED BRAT.
WHA!
BUT... BUT... I AM THE GREAT HERO KING OF ENGLAND!
WELL, LET'S LOOK AT THE FACTS, SHALL WE?
YOU WERE HARDLY EVER EVEN IN ENGLAND, PREFERRING YOUR LANDS IN FRANCE.
WELL, COME ON! ENGLAND IS A DUMP! ALWAYS COLD AND RAINING!

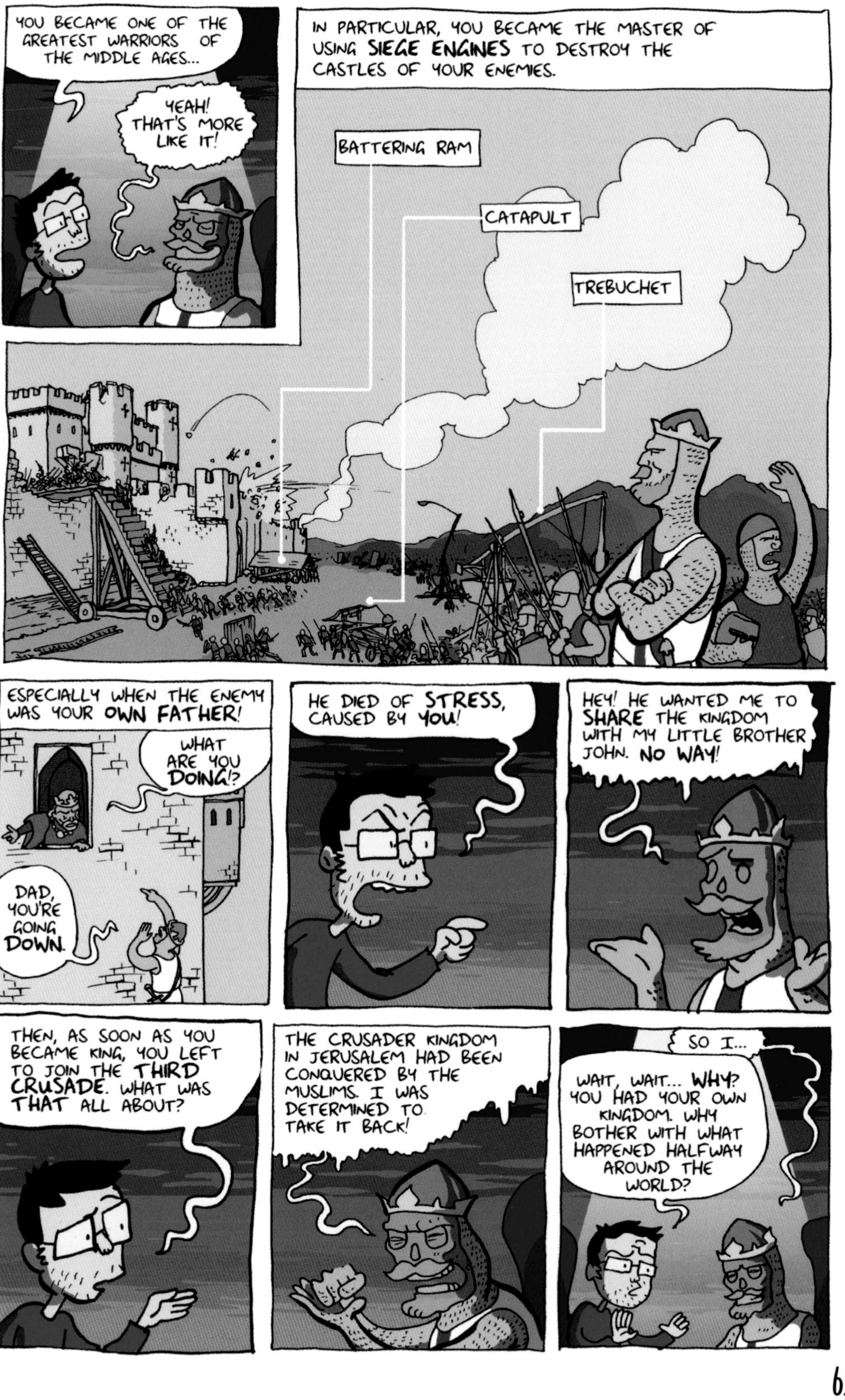

YOU BECAME ONE OF THE GREATEST WARRIORS OF THE MIDDLE AGES...
YEAH! THAT'S MORE LIKE IT!
IN PARTICULAR, YOU BECAME THE MASTER OF USING SIEGE ENGINES TO DESTROY THE CASTLES OF YOUR ENEMIES.
BATTERING RAM
CATAPULT
TREBUCHET
ESPECIALLY WHEN THE ENEMY WAS YOUR OWN FATHER!
WHAT ARE YOU DOING!?
DAD, YOU'RE GOING DOWN.
HE DIED OF STRESS, CAUSED BY YOU!
HEY! HE WANTED ME TO SHARE THE KINGDOM WITH MY LITTLE BROTHER JOHN. NO WAY!
THEN, AS SOON AS YOU BECAME KING, YOU LEFT TO JOIN THE THIRD CRUSADE. WHAT WAS THAT ALL ABOUT?
THE CRUSADER KINGDOM IN JERUSALEM HAD BEEN CONQUERED BY THE MUSLIMS. I WAS DETERMINED TO TAKE IT BACK!
SO I...
WAIT, WAIT... WHY? YOU HAD YOUR OWN KINGDOM. WHY BOTHER WITH WHAT HAPPENED HALFWAY AROUND THE WORLD?

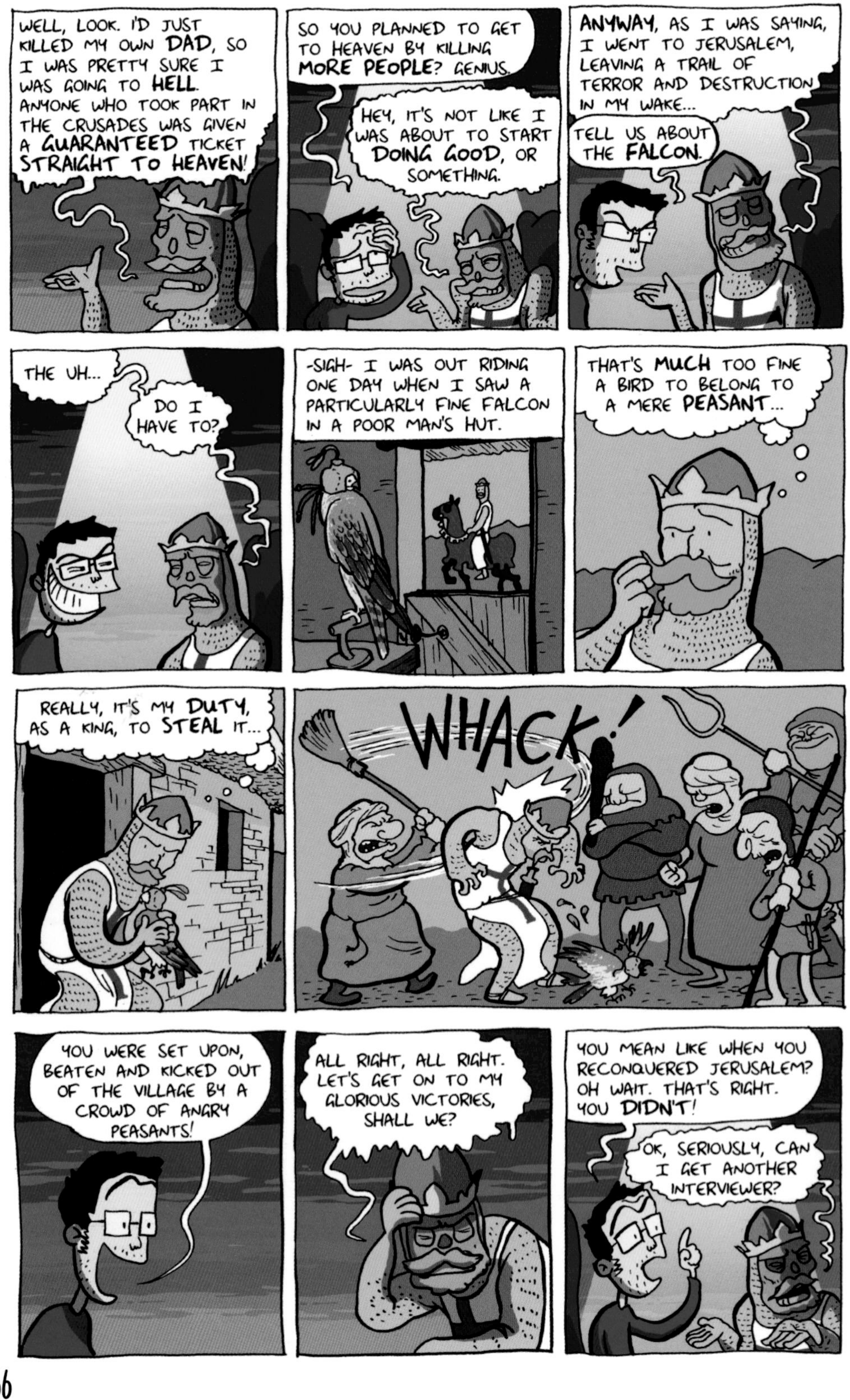
WELL, LOOK. I'D JUST KILLED MY OWN DAD, SO I WAS PRETTY SURE I WAS GOING TO HELL. ANYONE WHO TOOK PART IN THE CRUSADES WAS GIVEN A GUARANTEED TICKET STRAIGHT TO HEAVEN!
SO YOU PLANNED TO GET TO HEAVEN BY KILLING MORE PEOPLE? GENIUS.
HEY, IT'S NOT LIKE I WAS ABOUT TO START DOING GOOD, OR SOMETHING.
ANYWAY, AS I WAS SAYING, I WENT TO JERUSALEM, LEAVING A TRAIL OF TERROR AND DESTRUCTION IN MY WAKE...
TELL US ABOUT THE FALCON.
THE UH...
DO I HAVE TO?
-SIGH- I WAS OUT RIDING ONE DAY WHEN I SAW A PARTICULARLY FINE FALCON IN A POOR MAN'S HUT.
THAT'S MUCH TOO FINE A BIRD TO BELONG TO A MERE PEASANT...
REALLY, IT'S MY DUTY, AS A KING, TO STEAL IT...
WHACK!
YOU WERE SET UPON, BEATEN AND KICKED OUT OF THE VILLAGE BY A CROWD OF ANGRY PEASANTS!
ALL RIGHT, ALL RIGHT. LET'S GET ON TO MY GLORIOUS VICTORIES, SHALL WE?
YOU MEAN LIKE WHEN YOU RECONQUERED JERUSALEM? OH WAIT. THAT'S RIGHT. YOU DIDN'T!
OK, SERIOUSLY, CAN I GET ANOTHER INTERVIEWER?

YOU QUARRELED WITH YOUR ALLIES, SO THEY ALL LEFT, TAKING THEIR ARMIES WITH THEM.

THEY WERE ALL **IDIOTS!** THEY DIDN'T UNDERSTAND MILITARY STRATEGY!

WE HAD JUST ONE CITY. WE NEEDED TO BUILD MORE CASTLES AND BE READY FOR A LONG WAR, BUT THEY JUST WANTED TO ATTACK JERUSALEM AND GO HOME.

ACRE

HAIFA

ARSUF

JAFFA

JERUSALEM

ASCALON

PLUS, I HEARD MY LITTLE BROTHER JOHN WAS PLOTTING TO TAKE OVER MY KINGDOM.

SO YOU GAVE UP.

I MADE A **TACTICAL WITHDRAWAL!**

TO GET HOME, I HAD TO PASS THROUGH THE LANDS OF MY ENEMIES, SO I DISGUISED MYSELF AS A **RETURNING PILGRIM.**

SO... HOW DO I LOOK?

VERY GOOD, SIRE.

PEASANTY.

BUT YOU WERE RECOGNIZED BECAUSE YOU INSISTED ON EATING EXPENSIVE FOOD!

WHAT WAS IT AGAIN?

...ROAST CHICKEN...

...IT'S MY FAVORITE.

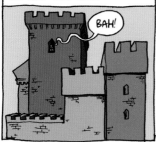

YOU WERE IMPRISONED, AND YOUR SUBJECTS HAD TO PAY A **KING'S RANSOM** TO GET YOU OUT!

BAH!

YOUR BROTHER JOHN TRIED TO PAY THEM TO **KEEP** YOU IN PRISON!

BUT BEFORE LONG, YOU WERE BACK HOME, AND BACK TO YOUR OLD WAYS, BEATING AND CHEATING ANYONE WHO EVEN LOOKED AT YOU FUNNY!

OK YOU KNOW WHAT? I'M OUTTA HERE.

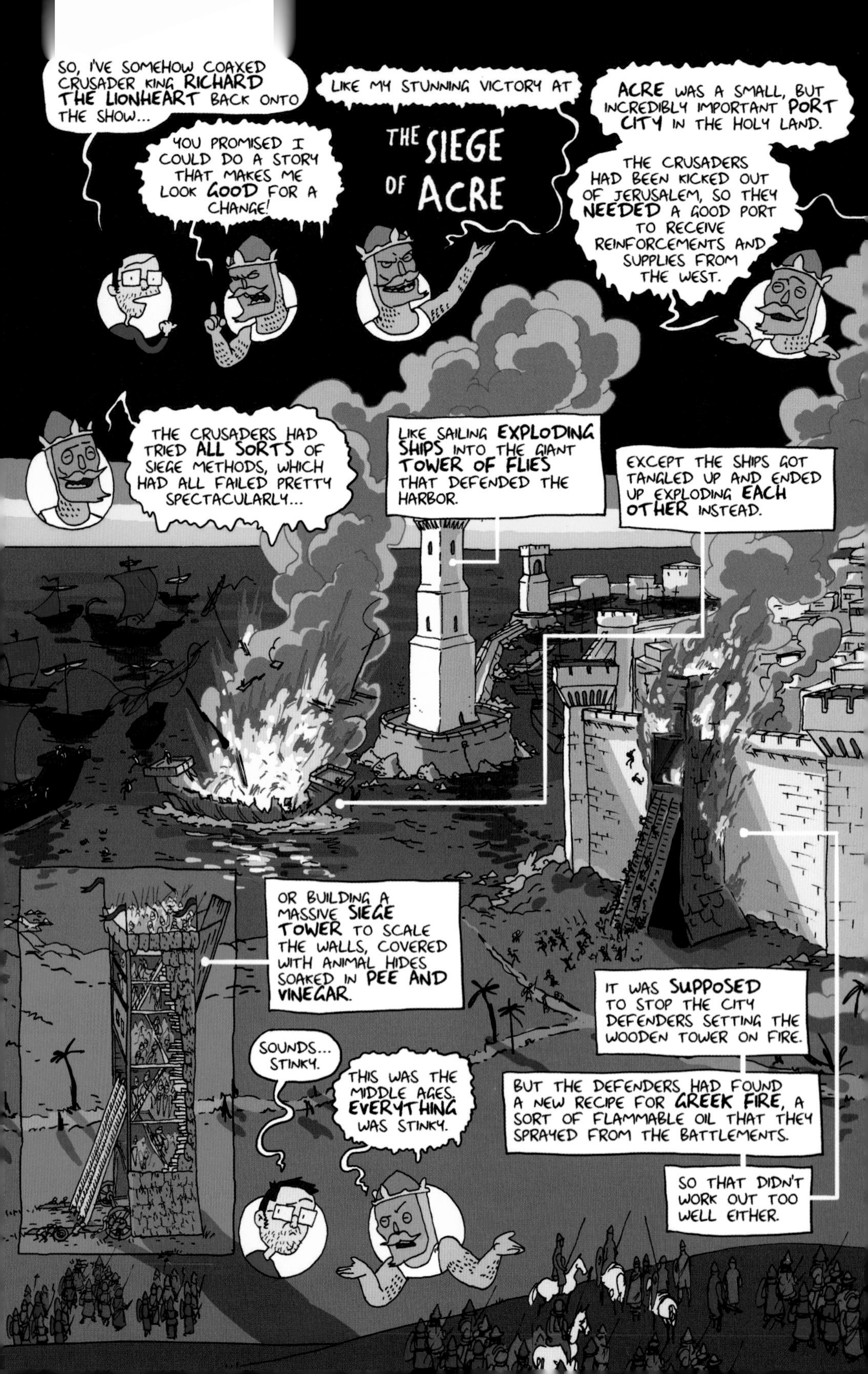
SO, I'VE SOMEHOW COAXED CRUSADER KING RICHARD THE LIONHEART BACK ONTO THE SHOW...
YOU PROMISED I COULD DO A STORY THAT MAKES ME LOOK GOOD FOR A CHANGE!
LIKE MY STUNNING VICTORY AT
THE SIEGE OF ACRE
ACRE WAS A SMALL, BUT INCREDIBLY IMPORTANT PORT CITY IN THE HOLY LAND.
THE CRUSADERS HAD BEEN KICKED OUT OF JERUSALEM, SO THEY NEEDED A GOOD PORT TO RECEIVE REINFORCEMENTS AND SUPPLIES FROM THE WEST.
THE CRUSADERS HAD TRIED ALL SORTS OF SIEGE METHODS, WHICH HAD ALL FAILED PRETTY SPECTACULARLY...
LIKE SAILING EXPLODING SHIPS INTO THE GIANT TOWER OF FLIES THAT DEFENDED THE HARBOR.
EXCEPT THE SHIPS GOT TANGLED UP AND ENDED UP EXPLODING EACH OTHER INSTEAD.
OR BUILDING A MASSIVE SIEGE TOWER TO SCALE THE WALLS, COVERED WITH ANIMAL HIDES SOAKED IN PEE AND VINEGAR.
SOUNDS... STINKY.
THIS WAS THE MIDDLE AGES. EVERYTHING WAS STINKY.
IT WAS SUPPOSED TO STOP THE CITY DEFENDERS SETTING THE WOODEN TOWER ON FIRE.
BUT THE DEFENDERS HAD FOUND A NEW RECIPE FOR GREEK FIRE, A SORT OF FLAMMABLE OIL THAT THEY SPRAYED FROM THE BATTLEMENTS.
SO THAT DIDN'T WORK OUT TOO WELL EITHER.

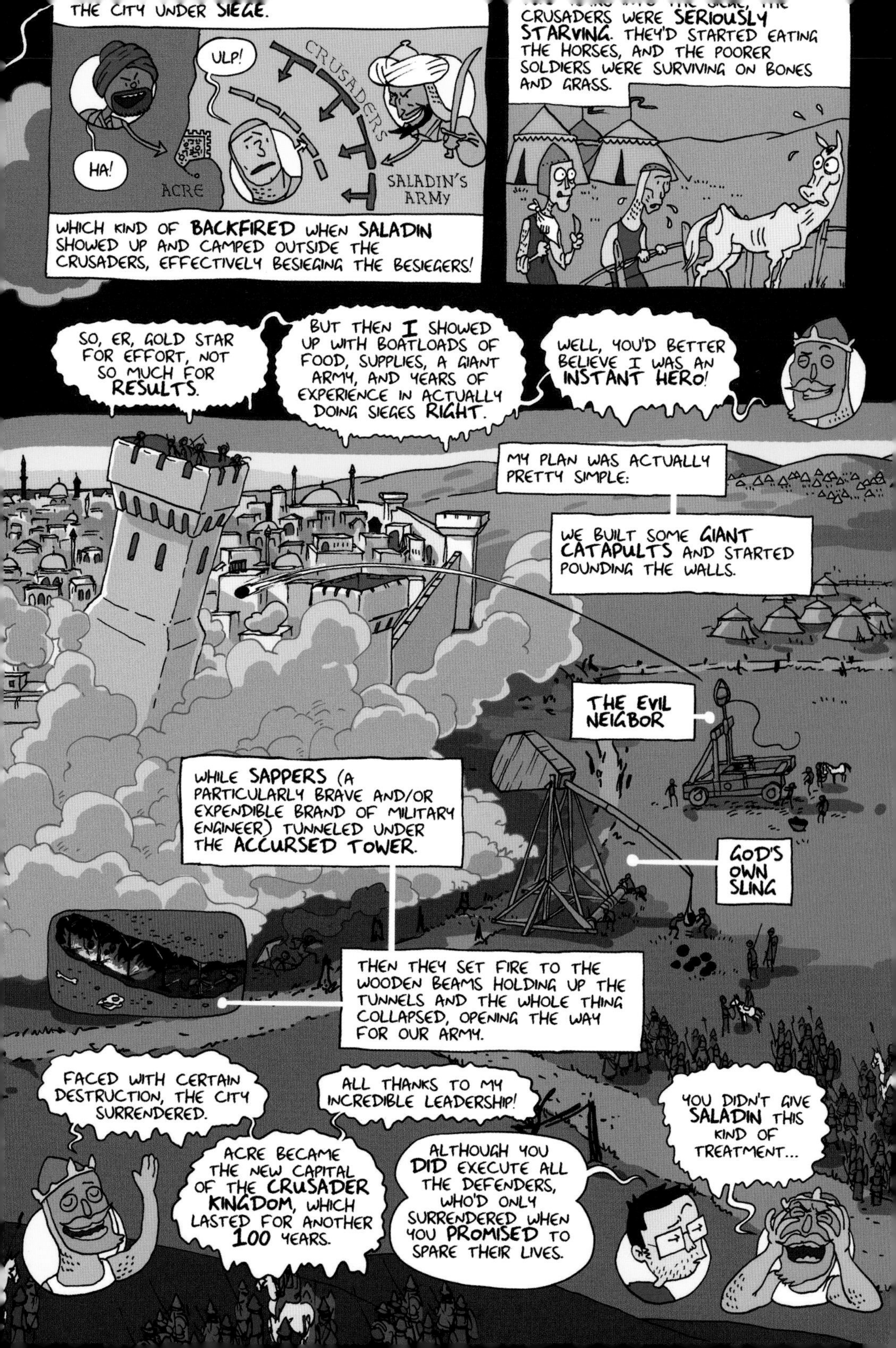

THE CITY UNDER SIEGE.
ULP!
CRUSADERS
HA!
ACRE
SALADIN'S ARMY
WHICH KIND OF BACKFIRED WHEN SALADIN SHOWED UP AND CAMPED OUTSIDE THE CRUSADERS, EFFECTIVELY BESIEGING THE BESIEGERS!
CRUSADERS WERE SERIOUSLY STARVING. THEY'D STARTED EATING THE HORSES, AND THE POORER SOLDIERS WERE SURVIVING ON BONES AND GRASS.
SO, ER, GOLD STAR FOR EFFORT, NOT SO MUCH FOR RESULTS.
BUT THEN I SHOWED UP WITH BOATLOADS OF FOOD, SUPPLIES, A GIANT ARMY, AND YEARS OF EXPERIENCE IN ACTUALLY DOING SIEGES RIGHT.
WELL, YOU'D BETTER BELIEVE I WAS AN INSTANT HERO!
MY PLAN WAS ACTUALLY PRETTY SIMPLE:
WE BUILT SOME GIANT CATAPULTS AND STARTED POUNDING THE WALLS.
THE EVIL NEIGBOR
WHILE SAPPERS (A PARTICULARLY BRAVE AND/OR EXPENDIBLE BRAND OF MILITARY ENGINEER) TUNNELED UNDER THE ACCURSED TOWER.
GOD'S OWN SLING
THEN THEY SET FIRE TO THE WOODEN BEAMS HOLDING UP THE TUNNELS AND THE WHOLE THING COLLAPSED, OPENING THE WAY FOR OUR ARMY.
FACED WITH CERTAIN DESTRUCTION, THE CITY SURRENDERED.
ALL THANKS TO MY INCREDIBLE LEADERSHIP!
ACRE BECAME THE NEW CAPITAL OF THE CRUSADER KINGDOM, WHICH LASTED FOR ANOTHER 100 YEARS.
ALTHOUGH YOU DID EXECUTE ALL THE DEFENDERS, WHO'D ONLY SURRENDERED WHEN YOU PROMISED TO SPARE THEIR LIVES.
YOU DIDN'T GIVE SALADIN THIS KIND OF TREATMENT...

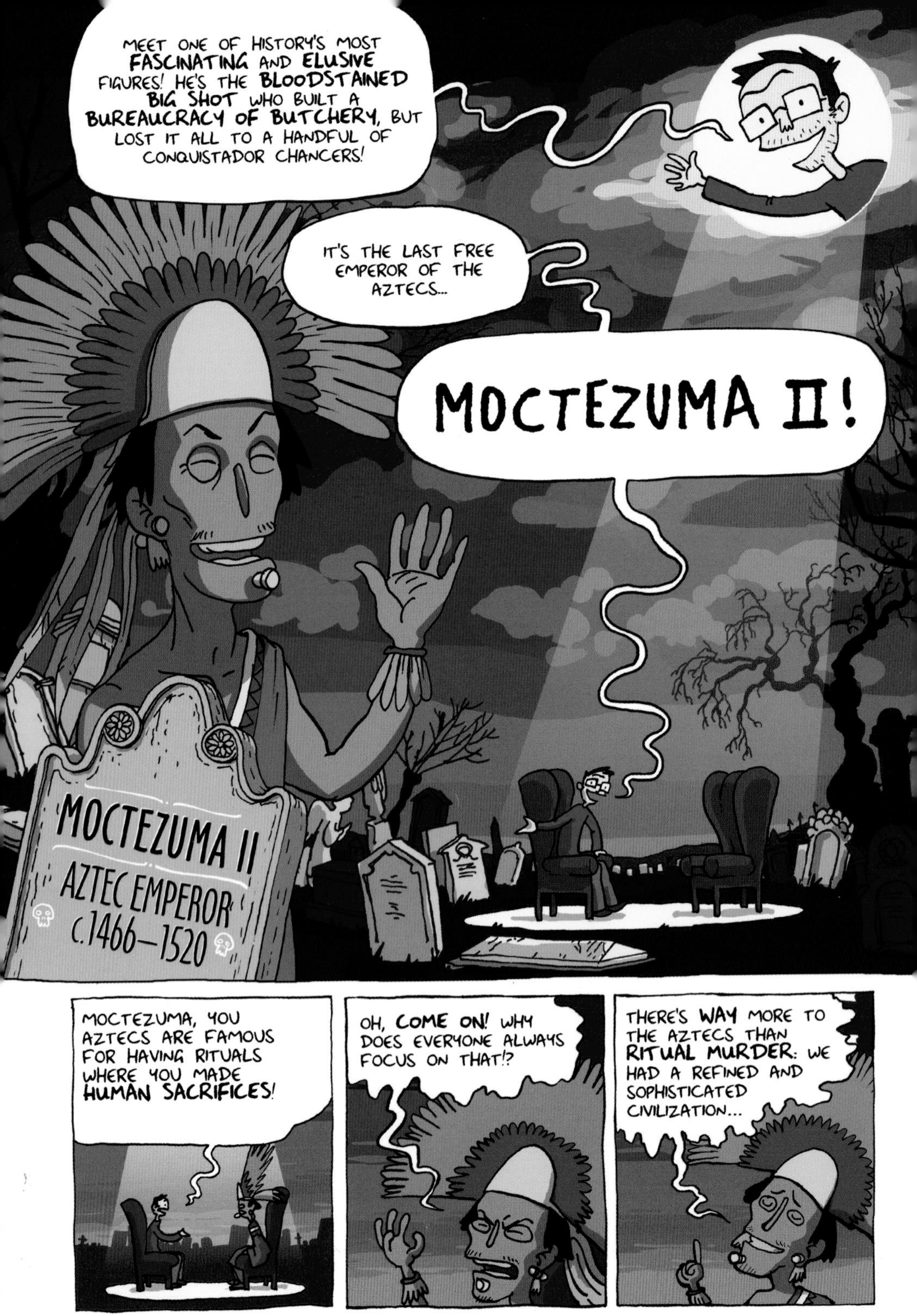
MEET ONE OF HISTORY'S MOST FASCINATING AND ELUSIVE FIGURES! HE'S THE BLOODSTAINED BIG SHOT WHO BUILT A BUREAUCRACY OF BUTCHERY, BUT LOST IT ALL TO A HANDFUL OF CONQUISTADOR CHANCERS!
IT'S THE LAST FREE EMPEROR OF THE AZTECS...
MOCTEZUMA II!
MOCTEZUMA II
AZTEC EMPEROR
c.1466–1520
MOCTEZUMA, YOU AZTECS ARE FAMOUS FOR HAVING RITUALS WHERE YOU MADE HUMAN SACRIFICES!
OH, COME ON! WHY DOES EVERYONE ALWAYS FOCUS ON THAT!?
THERE'S WAY MORE TO THE AZTECS THAN RITUAL MURDER: WE HAD A REFINED AND SOPHISTICATED CIVILIZATION...

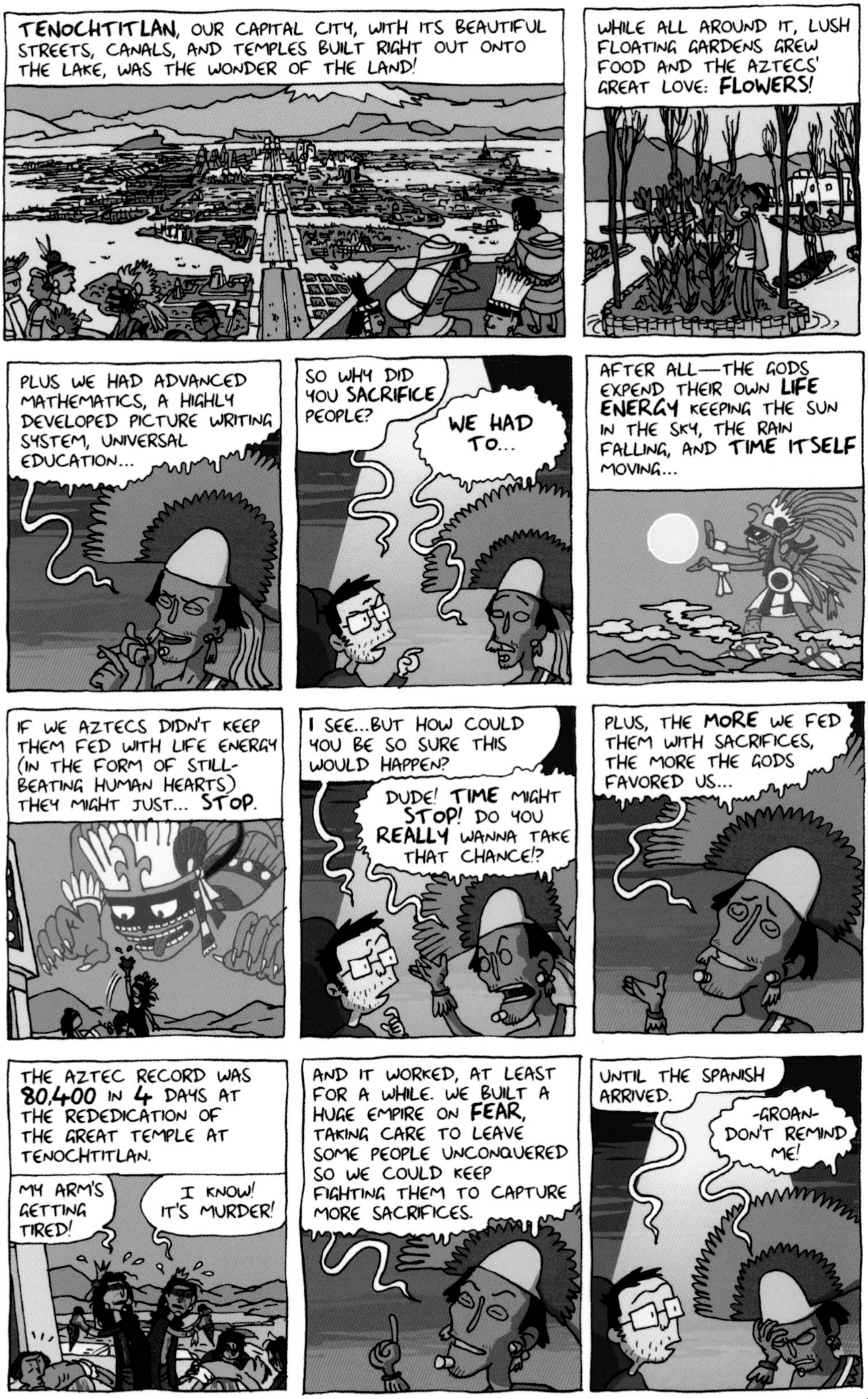
TENOCHTITLAN, OUR CAPITAL CITY, WITH ITS BEAUTIFUL STREETS, CANALS, AND TEMPLES BUILT RIGHT OUT ONTO THE LAKE, WAS THE WONDER OF THE LAND!
WHILE ALL AROUND IT, LUSH FLOATING GARDENS GREW FOOD AND THE AZTECS' GREAT LOVE: FLOWERS!
PLUS WE HAD ADVANCED MATHEMATICS, A HIGHLY DEVELOPED PICTURE WRITING SYSTEM, UNIVERSAL EDUCATION...
SO WHY DID YOU SACRIFICE PEOPLE?
WE HAD TO...
AFTER ALL—THE GODS EXPEND THEIR OWN LIFE ENERGY KEEPING THE SUN IN THE SKY, THE RAIN FALLING, AND TIME ITSELF MOVING...
IF WE AZTECS DIDN'T KEEP THEM FED WITH LIFE ENERGY (IN THE FORM OF STILL-BEATING HUMAN HEARTS) THEY MIGHT JUST... STOP.
I SEE...BUT HOW COULD YOU BE SO SURE THIS WOULD HAPPEN?
DUDE! TIME MIGHT STOP! DO YOU REALLY WANNA TAKE THAT CHANCE!?
PLUS, THE MORE WE FED THEM WITH SACRIFICES, THE MORE THE GODS FAVORED US...
THE AZTEC RECORD WAS 80,400 IN 4 DAYS AT THE REDEDICATION OF THE GREAT TEMPLE AT TENOCHTITLAN.
MY ARM'S GETTING TIRED!
I KNOW! IT'S MURDER!
AND IT WORKED, AT LEAST FOR A WHILE. WE BUILT A HUGE EMPIRE ON FEAR, TAKING CARE TO LEAVE SOME PEOPLE UNCONQUERED SO WE COULD KEEP FIGHTING THEM TO CAPTURE MORE SACRIFICES.
UNTIL THE SPANISH ARRIVED.
-GROAN- DON'T REMIND ME!

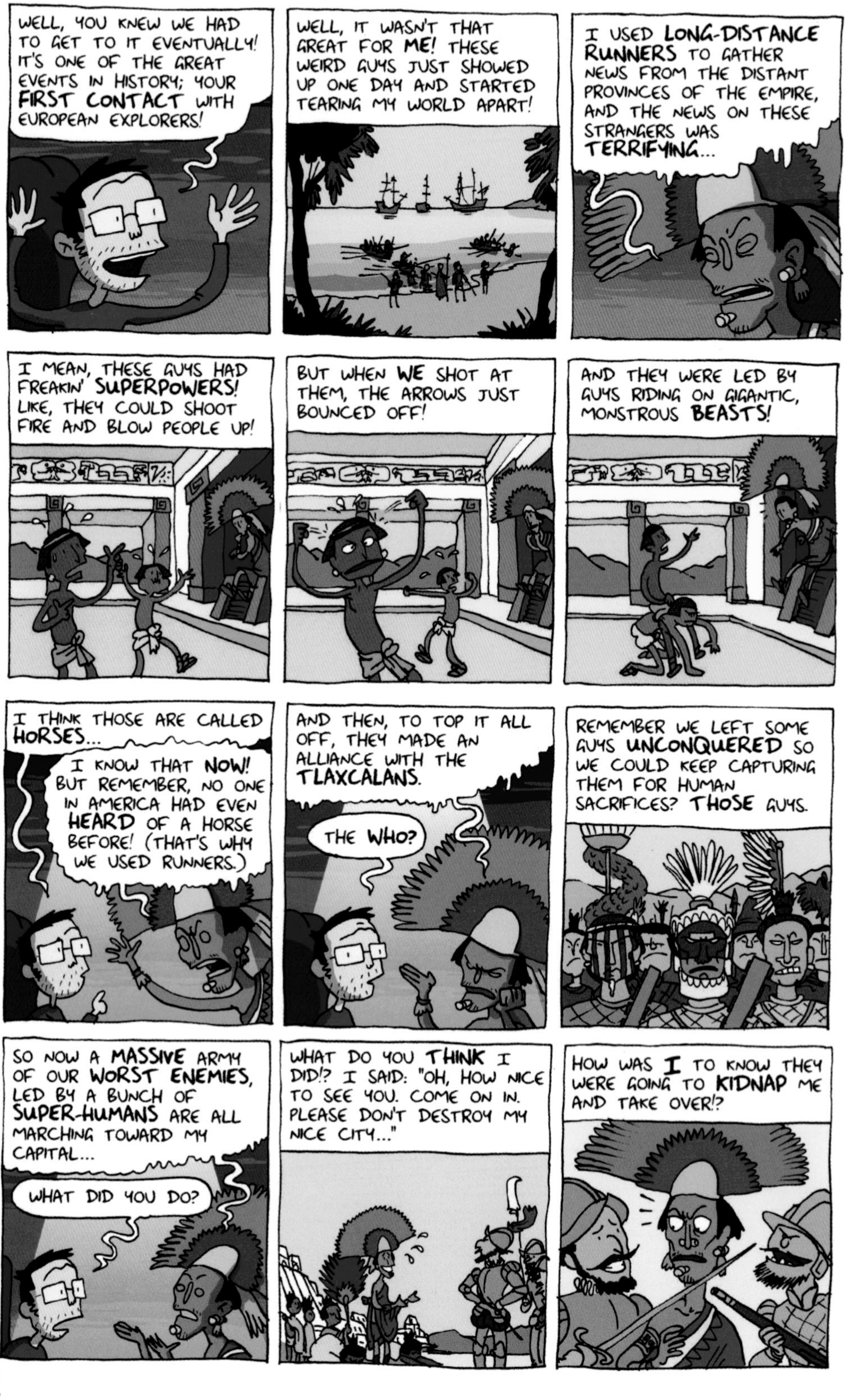
WELL, YOU KNEW WE HAD TO GET TO IT EVENTUALLY! IT'S ONE OF THE GREAT EVENTS IN HISTORY; YOUR FIRST CONTACT WITH EUROPEAN EXPLORERS!
WELL, IT WASN'T THAT GREAT FOR ME! THESE WEIRD GUYS JUST SHOWED UP ONE DAY AND STARTED TEARING MY WORLD APART!
I USED LONG-DISTANCE RUNNERS TO GATHER NEWS FROM THE DISTANT PROVINCES OF THE EMPIRE, AND THE NEWS ON THESE STRANGERS WAS TERRIFYING...
I MEAN, THESE GUYS HAD FREAKIN' SUPERPOWERS! LIKE, THEY COULD SHOOT FIRE AND BLOW PEOPLE UP!
BUT WHEN WE SHOT AT THEM, THE ARROWS JUST BOUNCED OFF!
AND THEY WERE LED BY GUYS RIDING ON GIGANTIC, MONSTROUS BEASTS!
I THINK THOSE ARE CALLED HORSES...
I KNOW THAT NOW! BUT REMEMBER, NO ONE IN AMERICA HAD EVEN HEARD OF A HORSE BEFORE! (THAT'S WHY WE USED RUNNERS.)
AND THEN, TO TOP IT ALL OFF, THEY MADE AN ALLIANCE WITH THE TLAXCALANS.
THE WHO?
REMEMBER WE LEFT SOME GUYS UNCONQUERED SO WE COULD KEEP CAPTURING THEM FOR HUMAN SACRIFICES? THOSE GUYS.
SO NOW A MASSIVE ARMY OF OUR WORST ENEMIES, LED BY A BUNCH OF SUPER-HUMANS ARE ALL MARCHING TOWARD MY CAPITAL...
WHAT DID YOU DO?
WHAT DO YOU THINK I DID!? I SAID: "OH, HOW NICE TO SEE YOU. COME ON IN. PLEASE DON'T DESTROY MY NICE CITY..."
HOW WAS I TO KNOW THEY WERE GOING TO KIDNAP ME AND TAKE OVER!?

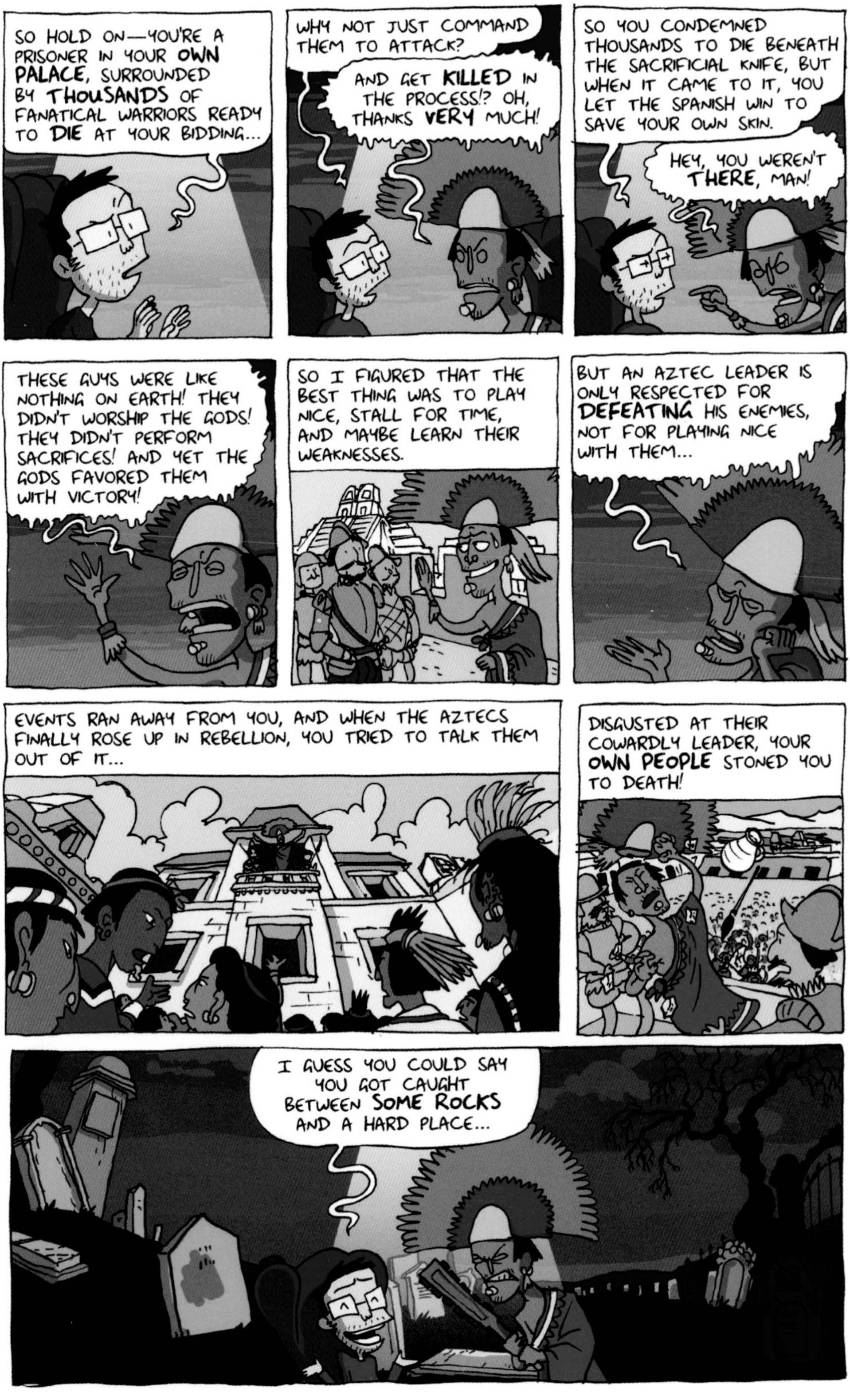
SO HOLD ON—YOU'RE A PRISONER IN YOUR OWN PALACE, SURROUNDED BY THOUSANDS OF FANATICAL WARRIORS READY TO DIE AT YOUR BIDDING...
WHY NOT JUST COMMAND THEM TO ATTACK?
AND GET KILLED IN THE PROCESS!? OH, THANKS VERY MUCH!
SO YOU CONDEMNED THOUSANDS TO DIE BENEATH THE SACRIFICIAL KNIFE, BUT WHEN IT CAME TO IT, YOU LET THE SPANISH WIN TO SAVE YOUR OWN SKIN.
HEY, YOU WEREN'T THERE, MAN!
THESE GUYS WERE LIKE NOTHING ON EARTH! THEY DIDN'T WORSHIP THE GODS! THEY DIDN'T PERFORM SACRIFICES! AND YET THE GODS FAVORED THEM WITH VICTORY!
SO I FIGURED THAT THE BEST THING WAS TO PLAY NICE, STALL FOR TIME, AND MAYBE LEARN THEIR WEAKNESSES.
BUT AN AZTEC LEADER IS ONLY RESPECTED FOR DEFEATING HIS ENEMIES, NOT FOR PLAYING NICE WITH THEM...
EVENTS RAN AWAY FROM YOU, AND WHEN THE AZTECS FINALLY ROSE UP IN REBELLION, YOU TRIED TO TALK THEM OUT OF IT...
DISGUSTED AT THEIR COWARDLY LEADER, YOUR OWN PEOPLE STONED YOU TO DEATH!
I GUESS YOU COULD SAY YOU GOT CAUGHT BETWEEN SOME ROCKS AND A HARD PLACE...

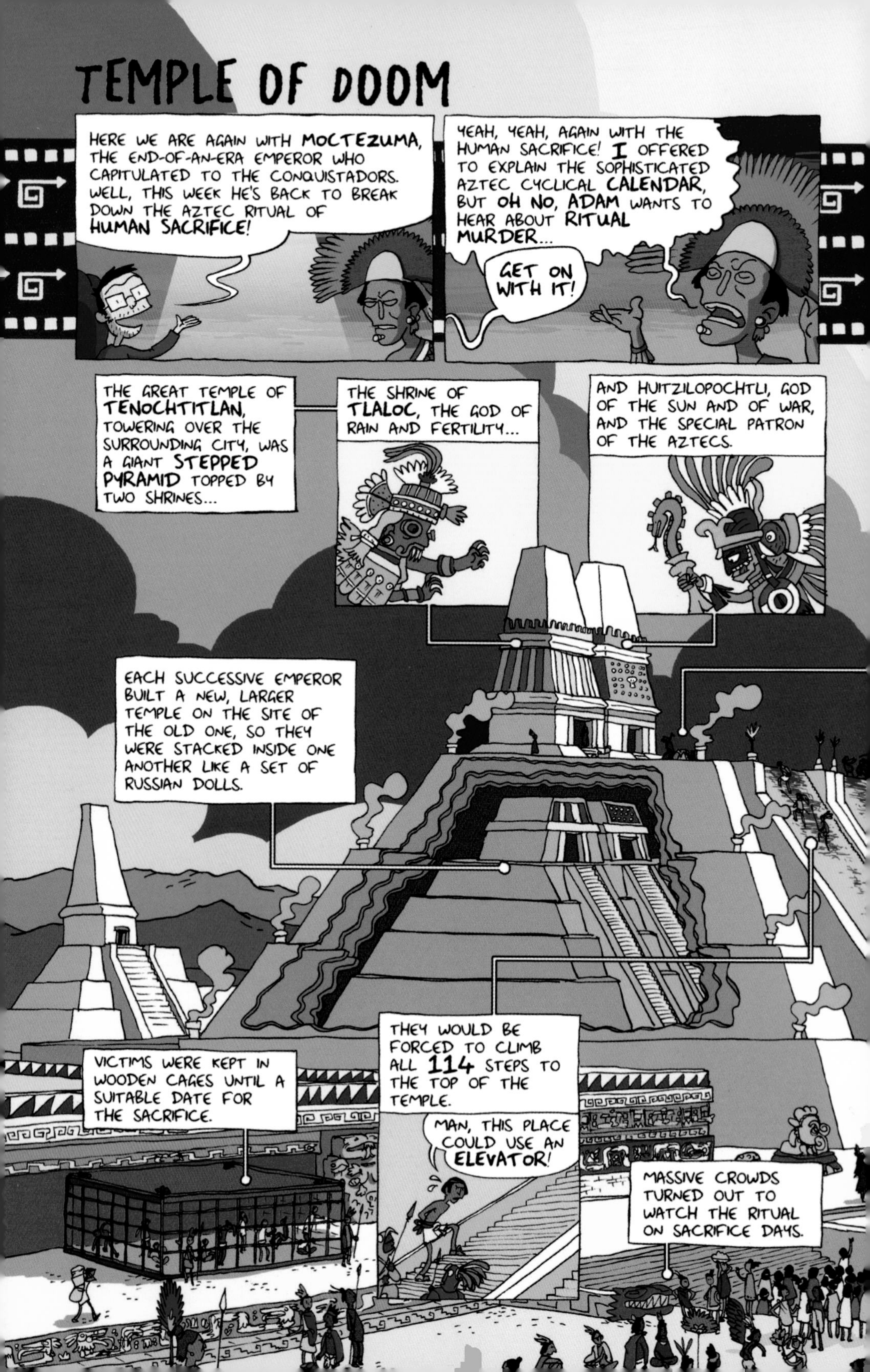
TEMPLE OF DOOM
HERE WE ARE AGAIN WITH MOCTEZUMA, THE END-OF-AN-ERA EMPEROR WHO CAPITULATED TO THE CONQUISTADORS. WELL, THIS WEEK HE'S BACK TO BREAK DOWN THE AZTEC RITUAL OF HUMAN SACRIFICE!
YEAH, YEAH, AGAIN WITH THE HUMAN SACRIFICE! I OFFERED TO EXPLAIN THE SOPHISTICATED AZTEC CYCLICAL CALENDAR, BUT OH NO, ADAM WANTS TO HEAR ABOUT RITUAL MURDER...
GET ON WITH IT!
THE GREAT TEMPLE OF TENOCHTITLAN, TOWERING OVER THE SURROUNDING CITY, WAS A GIANT STEPPED PYRAMID TOPPED BY TWO SHRINES...
THE SHRINE OF TLALOC, THE GOD OF RAIN AND FERTILITY...
AND HUITZILOPOCHTLI, GOD OF THE SUN AND OF WAR, AND THE SPECIAL PATRON OF THE AZTECS.
EACH SUCCESSIVE EMPEROR BUILT A NEW, LARGER TEMPLE ON THE SITE OF THE OLD ONE, SO THEY WERE STACKED INSIDE ONE ANOTHER LIKE A SET OF RUSSIAN DOLLS.
VICTIMS WERE KEPT IN WOODEN CAGES UNTIL A SUITABLE DATE FOR THE SACRIFICE.
THEY WOULD BE FORCED TO CLIMB ALL 114 STEPS TO THE TOP OF THE TEMPLE.
MAN, THIS PLACE COULD USE AN ELEVATOR!
MASSIVE CROWDS TURNED OUT TO WATCH THE RITUAL ON SACRIFICE DAYS.

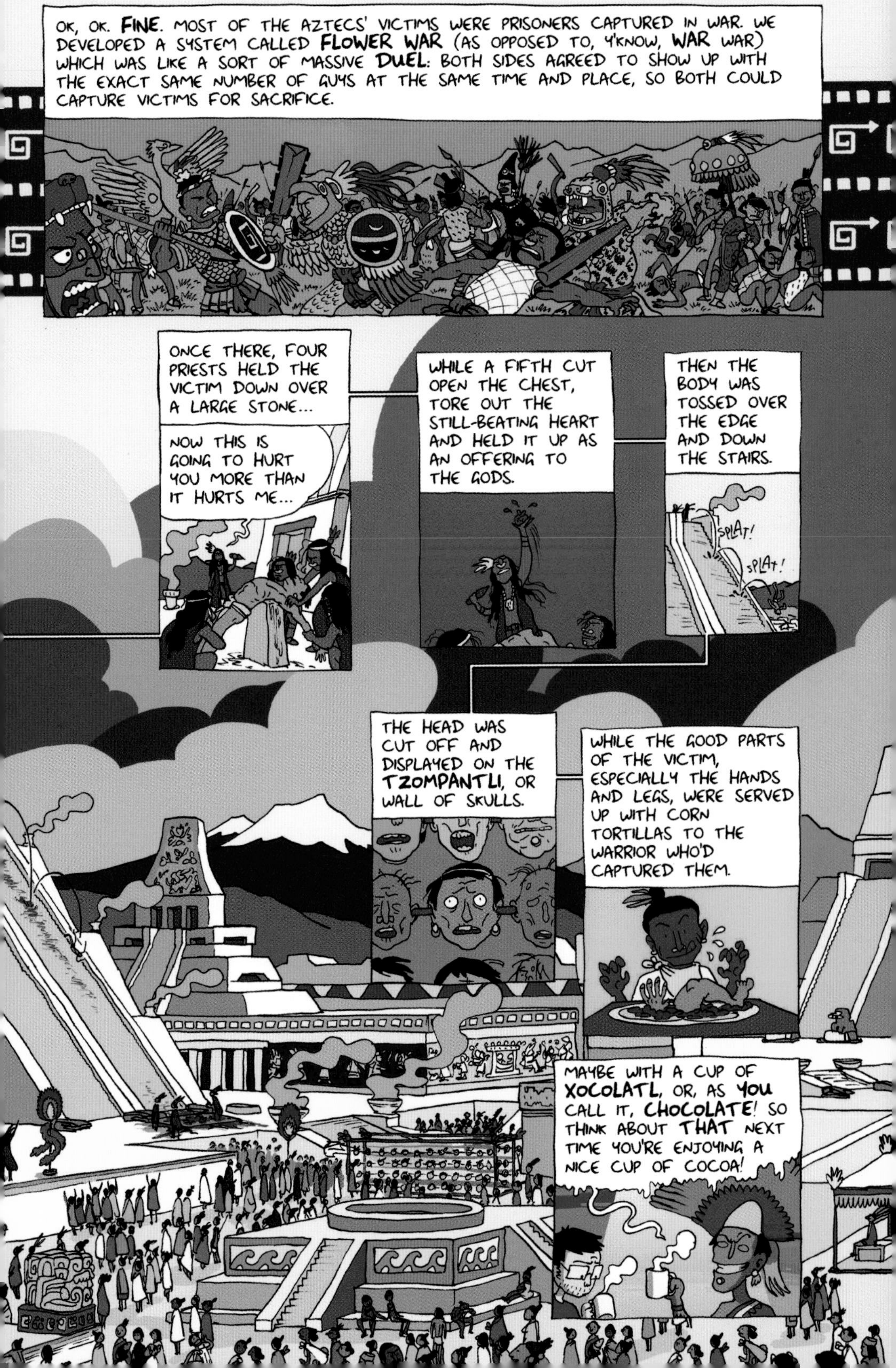
OK, OK. FINE. MOST OF THE AZTECS' VICTIMS WERE PRISONERS CAPTURED IN WAR. WE DEVELOPED A SYSTEM CALLED FLOWER WAR (AS OPPOSED TO, Y'KNOW, WAR WAR) WHICH WAS LIKE A SORT OF MASSIVE DUEL: BOTH SIDES AGREED TO SHOW UP WITH THE EXACT SAME NUMBER OF GUYS AT THE SAME TIME AND PLACE, SO BOTH COULD CAPTURE VICTIMS FOR SACRIFICE.
ONCE THERE, FOUR PRIESTS HELD THE VICTIM DOWN OVER A LARGE STONE...
NOW THIS IS GOING TO HURT YOU MORE THAN IT HURTS ME...
WHILE A FIFTH CUT OPEN THE CHEST, TORE OUT THE STILL-BEATING HEART AND HELD IT UP AS AN OFFERING TO THE GODS.
THEN THE BODY WAS TOSSED OVER THE EDGE AND DOWN THE STAIRS.
SPLAT!
SPLAT!
THE HEAD WAS CUT OFF AND DISPLAYED ON THE TZOMPANTLI, OR WALL OF SKULLS.
WHILE THE GOOD PARTS OF THE VICTIM, ESPECIALLY THE HANDS AND LEGS, WERE SERVED UP WITH CORN TORTILLAS TO THE WARRIOR WHO'D CAPTURED THEM.
MAYBE WITH A CUP OF XOCOLATL, OR, AS YOU CALL IT, CHOCOLATE! SO THINK ABOUT THAT NEXT TIME YOU'RE ENJOYING A NICE CUP OF COCOA!

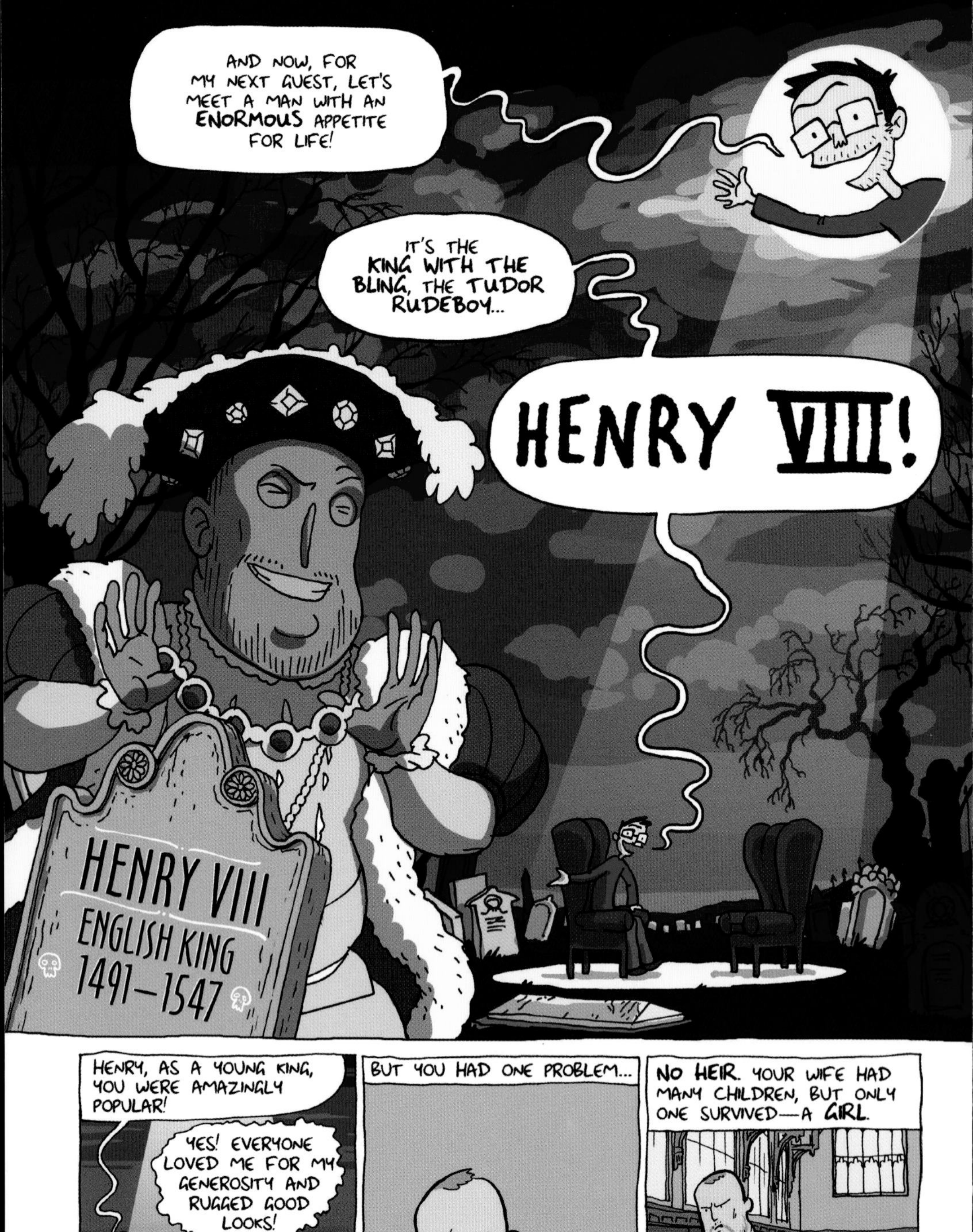
AND NOW, FOR MY NEXT GUEST, LET'S MEET A MAN WITH AN ENORMOUS APPETITE FOR LIFE!
IT'S THE KING WITH THE BLING, THE TUDOR RUDEBOY...
HENRY VIII!
HENRY VIII
ENGLISH KING
1491–1547

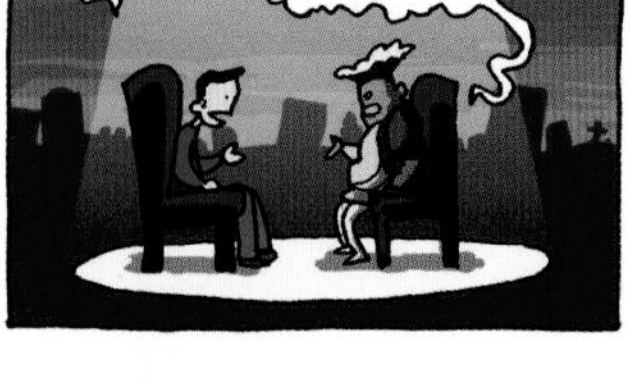
HENRY, AS A YOUNG KING, YOU WERE AMAZINGLY POPULAR!
YES! EVERYONE LOVED ME FOR MY GENEROSITY AND RUGGED GOOD LOOKS!

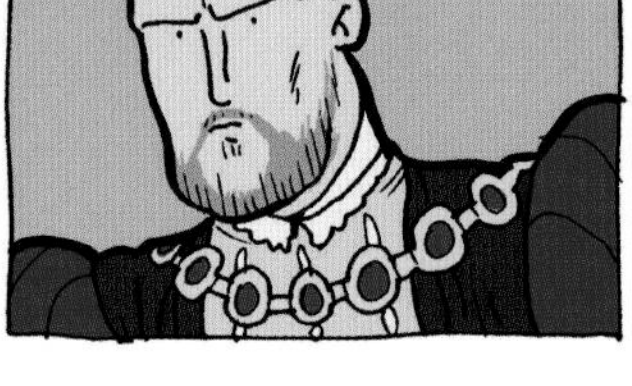
BUT YOU HAD ONE PROBLEM...

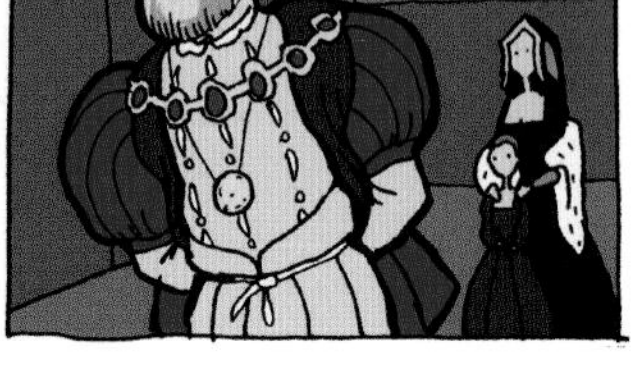
NO HEIR. YOUR WIFE HAD MANY CHILDREN, BUT ONLY ONE SURVIVED—A GIRL.

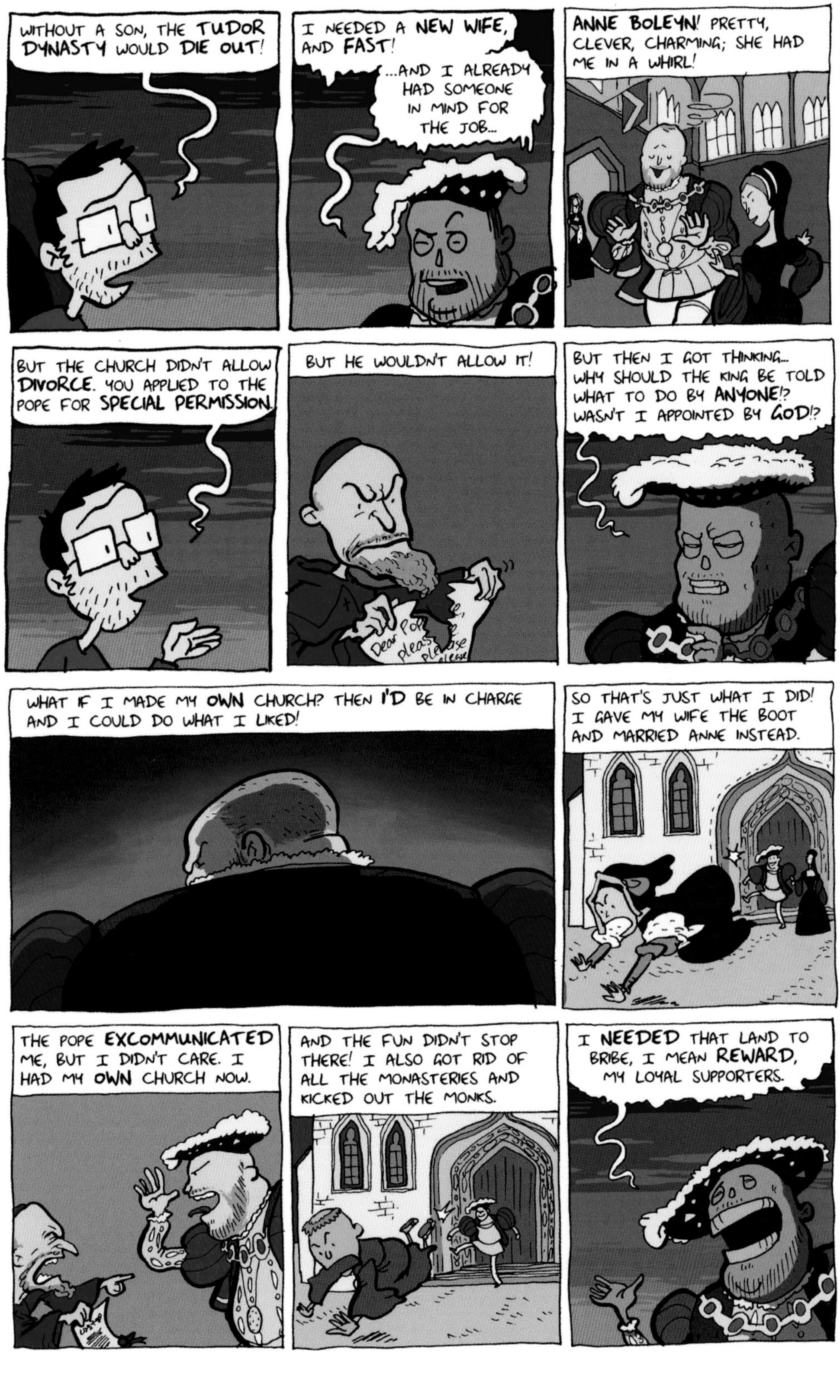
WITHOUT A SON, THE TUDOR DYNASTY WOULD DIE OUT!
I NEEDED A NEW WIFE, AND FAST!
...AND I ALREADY HAD SOMEONE IN MIND FOR THE JOB...
ANNE BOLEYN! PRETTY, CLEVER, CHARMING; SHE HAD ME IN A WHIRL!
BUT THE CHURCH DIDN'T ALLOW DIVORCE. YOU APPLIED TO THE POPE FOR SPECIAL PERMISSION.
BUT HE WOULDN'T ALLOW IT!
Dear Pope please please please
BUT THEN I GOT THINKING... WHY SHOULD THE KING BE TOLD WHAT TO DO BY ANYONE!? WASN'T I APPOINTED BY GOD!?
WHAT IF I MADE MY OWN CHURCH? THEN I'D BE IN CHARGE AND I COULD DO WHAT I LIKED!
SO THAT'S JUST WHAT I DID! I GAVE MY WIFE THE BOOT AND MARRIED ANNE INSTEAD.
THE POPE EXCOMMUNICATED ME, BUT I DIDN'T CARE. I HAD MY OWN CHURCH NOW.
AND THE FUN DIDN'T STOP THERE! I ALSO GOT RID OF ALL THE MONASTERIES AND KICKED OUT THE MONKS.
I NEEDED THAT LAND TO BRIBE, I MEAN REWARD, MY LOYAL SUPPORTERS.

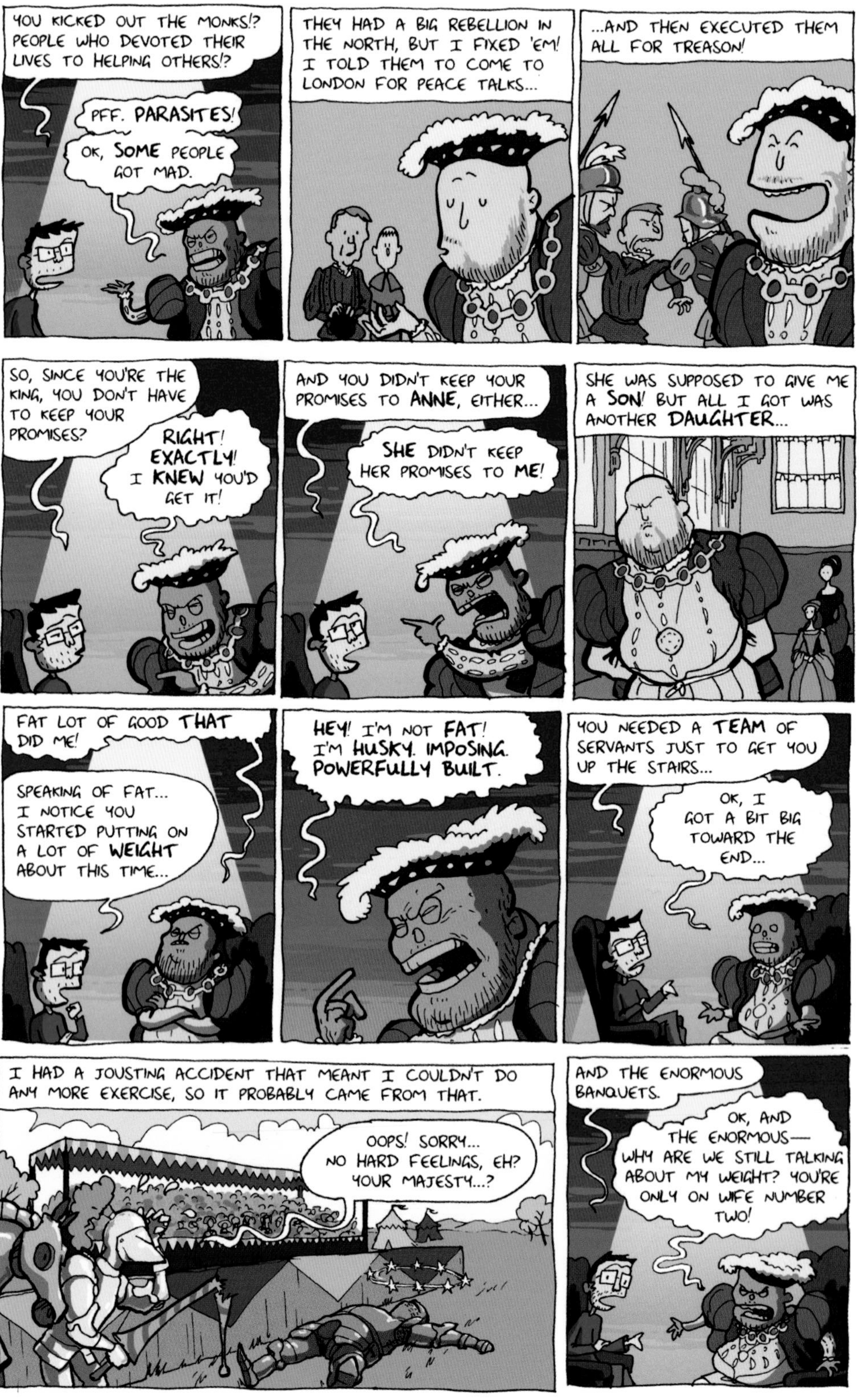
YOU KICKED OUT THE MONKS!? PEOPLE WHO DEVOTED THEIR LIVES TO HELPING OTHERS!?
PFF. PARASITES!
OK, SOME PEOPLE GOT MAD.
THEY HAD A BIG REBELLION IN THE NORTH, BUT I FIXED 'EM! I TOLD THEM TO COME TO LONDON FOR PEACE TALKS...
...AND THEN EXECUTED THEM ALL FOR TREASON!
SO, SINCE YOU'RE THE KING, YOU DON'T HAVE TO KEEP YOUR PROMISES?
RIGHT! EXACTLY! I KNEW YOU'D GET IT!
AND YOU DIDN'T KEEP YOUR PROMISES TO ANNE, EITHER...
SHE DIDN'T KEEP HER PROMISES TO ME!
SHE WAS SUPPOSED TO GIVE ME A SON! BUT ALL I GOT WAS ANOTHER DAUGHTER...
FAT LOT OF GOOD THAT DID ME!
SPEAKING OF FAT... I NOTICE YOU STARTED PUTTING ON A LOT OF WEIGHT ABOUT THIS TIME...
HEY! I'M NOT FAT! I'M HUSKY. IMPOSING. POWERFULLY BUILT.
YOU NEEDED A TEAM OF SERVANTS JUST TO GET YOU UP THE STAIRS...
OK, I GOT A BIT BIG TOWARD THE END...
I HAD A JOUSTING ACCIDENT THAT MEANT I COULDN'T DO ANY MORE EXERCISE, SO IT PROBABLY CAME FROM THAT.
OOPS! SORRY... NO HARD FEELINGS, EH? YOUR MAJESTY...?
AND THE ENORMOUS BANQUETS.
OK, AND THE ENORMOUS— WHY ARE WE STILL TALKING ABOUT MY WEIGHT? YOU'RE ONLY ON WIFE NUMBER TWO!

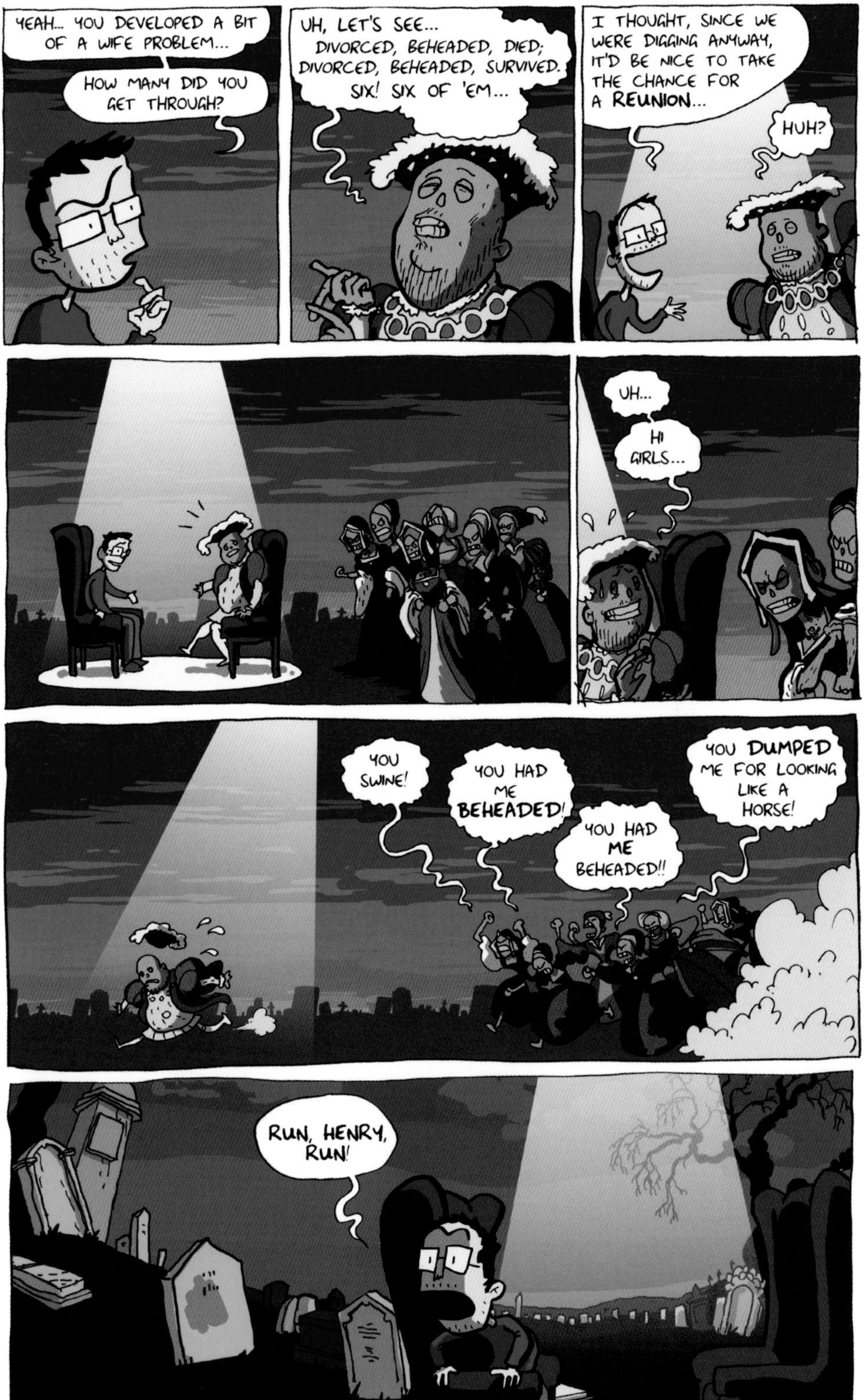
YEAH... YOU DEVELOPED A BIT OF A WIFE PROBLEM...
HOW MANY DID YOU GET THROUGH?
UH, LET'S SEE... DIVORCED, BEHEADED, DIED; DIVORCED, BEHEADED, SURVIVED. SIX! SIX OF 'EM...
I THOUGHT, SINCE WE WERE DIGGING ANYWAY, IT'D BE NICE TO TAKE THE CHANCE FOR A REUNION...
HUH?
UH...
HI GIRLS...
YOU SWINE!
YOU HAD ME BEHEADED!
YOU HAD ME BEHEADED!!
YOU DUMPED ME FOR LOOKING LIKE A HORSE!
RUN, HENRY, RUN!

FULL TILT
A HISTORY OF JOUSTING

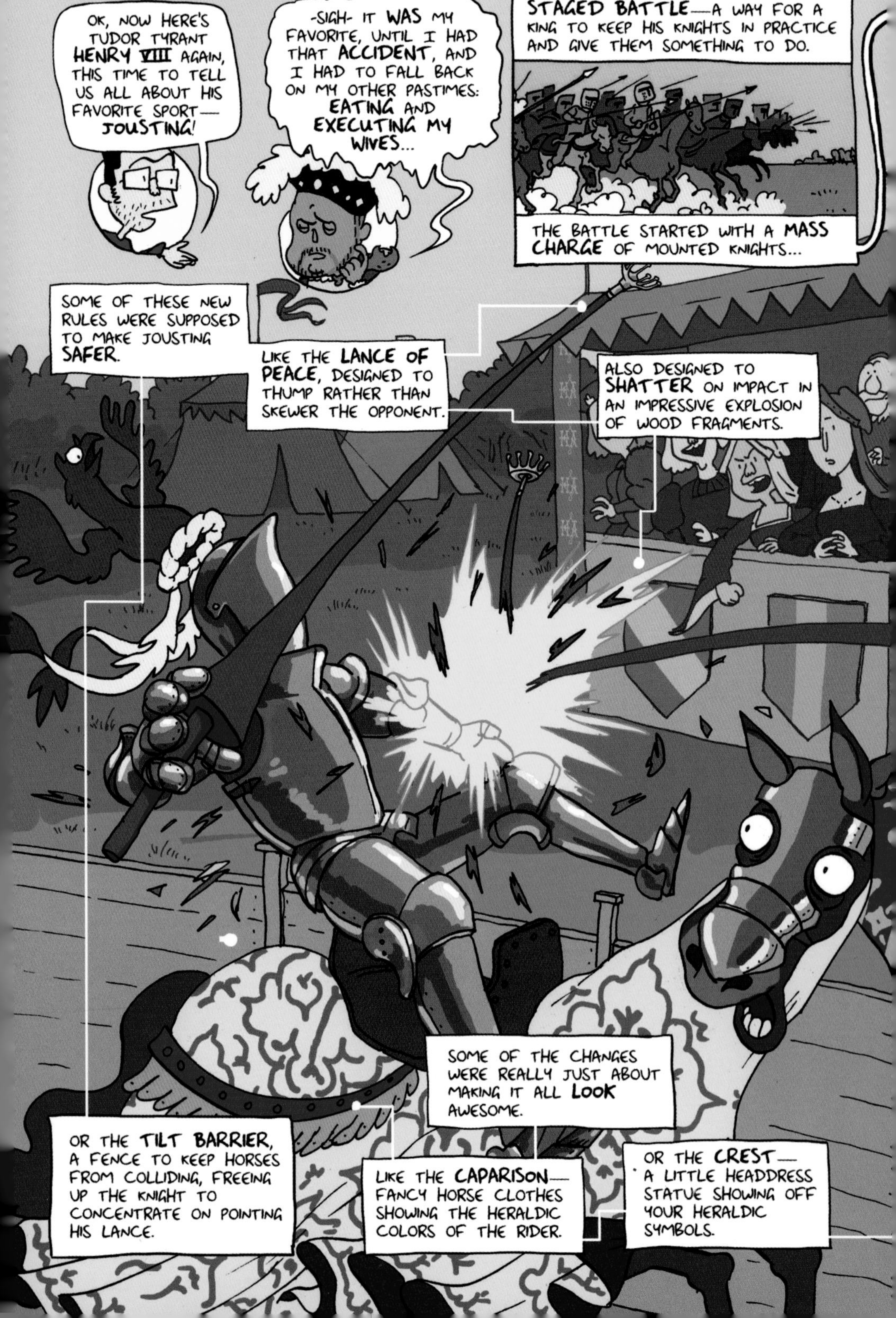

OK, NOW HERE'S TUDOR TYRANT HENRY VIII AGAIN, THIS TIME TO TELL US ALL ABOUT HIS FAVORITE SPORT—JOUSTING!
-SIGH- IT WAS MY FAVORITE, UNTIL I HAD THAT ACCIDENT, AND I HAD TO FALL BACK ON MY OTHER PASTIMES: EATING AND EXECUTING MY WIVES...
JOUSTING BEGAN AS A SORT OF STAGED BATTLE—A WAY FOR A KING TO KEEP HIS KNIGHTS IN PRACTICE AND GIVE THEM SOMETHING TO DO.
THE BATTLE STARTED WITH A MASS CHARGE OF MOUNTED KNIGHTS...
SOME OF THESE NEW RULES WERE SUPPOSED TO MAKE JOUSTING SAFER.
LIKE THE LANCE OF PEACE, DESIGNED TO THUMP RATHER THAN SKEWER THE OPPONENT.
ALSO DESIGNED TO SHATTER ON IMPACT IN AN IMPRESSIVE EXPLOSION OF WOOD FRAGMENTS.
OR THE TILT BARRIER, A FENCE TO KEEP HORSES FROM COLLIDING, FREEING UP THE KNIGHT TO CONCENTRATE ON POINTING HIS LANCE.
SOME OF THE CHANGES WERE REALLY JUST ABOUT MAKING IT ALL LOOK AWESOME.
LIKE THE CAPARISON—FANCY HORSE CLOTHES SHOWING THE HERALDIC COLORS OF THE RIDER.
OR THE CREST—A LITTLE HEADDRESS STATUE SHOWING OFF YOUR HERALDIC SYMBOLS.

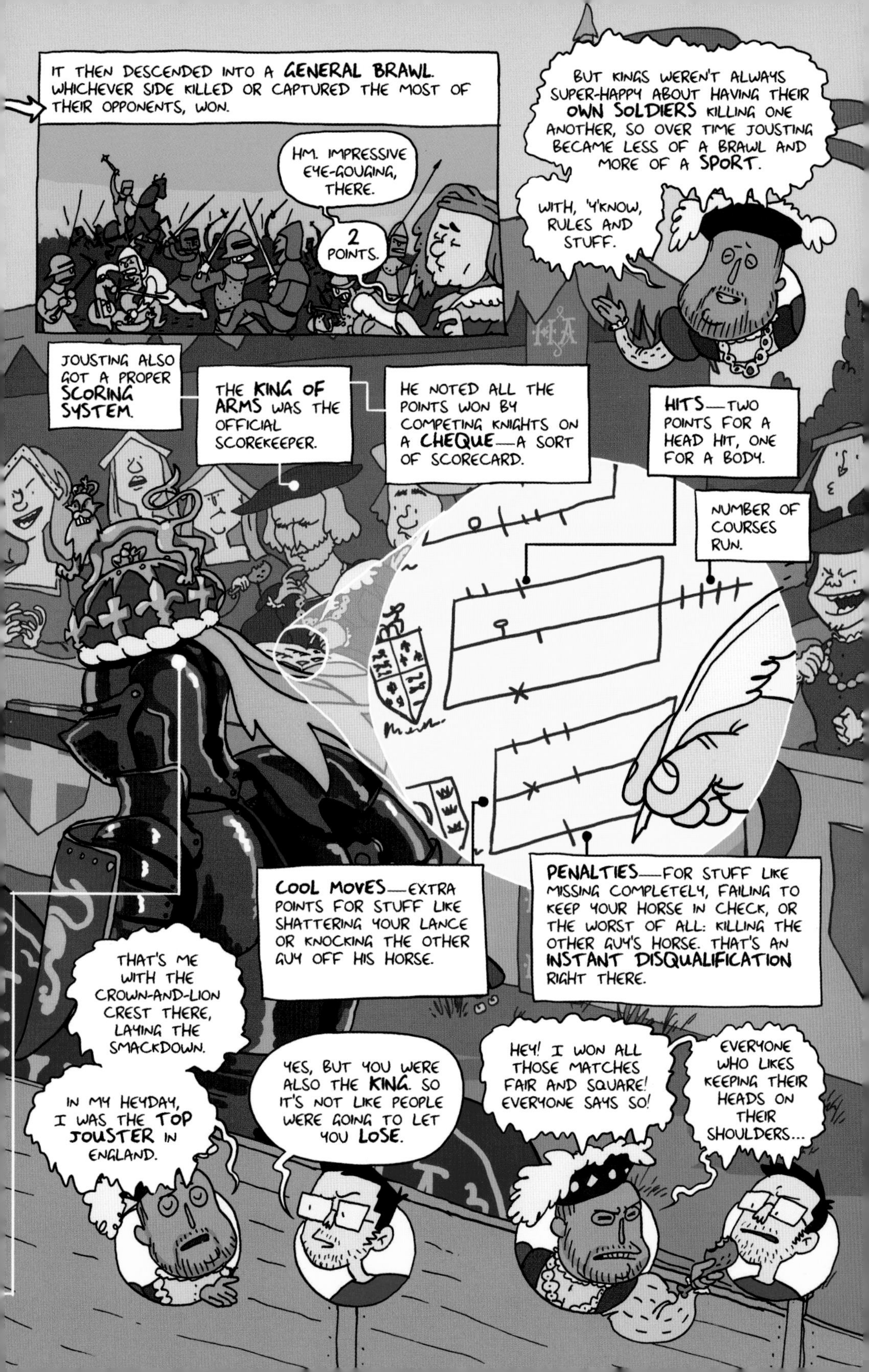
IT THEN DESCENDED INTO A GENERAL BRAWL. WHICHEVER SIDE KILLED OR CAPTURED THE MOST OF THEIR OPPONENTS, WON.
HM. IMPRESSIVE EYE-GOUGING, THERE.
2 POINTS.
BUT KINGS WEREN'T ALWAYS SUPER-HAPPY ABOUT HAVING THEIR OWN SOLDIERS KILLING ONE ANOTHER, SO OVER TIME JOUSTING BECAME LESS OF A BRAWL AND MORE OF A SPORT.
WITH, 'Y'KNOW, RULES AND STUFF.
JOUSTING ALSO GOT A PROPER SCORING SYSTEM.
THE KING OF ARMS WAS THE OFFICIAL SCOREKEEPER.
HE NOTED ALL THE POINTS WON BY COMPETING KNIGHTS ON A CHEQUE—A SORT OF SCORECARD.
HITS—TWO POINTS FOR A HEAD HIT, ONE FOR A BODY.
NUMBER OF COURSES RUN.
COOL MOVES—EXTRA POINTS FOR STUFF LIKE SHATTERING YOUR LANCE OR KNOCKING THE OTHER GUY OFF HIS HORSE.
PENALTIES—FOR STUFF LIKE MISSING COMPLETELY, FAILING TO KEEP YOUR HORSE IN CHECK, OR THE WORST OF ALL: KILLING THE OTHER GUY'S HORSE. THAT'S AN INSTANT DISQUALIFICATION RIGHT THERE.
THAT'S ME WITH THE CROWN-AND-LION CREST THERE, LAYING THE SMACKDOWN.
IN MY HEYDAY, I WAS THE TOP JOUSTER IN ENGLAND.
YES, BUT YOU WERE ALSO THE KING. SO IT'S NOT LIKE PEOPLE WERE GOING TO LET YOU LOSE.
HEY! I WON ALL THOSE MATCHES FAIR AND SQUARE! EVERYONE SAYS SO!
EVERYONE WHO LIKES KEEPING THEIR HEADS ON THEIR SHOULDERS...

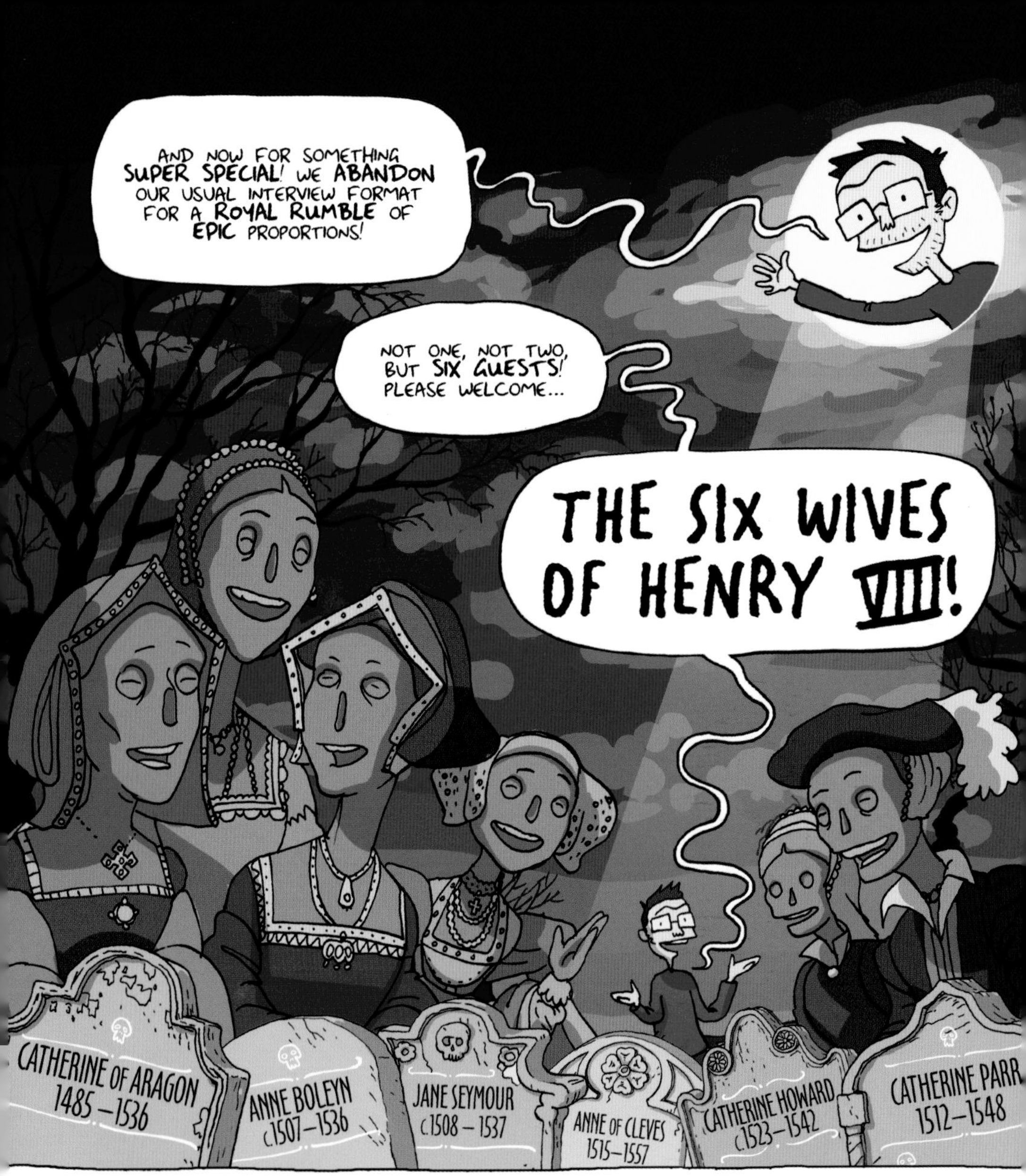
AND NOW FOR SOMETHING SUPER SPECIAL! WE ABANDON OUR USUAL INTERVIEW FORMAT FOR A ROYAL RUMBLE OF EPIC PROPORTIONS!
NOT ONE, NOT TWO, BUT SIX GUESTS! PLEASE WELCOME...
THE SIX WIVES OF HENRY VIII!
CATHERINE OF ARAGON 1485 – 1536
ANNE BOLEYN c.1507 – 1536
JANE SEYMOUR c.1508 – 1537
ANNE OF CLEVES 1515 – 1557
CATHERINE HOWARD c.1523 – 1542
CATHERINE PARR 1512 – 1548

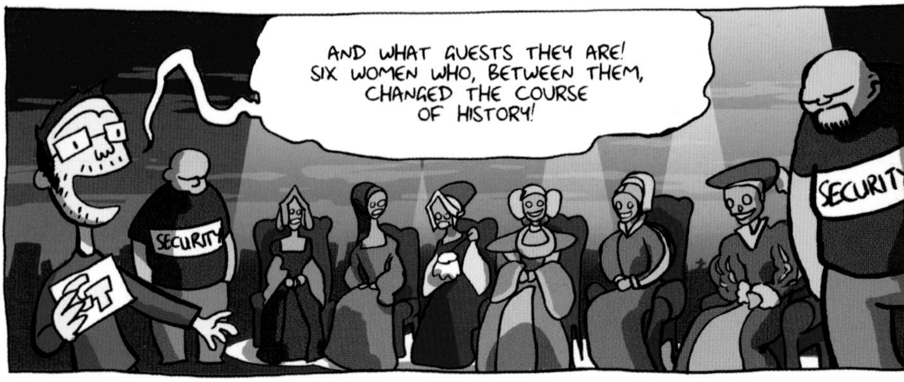
AND WHAT GUESTS THEY ARE! SIX WOMEN WHO, BETWEEN THEM, CHANGED THE COURSE OF HISTORY!
SECURITY
SECURITY

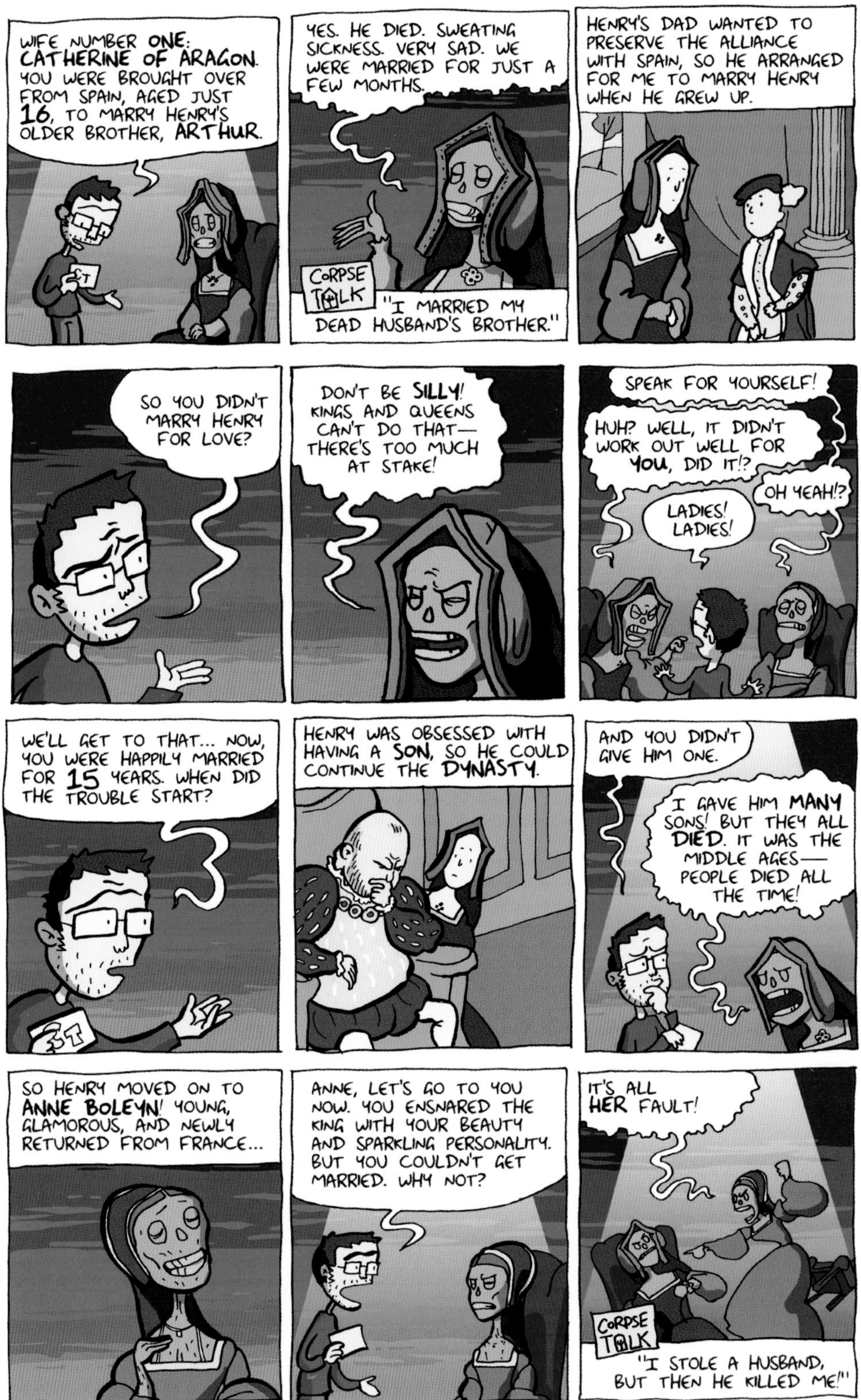
WIFE NUMBER ONE: CATHERINE OF ARAGON. YOU WERE BROUGHT OVER FROM SPAIN, AGED JUST 16, TO MARRY HENRY'S OLDER BROTHER, ARTHUR.
YES. HE DIED. SWEATING SICKNESS. VERY SAD. WE WERE MARRIED FOR JUST A FEW MONTHS.
CORPSE TALK
"I MARRIED MY DEAD HUSBAND'S BROTHER."
HENRY'S DAD WANTED TO PRESERVE THE ALLIANCE WITH SPAIN, SO HE ARRANGED FOR ME TO MARRY HENRY WHEN HE GREW UP.
SO YOU DIDN'T MARRY HENRY FOR LOVE?
DON'T BE SILLY! KINGS AND QUEENS CAN'T DO THAT— THERE'S TOO MUCH AT STAKE!
SPEAK FOR YOURSELF!
HUH? WELL, IT DIDN'T WORK OUT WELL FOR YOU, DID IT!?
OH YEAH!?
LADIES! LADIES!
WE'LL GET TO THAT... NOW, YOU WERE HAPPILY MARRIED FOR 15 YEARS. WHEN DID THE TROUBLE START?
HENRY WAS OBSESSED WITH HAVING A SON, SO HE COULD CONTINUE THE DYNASTY.
AND YOU DIDN'T GIVE HIM ONE.
I GAVE HIM MANY SONS! BUT THEY ALL DIED. IT WAS THE MIDDLE AGES— PEOPLE DIED ALL THE TIME!
SO HENRY MOVED ON TO ANNE BOLEYN! YOUNG, GLAMOROUS, AND NEWLY RETURNED FROM FRANCE...
ANNE, LET'S GO TO YOU NOW. YOU ENSNARED THE KING WITH YOUR BEAUTY AND SPARKLING PERSONALITY. BUT YOU COULDN'T GET MARRIED. WHY NOT?
IT'S ALL HER FAULT!
CORPSE TALK
"I STOLE A HUSBAND, BUT THEN HE KILLED ME!"

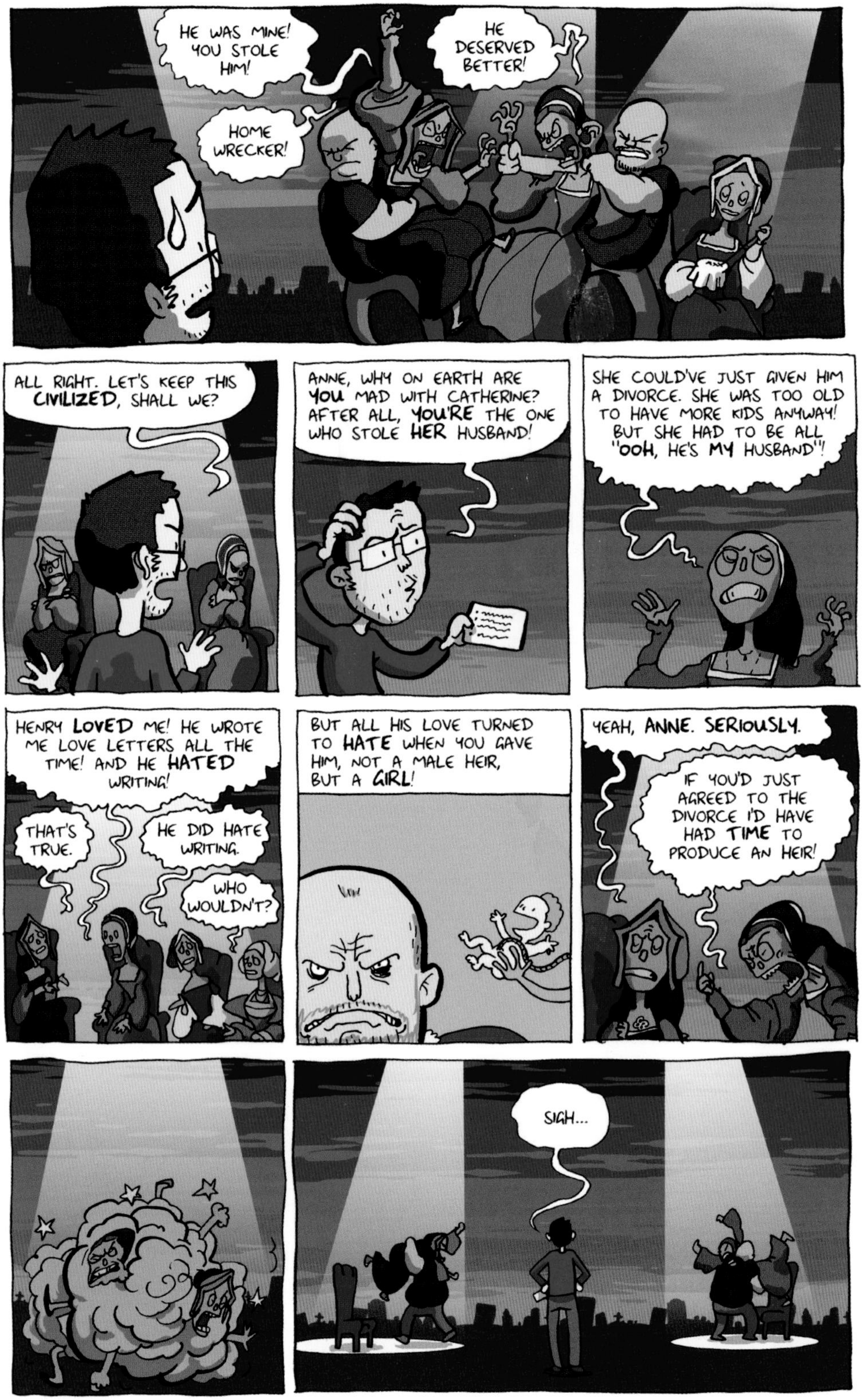
HE WAS MINE! YOU STOLE HIM!
HE DESERVED BETTER!
HOME WRECKER!
ALL RIGHT. LET'S KEEP THIS CIVILIZED, SHALL WE?
ANNE, WHY ON EARTH ARE YOU MAD WITH CATHERINE? AFTER ALL, YOU'RE THE ONE WHO STOLE HER HUSBAND!
SHE COULD'VE JUST GIVEN HIM A DIVORCE. SHE WAS TOO OLD TO HAVE MORE KIDS ANYWAY! BUT SHE HAD TO BE ALL "OOH, HE'S MY HUSBAND"!
HENRY LOVED ME! HE WROTE ME LOVE LETTERS ALL THE TIME! AND HE HATED WRITING!
THAT'S TRUE.
HE DID HATE WRITING.
WHO WOULDN'T?
BUT ALL HIS LOVE TURNED TO HATE WHEN YOU GAVE HIM, NOT A MALE HEIR, BUT A GIRL!
YEAH, ANNE. SERIOUSLY.
IF YOU'D JUST AGREED TO THE DIVORCE I'D HAVE HAD TIME TO PRODUCE AN HEIR!
SIGH...

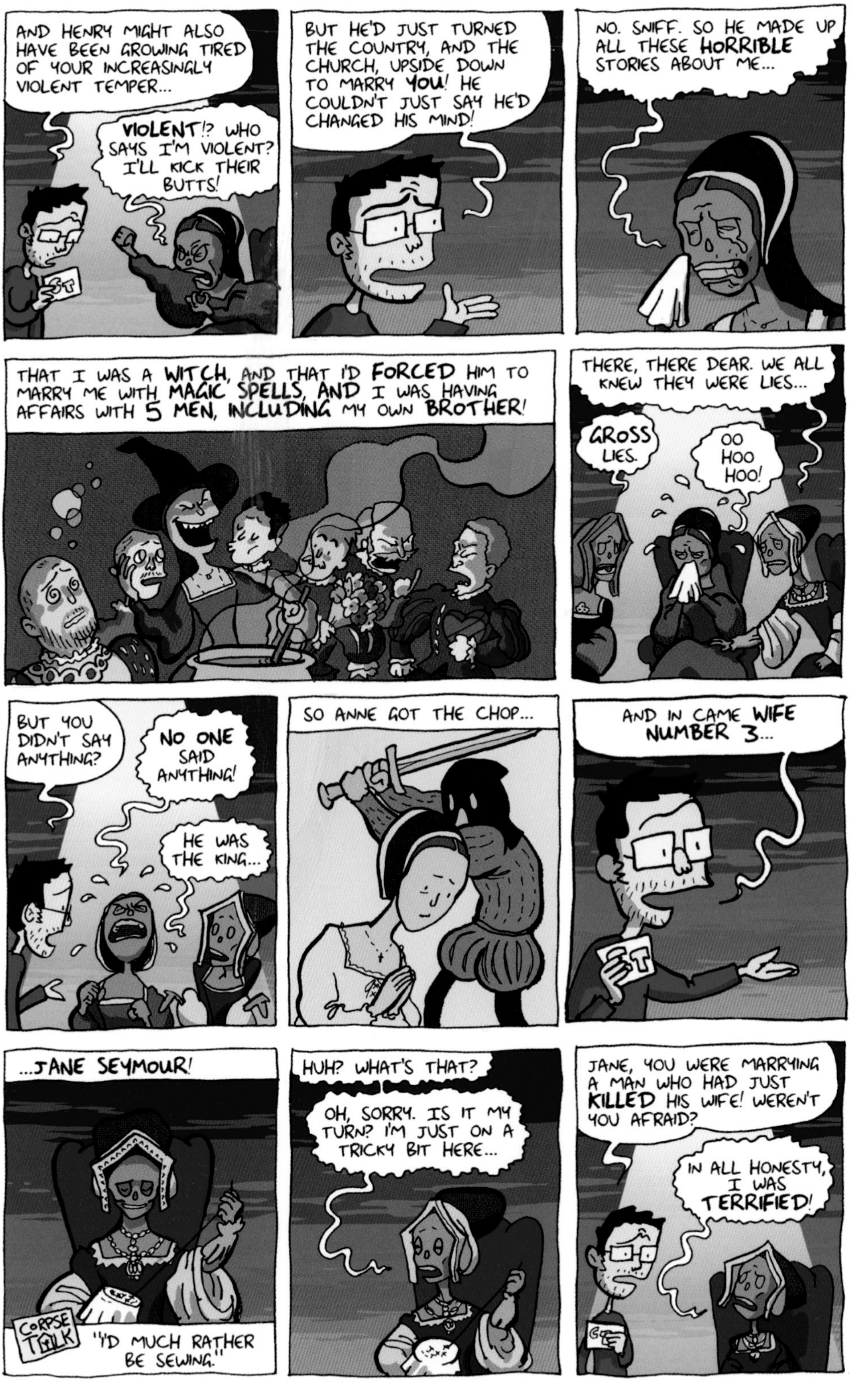
AND HENRY MIGHT ALSO HAVE BEEN GROWING TIRED OF YOUR INCREASINGLY VIOLENT TEMPER...
VIOLENT!? WHO SAYS I'M VIOLENT? I'LL KICK THEIR BUTTS!
BUT HE'D JUST TURNED THE COUNTRY, AND THE CHURCH, UPSIDE DOWN TO MARRY YOU! HE COULDN'T JUST SAY HE'D CHANGED HIS MIND!
NO. SNIFF. SO HE MADE UP ALL THESE HORRIBLE STORIES ABOUT ME...
THAT I WAS A WITCH, AND THAT I'D FORCED HIM TO MARRY ME WITH MAGIC SPELLS, AND I WAS HAVING AFFAIRS WITH 5 MEN, INCLUDING MY OWN BROTHER!
THERE, THERE DEAR. WE ALL KNEW THEY WERE LIES...
GROSS LIES.
OO HOO HOO!
BUT YOU DIDN'T SAY ANYTHING?
NO ONE SAID ANYTHING!
HE WAS THE KING...
SO ANNE GOT THE CHOP...
AND IN CAME WIFE NUMBER 3...
...JANE SEYMOUR!
CORPSE TALK
"I'D MUCH RATHER BE SEWING."
HUH? WHAT'S THAT?
OH, SORRY. IS IT MY TURN? I'M JUST ON A TRICKY BIT HERE...
JANE, YOU WERE MARRYING A MAN WHO HAD JUST KILLED HIS WIFE! WEREN'T YOU AFRAID?
IN ALL HONESTY, I WAS TERRIFIED!

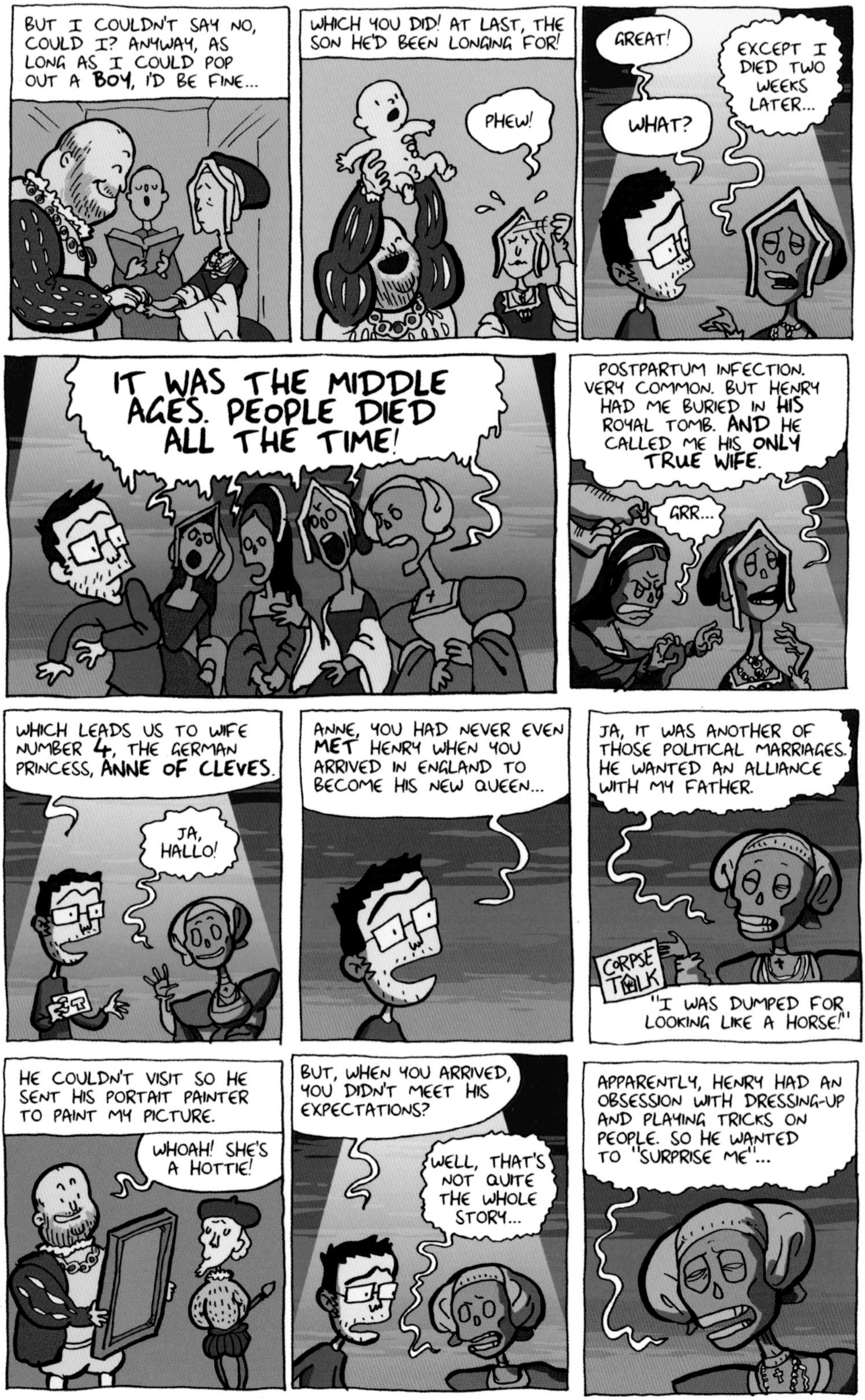

BUT I COULDN'T SAY NO, COULD I? ANYWAY, AS LONG AS I COULD POP OUT A BOY, I'D BE FINE...
WHICH YOU DID! AT LAST, THE SON HE'D BEEN LONGING FOR!
PHEW!
GREAT!
WHAT?
EXCEPT I DIED TWO WEEKS LATER...
IT WAS THE MIDDLE AGES. PEOPLE DIED ALL THE TIME!
POSTPARTUM INFECTION. VERY COMMON. BUT HENRY HAD ME BURIED IN HIS ROYAL TOMB. AND HE CALLED ME HIS ONLY TRUE WIFE.
GRR...
WHICH LEADS US TO WIFE NUMBER 4, THE GERMAN PRINCESS, ANNE OF CLEVES.
JA, HALLO!
ANNE, YOU HAD NEVER EVEN MET HENRY WHEN YOU ARRIVED IN ENGLAND TO BECOME HIS NEW QUEEN...
JA, IT WAS ANOTHER OF THOSE POLITICAL MARRIAGES. HE WANTED AN ALLIANCE WITH MY FATHER.
CORPSE TALK
"I WAS DUMPED FOR LOOKING LIKE A HORSE!"
HE COULDN'T VISIT SO HE SENT HIS PORTAIT PAINTER TO PAINT MY PICTURE.
WHOAH! SHE'S A HOTTIE!
BUT, WHEN YOU ARRIVED, YOU DIDN'T MEET HIS EXPECTATIONS?
WELL, THAT'S NOT QUITE THE WHOLE STORY...
APPARENTLY, HENRY HAD AN OBSESSION WITH DRESSING-UP AND PLAYING TRICKS ON PEOPLE. SO HE WANTED TO "SURPRISE ME"...

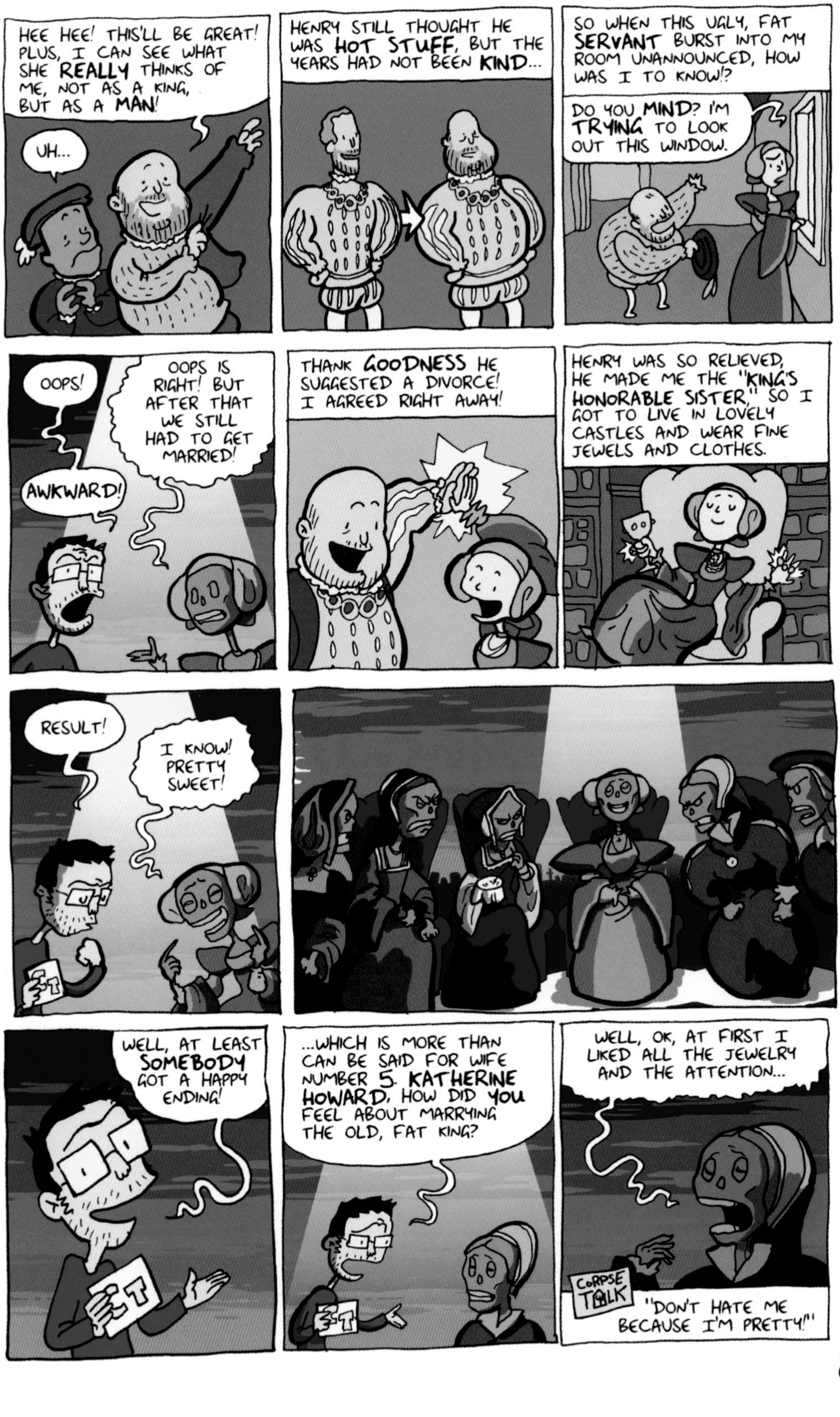
HEE HEE! THIS'LL BE GREAT! PLUS, I CAN SEE WHAT SHE REALLY THINKS OF ME, NOT AS A KING, BUT AS A MAN!
UH...
HENRY STILL THOUGHT HE WAS HOT STUFF, BUT THE YEARS HAD NOT BEEN KIND...
SO WHEN THIS UGLY, FAT SERVANT BURST INTO MY ROOM UNANNOUNCED, HOW WAS I TO KNOW!?
DO YOU MIND? I'M TRYING TO LOOK OUT THIS WINDOW.
OOPS!
AWKWARD!
OOPS IS RIGHT! BUT AFTER THAT WE STILL HAD TO GET MARRIED!
THANK GOODNESS HE SUGGESTED A DIVORCE! I AGREED RIGHT AWAY!
HENRY WAS SO RELIEVED, HE MADE ME THE "KING'S HONORABLE SISTER," SO I GOT TO LIVE IN LOVELY CASTLES AND WEAR FINE JEWELS AND CLOTHES.
RESULT!
I KNOW! PRETTY SWEET!
WELL, AT LEAST SOMEBODY GOT A HAPPY ENDING!
...WHICH IS MORE THAN CAN BE SAID FOR WIFE NUMBER 5, KATHERINE HOWARD. HOW DID YOU FEEL ABOUT MARRYING THE OLD, FAT KING?
WELL, OK, AT FIRST I LIKED ALL THE JEWELRY AND THE ATTENTION...
CORPSE TALK
"DON'T HATE ME BECAUSE I'M PRETTY!"

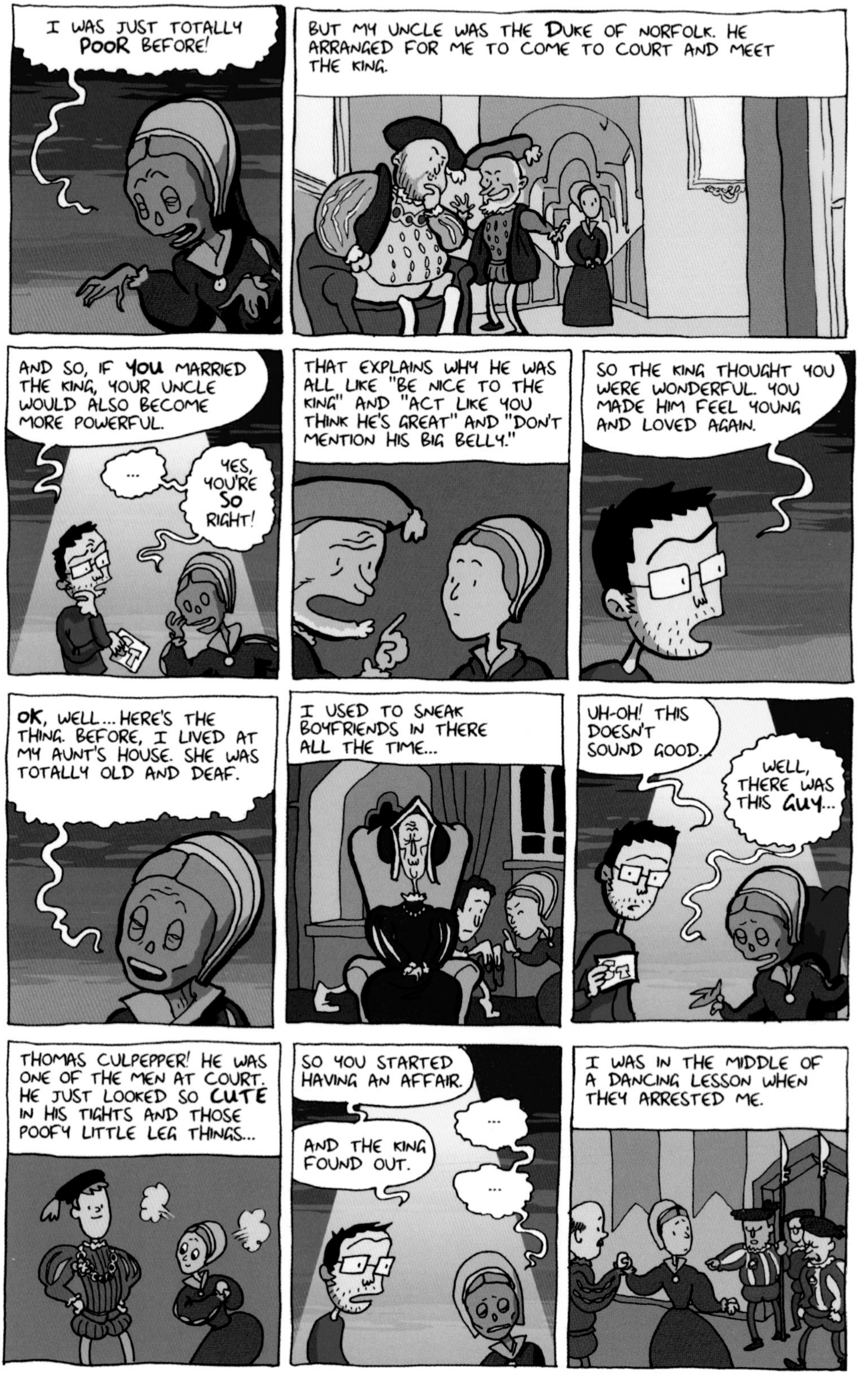
I WAS JUST TOTALLY POOR BEFORE!
BUT MY UNCLE WAS THE DUKE OF NORFOLK. HE ARRANGED FOR ME TO COME TO COURT AND MEET THE KING.
AND SO, IF YOU MARRIED THE KING, YOUR UNCLE WOULD ALSO BECOME MORE POWERFUL.
...
YES, YOU'RE SO RIGHT!
THAT EXPLAINS WHY HE WAS ALL LIKE "BE NICE TO THE KING" AND "ACT LIKE YOU THINK HE'S GREAT" AND "DON'T MENTION HIS BIG BELLY."
SO THE KING THOUGHT YOU WERE WONDERFUL. YOU MADE HIM FEEL YOUNG AND LOVED AGAIN.
OK, WELL... HERE'S THE THING. BEFORE, I LIVED AT MY AUNT'S HOUSE. SHE WAS TOTALLY OLD AND DEAF.
I USED TO SNEAK BOYFRIENDS IN THERE ALL THE TIME...
UH-OH! THIS DOESN'T SOUND GOOD...
WELL, THERE WAS THIS GUY...
THOMAS CULPEPPER! HE WAS ONE OF THE MEN AT COURT. HE JUST LOOKED SO CUTE IN HIS TIGHTS AND THOSE POOFY LITTLE LEG THINGS...
SO YOU STARTED HAVING AN AFFAIR.
AND THE KING FOUND OUT.
...
...
I WAS IN THE MIDDLE OF A DANCING LESSON WHEN THEY ARRESTED ME.

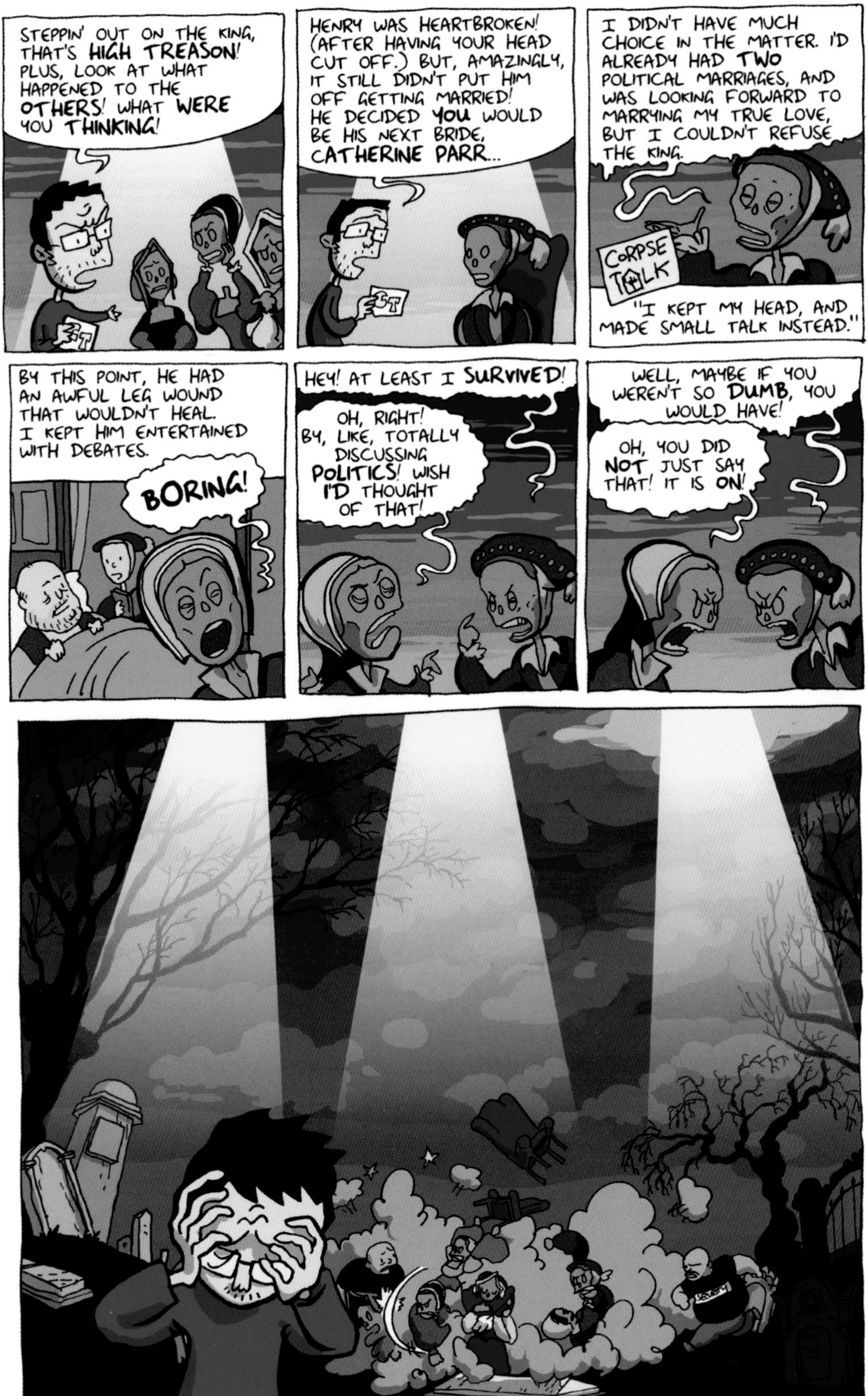
STEPPIN' OUT ON THE KING, THAT'S HIGH TREASON! PLUS, LOOK AT WHAT HAPPENED TO THE OTHERS! WHAT WERE YOU THINKING!
HENRY WAS HEARTBROKEN! (AFTER HAVING YOUR HEAD CUT OFF.) BUT, AMAZINGLY, IT STILL DIDN'T PUT HIM OFF GETTING MARRIED! HE DECIDED YOU WOULD BE HIS NEXT BRIDE, CATHERINE PARR...
I DIDN'T HAVE MUCH CHOICE IN THE MATTER. I'D ALREADY HAD TWO POLITICAL MARRIAGES, AND WAS LOOKING FORWARD TO MARRYING MY TRUE LOVE, BUT I COULDN'T REFUSE THE KING.
CORPSE TALK
"I KEPT MY HEAD, AND MADE SMALL TALK INSTEAD."
BY THIS POINT, HE HAD AN AWFUL LEG WOUND THAT WOULDN'T HEAL. I KEPT HIM ENTERTAINED WITH DEBATES.
BORING!
HEY! AT LEAST I SURVIVED!
OH, RIGHT! BY, LIKE, TOTALLY DISCUSSING POLITICS! WISH I'D THOUGHT OF THAT!
WELL, MAYBE IF YOU WEREN'T SO DUMB, YOU WOULD HAVE!
OH, YOU DID NOT JUST SAY THAT! IT IS ON!
SECURITY

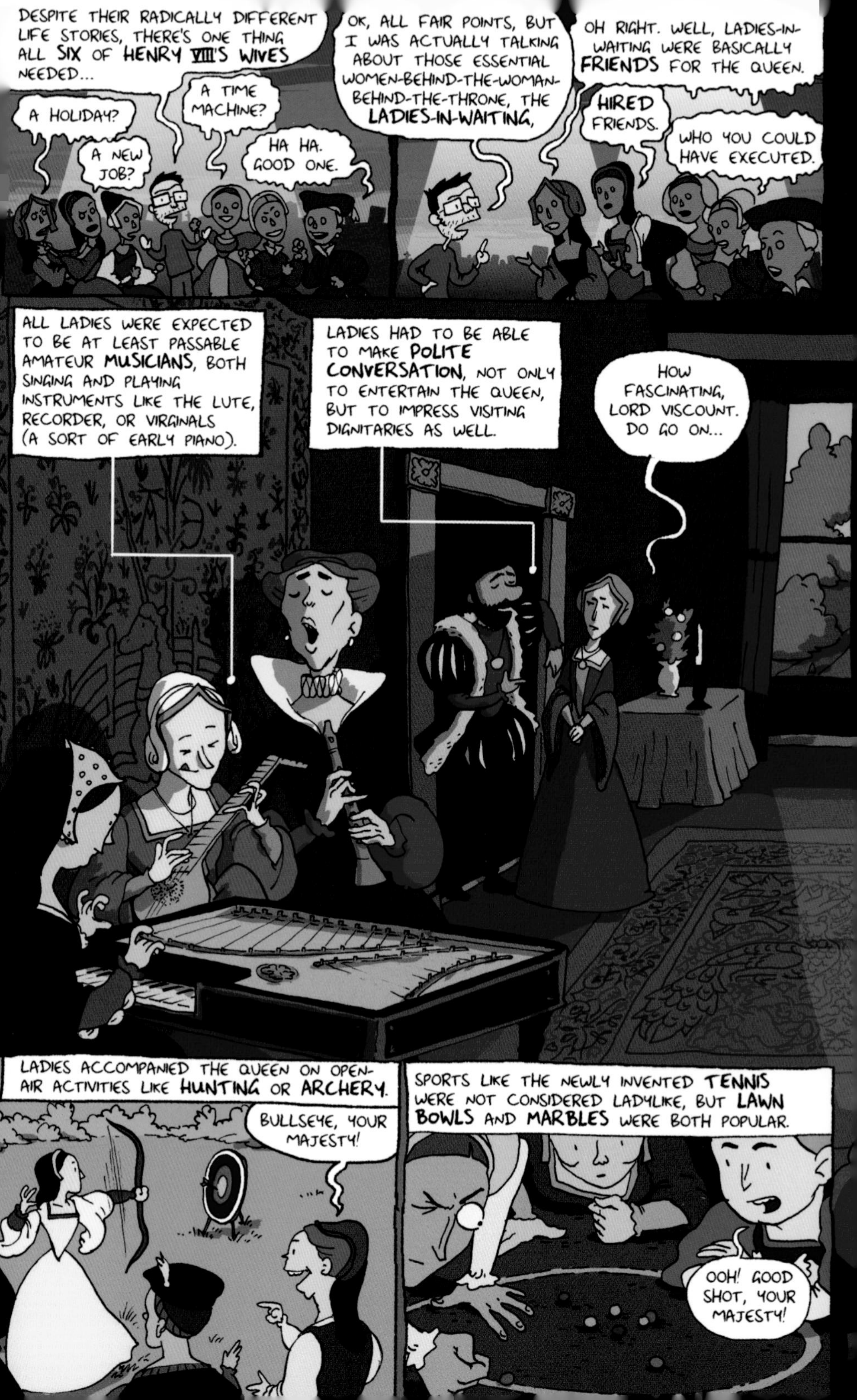

DESPITE THEIR RADICALLY DIFFERENT LIFE STORIES, THERE'S ONE THING ALL SIX OF HENRY VIII'S WIVES NEEDED...
A HOLIDAY?
A NEW JOB?
A TIME MACHINE?
HA HA. GOOD ONE.
OK, ALL FAIR POINTS, BUT I WAS ACTUALLY TALKING ABOUT THOSE ESSENTIAL WOMEN-BEHIND-THE-WOMAN-BEHIND-THE-THRONE, THE LADIES-IN-WAITING.
OH RIGHT. WELL, LADIES-IN-WAITING WERE BASICALLY FRIENDS FOR THE QUEEN.
HIRED FRIENDS.
WHO YOU COULD HAVE EXECUTED.
ALL LADIES WERE EXPECTED TO BE AT LEAST PASSABLE AMATEUR MUSICIANS, BOTH SINGING AND PLAYING INSTRUMENTS LIKE THE LUTE, RECORDER, OR VIRGINALS (A SORT OF EARLY PIANO).
LADIES HAD TO BE ABLE TO MAKE POLITE CONVERSATION, NOT ONLY TO ENTERTAIN THE QUEEN, BUT TO IMPRESS VISITING DIGNITARIES AS WELL.
HOW FASCINATING, LORD VISCOUNT. DO GO ON...
LADIES ACCOMPANIED THE QUEEN ON OPEN-AIR ACTIVITIES LIKE HUNTING OR ARCHERY.
BULLSEYE, YOUR MAJESTY!
SPORTS LIKE THE NEWLY INVENTED TENNIS WERE NOT CONSIDERED LADYLIKE, BUT LAWN BOWLS AND MARBLES WERE BOTH POPULAR.
OOH! GOOD SHOT, YOUR MAJESTY!

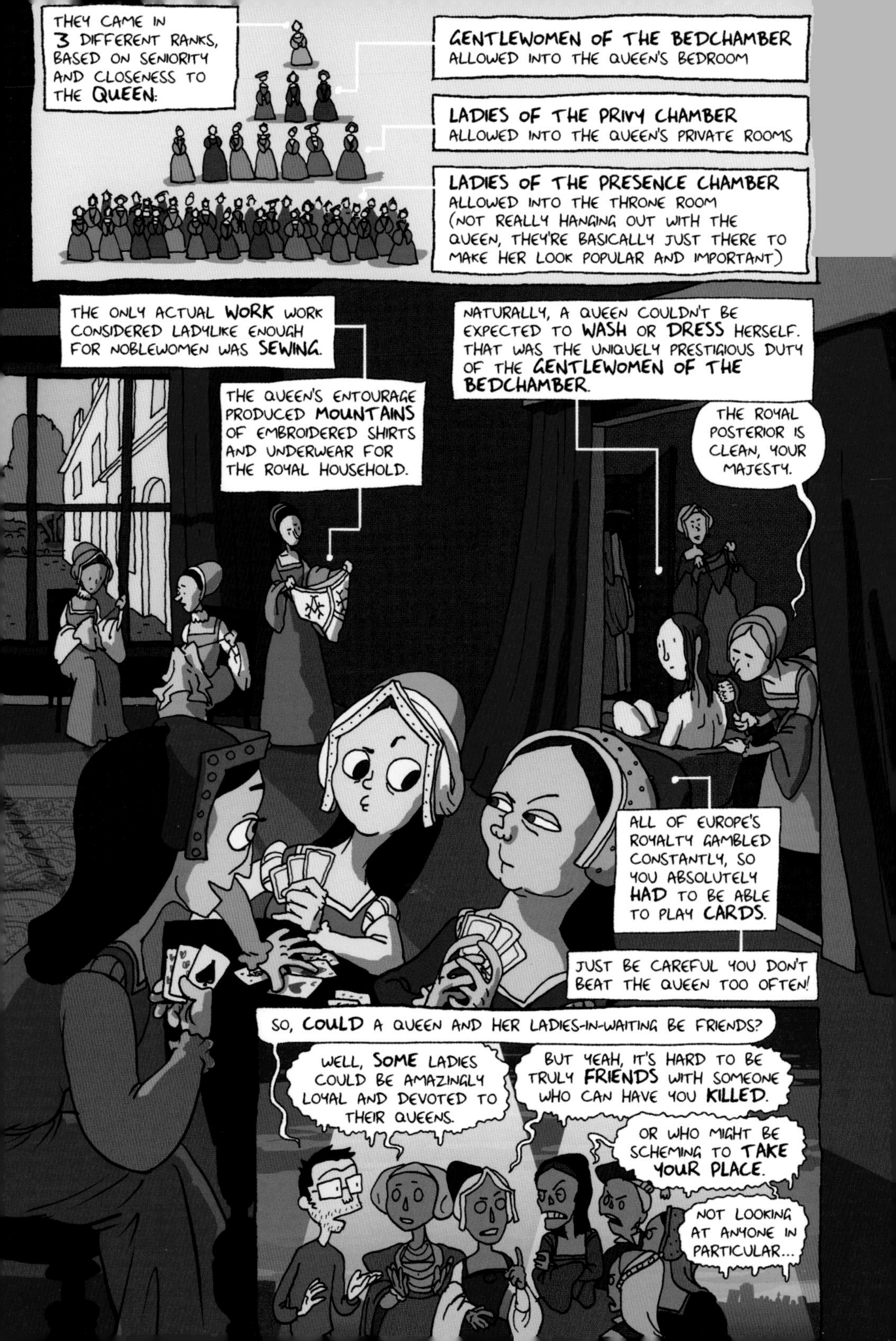
THEY CAME IN 3 DIFFERENT RANKS, BASED ON SENIORITY AND CLOSENESS TO THE QUEEN:
GENTLEWOMEN OF THE BEDCHAMBER
ALLOWED INTO THE QUEEN'S BEDROOM
LADIES OF THE PRIVY CHAMBER
ALLOWED INTO THE QUEEN'S PRIVATE ROOMS
LADIES OF THE PRESENCE CHAMBER
ALLOWED INTO THE THRONE ROOM (NOT REALLY HANGING OUT WITH THE QUEEN, THEY'RE BASICALLY JUST THERE TO MAKE HER LOOK POPULAR AND IMPORTANT)
THE ONLY ACTUAL WORK WORK CONSIDERED LADYLIKE ENOUGH FOR NOBLEWOMEN WAS SEWING.
THE QUEEN'S ENTOURAGE PRODUCED MOUNTAINS OF EMBROIDERED SHIRTS AND UNDERWEAR FOR THE ROYAL HOUSEHOLD.
NATURALLY, A QUEEN COULDN'T BE EXPECTED TO WASH OR DRESS HERSELF. THAT WAS THE UNIQUELY PRESTIGIOUS DUTY OF THE GENTLEWOMEN OF THE BEDCHAMBER.
THE ROYAL POSTERIOR IS CLEAN, YOUR MAJESTY.
ALL OF EUROPE'S ROYALTY GAMBLED CONSTANTLY, SO YOU ABSOLUTELY HAD TO BE ABLE TO PLAY CARDS.
JUST BE CAREFUL YOU DON'T BEAT THE QUEEN TOO OFTEN!
SO, COULD A QUEEN AND HER LADIES-IN-WAITING BE FRIENDS?
WELL, SOME LADIES COULD BE AMAZINGLY LOYAL AND DEVOTED TO THEIR QUEENS.
BUT YEAH, IT'S HARD TO BE TRULY FRIENDS WITH SOMEONE WHO CAN HAVE YOU KILLED.
OR WHO MIGHT BE SCHEMING TO TAKE YOUR PLACE.
NOT LOOKING AT ANYONE IN PARTICULAR...

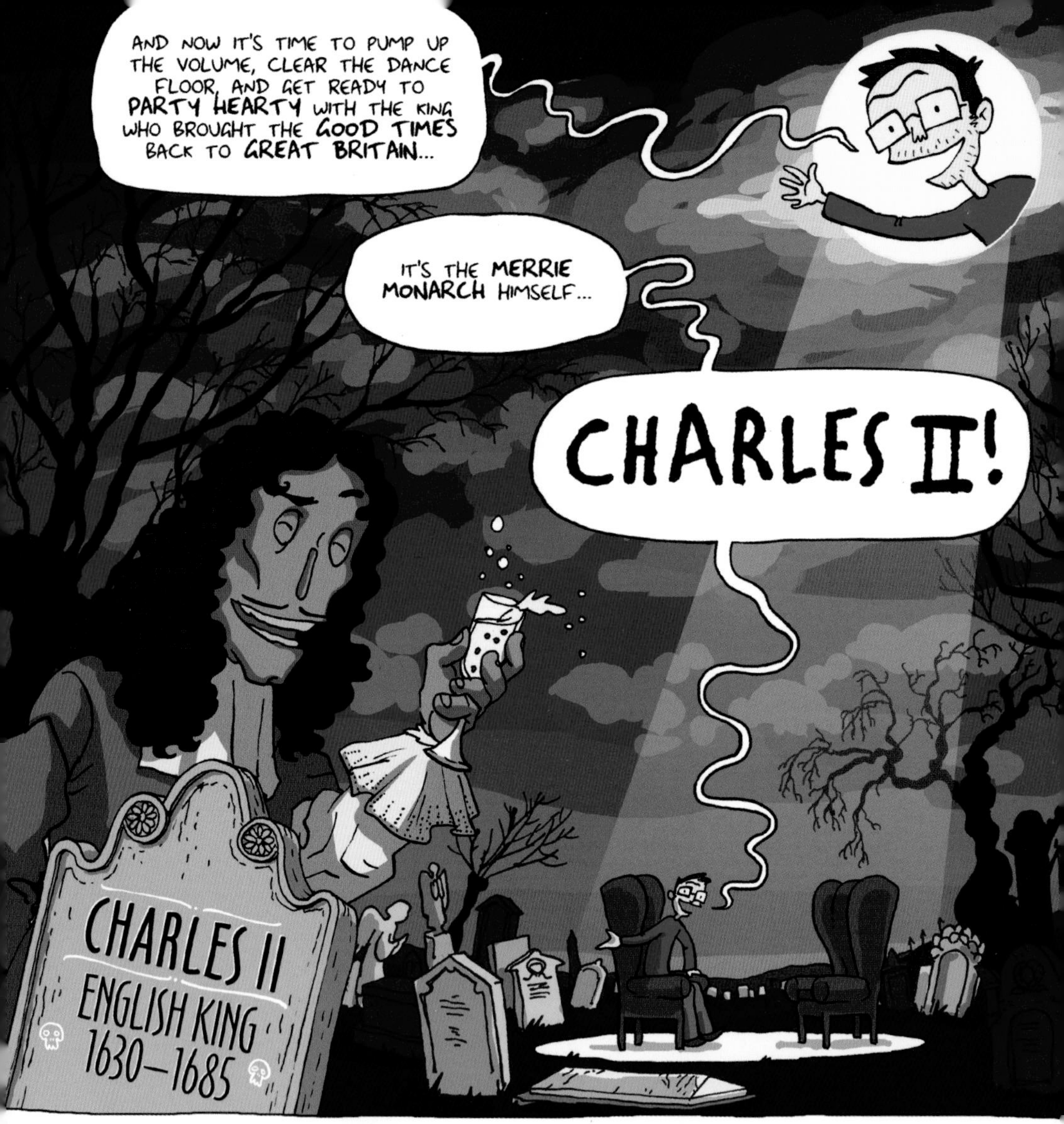
AND NOW IT'S TIME TO PUMP UP THE VOLUME, CLEAR THE DANCE FLOOR, AND GET READY TO PARTY HEARTY WITH THE KING WHO BROUGHT THE GOOD TIMES BACK TO GREAT BRITAIN...
IT'S THE MERRIE MONARCH HIMSELF...
CHARLES II!
CHARLES II
ENGLISH KING
1630–1685

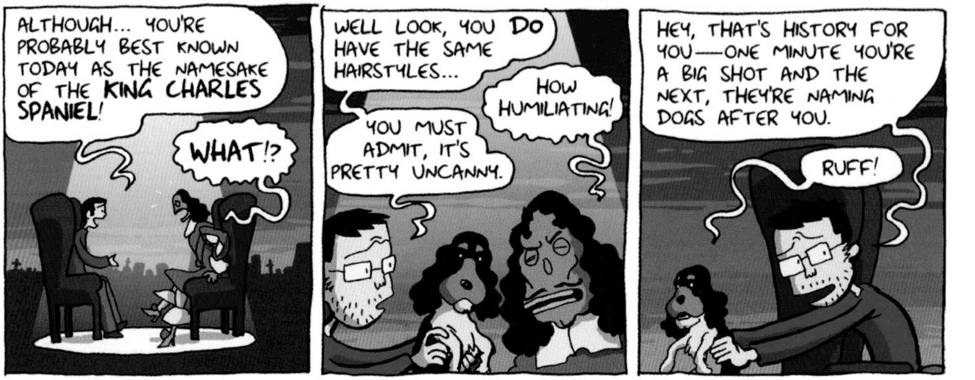
ALTHOUGH... YOU'RE PROBABLY BEST KNOWN TODAY AS THE NAMESAKE OF THE KING CHARLES SPANIEL!
WHAT!?
WELL LOOK, YOU DO HAVE THE SAME HAIRSTYLES...
YOU MUST ADMIT, IT'S PRETTY UNCANNY.
HOW HUMILIATING!
HEY, THAT'S HISTORY FOR YOU—ONE MINUTE YOU'RE A BIG SHOT AND THE NEXT, THEY'RE NAMING DOGS AFTER YOU.
RUFF!

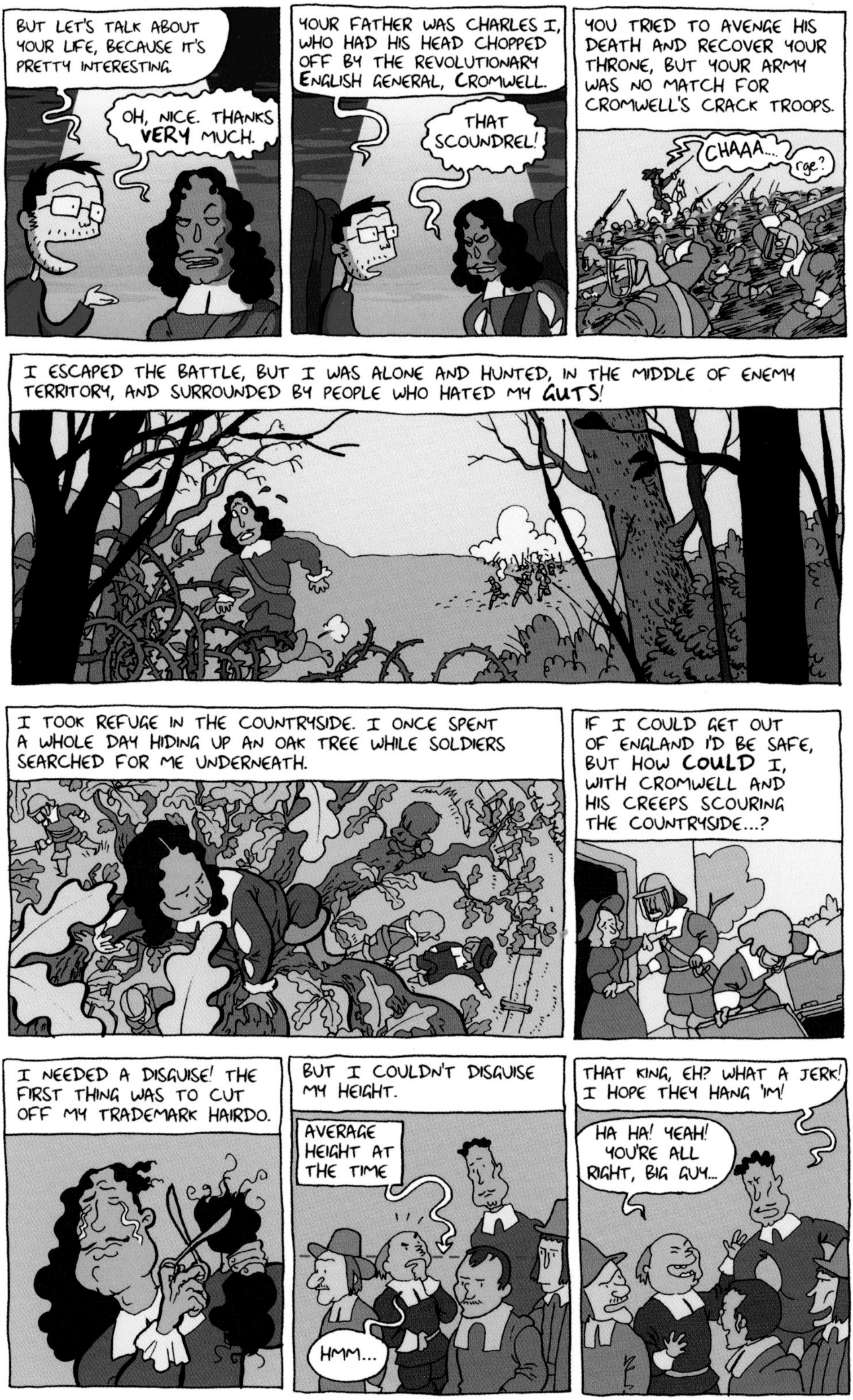

BUT LET'S TALK ABOUT YOUR LIFE, BECAUSE IT'S PRETTY INTERESTING.
OH, NICE. THANKS VERY MUCH.
YOUR FATHER WAS CHARLES I, WHO HAD HIS HEAD CHOPPED OFF BY THE REVOLUTIONARY ENGLISH GENERAL, CROMWELL.
THAT SCOUNDREL!
YOU TRIED TO AVENGE HIS DEATH AND RECOVER YOUR THRONE, BUT YOUR ARMY WAS NO MATCH FOR CROMWELL'S CRACK TROOPS.
CHAAA...
rge?
I ESCAPED THE BATTLE, BUT I WAS ALONE AND HUNTED, IN THE MIDDLE OF ENEMY TERRITORY, AND SURROUNDED BY PEOPLE WHO HATED MY GUTS!
I TOOK REFUGE IN THE COUNTRYSIDE. I ONCE SPENT A WHOLE DAY HIDING UP AN OAK TREE WHILE SOLDIERS SEARCHED FOR ME UNDERNEATH.
IF I COULD GET OUT OF ENGLAND I'D BE SAFE, BUT HOW COULD I, WITH CROMWELL AND HIS CREEPS SCOURING THE COUNTRYSIDE...?
I NEEDED A DISGUISE! THE FIRST THING WAS TO CUT OFF MY TRADEMARK HAIRDO.
BUT I COULDN'T DISGUISE MY HEIGHT.
AVERAGE HEIGHT AT THE TIME
HMM...
THAT KING, EH? WHAT A JERK! I HOPE THEY HANG 'IM!
HA HA! YEAH! YOU'RE ALL RIGHT, BIG GUY...

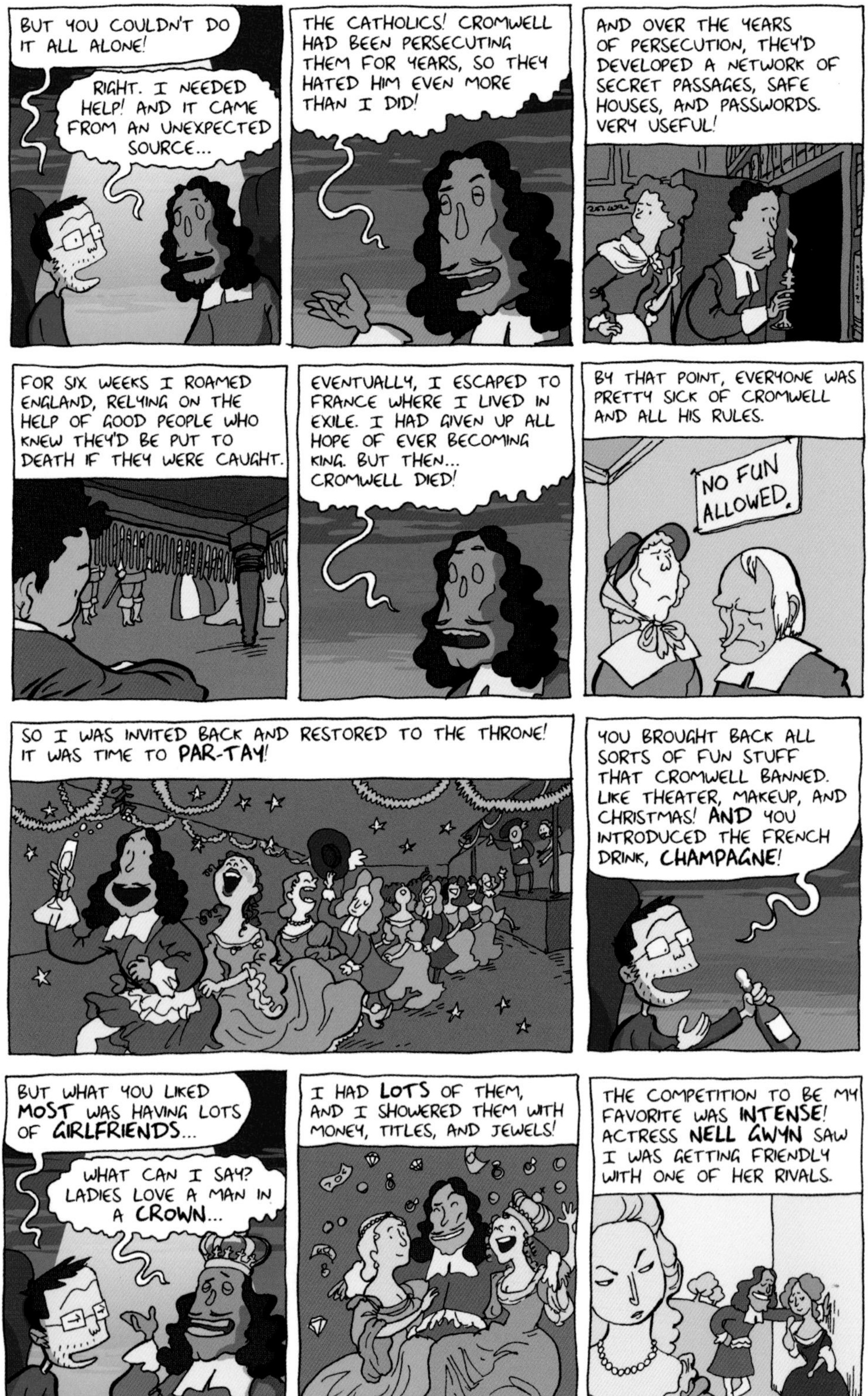
BUT YOU COULDN'T DO IT ALL ALONE!
RIGHT. I NEEDED HELP! AND IT CAME FROM AN UNEXPECTED SOURCE...
THE CATHOLICS! CROMWELL HAD BEEN PERSECUTING THEM FOR YEARS, SO THEY HATED HIM EVEN MORE THAN I DID!
AND OVER THE YEARS OF PERSECUTION, THEY'D DEVELOPED A NETWORK OF SECRET PASSAGES, SAFE HOUSES, AND PASSWORDS. VERY USEFUL!
FOR SIX WEEKS I ROAMED ENGLAND, RELYING ON THE HELP OF GOOD PEOPLE WHO KNEW THEY'D BE PUT TO DEATH IF THEY WERE CAUGHT.
EVENTUALLY, I ESCAPED TO FRANCE WHERE I LIVED IN EXILE. I HAD GIVEN UP ALL HOPE OF EVER BECOMING KING. BUT THEN... CROMWELL DIED!
BY THAT POINT, EVERYONE WAS PRETTY SICK OF CROMWELL AND ALL HIS RULES.
NO FUN ALLOWED.
SO I WAS INVITED BACK AND RESTORED TO THE THRONE! IT WAS TIME TO PAR-TAY!
YOU BROUGHT BACK ALL SORTS OF FUN STUFF THAT CROMWELL BANNED. LIKE THEATER, MAKEUP, AND CHRISTMAS! AND YOU INTRODUCED THE FRENCH DRINK, CHAMPAGNE!
BUT WHAT YOU LIKED MOST WAS HAVING LOTS OF GIRLFRIENDS...
WHAT CAN I SAY? LADIES LOVE A MAN IN A CROWN...
I HAD LOTS OF THEM, AND I SHOWERED THEM WITH MONEY, TITLES, AND JEWELS!
THE COMPETITION TO BE MY FAVORITE WAS INTENSE! ACTRESS NELL GWYN SAW I WAS GETTING FRIENDLY WITH ONE OF HER RIVALS.

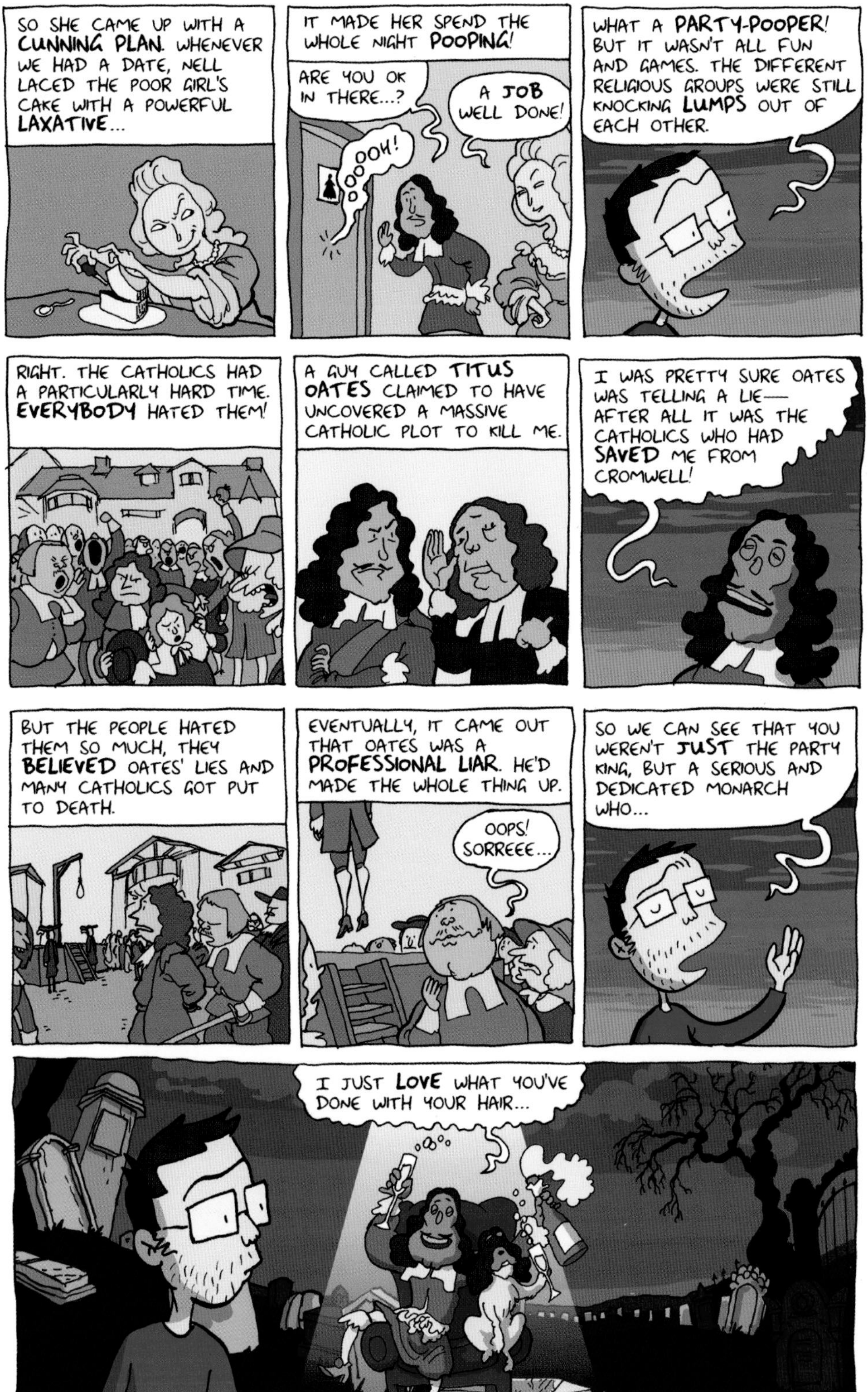
SO SHE CAME UP WITH A CUNNING PLAN. WHENEVER WE HAD A DATE, NELL LACED THE POOR GIRL'S CAKE WITH A POWERFUL LAXATIVE...
IT MADE HER SPEND THE WHOLE NIGHT POOPING!
ARE YOU OK IN THERE...?
OOOH!
A JOB WELL DONE!
WHAT A PARTY-POOPER! BUT IT WASN'T ALL FUN AND GAMES. THE DIFFERENT RELIGIOUS GROUPS WERE STILL KNOCKING LUMPS OUT OF EACH OTHER.
RIGHT. THE CATHOLICS HAD A PARTICULARLY HARD TIME. EVERYBODY HATED THEM!
A GUY CALLED TITUS OATES CLAIMED TO HAVE UNCOVERED A MASSIVE CATHOLIC PLOT TO KILL ME.
I WAS PRETTY SURE OATES WAS TELLING A LIE— AFTER ALL IT WAS THE CATHOLICS WHO HAD SAVED ME FROM CROMWELL!
BUT THE PEOPLE HATED THEM SO MUCH, THEY BELIEVED OATES' LIES AND MANY CATHOLICS GOT PUT TO DEATH.
EVENTUALLY, IT CAME OUT THAT OATES WAS A PROFESSIONAL LIAR. HE'D MADE THE WHOLE THING UP.
OOPS! SORREEE...
SO WE CAN SEE THAT YOU WEREN'T JUST THE PARTY KING, BUT A SERIOUS AND DEDICATED MONARCH WHO...
I JUST LOVE WHAT YOU'VE DONE WITH YOUR HAIR...

A MEMOIR ON MONARCHY

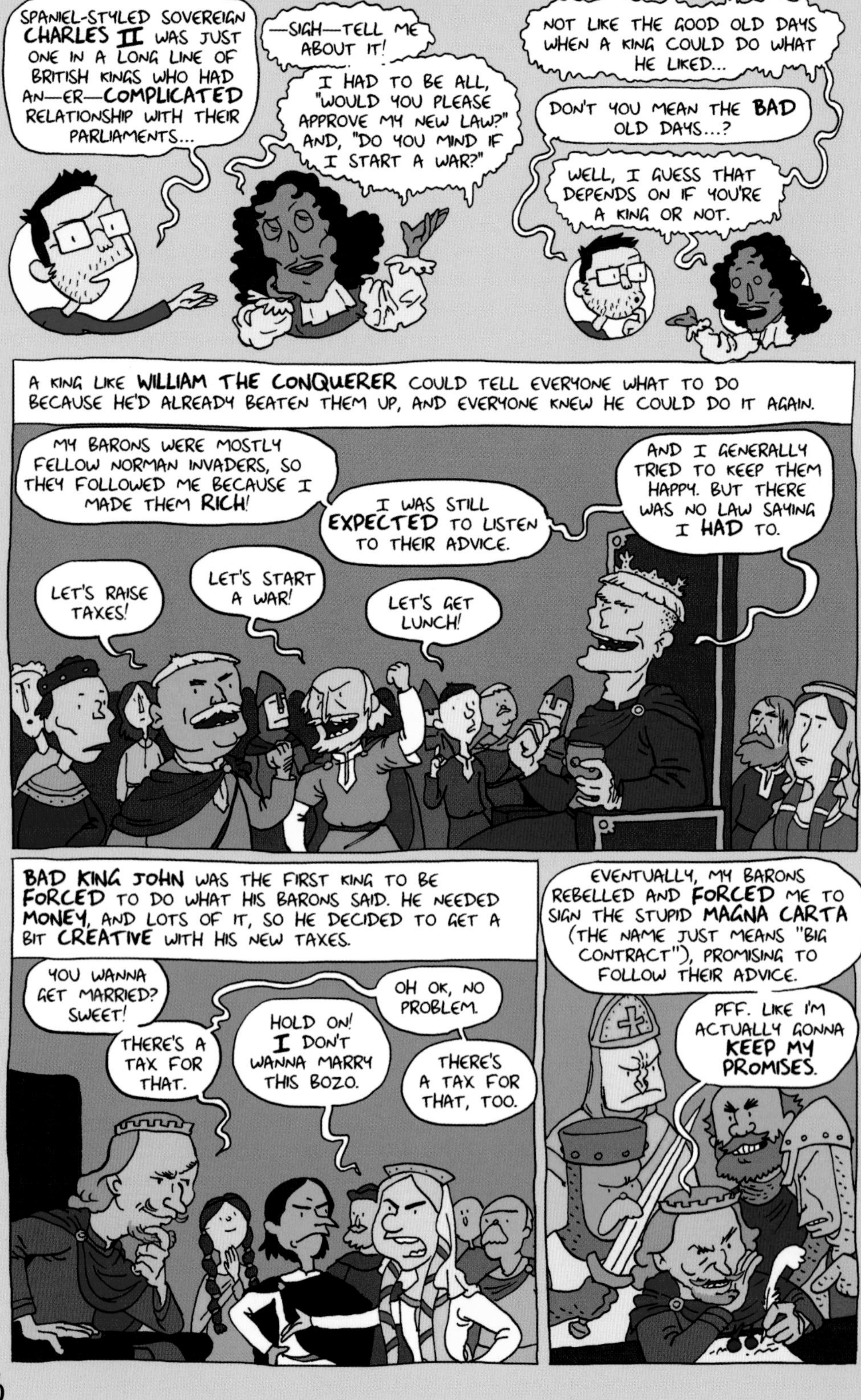

SPANIEL-STYLED SOVEREIGN CHARLES II WAS JUST ONE IN A LONG LINE OF BRITISH KINGS WHO HAD AN—ER—COMPLICATED RELATIONSHIP WITH THEIR PARLIAMENTS...
—SIGH—TELL ME ABOUT IT!
I HAD TO BE ALL, "WOULD YOU PLEASE APPROVE MY NEW LAW?" AND, "DO YOU MIND IF I START A WAR?"
NOT LIKE THE GOOD OLD DAYS WHEN A KING COULD DO WHAT HE LIKED...
DON'T YOU MEAN THE BAD OLD DAYS...?
WELL, I GUESS THAT DEPENDS ON IF YOU'RE A KING OR NOT.
A KING LIKE WILLIAM THE CONQUERER COULD TELL EVERYONE WHAT TO DO BECAUSE HE'D ALREADY BEATEN THEM UP, AND EVERYONE KNEW HE COULD DO IT AGAIN.
MY BARONS WERE MOSTLY FELLOW NORMAN INVADERS, SO THEY FOLLOWED ME BECAUSE I MADE THEM RICH!
I WAS STILL EXPECTED TO LISTEN TO THEIR ADVICE.
AND I GENERALLY TRIED TO KEEP THEM HAPPY. BUT THERE WAS NO LAW SAYING I HAD TO.
LET'S RAISE TAXES!
LET'S START A WAR!
LET'S GET LUNCH!
BAD KING JOHN WAS THE FIRST KING TO BE FORCED TO DO WHAT HIS BARONS SAID. HE NEEDED MONEY, AND LOTS OF IT, SO HE DECIDED TO GET A BIT CREATIVE WITH HIS NEW TAXES.
YOU WANNA GET MARRIED? SWEET!
THERE'S A TAX FOR THAT.
HOLD ON! I DON'T WANNA MARRY THIS BOZO.
OH OK, NO PROBLEM.
THERE'S A TAX FOR THAT, TOO.
EVENTUALLY, MY BARONS REBELLED AND FORCED ME TO SIGN THE STUPID MAGNA CARTA (THE NAME JUST MEANS "BIG CONTRACT"), PROMISING TO FOLLOW THEIR ADVICE.
PFF. LIKE I'M ACTUALLY GONNA KEEP MY PROMISES.

JOHN'S SON **HENRY III** CARRIED ON THE FAMILY TRADITION OF CHEESING OFF THE BARONS, THIS TIME BY GIVING ALL THE CUSHY JOBS TO HIS BUDDIES. HE ACTUALLY GOT CAPTURED AND REPLACED FOR A WHILE BY REBEL BARON **SIMON DE MONTFORT**.

THE KING SHOULD RULE FOR THE GOOD OF **ALL**, NOT JUST HIS FAVORITES!

YOU WERE HAPPY ENOUGH WHEN **YOU** WERE THE ONE GETTING THE FAVORS...

I WAS ALSO THE FIRST RULER TO INCLUDE **COMMONERS** IN MY PARLIAMENT.

SEE? I'M A MAN OF THE PEOPLE!

NOT AT ALL AN ILLEGAL USURPER DRUNK ON POWER, NO SIRREE!

BY THE TIME OF **HENRY VIII**, IT WAS STANDARD PRACTICE FOR THE KING TO CALL A PARLIAMENT OF BOTH LORDS **AND** COMMONS WHEN HE WANTED TO CHANGE A LAW.

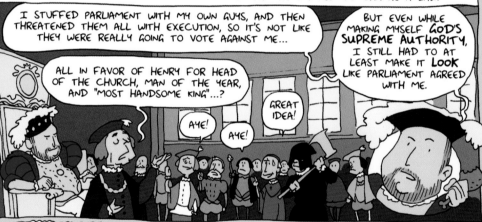

I STUFFED PARLIAMENT WITH MY OWN GUYS, AND THEN THREATENED THEM ALL WITH EXECUTION, SO IT'S NOT LIKE THEY WERE REALLY GOING TO VOTE AGAINST ME...

BUT EVEN WHILE MAKING MYSELF **GOD'S SUPREME AUTHORITY**, I STILL HAD TO AT LEAST MAKE IT **LOOK** LIKE PARLIAMENT AGREED WITH ME.

ALL IN FAVOR OF HENRY FOR HEAD OF THE CHURCH, MAN OF THE YEAR, AND "MOST HANDSOME KING"...?

AYE!

AYE!

GREAT IDEA!

OK, SO, HENRY ALWAYS HAD A BIT OF AN EGO PROBLEM.

BUT THIS THING ABOUT MAKING HIM THE HEAD OF THE CHURCH WAS JUST ONE PART OF A MASSIVE RELIGIOUS MOVEMENT SWEEPING EUROPE...

THE **PROTESTANT REFORMATION**.

HENRY'S NEW CHURCH STILL LOOKED A LOT LIKE THE OLD ONE, JUST WITH **HIM** AT THE TOP INSTEAD OF THE POPE.

BUT OTHER, MORE RADICAL CHURCHES ARGUED THAT ALL PEOPLE ARE EQUAL BEFORE GOD.

AND FROM THERE IT WAS A SHORT STEP TO ARGUING THAT PEOPLE SHOULD HAVE AN EQUAL SAY IN HOW THINGS ARE RUN.

THESE TWO IDEAS BECAME MORE AND MORE EXTREME UNTIL THEY CAME TO A HEAD IN THE REIGN OF MY DAD, **CHARLES I**...

I'M APPOINTED BY **GOD**!

YOU ALL HAVE TO DO WHAT I SAY!

CHARLES AND HIS PARLIAMENT ENDED UP FIGHTING THE **ENGLISH CIVIL WAR** OVER WHO GOT THE FINAL SAY IN RUNNING THE COUNTRY.

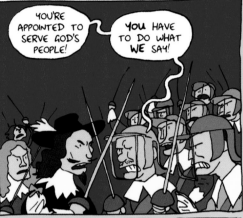

YOU'RE APPOINTED TO SERVE GOD'S PEOPLE!

YOU HAVE TO DO WHAT **WE** SAY!

BUT EVEN AFTER LOSING, CHARLES I KEPT INSISTING HE COULD DO WHATEVER HE LIKED, SO IN THE END THEY **EXECUTED** HIM.

I'M STILL RIGHT, YOU KNOW...

THE HEAD OF PARLIAMENT'S REBEL ARMY, **OLIVER CROMWELL**, TOOK OVER AND BECAME **ROYAL PROTECTOR**.

NO CROWN.

JUST RAW, NAKED POWER PLEASE.

AND THAT COULD'VE BEEN THAT. NO MORE KINGS, JUST A PURITANICAL, RELIGIOUSLY INSPIRED **DICTATORSHIP**.

BUT IT DIDN'T TAKE LONG FOR EVERYONE TO GET PRETTY SICK OF PURITANS LIKE CROMWELL, SINCE THEY BASICALLY BANNED EVERYTHING **FUN**.

NO PARTIES

NO THEATER

NO ENJOYING YOURSELF

SO WHAT **CAN WE** DO?

READ THE BIBLE.

HERE YOU GO.

AND THEN AFTER CROMWELL DIED, HIS SON DIDN'T REALLY WANT THE JOB.

SO THEY ASKED **ME** TO COME BACK!

YAY! CHAMPAGNE AND PARDONS FOR EVERYONE!

THE PEOPLE WHO WANTED A KING LIKED ME BECAUSE, HEY, I WAS A KING.

AND THE PEOPLE WHO WANTED PARLIAMENT RUNNING THINGS LIKED ME BECAUSE I MOSTLY LET THEM RUN THINGS.

BUT MY BROTHER **JAMES II** WAS MUCH MORE INTO THE WHOLE I-CAN-DO-WHAT-I-LIKE THING, SO WHEN HE TOOK OVER, IT WAS THE SAME THING ALL OVER AGAIN.

MAY I REMIND YOU THAT I'M APPOINTED BY GOD...

THIS **AGAIN**...?

WHAT IS **WITH** THESE GUYS!?

THAT WHOLE KILLING-THE-KING THING HAD LEFT A BAD TASTE IN EVERYONE'S MOUTHS, SO THEY JUST CHASED HIM OUT OF THE COUNTRY, AND INVITED HIS DAUGHTER **MARY**, ALONG WITH HER HUSBAND, THE JUICILY NAMED DUTCH PRINCE **WILLIAM OF ORANGE**, TO TAKE OVER.

SO, LOOK, THIS TIME, YOU **REALLY** HAVE TO DO WHAT WE SAY.

THEY AGREED TO RULE TOGETHER, IN RETURN FOR SIGNING THE **BILL OF RIGHTS**, BASICALLY PROMISING TO LET PARLIAMENT RUN THE COUNTRY ON THEIR BEHALF.

Free Elections.

Regular Parliaments.

Parliament Makes all the Laws.

No Killing People for Being Mean about the Royal Family.

AND THAT'S STILL ROUGHLY THE SYSTEM WE HAVE TODAY.

TECHNICALLY THE **HEAD OF STATE**...

Monarch

BUT PRACTICALLY SPEAKING DOES WHAT PARLIAMENT SAYS.

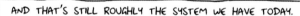

House of Commons

House of Lords

VOTES ON NEW LAWS AND RUNS THE COUNTRY.

MEMBERS ARE VOTED FOR IN GENERAL ELECTIONS.

REVIEWS NEW LAWS FROM THE COMMONS.

THESE DAYS, MOST LORDS ARE **APPOINTED** BY THE PRIME MINISTER.

—SIGH—

SO GONE ARE THE DAY OF "OFF WITH THEIR HEADS!" OR "LET'S ALL INVADE FRANCE!"

STILL, I GUESS IT LEAVES MORE TIME FOR PARTYING...

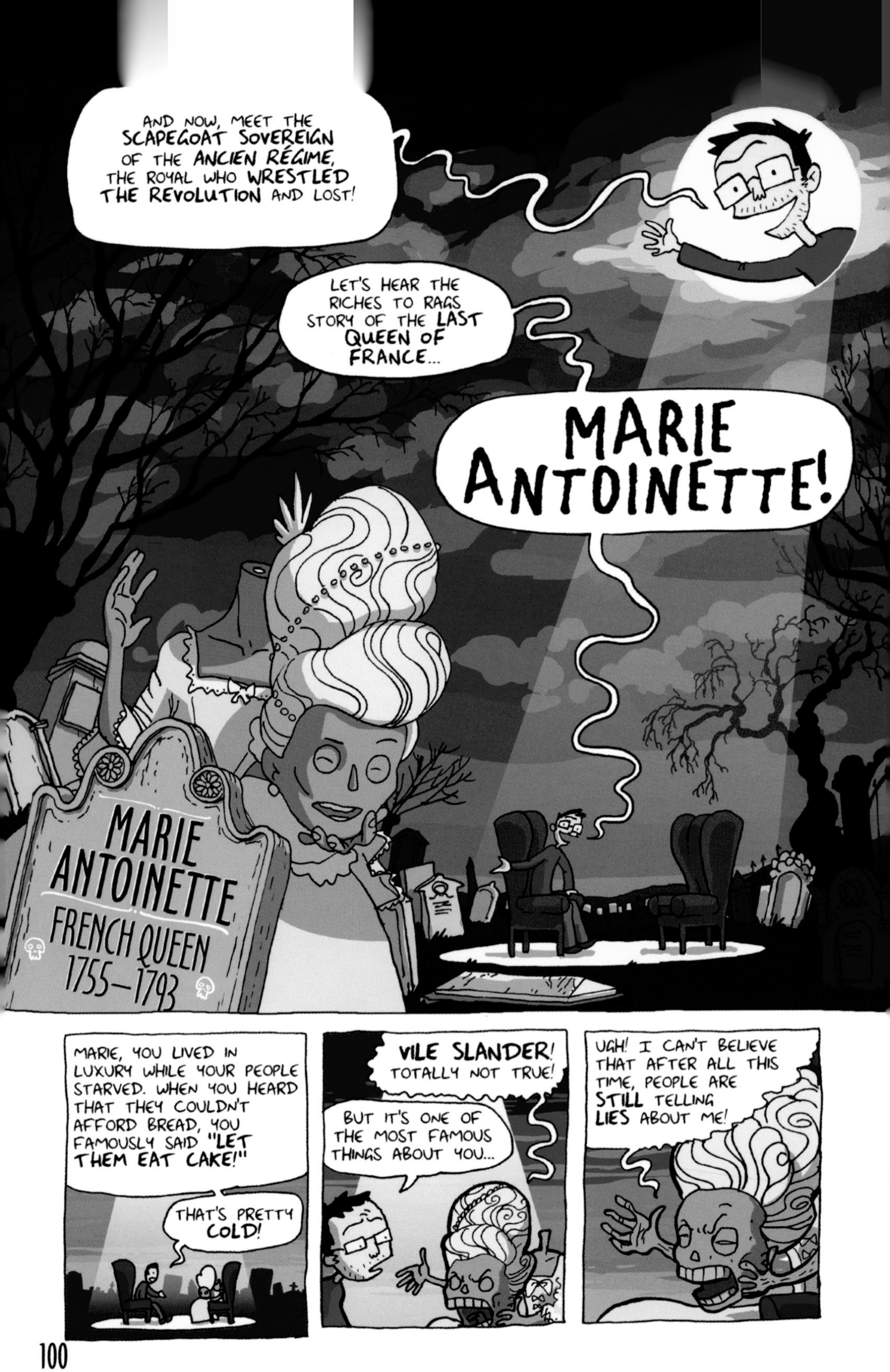
AND NOW, MEET THE SCAPEGOAT SOVEREIGN OF THE ANCIEN RÉGIME, THE ROYAL WHO WRESTLED THE REVOLUTION AND LOST!
LET'S HEAR THE RICHES TO RAGS STORY OF THE LAST QUEEN OF FRANCE...
MARIE ANTOINETTE!
MARIE ANTOINETTE
FRENCH QUEEN
1755–1793
MARIE, YOU LIVED IN LUXURY WHILE YOUR PEOPLE STARVED. WHEN YOU HEARD THAT THEY COULDN'T AFFORD BREAD, YOU FAMOUSLY SAID "LET THEM EAT CAKE!"
THAT'S PRETTY COLD!
VILE SLANDER! TOTALLY NOT TRUE!
BUT IT'S ONE OF THE MOST FAMOUS THINGS ABOUT YOU...
UGH! I CAN'T BELIEVE THAT AFTER ALL THIS TIME, PEOPLE ARE STILL TELLING LIES ABOUT ME!

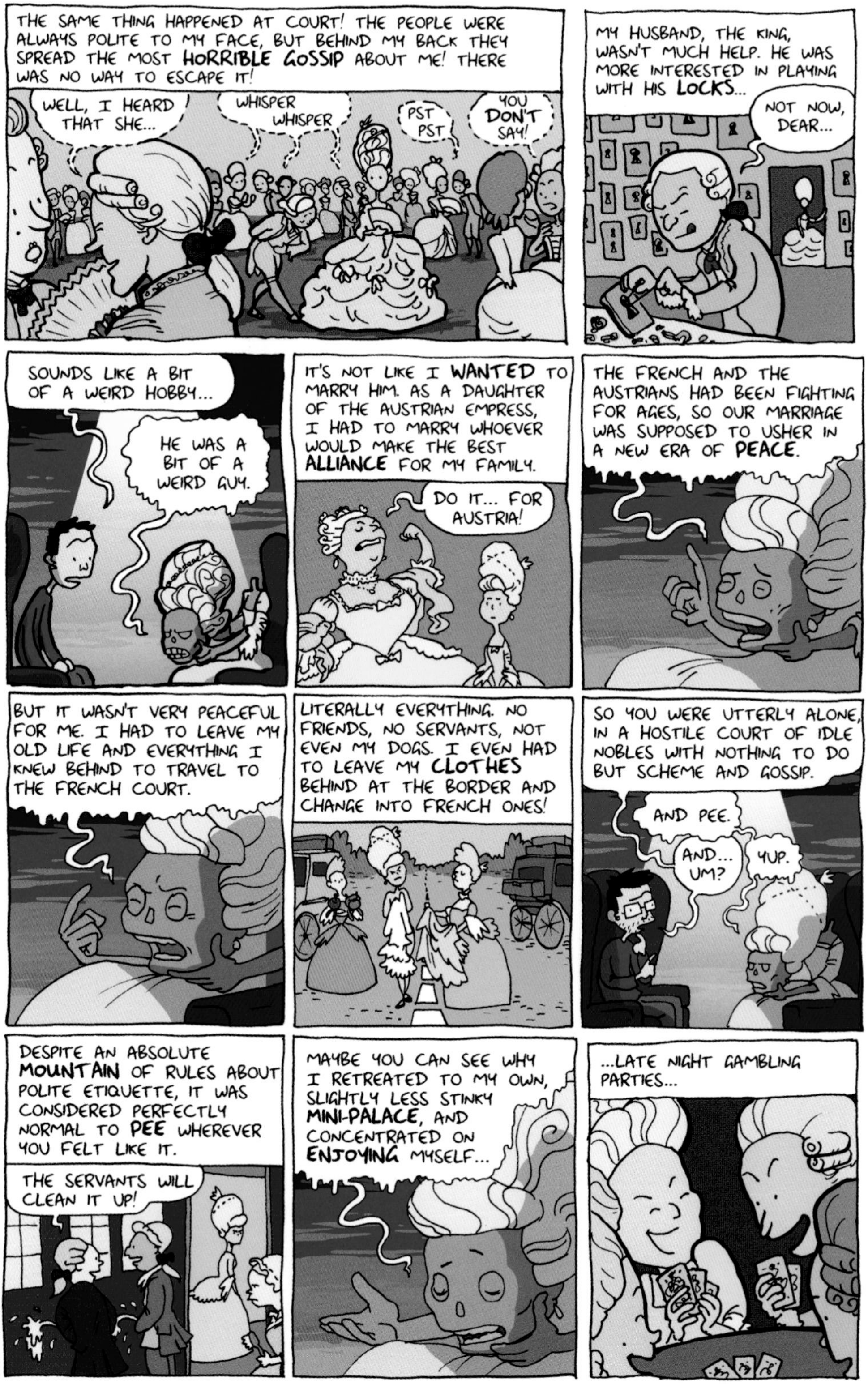
THE SAME THING HAPPENED AT COURT! THE PEOPLE WERE ALWAYS POLITE TO MY FACE, BUT BEHIND MY BACK THEY SPREAD THE MOST HORRIBLE GOSSIP ABOUT ME! THERE WAS NO WAY TO ESCAPE IT!
WELL, I HEARD THAT SHE...
WHISPER WHISPER
PST PST
YOU DON'T SAY!
MY HUSBAND, THE KING, WASN'T MUCH HELP. HE WAS MORE INTERESTED IN PLAYING WITH HIS LOCKS...
NOT NOW, DEAR...
SOUNDS LIKE A BIT OF A WEIRD HOBBY...
HE WAS A BIT OF A WEIRD GUY.
IT'S NOT LIKE I WANTED TO MARRY HIM. AS A DAUGHTER OF THE AUSTRIAN EMPRESS, I HAD TO MARRY WHOEVER WOULD MAKE THE BEST ALLIANCE FOR MY FAMILY.
DO IT... FOR AUSTRIA!
THE FRENCH AND THE AUSTRIANS HAD BEEN FIGHTING FOR AGES, SO OUR MARRIAGE WAS SUPPOSED TO USHER IN A NEW ERA OF PEACE.
BUT IT WASN'T VERY PEACEFUL FOR ME. I HAD TO LEAVE MY OLD LIFE AND EVERYTHING I KNEW BEHIND TO TRAVEL TO THE FRENCH COURT.
LITERALLY EVERYTHING. NO FRIENDS, NO SERVANTS, NOT EVEN MY DOGS. I EVEN HAD TO LEAVE MY CLOTHES BEHIND AT THE BORDER AND CHANGE INTO FRENCH ONES!
SO YOU WERE UTTERLY ALONE, IN A HOSTILE COURT OF IDLE NOBLES WITH NOTHING TO DO BUT SCHEME AND GOSSIP.
AND PEE.
AND... UM?
YUP.
DESPITE AN ABSOLUTE MOUNTAIN OF RULES ABOUT POLITE ETIQUETTE, IT WAS CONSIDERED PERFECTLY NORMAL TO PEE WHEREVER YOU FELT LIKE IT.
THE SERVANTS WILL CLEAN IT UP!
MAYBE YOU CAN SEE WHY I RETREATED TO MY OWN, SLIGHTLY LESS STINKY MINI-PALACE, AND CONCENTRATED ON ENJOYING MYSELF...
...LATE NIGHT GAMBLING PARTIES...

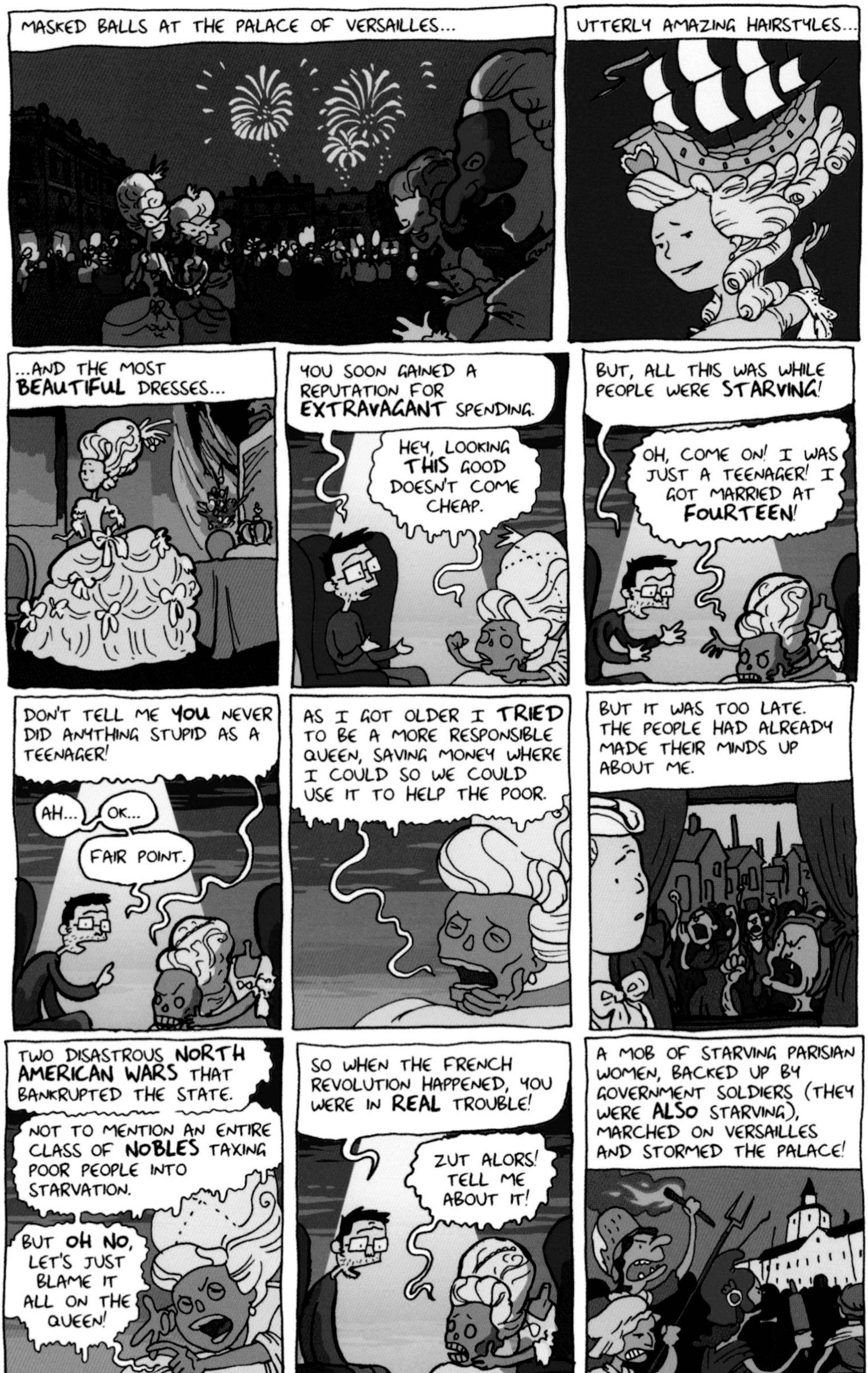
MASKED BALLS AT THE PALACE OF VERSAILLES...
UTTERLY AMAZING HAIRSTYLES...
...AND THE MOST BEAUTIFUL DRESSES...
YOU SOON GAINED A REPUTATION FOR EXTRAVAGANT SPENDING.
HEY, LOOKING THIS GOOD DOESN'T COME CHEAP.
BUT, ALL THIS WAS WHILE PEOPLE WERE STARVING!
OH, COME ON! I WAS JUST A TEENAGER! I GOT MARRIED AT FOURTEEN!
DON'T TELL ME YOU NEVER DID ANYTHING STUPID AS A TEENAGER!
AH...
OK...
FAIR POINT.
AS I GOT OLDER I TRIED TO BE A MORE RESPONSIBLE QUEEN, SAVING MONEY WHERE I COULD SO WE COULD USE IT TO HELP THE POOR.
BUT IT WAS TOO LATE. THE PEOPLE HAD ALREADY MADE THEIR MINDS UP ABOUT ME.
TWO DISASTROUS NORTH AMERICAN WARS THAT BANKRUPTED THE STATE.
NOT TO MENTION AN ENTIRE CLASS OF NOBLES TAXING POOR PEOPLE INTO STARVATION.
BUT OH NO, LET'S JUST BLAME IT ALL ON THE QUEEN!
SO WHEN THE FRENCH REVOLUTION HAPPENED, YOU WERE IN REAL TROUBLE!
ZUT ALORS! TELL ME ABOUT IT!
A MOB OF STARVING PARISIAN WOMEN, BACKED UP BY GOVERNMENT SOLDIERS (THEY WERE ALSO STARVING), MARCHED ON VERSAILLES AND STORMED THE PALACE!

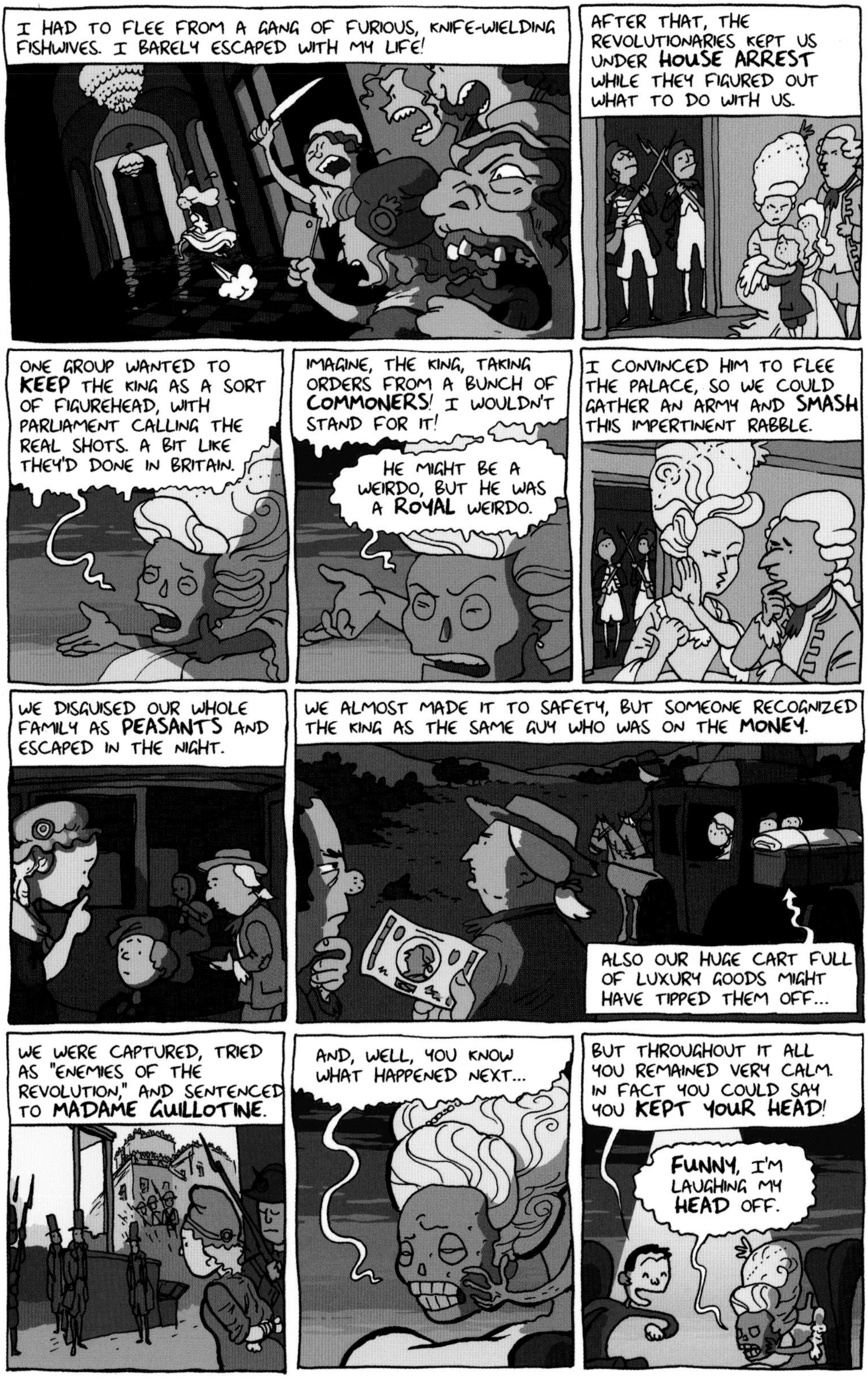
I HAD TO FLEE FROM A GANG OF FURIOUS, KNIFE-WIELDING FISHWIVES. I BARELY ESCAPED WITH MY LIFE!
AFTER THAT, THE REVOLUTIONARIES KEPT US UNDER HOUSE ARREST WHILE THEY FIGURED OUT WHAT TO DO WITH US.
ONE GROUP WANTED TO KEEP THE KING AS A SORT OF FIGUREHEAD, WITH PARLIAMENT CALLING THE REAL SHOTS. A BIT LIKE THEY'D DONE IN BRITAIN.
IMAGINE, THE KING, TAKING ORDERS FROM A BUNCH OF COMMONERS! I WOULDN'T STAND FOR IT!
HE MIGHT BE A WEIRDO, BUT HE WAS A ROYAL WEIRDO.
I CONVINCED HIM TO FLEE THE PALACE, SO WE COULD GATHER AN ARMY AND SMASH THIS IMPERTINENT RABBLE.
WE DISGUISED OUR WHOLE FAMILY AS PEASANTS AND ESCAPED IN THE NIGHT.
WE ALMOST MADE IT TO SAFETY, BUT SOMEONE RECOGNIZED THE KING AS THE SAME GUY WHO WAS ON THE MONEY.
ALSO OUR HUGE CART FULL OF LUXURY GOODS MIGHT HAVE TIPPED THEM OFF...
WE WERE CAPTURED, TRIED AS "ENEMIES OF THE REVOLUTION," AND SENTENCED TO MADAME GUILLOTINE.
AND, WELL, YOU KNOW WHAT HAPPENED NEXT...
BUT THROUGHOUT IT ALL YOU REMAINED VERY CALM. IN FACT YOU COULD SAY YOU KEPT YOUR HEAD!
FUNNY, I'M LAUGHING MY HEAD OFF.

DECAPITATION STATIONS

TEEN QUEEN **MARIE ANTOINETTE** LOST HER HEAD TO THAT QUINTESSENTIAL SYMBOL OF THE FRENCH REVOLUTION: THE **GUILLOTINE.**

UGH. DON'T REMIND ME.

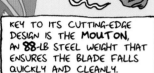

NAMED AFTER THE REVOLUTIONARY WHO FIRST PROPOSED IT: **DR JOSEPH-IGNACE GUILLOTIN.**

PERSONALLY, I THOUGHT **ANY** FORM OF THE DEATH PENALTY WAS **CRUEL.**

BUT, I ARGUED, IF WE **ARE** GOING TO KILL PEOPLE, LET'S AT LEAST MAKE IT AS **HUMANE** AS POSSIBLE.

THE GUILLOTINE WAS **SCIENTIFICALLY DESIGNED** TO BE QUICK, PAINLESS, AND OFFER AN **EQUAL-RIGHTS EXECUTION** TO ALL CITIZENS.

KEY TO ITS CUTTING-EDGE DESIGN IS THE **MOUTON,** AN **88-LB** STEEL WEIGHT THAT ENSURES THE BLADE FALLS QUICKLY AND CLEANLY.

THE RAZOR-SHARP STEEL **BLADE** DROPS OVER **2** YARDS TO REACH SPEEDS OF **40** MPH.

AT THAT SPEED THE GUILLOTINE CAN SLICE THROUGH A NECK IN **0.005** SECONDS!

FAST ENOUGH THAT YOU WON'T FEEL A THING!

THE **LUNETTE** IS MADE OF TWO HALF MOONS THAT SLIDE TOGETHER TO HOLD THE HEAD IN PLACE.

DURING THE FRENCH REVOLUTION, THE GUILLOTINE EXECUTED OVER **15,000** FRENCH CITIZENS.

AT THE HEIGHT OF THE SO-CALLED **REIGN OF TERROR,** **3,000** PEOPLE WERE GUILLOTINED IN **ONE MONTH.**

THE REGULAR EXECUTIONS BECAME SOMETHING OF A **SPECTATOR SPORT.**

SOME WOMEN EVEN BROUGHT THEIR KNITTING.

THE **BASCULE,** (A WOODEN BENCH SUPPORTING THE BODY) STARTS UPRIGHT AND IS THEN FOLDED DOWN INTO PLACE.

GRAND PANIER— A BIG BASKET FOR CATCHING THE BODY.

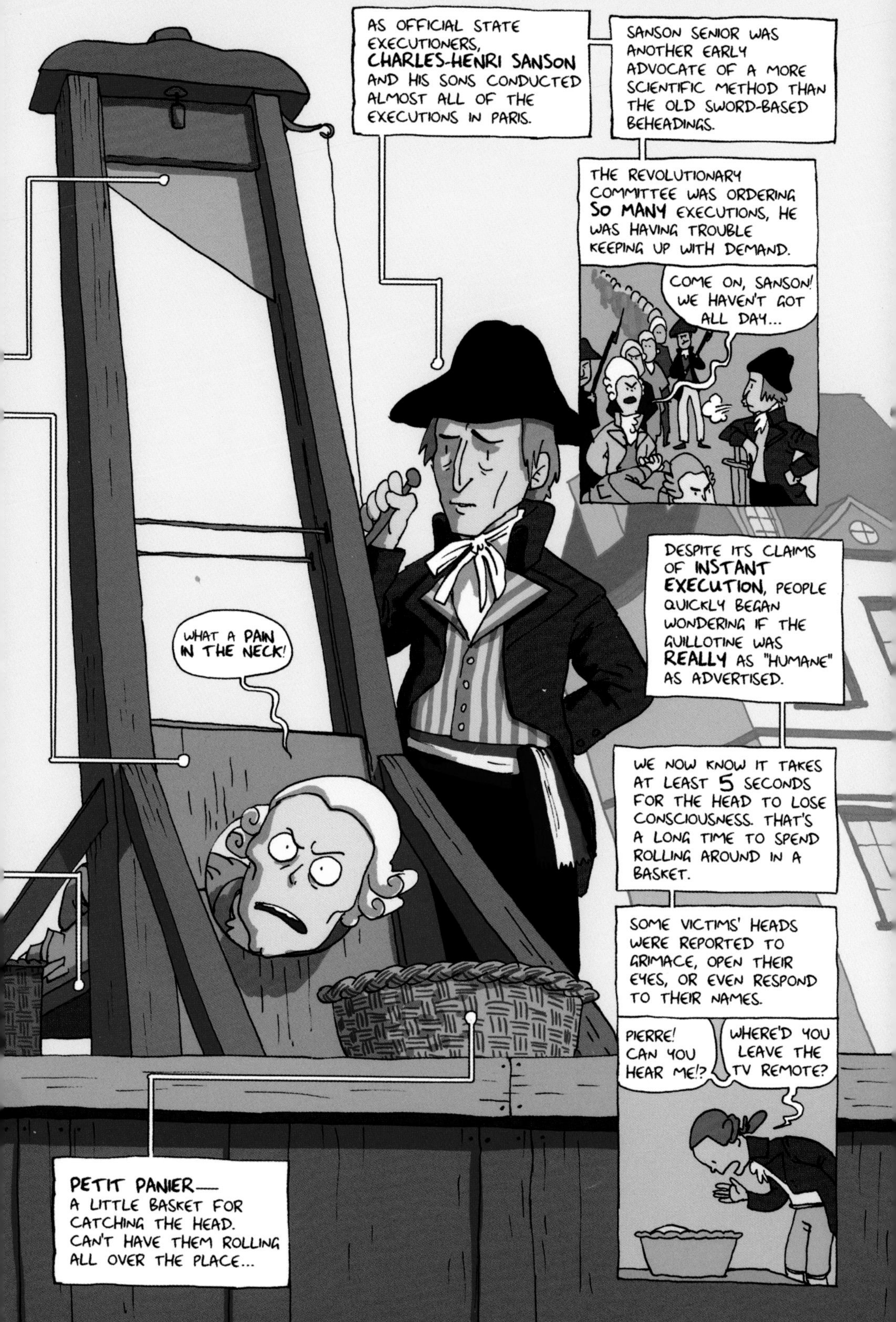
AS OFFICIAL STATE EXECUTIONERS, CHARLES-HENRI SANSON AND HIS SONS CONDUCTED ALMOST ALL OF THE EXECUTIONS IN PARIS.
SANSON SENIOR WAS ANOTHER EARLY ADVOCATE OF A MORE SCIENTIFIC METHOD THAN THE OLD SWORD-BASED BEHEADINGS.
THE REVOLUTIONARY COMMITTEE WAS ORDERING SO MANY EXECUTIONS, HE WAS HAVING TROUBLE KEEPING UP WITH DEMAND.
COME ON, SANSON! WE HAVEN'T GOT ALL DAY...
WHAT A PAIN IN THE NECK!
DESPITE ITS CLAIMS OF INSTANT EXECUTION, PEOPLE QUICKLY BEGAN WONDERING IF THE GUILLOTINE WAS REALLY AS "HUMANE" AS ADVERTISED.
WE NOW KNOW IT TAKES AT LEAST 5 SECONDS FOR THE HEAD TO LOSE CONSCIOUSNESS. THAT'S A LONG TIME TO SPEND ROLLING AROUND IN A BASKET.
SOME VICTIMS' HEADS WERE REPORTED TO GRIMACE, OPEN THEIR EYES, OR EVEN RESPOND TO THEIR NAMES.
PIERRE! CAN YOU HEAR ME!?
WHERE'D YOU LEAVE THE TV REMOTE?
PETIT PANIER— A LITTLE BASKET FOR CATCHING THE HEAD. CAN'T HAVE THEM ROLLING ALL OVER THE PLACE...

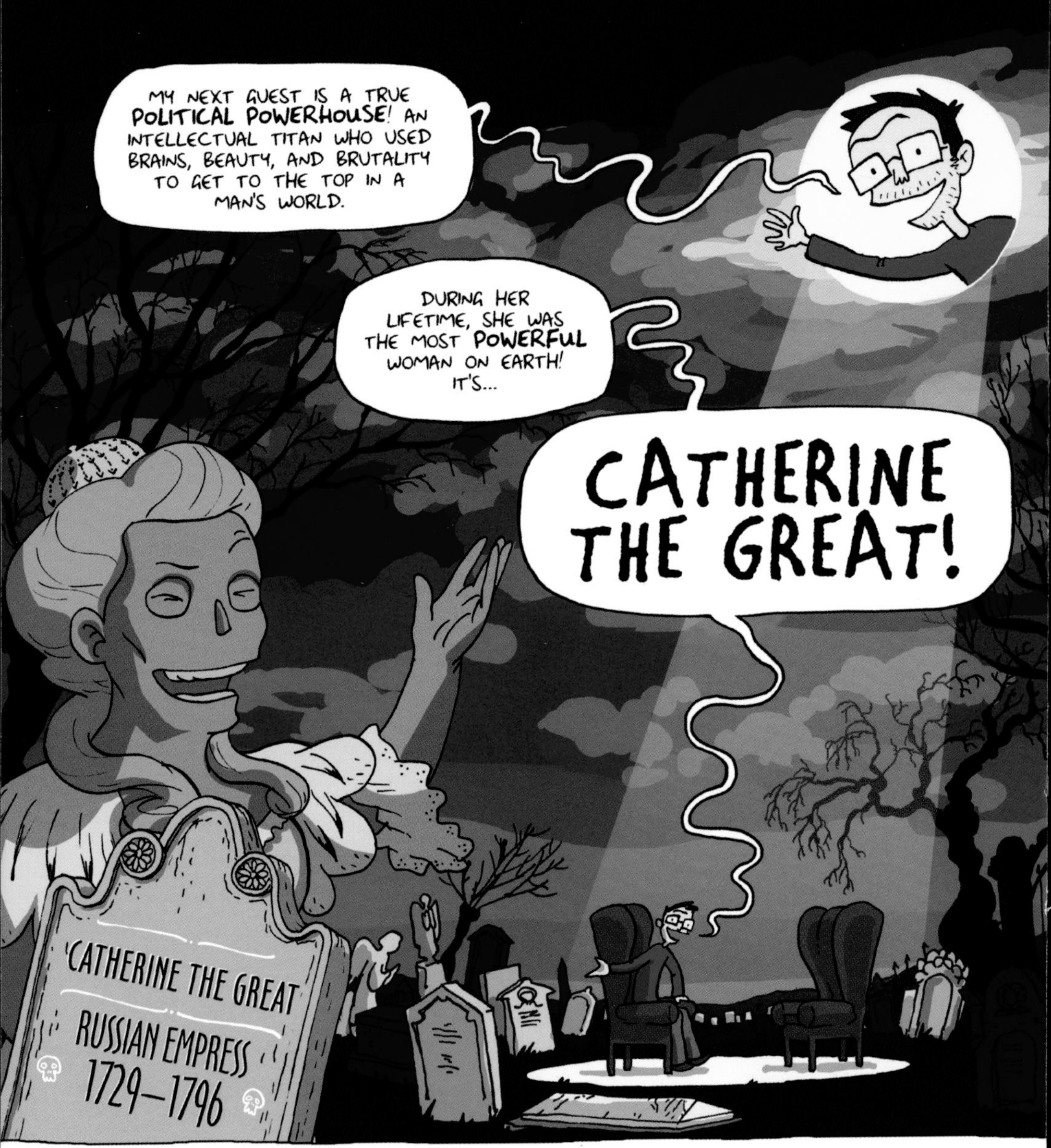
MY NEXT GUEST IS A TRUE POLITICAL POWERHOUSE! AN INTELLECTUAL TITAN WHO USED BRAINS, BEAUTY, AND BRUTALITY TO GET TO THE TOP IN A MAN'S WORLD.
DURING HER LIFETIME, SHE WAS THE MOST POWERFUL WOMAN ON EARTH! IT'S...
CATHERINE THE GREAT!
CATHERINE THE GREAT
RUSSIAN EMPRESS
1729–1796

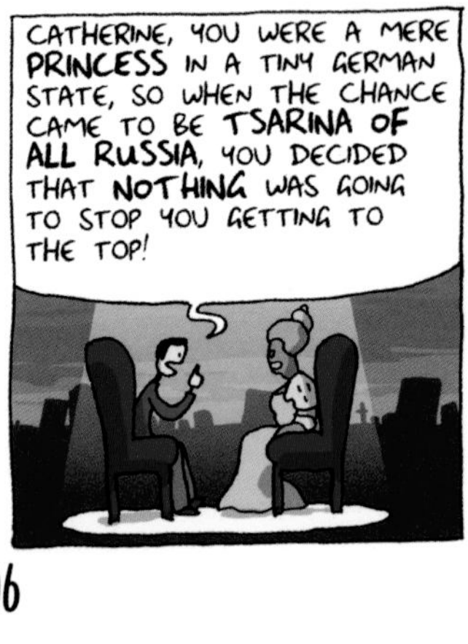
CATHERINE, YOU WERE A MERE PRINCESS IN A TINY GERMAN STATE, SO WHEN THE CHANCE CAME TO BE TSARINA OF ALL RUSSIA, YOU DECIDED THAT NOTHING WAS GOING TO STOP YOU GETTING TO THE TOP!

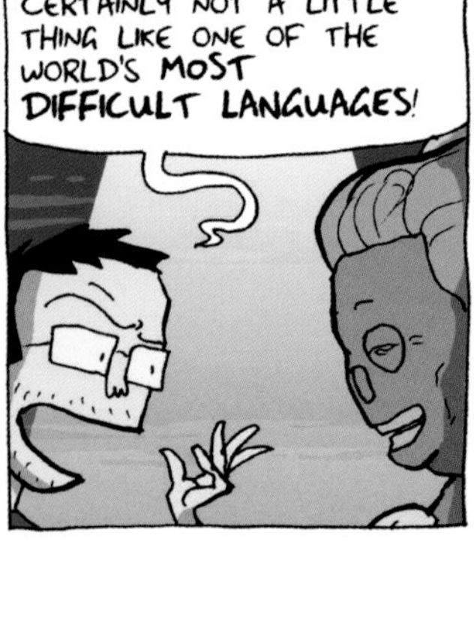
CERTAINLY NOT A LITTLE THING LIKE ONE OF THE WORLD'S MOST DIFFICULT LANGUAGES!

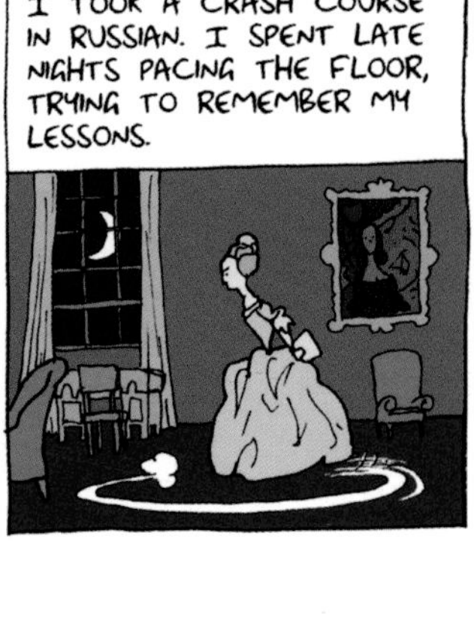
I TOOK A CRASH COURSE IN RUSSIAN. I SPENT LATE NIGHTS PACING THE FLOOR, TRYING TO REMEMBER MY LESSONS.

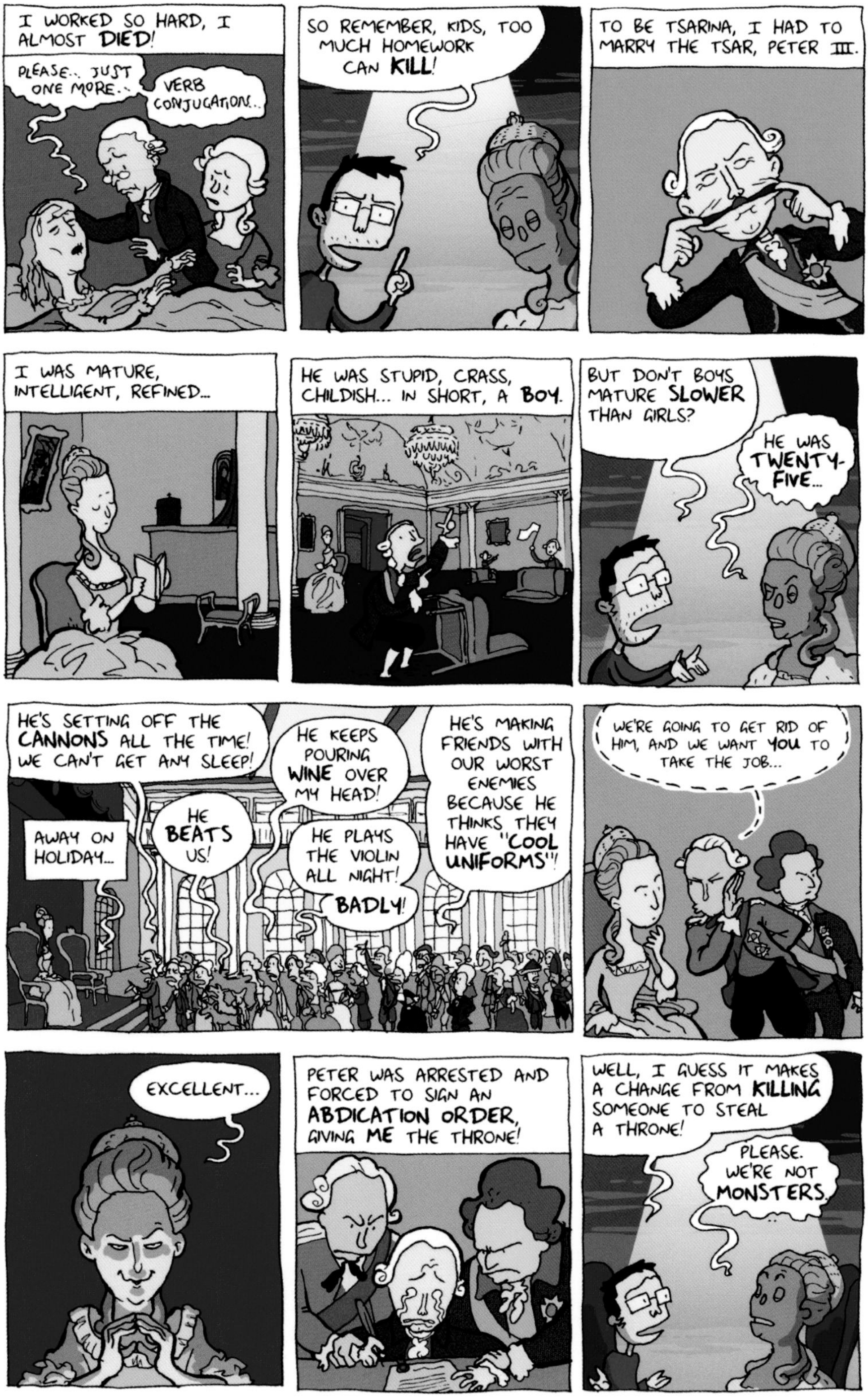
I WORKED SO HARD, I ALMOST DIED!
PLEASE... JUST ONE MORE...
VERB CONJUGATION...
SO REMEMBER, KIDS, TOO MUCH HOMEWORK CAN KILL!
TO BE TSARINA, I HAD TO MARRY THE TSAR, PETER III.
I WAS MATURE, INTELLIGENT, REFINED...
HE WAS STUPID, CRASS, CHILDISH... IN SHORT, A BOY.
BUT DON'T BOYS MATURE SLOWER THAN GIRLS?
HE WAS TWENTY-FIVE...
HE'S SETTING OFF THE CANNONS ALL THE TIME! WE CAN'T GET ANY SLEEP!
HE KEEPS POURING WINE OVER MY HEAD!
HE'S MAKING FRIENDS WITH OUR WORST ENEMIES BECAUSE HE THINKS THEY HAVE "COOL UNIFORMS"!
AWAY ON HOLIDAY...
HE BEATS US!
HE PLAYS THE VIOLIN ALL NIGHT!
BADLY!
WE'RE GOING TO GET RID OF HIM, AND WE WANT YOU TO TAKE THE JOB...
EXCELLENT...
PETER WAS ARRESTED AND FORCED TO SIGN AN ABDICATION ORDER, GIVING ME THE THRONE!
WELL, I GUESS IT MAKES A CHANGE FROM KILLING SOMEONE TO STEAL A THRONE!
PLEASE. WE'RE NOT MONSTERS.
..

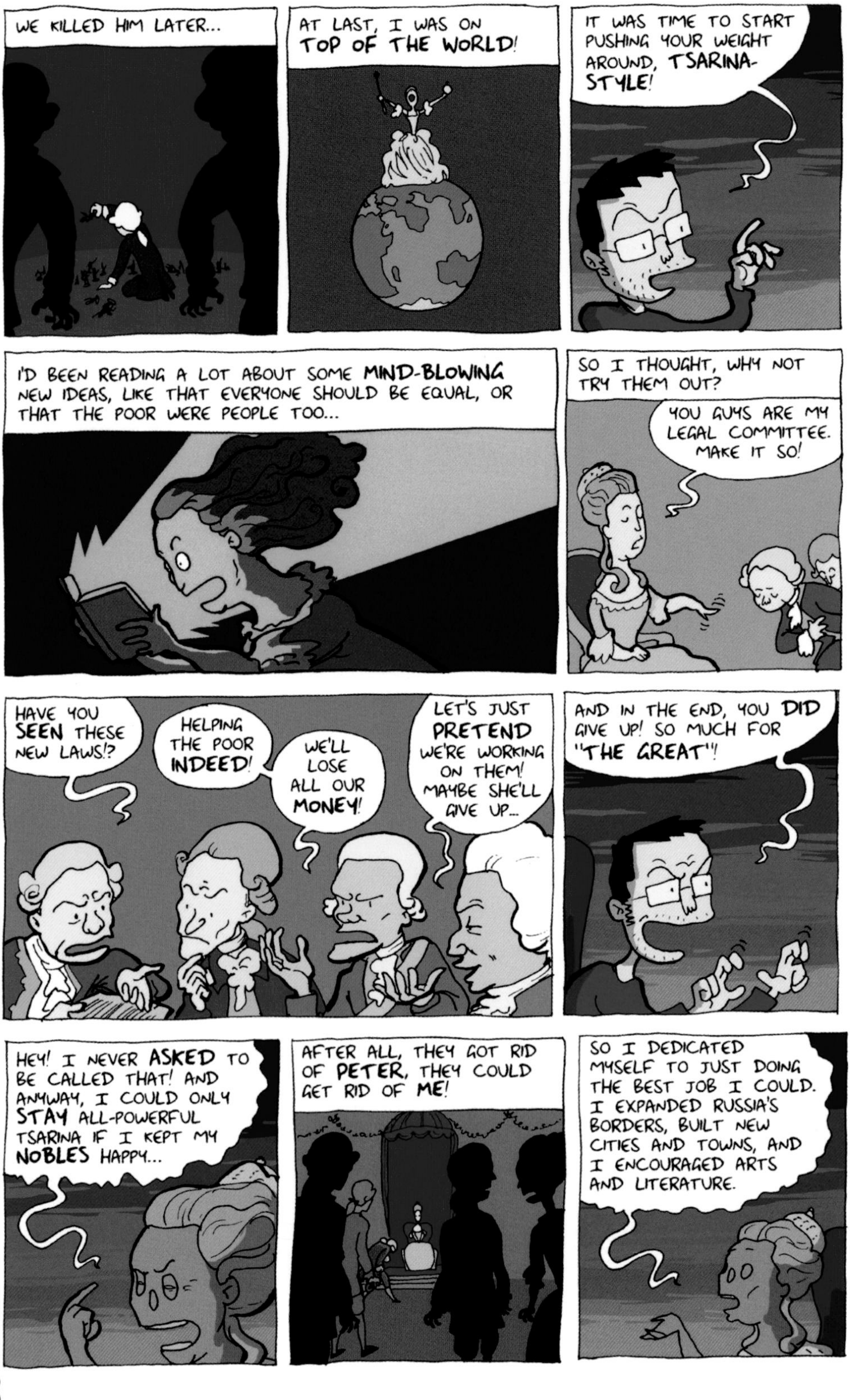
WE KILLED HIM LATER...
AT LAST, I WAS ON TOP OF THE WORLD!
IT WAS TIME TO START PUSHING YOUR WEIGHT AROUND, TSARINA-STYLE!
I'D BEEN READING A LOT ABOUT SOME MIND-BLOWING NEW IDEAS, LIKE THAT EVERYONE SHOULD BE EQUAL, OR THAT THE POOR WERE PEOPLE TOO...
SO I THOUGHT, WHY NOT TRY THEM OUT?
YOU GUYS ARE MY LEGAL COMMITTEE. MAKE IT SO!
HAVE YOU SEEN THESE NEW LAWS!?
HELPING THE POOR INDEED!
WE'LL LOSE ALL OUR MONEY!
LET'S JUST PRETEND WE'RE WORKING ON THEM! MAYBE SHE'LL GIVE UP...
AND IN THE END, YOU DID GIVE UP! SO MUCH FOR "THE GREAT"!
HEY! I NEVER ASKED TO BE CALLED THAT! AND ANYWAY, I COULD ONLY STAY ALL-POWERFUL TSARINA IF I KEPT MY NOBLES HAPPY...
AFTER ALL, THEY GOT RID OF PETER, THEY COULD GET RID OF ME!
SO I DEDICATED MYSELF TO JUST DOING THE BEST JOB I COULD. I EXPANDED RUSSIA'S BORDERS, BUILT NEW CITIES AND TOWNS, AND I ENCOURAGED ARTS AND LITERATURE.

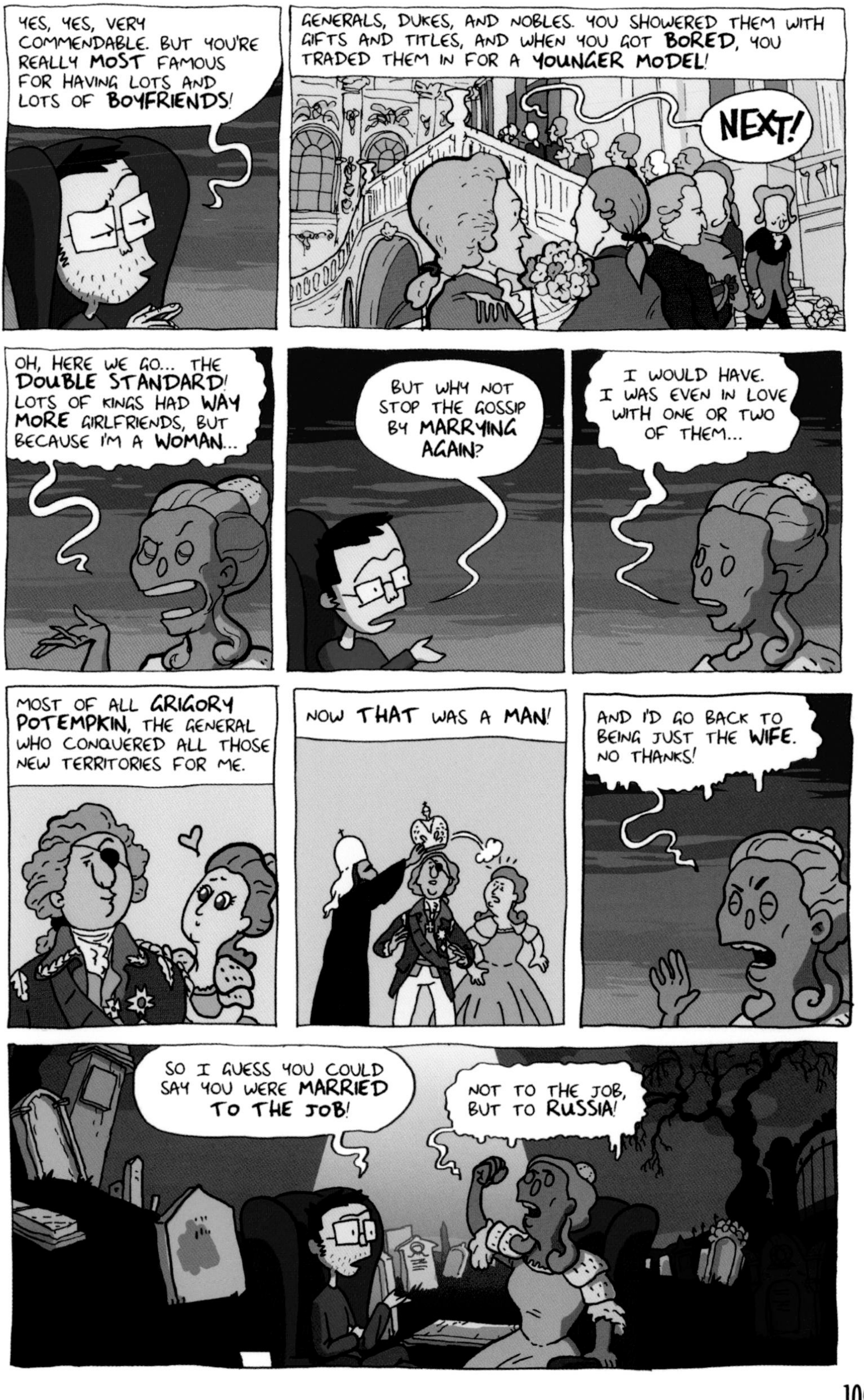
YES, YES, VERY COMMENDABLE. BUT YOU'RE REALLY MOST FAMOUS FOR HAVING LOTS AND LOTS OF BOYFRIENDS!
GENERALS, DUKES, AND NOBLES. YOU SHOWERED THEM WITH GIFTS AND TITLES, AND WHEN YOU GOT BORED, YOU TRADED THEM IN FOR A YOUNGER MODEL!
NEXT!
OH, HERE WE GO... THE DOUBLE STANDARD! LOTS OF KINGS HAD WAY MORE GIRLFRIENDS, BUT BECAUSE I'M A WOMAN...
BUT WHY NOT STOP THE GOSSIP BY MARRYING AGAIN?
I WOULD HAVE. I WAS EVEN IN LOVE WITH ONE OR TWO OF THEM...
MOST OF ALL GRIGORY POTEMPKIN, THE GENERAL WHO CONQUERED ALL THOSE NEW TERRITORIES FOR ME.
NOW THAT WAS A MAN!
AND I'D GO BACK TO BEING JUST THE WIFE. NO THANKS!
SO I GUESS YOU COULD SAY YOU WERE MARRIED TO THE JOB!
NOT TO THE JOB, BUT TO RUSSIA!

TSARS IN THEIR EYES

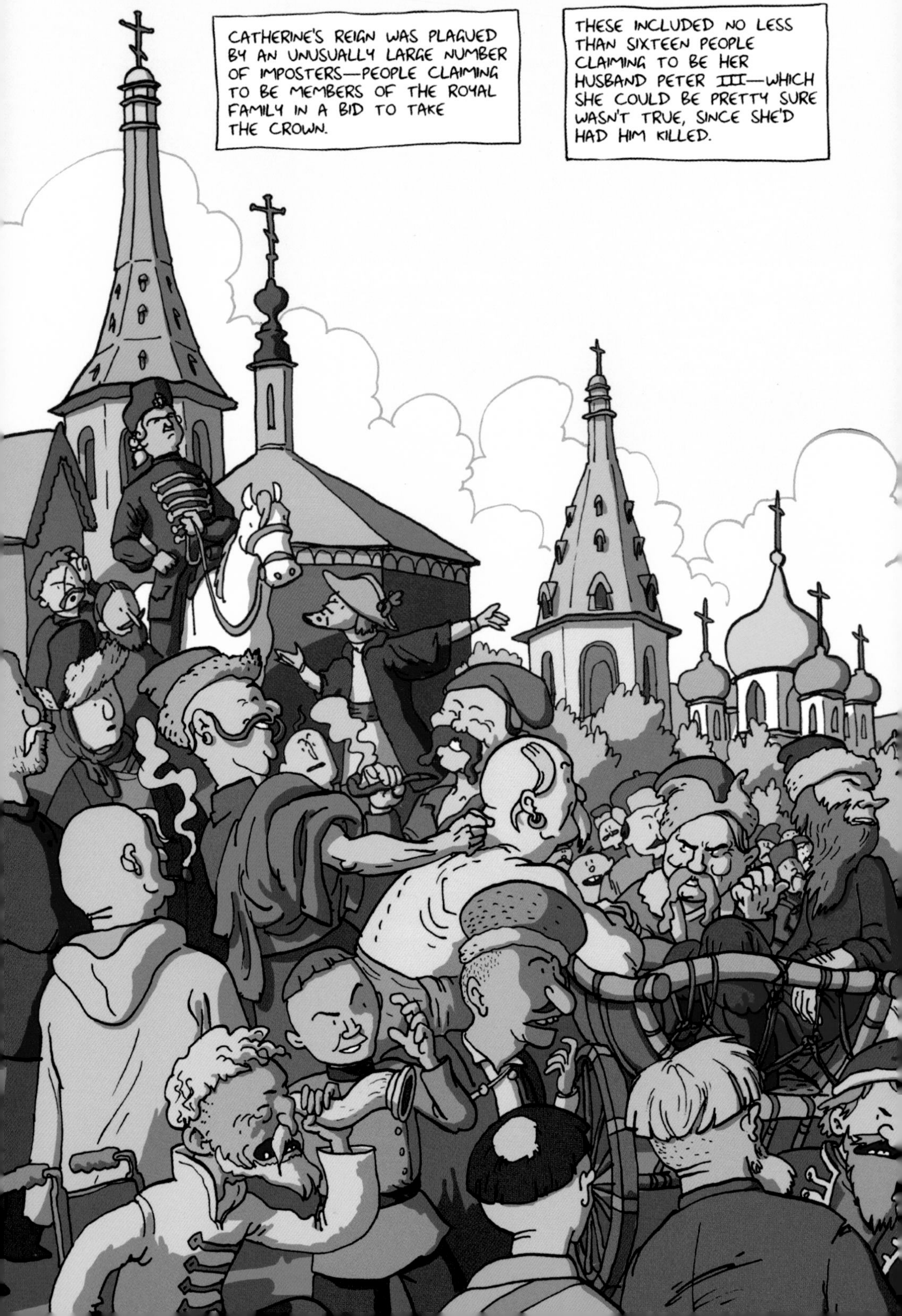
CATHERINE'S REIGN WAS PLAGUED BY AN UNUSUALLY LARGE NUMBER OF IMPOSTERS—PEOPLE CLAIMING TO BE MEMBERS OF THE ROYAL FAMILY IN A BID TO TAKE THE CROWN.
THESE INCLUDED NO LESS THAN SIXTEEN PEOPLE CLAIMING TO BE HER HUSBAND PETER III—WHICH SHE COULD BE PRETTY SURE WASN'T TRUE, SINCE SHE'D HAD HIM KILLED.

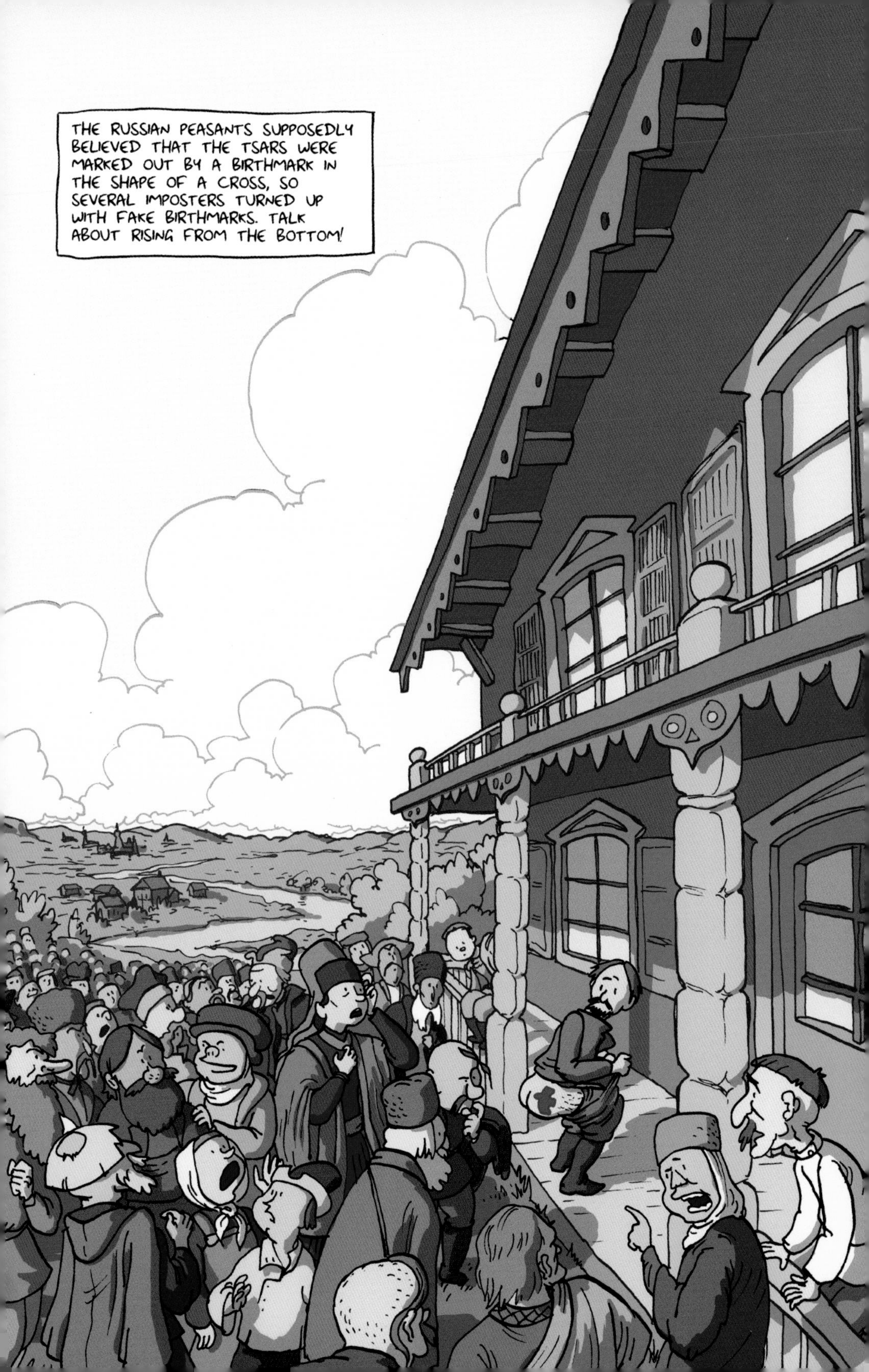
THE RUSSIAN PEASANTS SUPPOSEDLY BELIEVED THAT THE TSARS WERE MARKED OUT BY A BIRTHMARK IN THE SHAPE OF A CROSS, SO SEVERAL IMPOSTERS TURNED UP WITH FAKE BIRTHMARKS. TALK ABOUT RISING FROM THE BOTTOM!

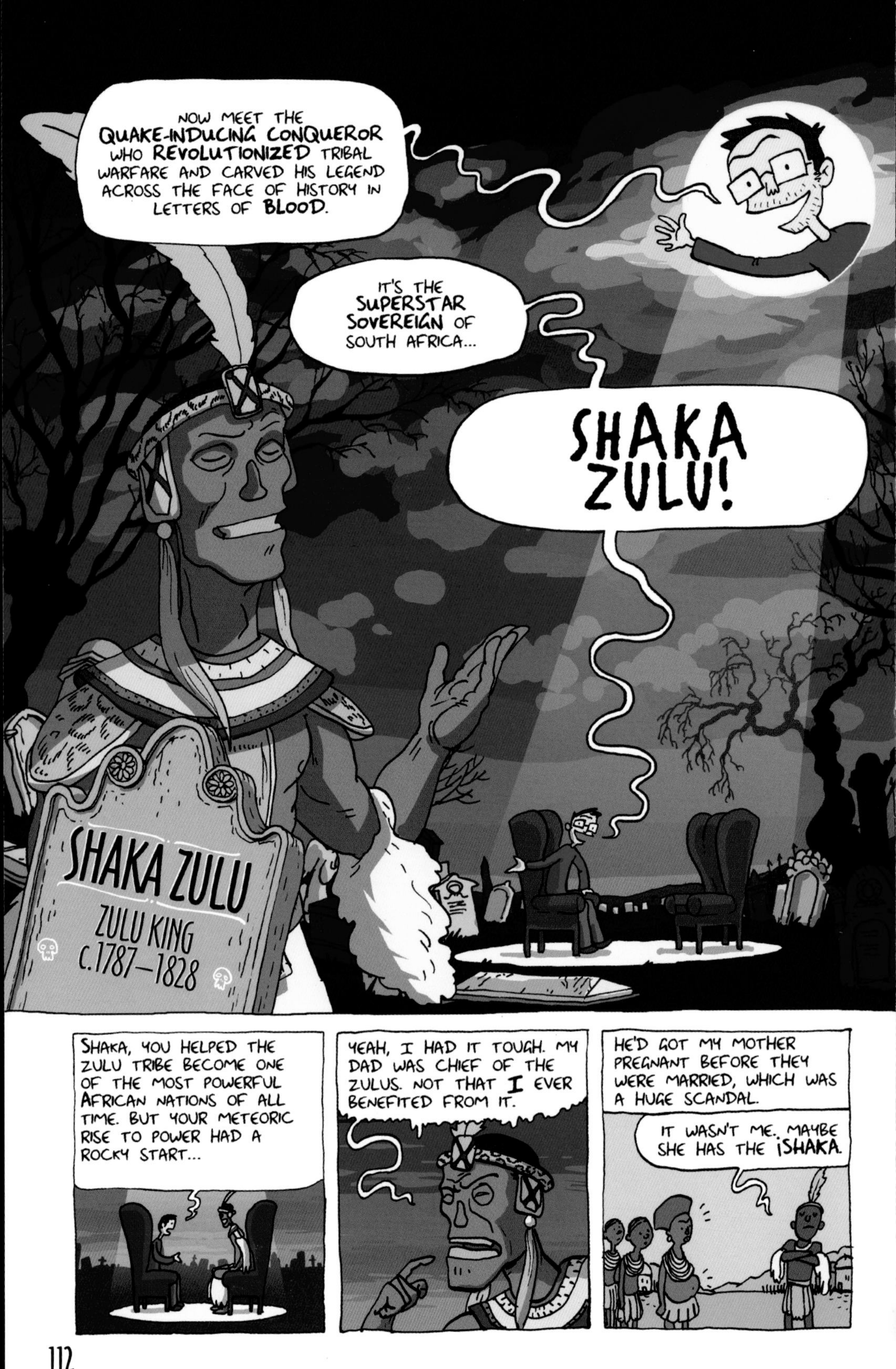
NOW MEET THE QUAKE-INDUCING CONQUEROR WHO REVOLUTIONIZED TRIBAL WARFARE AND CARVED HIS LEGEND ACROSS THE FACE OF HISTORY IN LETTERS OF BLOOD.
IT'S THE SUPERSTAR SOVEREIGN OF SOUTH AFRICA...
SHAKA ZULU!
SHAKA ZULU
ZULU KING
c.1787–1828
SHAKA, YOU HELPED THE ZULU TRIBE BECOME ONE OF THE MOST POWERFUL AFRICAN NATIONS OF ALL TIME. BUT YOUR METEORIC RISE TO POWER HAD A ROCKY START...
YEAH, I HAD IT TOUGH. MY DAD WAS CHIEF OF THE ZULUS. NOT THAT I EVER BENEFITED FROM IT.
HE'D GOT MY MOTHER PREGNANT BEFORE THEY WERE MARRIED, WHICH WAS A HUGE SCANDAL.
IT WASN'T ME. MAYBE SHE HAS THE iSHAKA.

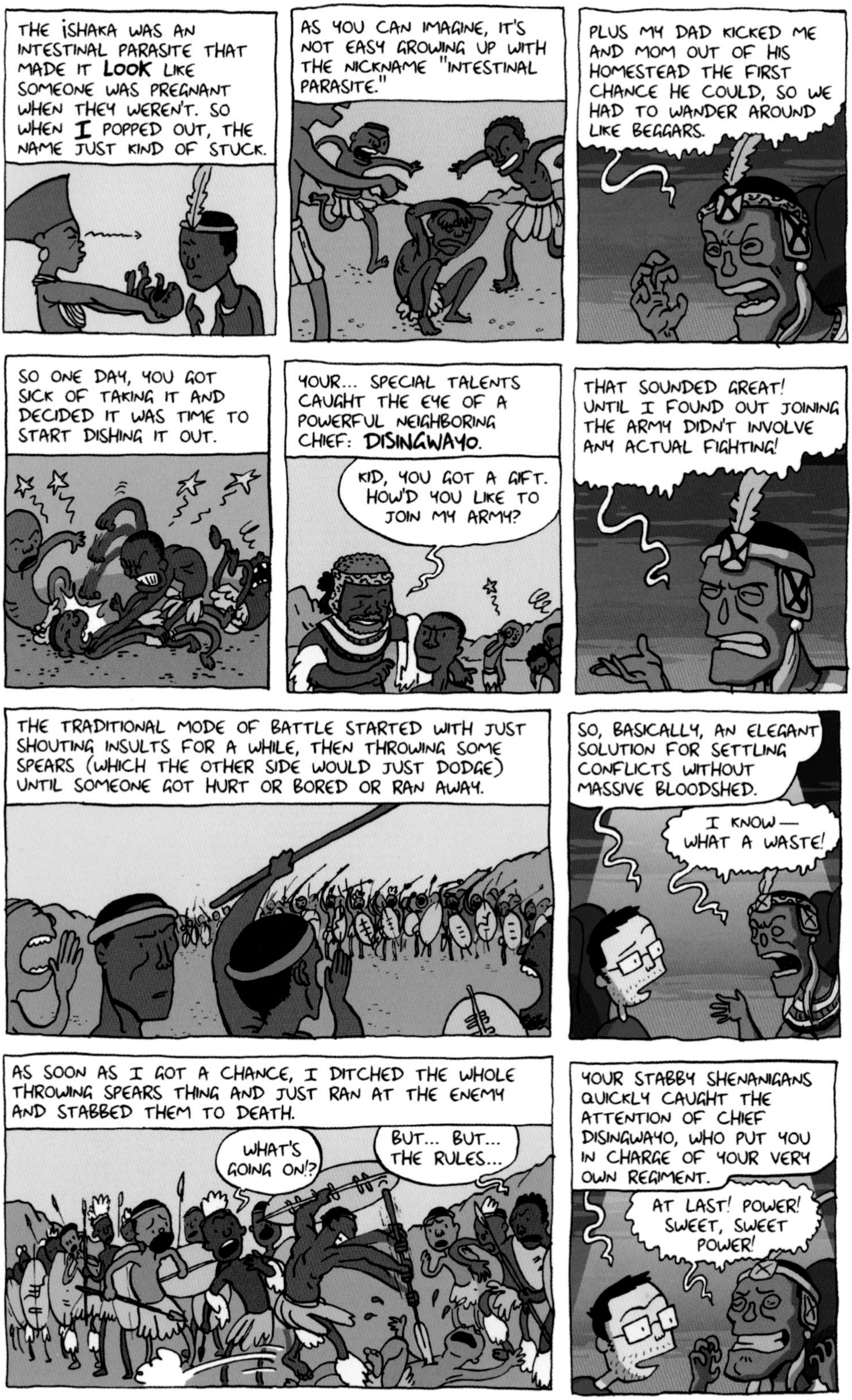
THE iSHAKA WAS AN INTESTINAL PARASITE THAT MADE IT LOOK LIKE SOMEONE WAS PREGNANT WHEN THEY WEREN'T. SO WHEN I POPPED OUT, THE NAME JUST KIND OF STUCK.
AS YOU CAN IMAGINE, IT'S NOT EASY GROWING UP WITH THE NICKNAME "INTESTINAL PARASITE."
PLUS MY DAD KICKED ME AND MOM OUT OF HIS HOMESTEAD THE FIRST CHANCE HE COULD, SO WE HAD TO WANDER AROUND LIKE BEGGARS.
SO ONE DAY, YOU GOT SICK OF TAKING IT AND DECIDED IT WAS TIME TO START DISHING IT OUT.
YOUR... SPECIAL TALENTS CAUGHT THE EYE OF A POWERFUL NEIGHBORING CHIEF: DISINGWAYO.
KID, YOU GOT A GIFT. HOW'D YOU LIKE TO JOIN MY ARMY?
THAT SOUNDED GREAT! UNTIL I FOUND OUT JOINING THE ARMY DIDN'T INVOLVE ANY ACTUAL FIGHTING!
THE TRADITIONAL MODE OF BATTLE STARTED WITH JUST SHOUTING INSULTS FOR A WHILE, THEN THROWING SOME SPEARS (WHICH THE OTHER SIDE WOULD JUST DODGE) UNTIL SOMEONE GOT HURT OR BORED OR RAN AWAY.
SO, BASICALLY, AN ELEGANT SOLUTION FOR SETTLING CONFLICTS WITHOUT MASSIVE BLOODSHED.
I KNOW— WHAT A WASTE!
AS SOON AS I GOT A CHANCE, I DITCHED THE WHOLE THROWING SPEARS THING AND JUST RAN AT THE ENEMY AND STABBED THEM TO DEATH.
WHAT'S GOING ON!?
BUT... BUT... THE RULES...
YOUR STABBY SHENANIGANS QUICKLY CAUGHT THE ATTENTION OF CHIEF DISINGWAYO, WHO PUT YOU IN CHARGE OF YOUR VERY OWN REGIMENT.
AT LAST! POWER! SWEET, SWEET POWER!

I TRAINED MY NEW UNDERLINGS WITH 50-MILE-A-DAY BAREFOOT RUNS ACROSS THE BAKING, ROCKY SAVANNAH TO TOUGHEN THEM UP.

ANYONE WHO COMPLAINED WAS PUT TO DEATH. ANYONE WHO DROPPED HIS WEAPON WAS PUT TO DEATH. ANYONE WHO LOOKED TIRED WAS...

I GET IT...

WELL, IT WORKED. I FORGED THEM INTO AN UNSTOPPABLE ARMY OF KILLING MACHINES, AFRAID OF ONLY ONE THING IN THE WORLD: **ME!**

BUT THIS WAS JUST THE **FIRST** STEP IN MY **MASTER PLAN**. WITH MY NEW SUPER-SOLDIERS, I WAS READY FOR PHASE TWO: THE BUFFALO'S HORNS!

THE WHAT NOW?

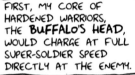

FIRST, MY CORE OF HARDENED WARRIORS, THE **BUFFALO'S HEAD**, WOULD CHARGE AT FULL SUPER-SOLDIER SPEED DIRECTLY AT THE ENEMY.

THEN, OUT FROM BEHIND THEM WOULD SPRING THE TWO **BUFFALO'S HORNS**, ENCLOSING THE ENEMY IN AN IMPENETRABLE STOCKADE OF **STABBINGS**.

SOUNDS PRETTY BRUTAL.

BRUTAL, MAYBE, BUT THE GREAT SHAKA COULD ALSO SHOW **MERCY**. I ALWAYS OFFERED MY DEFEATED ENEMIES THE CHANCE TO JOIN THE ZULUS.

LUCKY THEM...

HEY, IT **WAS** LUCKY FOR THEM!

NOT ONLY DID THEY GET TO AVOID A VIOLENT, POINTY DEATH, BUT THEY BECAME PROUD MEMBERS OF THE MIGHTY **ZULU NATION!**

YOU SEE BEFORE SHAKA, THERE **WAS** NO ZULU NATION, BUT INSTEAD A BUNCH OF CHIEFTAINS, RULING OVER VILLAGES.

PEOPLE WERE LOYAL TO THEIR VILLAGE AND THEIR FAMILY, BUT THEY WERE ALWAYS FIGHTING OTHER VILLAGES OVER STUFF LIKE CATTLE OR WOMEN.

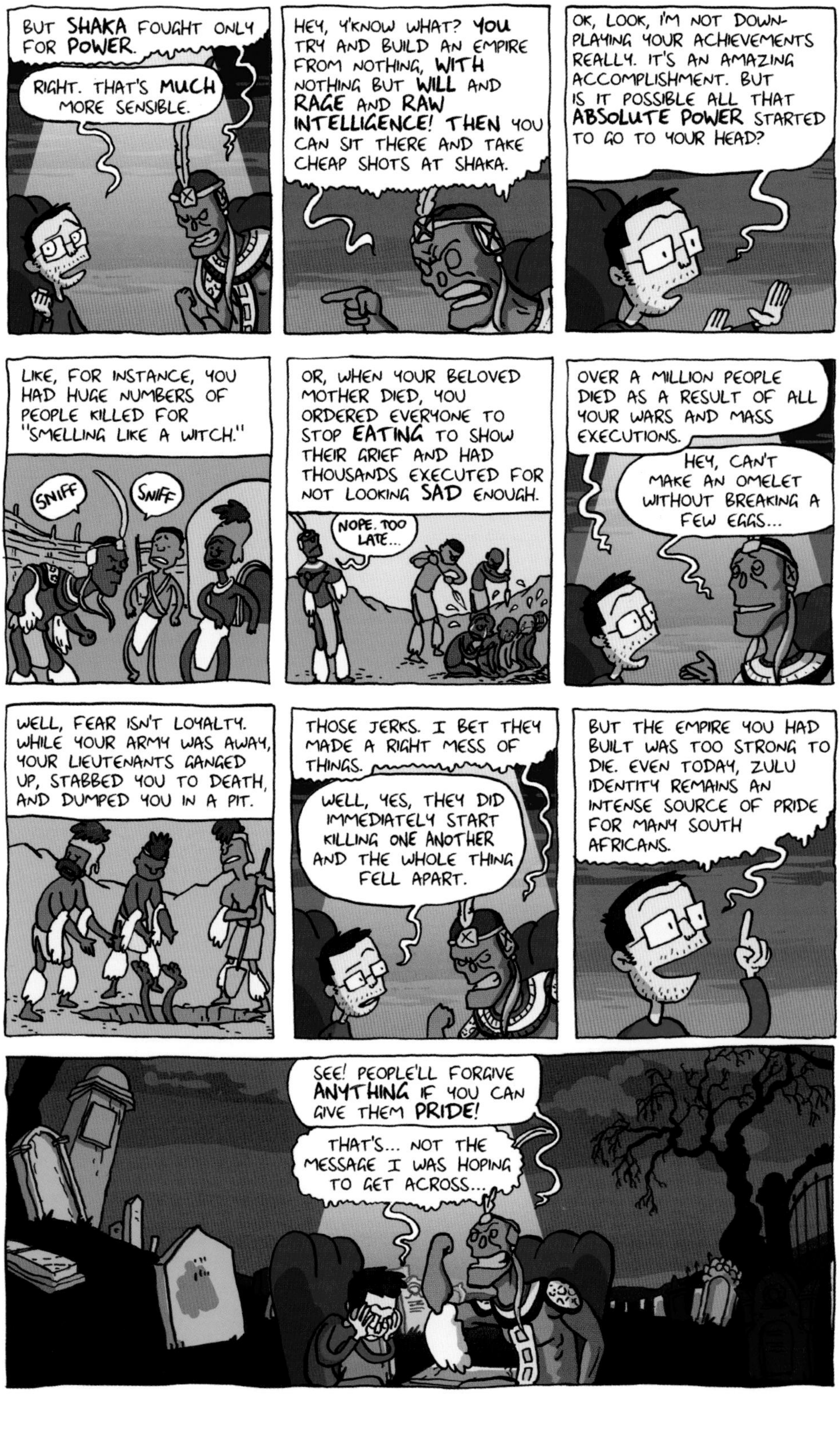
BUT SHAKA FOUGHT ONLY FOR POWER.
RIGHT. THAT'S MUCH MORE SENSIBLE.
HEY, Y'KNOW WHAT? YOU TRY AND BUILD AN EMPIRE FROM NOTHING, WITH NOTHING BUT WILL AND RAGE AND RAW INTELLIGENCE! THEN YOU CAN SIT THERE AND TAKE CHEAP SHOTS AT SHAKA.
OK, LOOK, I'M NOT DOWN-PLAYING YOUR ACHIEVEMENTS REALLY. IT'S AN AMAZING ACCOMPLISHMENT. BUT IS IT POSSIBLE ALL THAT ABSOLUTE POWER STARTED TO GO TO YOUR HEAD?
LIKE, FOR INSTANCE, YOU HAD HUGE NUMBERS OF PEOPLE KILLED FOR "SMELLING LIKE A WITCH."
SNIFF
SNIFF
OR, WHEN YOUR BELOVED MOTHER DIED, YOU ORDERED EVERYONE TO STOP EATING TO SHOW THEIR GRIEF AND HAD THOUSANDS EXECUTED FOR NOT LOOKING SAD ENOUGH.
NOPE. TOO LATE...
OVER A MILLION PEOPLE DIED AS A RESULT OF ALL YOUR WARS AND MASS EXECUTIONS.
HEY, CAN'T MAKE AN OMELET WITHOUT BREAKING A FEW EGGS...
WELL, FEAR ISN'T LOYALTY. WHILE YOUR ARMY WAS AWAY, YOUR LIEUTENANTS GANGED UP, STABBED YOU TO DEATH, AND DUMPED YOU IN A PIT.
THOSE JERKS. I BET THEY MADE A RIGHT MESS OF THINGS.
WELL, YES, THEY DID IMMEDIATELY START KILLING ONE ANOTHER AND THE WHOLE THING FELL APART.
BUT THE EMPIRE YOU HAD BUILT WAS TOO STRONG TO DIE. EVEN TODAY, ZULU IDENTITY REMAINS AN INTENSE SOURCE OF PRIDE FOR MANY SOUTH AFRICANS.
SEE! PEOPLE'LL FORGIVE ANYTHING IF YOU CAN GIVE THEM PRIDE!
THAT'S... NOT THE MESSAGE I WAS HOPING TO GET ACROSS...

The Battle of iSandlwana

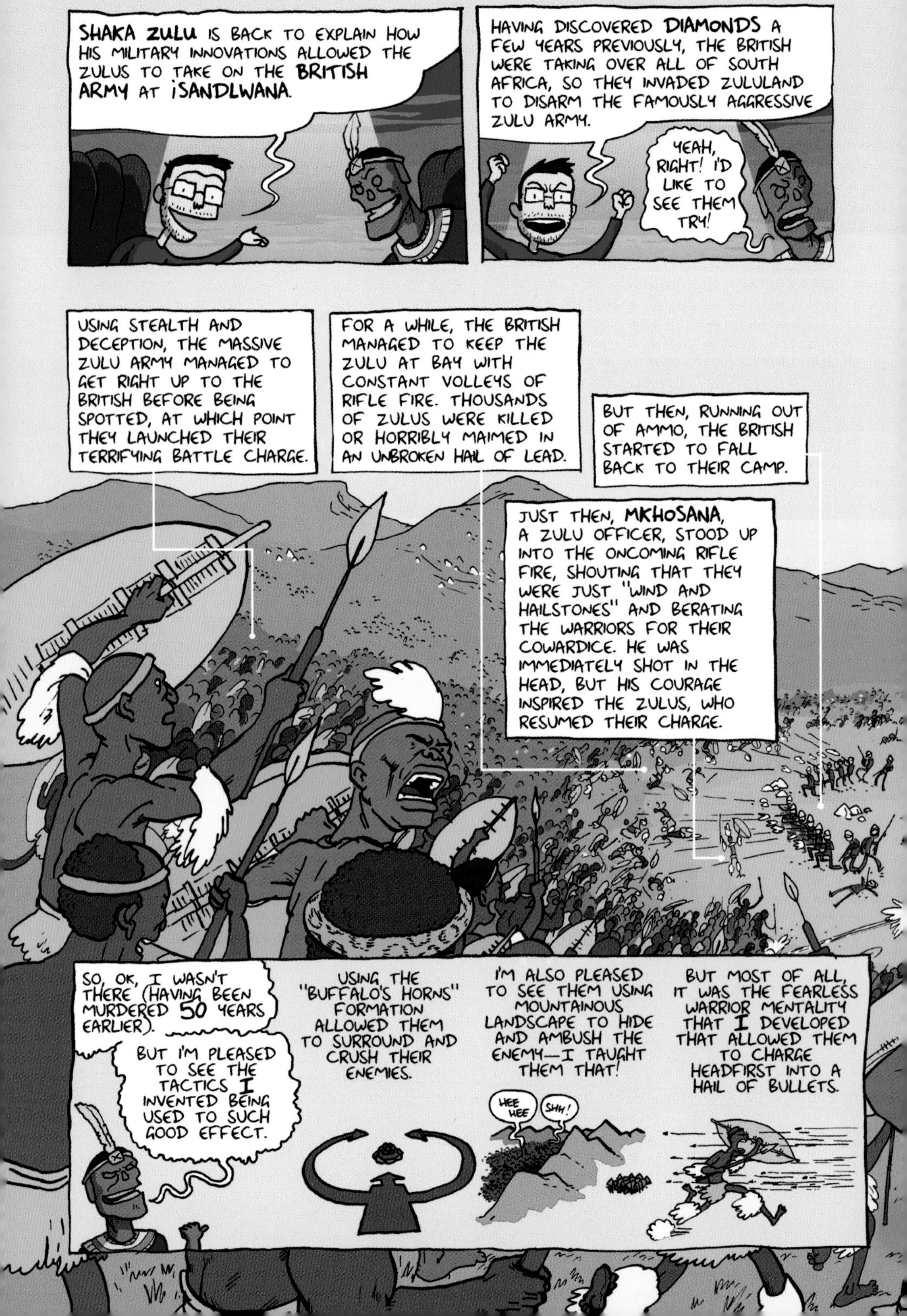
SHAKA ZULU IS BACK TO EXPLAIN HOW HIS MILITARY INNOVATIONS ALLOWED THE ZULUS TO TAKE ON THE BRITISH ARMY AT iSANDLWANA.
HAVING DISCOVERED DIAMONDS A FEW YEARS PREVIOUSLY, THE BRITISH WERE TAKING OVER ALL OF SOUTH AFRICA, SO THEY INVADED ZULULAND TO DISARM THE FAMOUSLY AGGRESSIVE ZULU ARMY.
YEAH, RIGHT! I'D LIKE TO SEE THEM TRY!
USING STEALTH AND DECEPTION, THE MASSIVE ZULU ARMY MANAGED TO GET RIGHT UP TO THE BRITISH BEFORE BEING SPOTTED, AT WHICH POINT THEY LAUNCHED THEIR TERRIFYING BATTLE CHARGE.
FOR A WHILE, THE BRITISH MANAGED TO KEEP THE ZULU AT BAY WITH CONSTANT VOLLEYS OF RIFLE FIRE. THOUSANDS OF ZULUS WERE KILLED OR HORRIBLY MAIMED IN AN UNBROKEN HAIL OF LEAD.
BUT THEN, RUNNING OUT OF AMMO, THE BRITISH STARTED TO FALL BACK TO THEIR CAMP.
JUST THEN, MKHOSANA, A ZULU OFFICER, STOOD UP INTO THE ONCOMING RIFLE FIRE, SHOUTING THAT THEY WERE JUST "WIND AND HAILSTONES" AND BERATING THE WARRIORS FOR THEIR COWARDICE. HE WAS IMMEDIATELY SHOT IN THE HEAD, BUT HIS COURAGE INSPIRED THE ZULUS, WHO RESUMED THEIR CHARGE.
SO, OK, I WASN'T THERE (HAVING BEEN MURDERED 50 YEARS EARLIER).
BUT I'M PLEASED TO SEE THE TACTICS I INVENTED BEING USED TO SUCH GOOD EFFECT.
USING THE "BUFFALO'S HORNS" FORMATION ALLOWED THEM TO SURROUND AND CRUSH THEIR ENEMIES.
I'M ALSO PLEASED TO SEE THEM USING MOUNTAINOUS LANDSCAPE TO HIDE AND AMBUSH THE ENEMY—I TAUGHT THEM THAT!
HEE HEE
SHH!
BUT MOST OF ALL, IT WAS THE FEARLESS WARRIOR MENTALITY THAT I DEVELOPED THAT ALLOWED THEM TO CHARGE HEADFIRST INTO A HAIL OF BULLETS.

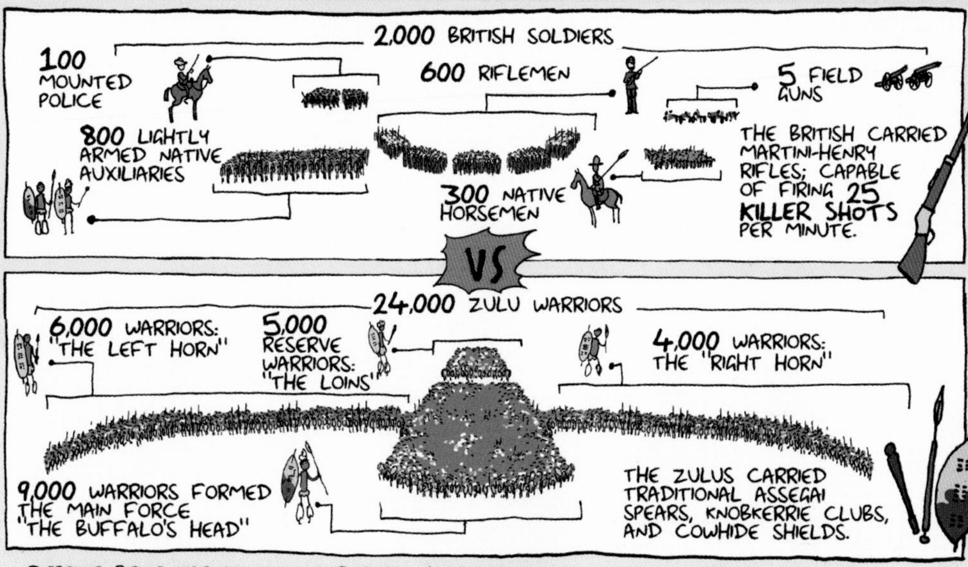
2,000 BRITISH SOLDIERS
100 MOUNTED POLICE
600 RIFLEMEN
5 FIELD GUNS
800 LIGHTLY ARMED NATIVE AUXILIARIES
300 NATIVE HORSEMEN
THE BRITISH CARRIED MARTINI-HENRY RIFLES; CAPABLE OF FIRING 25 KILLER SHOTS PER MINUTE.
VS
24,000 ZULU WARRIORS
6,000 WARRIORS: "THE LEFT HORN"
5,000 RESERVE WARRIORS: "THE LOINS"
4,000 WARRIORS: THE "RIGHT HORN"
9,000 WARRIORS FORMED THE MAIN FORCE "THE BUFFALO'S HEAD"
THE ZULUS CARRIED TRADITIONAL ASSEGAI SPEARS, KNOBKERRIE CLUBS, AND COWHIDE SHIELDS.

DESPITE BEING VASTLY OUTNUMBERED, THEIR FIREARMS MADE THE BRITISH CONFIDENT OF AN EASY VICTORY. MAYBE A LITTLE **TOO** CONFIDENT...

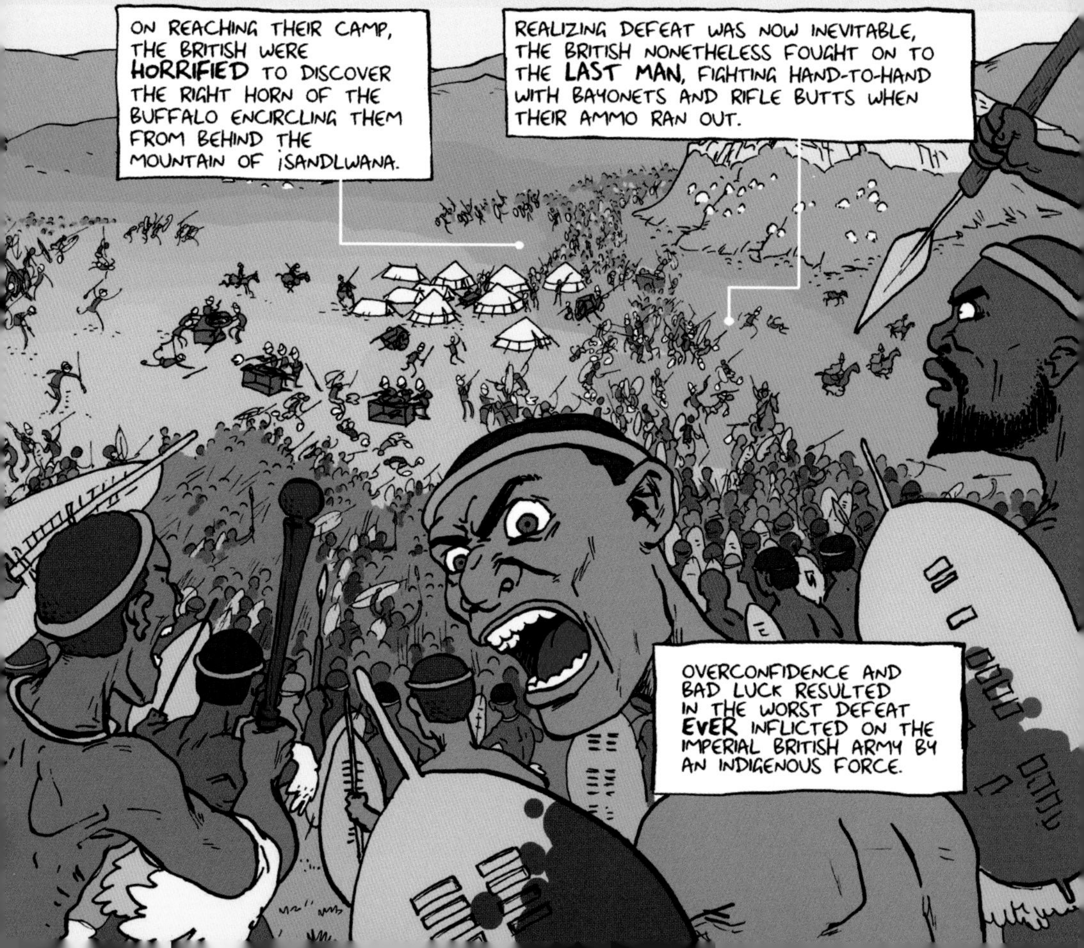
ON REACHING THEIR CAMP, THE BRITISH WERE HORRIFIED TO DISCOVER THE RIGHT HORN OF THE BUFFALO ENCIRCLING THEM FROM BEHIND THE MOUNTAIN OF ISANDLWANA.
REALIZING DEFEAT WAS NOW INEVITABLE, THE BRITISH NONETHELESS FOUGHT ON TO THE LAST MAN, FIGHTING HAND-TO-HAND WITH BAYONETS AND RIFLE BUTTS WHEN THEIR AMMO RAN OUT.
OVERCONFIDENCE AND BAD LUCK RESULTED IN THE WORST DEFEAT EVER INFLICTED ON THE IMPERIAL BRITISH ARMY BY AN INDIGENOUS FORCE.

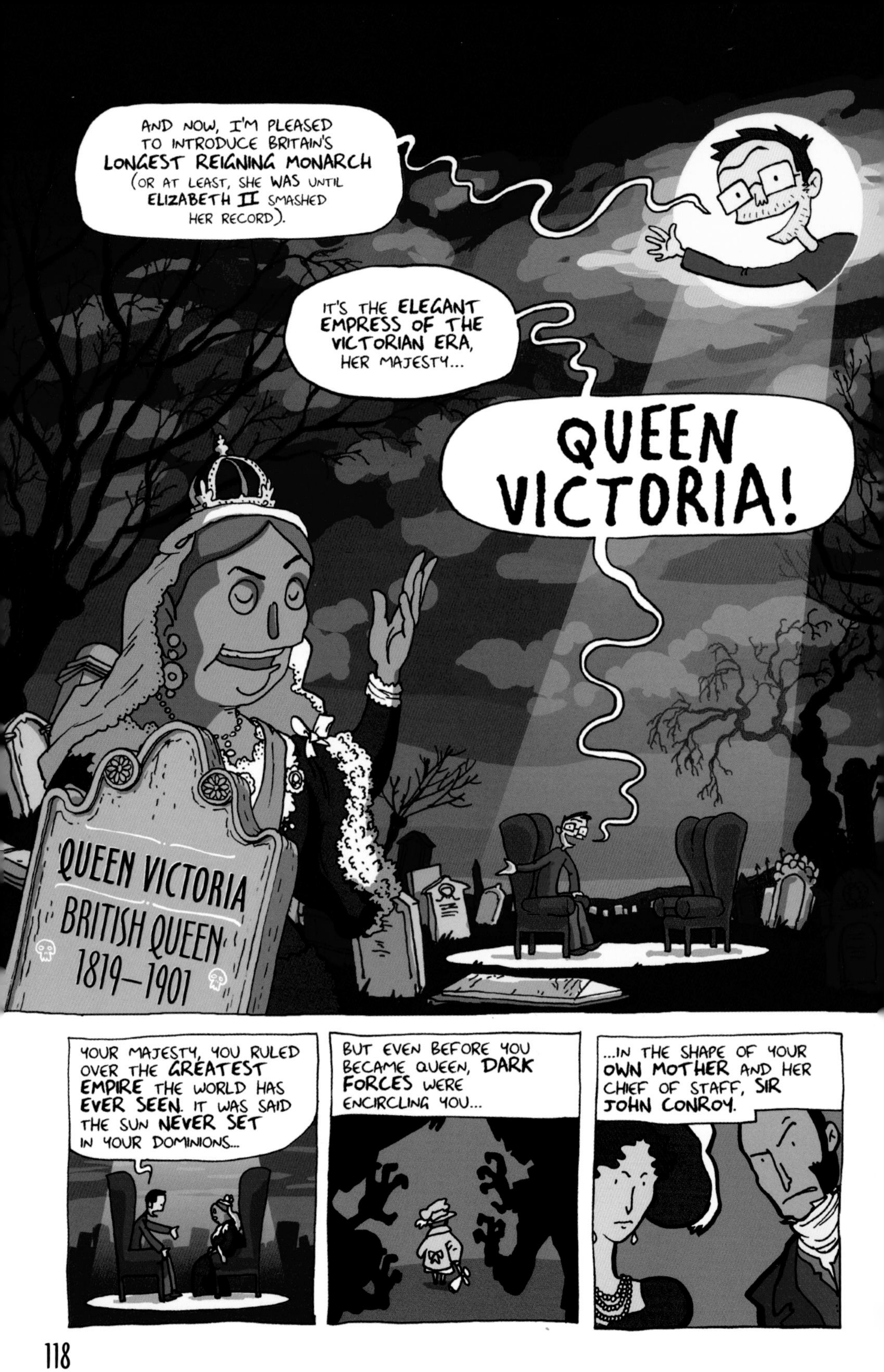
AND NOW, I'M PLEASED TO INTRODUCE BRITAIN'S **LONGEST REIGNING MONARCH** (OR AT LEAST, SHE **WAS** UNTIL **ELIZABETH II** SMASHED HER RECORD).
IT'S THE **ELEGANT EMPRESS OF THE VICTORIAN ERA,** HER MAJESTY...
QUEEN VICTORIA!
QUEEN VICTORIA
BRITISH QUEEN
1819–1901
YOUR MAJESTY, YOU RULED OVER THE **GREATEST EMPIRE** THE WORLD HAS **EVER SEEN**. IT WAS SAID THE SUN **NEVER SET** IN YOUR DOMINIONS...
BUT EVEN BEFORE YOU BECAME QUEEN, **DARK FORCES** WERE ENCIRCLING YOU...
...IN THE SHAPE OF YOUR **OWN MOTHER** AND HER CHIEF OF STAFF, **SIR JOHN CONROY**.

BETWEEN THEM, THEY MADE MY LIFE **MISERABLE**. THEY SAID IT WAS FOR MY OWN GOOD...

BUT REALLY, THEY HOPED TO BECOME THE **POWER BEHIND THE THRONE**.

SO THEY DEVISED A SYSTEM TO TRAIN ME TO BE **COMPLETELY DEPENDENT** ON THEM!

OOH! **DASTARDLY!**

THEY KEPT ME LOCKED AWAY IN KENSINGTON PALACE. I NEVER SAW MY FAMILY AND I NEVER HAD ANY FRIENDS!

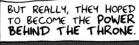

BUT AT THE SAME TIME, I WAS NEVER ALLOWED TO BE ALONE...

DEAR DIARY...

I HAD TO SLEEP IN MY **MOTHER'S** ROOM...

I EVEN HAD TO BE HELPED UP AND DOWN **STAIRS**!

THANK GOODNESS I'M HERE TO PROTECT YOU!

IN SHORT, I HAD NO PRIVACY AT ALL!

HAVE ANOTHER PIECE OF TOILET PAPER, DEAR.

MOTHER!

BUT THEIR PLAN **BACKFIRED!**

TOO RIGHT IT DID! I GREW TO **HATE** THEM, AND THEIR **STUPID RULES!**

SIR JOHN EVEN TRIED TO **FORCE** ME TO MAKE HIM MY PRIVATE SECRETARY.

JUST **SIGN** IT, YOU STUPID GIRL!

NEVER!

I WAS TO BECOME QUEEN WHEN MY UNCLE, THE KING, DIED. IF IT HAPPENED BEFORE I TURNED **18**, MY MOTHER WOULD GET TO RULE IN MY PLACE!

THE KING HATED THEM TOO, SO HE SWORE TO LIVE **LONG ENOUGH** TO **FOIL** THEIR PLANS!

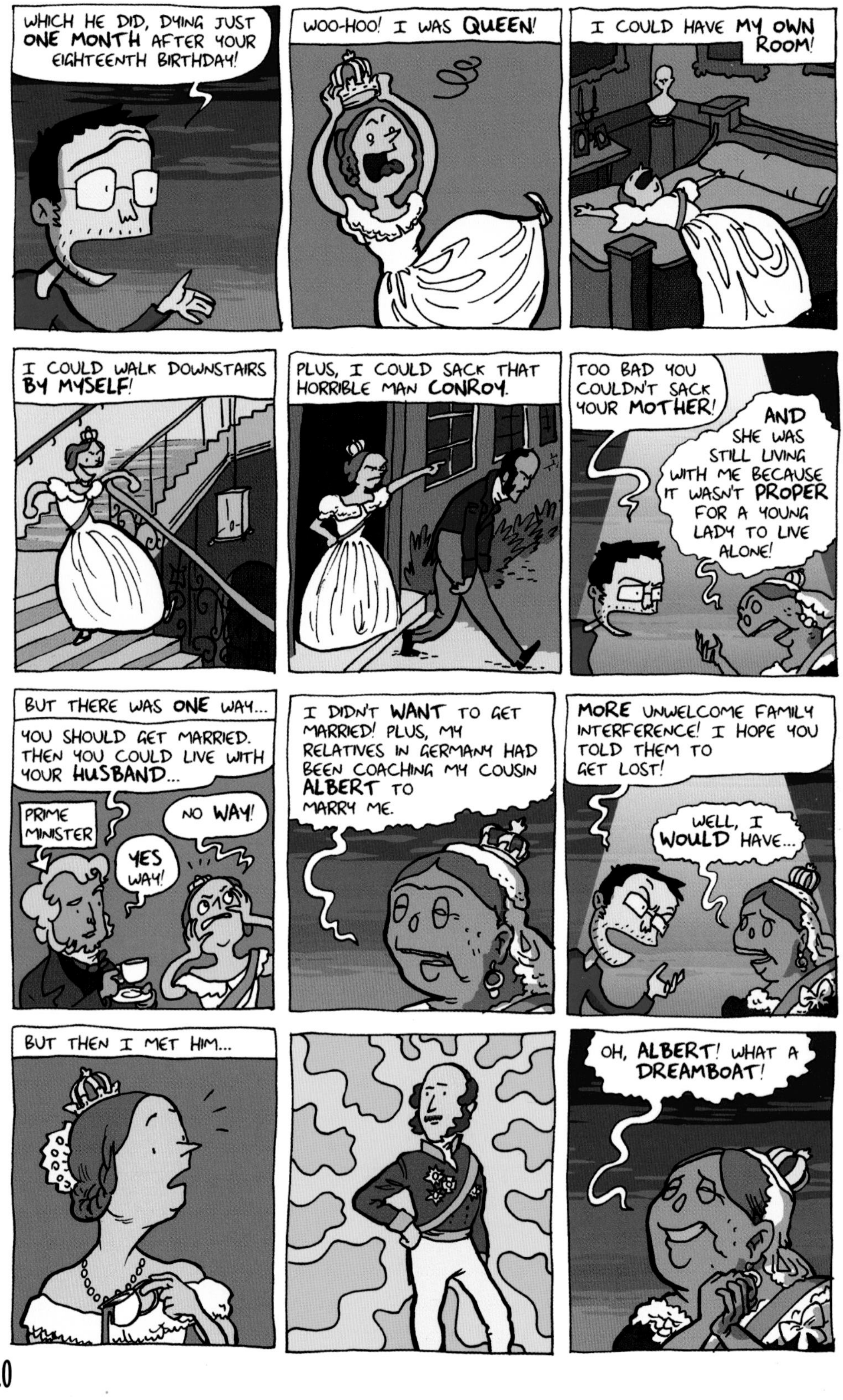
WHICH HE DID, DYING JUST ONE MONTH AFTER YOUR EIGHTEENTH BIRTHDAY!
WOO-HOO! I WAS QUEEN!
I COULD HAVE MY OWN ROOM!
I COULD WALK DOWNSTAIRS BY MYSELF!
PLUS, I COULD SACK THAT HORRIBLE MAN CONROY.
TOO BAD YOU COULDN'T SACK YOUR MOTHER!
AND SHE WAS STILL LIVING WITH ME BECAUSE IT WASN'T PROPER FOR A YOUNG LADY TO LIVE ALONE!
BUT THERE WAS ONE WAY...
YOU SHOULD GET MARRIED. THEN YOU COULD LIVE WITH YOUR HUSBAND...
PRIME MINISTER
NO WAY!
YES WAY!
I DIDN'T WANT TO GET MARRIED! PLUS, MY RELATIVES IN GERMANY HAD BEEN COACHING MY COUSIN ALBERT TO MARRY ME.
MORE UNWELCOME FAMILY INTERFERENCE! I HOPE YOU TOLD THEM TO GET LOST!
WELL, I WOULD HAVE...
BUT THEN I MET HIM...
OH, ALBERT! WHAT A DREAMBOAT!

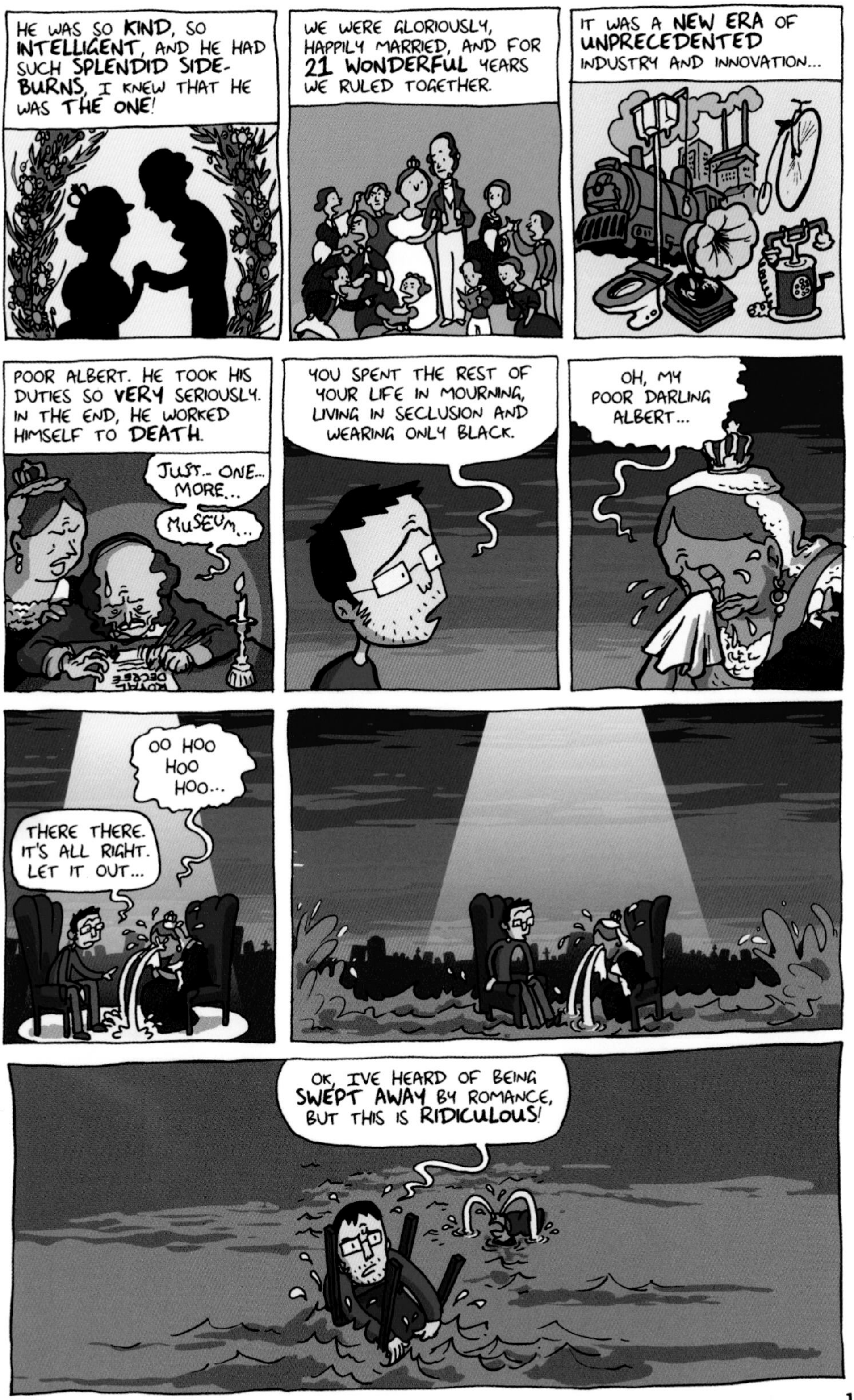
HE WAS SO KIND, SO INTELLIGENT, AND HE HAD SUCH SPLENDID SIDE-BURNS, I KNEW THAT HE WAS THE ONE!
WE WERE GLORIOUSLY, HAPPILY MARRIED, AND FOR 21 WONDERFUL YEARS WE RULED TOGETHER.
IT WAS A NEW ERA OF UNPRECEDENTED INDUSTRY AND INNOVATION...
POOR ALBERT. HE TOOK HIS DUTIES SO VERY SERIOUSLY. IN THE END, HE WORKED HIMSELF TO DEATH.
JUST... ONE... MORE...
MUSEUM...
ROYAL DECREE
YOU SPENT THE REST OF YOUR LIFE IN MOURNING, LIVING IN SECLUSION AND WEARING ONLY BLACK.
OH, MY POOR DARLING ALBERT...
OO HOO HOO HOO...
THERE THERE. IT'S ALL RIGHT. LET IT OUT...
OK, IVE HEARD OF BEING SWEPT AWAY BY ROMANCE, BUT THIS IS RIDICULOUS!

GAME OF THRONES

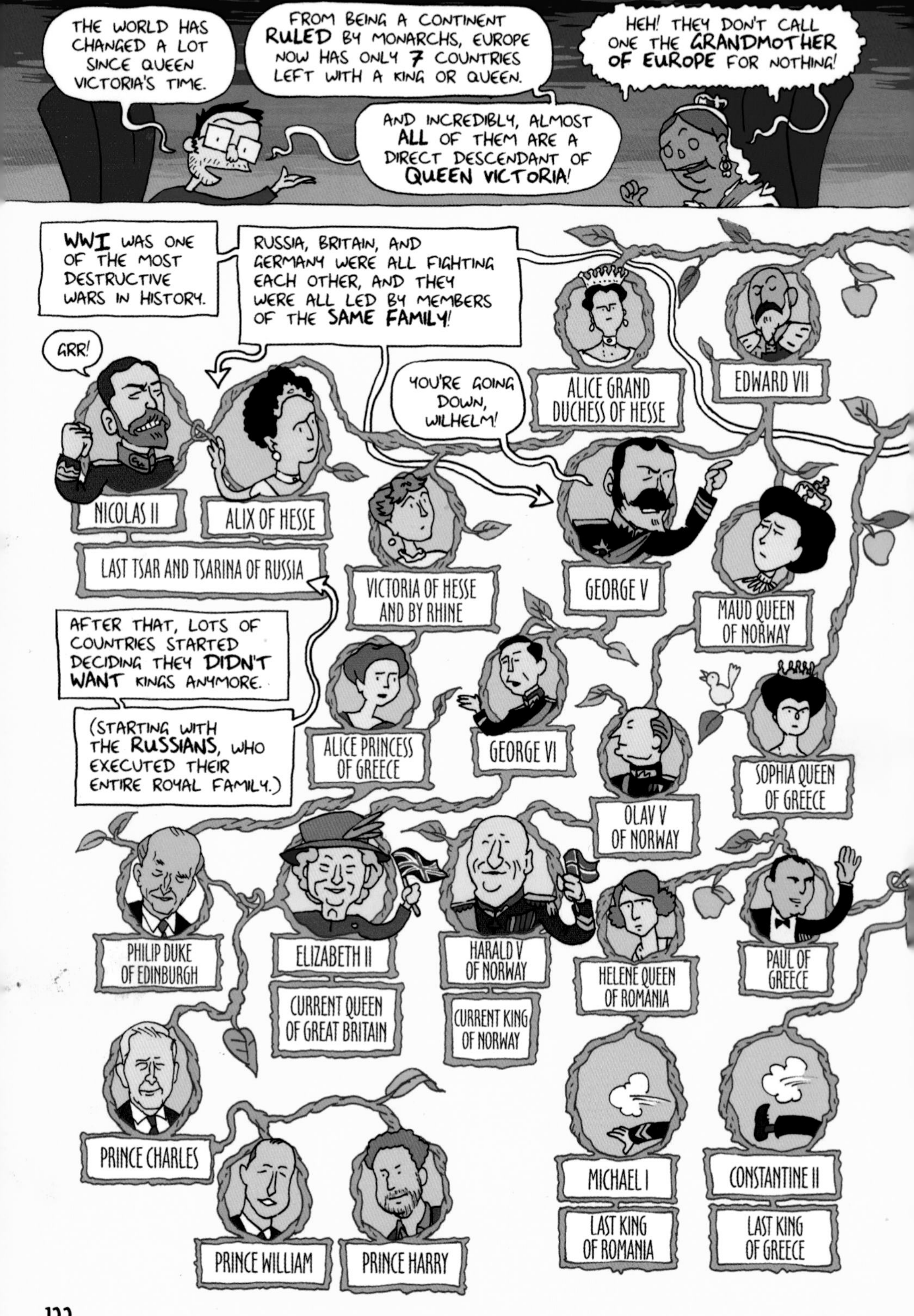

THE WORLD HAS CHANGED A LOT SINCE QUEEN VICTORIA'S TIME.
FROM BEING A CONTINENT **RULED** BY MONARCHS, EUROPE NOW HAS ONLY **7** COUNTRIES LEFT WITH A KING OR QUEEN.
AND INCREDIBLY, ALMOST **ALL** OF THEM ARE A DIRECT DESCENDANT OF **QUEEN VICTORIA**!
HEH! THEY DON'T CALL ONE THE **GRANDMOTHER OF EUROPE** FOR NOTHING!
WWI WAS ONE OF THE MOST DESTRUCTIVE WARS IN HISTORY.
RUSSIA, BRITAIN, AND GERMANY WERE ALL FIGHTING EACH OTHER, AND THEY WERE ALL LED BY MEMBERS OF THE **SAME FAMILY**!
GRR!
YOU'RE GOING DOWN, WILHELM!
ALICE GRAND DUCHESS OF HESSE
EDWARD VII
NICOLAS II
ALIX OF HESSE
LAST TSAR AND TSARINA OF RUSSIA
VICTORIA OF HESSE AND BY RHINE
GEORGE V
MAUD QUEEN OF NORWAY
AFTER THAT, LOTS OF COUNTRIES STARTED DECIDING THEY **DIDN'T WANT** KINGS ANYMORE.
(STARTING WITH THE **RUSSIANS**, WHO EXECUTED THEIR ENTIRE ROYAL FAMILY.)
ALICE PRINCESS OF GREECE
GEORGE VI
OLAV V OF NORWAY
SOPHIA QUEEN OF GREECE
PHILIP DUKE OF EDINBURGH
ELIZABETH II
CURRENT QUEEN OF GREAT BRITAIN
HARALD V OF NORWAY
CURRENT KING OF NORWAY
HELENE QUEEN OF ROMANIA
PAUL OF GREECE
PRINCE CHARLES
PRINCE WILLIAM
PRINCE HARRY
MICHAEL I
LAST KING OF ROMANIA
CONSTANTINE II
LAST KING OF GREECE

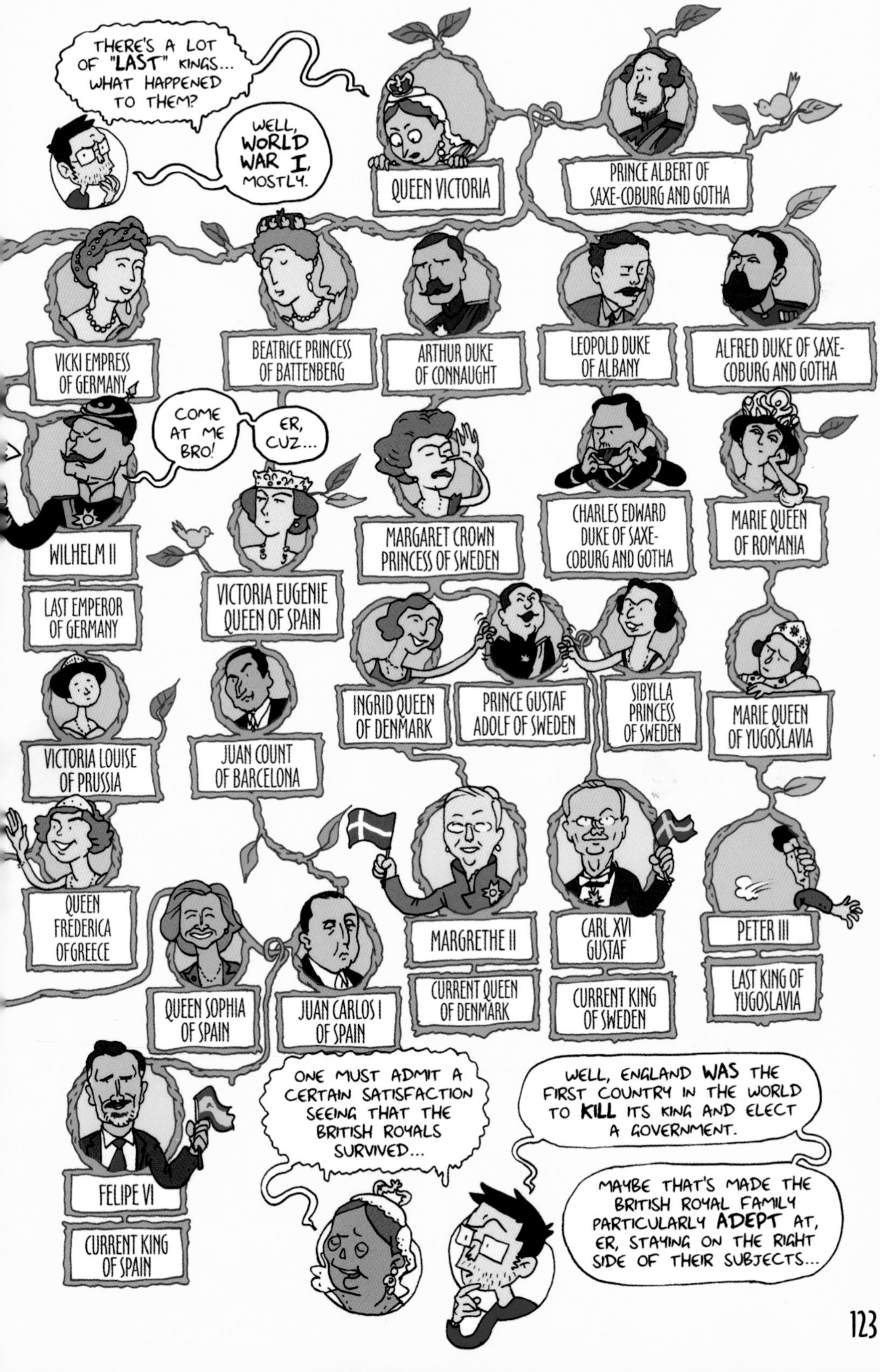

THERE'S A LOT OF "LAST" KINGS... WHAT HAPPENED TO THEM?
WELL, WORLD WAR I, MOSTLY.
QUEEN VICTORIA
PRINCE ALBERT OF SAXE-COBURG AND GOTHA
VICKI EMPRESS OF GERMANY
BEATRICE PRINCESS OF BATTENBERG
ARTHUR DUKE OF CONNAUGHT
LEOPOLD DUKE OF ALBANY
ALFRED DUKE OF SAXE-COBURG AND GOTHA
COME AT ME BRO!
ER, CUZ...
WILHELM II
LAST EMPEROR OF GERMANY
VICTORIA EUGENIE QUEEN OF SPAIN
MARGARET CROWN PRINCESS OF SWEDEN
CHARLES EDWARD DUKE OF SAXE-COBURG AND GOTHA
MARIE QUEEN OF ROMANIA
INGRID QUEEN OF DENMARK
PRINCE GUSTAF ADOLF OF SWEDEN
SIBYLLA PRINCESS OF SWEDEN
MARIE QUEEN OF YUGOSLAVIA
VICTORIA LOUISE OF PRUSSIA
JUAN COUNT OF BARCELONA
QUEEN FREDERICA OFGREECE
QUEEN SOPHIA OF SPAIN
JUAN CARLOS I OF SPAIN
MARGRETHE II
CURRENT QUEEN OF DENMARK
CARL XVI GUSTAF
CURRENT KING OF SWEDEN
PETER III
LAST KING OF YUGOSLAVIA
FELIPE VI
CURRENT KING OF SPAIN
ONE MUST ADMIT A CERTAIN SATISFACTION SEEING THAT THE BRITISH ROYALS SURVIVED...
WELL, ENGLAND WAS THE FIRST COUNTRY IN THE WORLD TO KILL ITS KING AND ELECT A GOVERNMENT.
MAYBE THAT'S MADE THE BRITISH ROYAL FAMILY PARTICULARLY ADEPT AT, ER, STAYING ON THE RIGHT SIDE OF THEIR SUBJECTS...

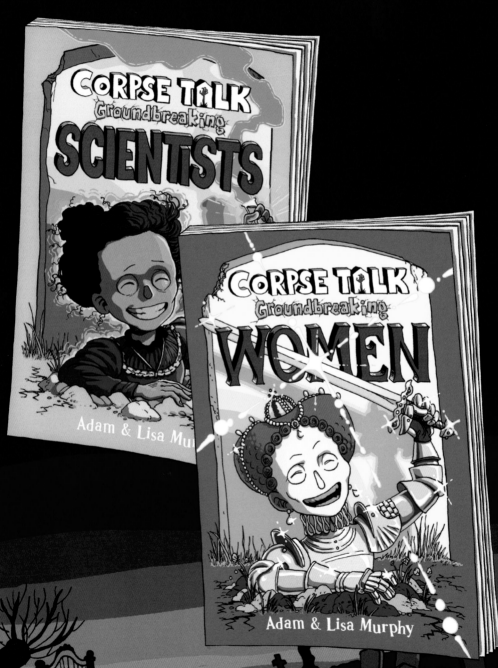

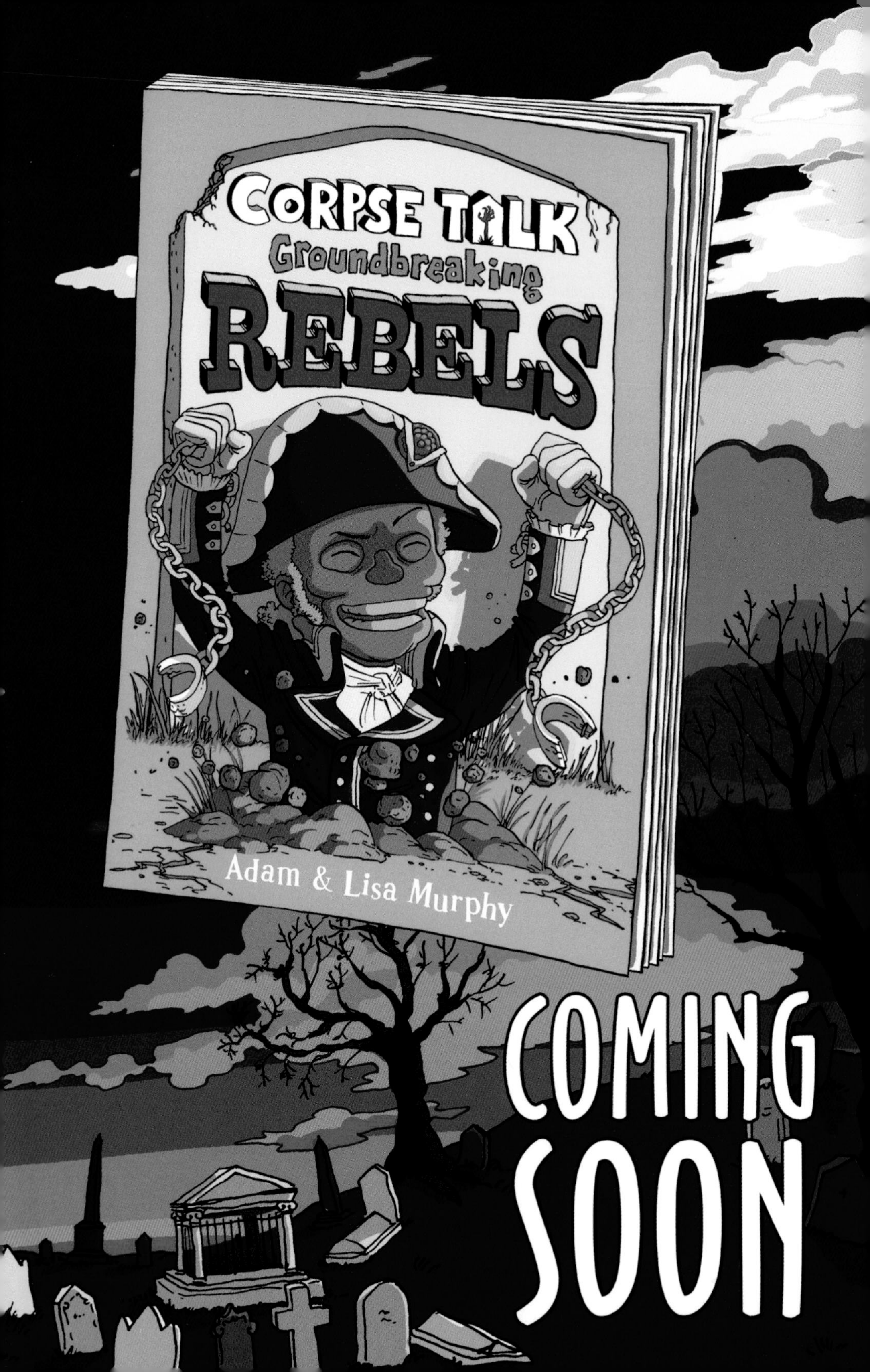
CORPSE TALK
Groundbreaking
REBELS
Adam & Lisa Murphy
COMING
SOON

Glossary

ABDICATION   THE ACT OF GIVING UP THE THRONE BY A KING OR QUEEN.

BARBARIAN   INSULTING WORD INVENTED BY THE ANCIENT GREEKS AND ROMANS TO DESCRIBE PEOPLE FROM A FOREIGN LAND WHO THEY THOUGHT WERE LESS CIVILIZED.

BYZANTINE   RELATING TO THE BYZANTINE THE EMPIRE, EASTERN PART OF THE ROMAN EMPIRE, BASED AROUND ITS CAPITAL CITY, CONSTANTINOPLE (TODAY ISTANBUL IN TURKEY). UNLIKE IN THE WEST, THIS EASTERN PART OF ROMAN EMPIRE SURVIVED THROUGHOUT THE MIDDLE AGES.

CATHOLIC   A MEMBER OF THE CATHOLIC CHURCH—THE BRANCH OF THE CHRISTIAN RELIGION THAT ACCEPTS THE POPE AS ITS LEADER.

CHIVALRY   CODE OF CONDUCT FOR KNIGHTS IN THE MIDDLE AGES, REQUIRING BRAVERY, HONESTY, FAIRNESS, AND POLITENESS.

CHRISTENDOM   WORD ONCE USED TO DESCRIBE LANDS WHERE CHRISTIANITY WAS THE MAIN RELIGION.

CIVILIZED   A SOCIETY WITH A LOT OF SOCIAL AND TECHNOLOGICAL COMPLEXITY. BEHAVIOR CONSIDERED POLITE AND KIND BY SUCH A SOCIETY. THE WORD IS OFTEN USED BY ONE GROUP OF PEOPLE TO DESCRIBE THEMSELVES AS SUPERIOR TO ANOTHER GROUP.

CIVIL WAR   WAR BETWEEN PEOPLE OF THE SAME COUNTRY.

CONQUISTADORS   LEADERS IN THE 16TH CENTURY SPANISH CONQUEST OF PARTS OF CENTRAL AND SOUTH AMERICA.

COURT   PLACE WHERE A KING, QUEEN, OR OTHER RULER LIVES AND CARRIES OUT CEREMONIAL AND ADMINISTRATIVE DUTIES.

CRUSADES   SERIES OF WARS FOUGHT BY CHRISTIANS IN THE 11TH–13TH CENTURIES, TRYING TO RECONQUER LANDS FROM MUSLIMS IN THE MIDDLE EAST.

DICTATORSHIP   COUNTRY OR STATE RULED BY A DICTATOR—AN ABSOLUTE RULER WHOSE WORD IS LAW, USUALLY ONE WHO TOOK POWER BY FORCE.

EMPIRE   A STATE FORMED BY ONE COUNTRY CONQUERING AND RULING A LOT OF DIFFERENT COUNTRIES, PEOPLES, OR LANDS.

GLADIATOR   IN ANCIENT ROME, A MAN TRAINED TO FIGHT AGAINST OTHER MEN OR WILD ANIMALS FOR ENTERTAINMENT.

IMPERIAL   THINGS OR PEOPLE CONNECTED TO AN EMPIRE.

INCENSE   A SPICE OR GUM BURNED FOR THE SWEET SMELL IT RELEASES, OFTEN DURING RELIGIOUS CEREMONIES.

INDIGENOUS THE FIRST PEOPLE WHO LIVE OR HAVE LIVED IN A PARTICULAR COUNTRY OR AREA.

ISLAM RELIGION FOLLOWED BY MUSLIM PEOPLE, BASED AROUND THE WORSHIP OF A SINGLE GOD, AND FOLLOWING THE TEACHINGS OF THE PROPHET MUHAMMAD.

KURDISH THE KURDISH PEOPLE ARE A STATELESS ETHNIC GROUP FROM WESTERN ASIA, ORIGINATING IN THE AREA BORDERING TURKEY, IRAN, IRAQ, AND SYRIA.

MIDDLE AGES COMMON TERM FOR THE PERIOD OF HISTORY IN THE MIDDLE OF THE ANCIENT AND MODERN ERAS: FROM ROUGHLY THE 5TH–15TH CENTURY CE.

MONARCH A KING OR QUEEN.

NOMAD A PERSON WHO BELONGS TO A COMMUNITY THAT MOVES FROM PLACE TO PLACE. NOMADIC SOCIETY IS OFTEN BASED ON HERDING ANIMALS RATHER THAN FARMING CROPS.

PAGAN A PERSON WHO BELIEVES IN A RELIGION WHICH INCLUDES MULTIPLE GODS OR DEITIES. ORIGINALLY USED IN AN INSULTING OR DEROGATORY WAY.

PARLIAMENT GROUP OF PEOPLE IN GOVERNMENT WHO MAKE AND PASS LAWS. HISTORICALLY, EARLY PARLIAMENTS WERE A GATHERING OF NOBLES WHO ADVISED THE KING.

POTENTATE A RULER WITH GREAT POWER.

PROTESTANT A MEMBER OF ONE OF THE CHRISTIAN CHURCHES THAT SEPARATED FROM THE CATHOLIC CHURCH IN THE 16TH CENTURY IN PROTEST AT WHAT THEY SAW AS THE CORRUPTION AND HYPOCRISY OF THE CATHOLIC CHURCH.

QUR'AN THE HOLY BOOK OF ISLAM, BELIEVED TO BE THE WORDS OF GOD, AS REVEALED TO THE PROPHET MUHAMMAD.

SOVEREIGN THE QUEEN, KING, OR OTHER ROYAL RULER OF A COUNTRY.

SUBJECTS PEOPLE WHO ARE RULED BY A MONARCH.

SUCCESSION THE PROCESS BY WHICH ONE RULER INHERITS THE TITLE OR OFFICE OF ANOTHER.

TREASON THE CRIME OF BETRAYING ONE'S RULER OR COUNTRY.

UNCIVILIZED UNACCEPTABLE BEHAVIOR, EITHER BECAUSE IT IS RUDE OR CRUEL, OR BECAUSE IT IS ASSOCIATED WITH ANOTHER GROUP OF PEOPLE WHO ARE CONSIDERED TO BE LESS CIVILIZED.

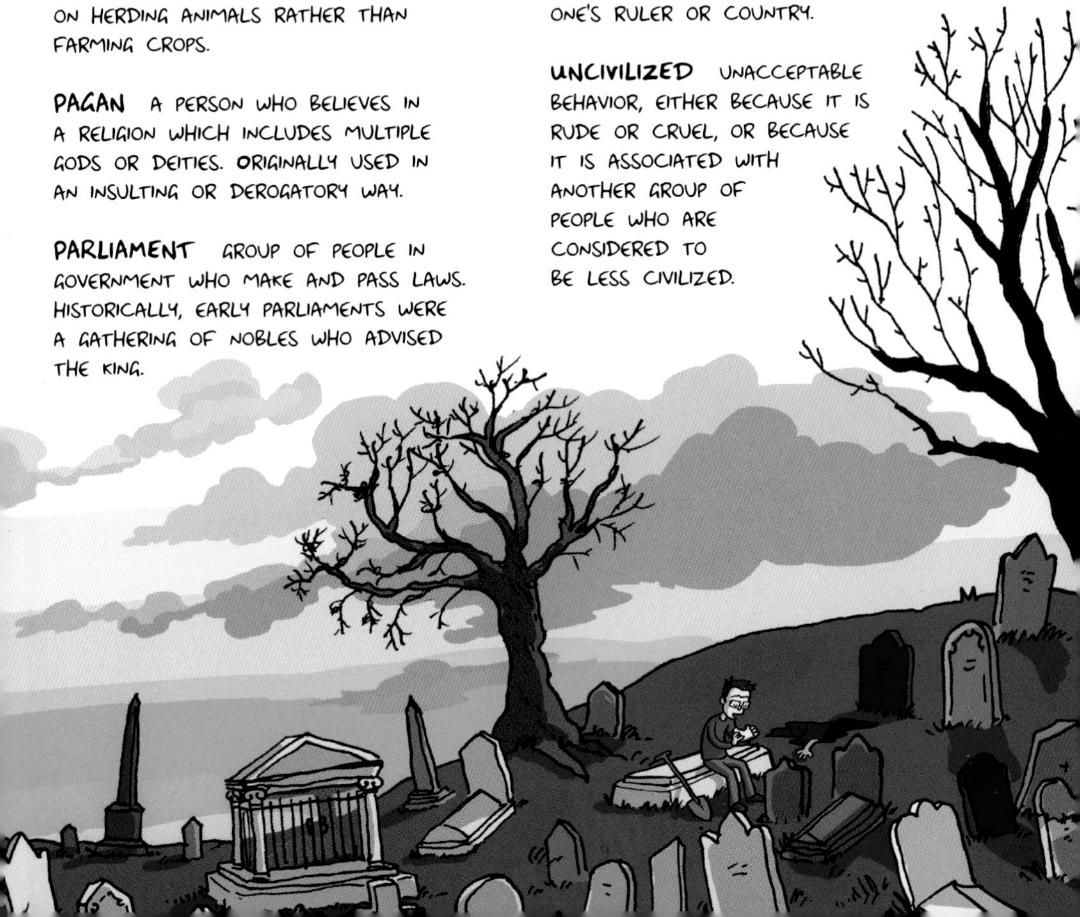

For Rowan and Mhari

Design and adaptation Paul Duffield
With special thanks to Tom Fickling,
Anthony Hinton, and Joe Brady
Senior Editor Marie Greenwood
US Senior Editor Shannon Beatty
Project Editor Kritika Gupta
Project Art Editor Jaileen Kaur
DTP Designer Dheeraj Singh
Senior Production Editor Robert Dunn
Senior Production Controller Inderjit Bhullar
Managing Editors Laura Gilbert , Monica Saigal
Managing Art Editor Romi Chakraborty
Delhi Creative Heads Glenda Fernandes, Malavika Talukder
Publishing Manager Francesca Young
Creative Director Helen Senior
Publishing Director Sarah Larter

First American Edition, 2021
Published in the United States by DK Publishing
1450 Broadway, Suite 801, New York, NY 10018

Text and Illustrations © Adam & Lisa Murphy, 2018, 2021

DK, a Division of Penguin Random House LLC
21 22 23 24 25 10 9 8 7 6 5 4 3 2 1
001–321700–Apr/2021

Published in Great Britain by Dorling Kindersley Limited

A catalog record for this book
is available from the Library of Congress.
ISBN: 978-0-7440-2766-2 (Paperback)
ISBN: 978-0-7440-2767-9 (Hardback)

DK books are available at special discounts when purchased in bulk
for sales promotions, premiums, fund-raising, or educational use.
For details, contact: DK Publishing Special Markets,
1450 Broadway, Suite 801, New York, NY 10018
SpecialSales@dk.com

Printed and bound in China

For the curious
www.dk.com

This book was made with Forest Stewardship
Council™ certified paper—one small step in DK's
commitment to a sustainable future. For more
information go to www.dk.com/our-green-pledge